CHAMPION *of* CIVIL RIGHTS

SOUTHERN BIOGRAPHY SERIES
Bertram Wyatt-Brown, Series Editor

CHAMPION
of CIVIL RIGHTS
Judge John Minor Wisdom

JOEL WILLIAM FRIEDMAN

LOUISIANA STATE UNIVERSITY PRESS
BATON ROUGE

Published by Louisiana State University Press
Copyright © 2009 by Louisiana State University Press
All rights reserved
Manufactured in the United States of America
Louisiana Paperback Edition, 2013

Designer: Tammi deGeneres
Typefaces: Metalcut, Arno Pro, Goudy Old Style
Typesetter: J. Jarrett Engineering, Inc.

Library of Congress Cataloging-in-Publication Data

Friedman, Joel William, 1951–
    Champion of civil rights : Judge John Minor Wisdom / Joel William Friedman.
        p. cm. – (Southern biography series)
    Includes index.
    ISBN 978-0-8071-3384-2 (cloth : alk. paper) 1. Wisdom, John Minor, 1905–1999. 2. Judges—United
States—Biography. 3. United States. Circuit Court (5th Circuit) 4. Civil rights—United States—History.
I. Title.
    KF373.W516F75 2009
    347.73'14092—dc22
    [B]

                                                                                          2008017155

ISBN 978-0-8071-5446-5 (pbk. : alk. paper) — ISBN 978-0-8071-3482-5 (pdf) —
ISBN 978-0-8071-4915-7 (epub) — ISBN 978-0-8071-4916-4 (mobi)

To my parents

CONTENTS

INTRODUCTION

This is a book about Wisdom. And about wisdom. And also about courage, intellectual rigor, and honesty, and about one man's lifelong commitment to fairness.

The chronicle of the civil rights movement in the United States, including the role played by many individuals whose names have become linked in the public mind to this transformative series of events, has been well documented. The slow and not altogether steady pace by which American society came to grips with the consequences of over a century's worth of racial discrimination is a vitally important part of the country's history whose lessons deserve constant reassessment. And though the move to an integrated society has been and remains a matter of national concern, nowhere were the stakes higher or the events more compelling than in the Deep South. The multifaceted campaign to remove the barriers that historically had blocked African Americans from full participation in most, if not all, sectors of American society had many heroes. This is the story of one of the pivotal figures in one of the central components of the desegregation efforts that coalesced during the second half of the twentieth century.

The declaration by the U.S. Supreme Court in 1954 that the maintenance of racially segregated public schools was unconstitutional and had to be abandoned "with all deliberate speed" was the impetus for decades of governmental action directed at integrating this and other public services. But as the Court itself acknowledged, the prime responsibility for enforcing its broad desegregation mandate in *Brown v.*

Board of Education fell to the federal trial and appellate court judges. Moreover, even though the bane of segregation extended north of the Mason-Dixon Line, the pervasive legacy of Jim Crow in the southern states meant that vigorous action by judges in this region was essential to any meaningful implementation of the Court's desegregation decree in *Brown*.

The initial responsibility for bringing the desegregation rule of law to various sectors of the public arena fell to the federal district judges. With a few notable exceptions, including District Judges J. Skelly Wright of New Orleans, Louisiana, and Frank M. Johnson, Jr., of Montgomery, Alabama, most federal trial judges in the South were only too eager to take advantage of every opportunity to thwart, or at least, impede, every effort to integrate the public institutions within their jurisdiction. Until 1981, the responsibility for reviewing the decisions of the trial judges in Texas, Louisiana, Mississippi, Alabama, Georgia, and Florida fell to one court—the U.S. Fifth Circuit Court of Appeals. Consequently, it was this court that issued the decrees that compelled the integration of schools and voting rolls across the Deep South.

Unlike trial courts, where a single judge sits alone to resolve the legal issues posed in a case, the Fifth Circuit, like all the federal circuit courts of appeal, sat, at least initially, in panels of three to resolve the appeal in every case. Consequently, no individual member of the Fifth Circuit had the unilateral authority to rule on behalf of this court. During this crucial time in the history of the United States, four members of the Fifth Circuit stood out as its most consistent champions of civil rights. Without the courageous stands taken by Richard Rives of Alabama, Elbert Tuttle of Georgia, and John Brown of Texas, this struggle for equality surely would have traveled a more circuitous course. But even within this pantheon of legal giants, one colleague stood out as their intellectual and scholarly leader. Time and again, when the Fifth Circuit was called upon to resolve its most sensitive, controversial, and momentous cases, the judge chosen to give voice to these jurists' collective judgment was invariably the same man.

The scion of two lines of Virginia landed aristocrats who could document their arrival in the United States in the seventeenth century, John Minor Wisdom was born into a family of privilege and social position in the highly structured early-twentieth-century society of New Orleans. He married a woman who had grown up on a huge sugar plantation and whose great-grandfather had been an original member of the Loui-

siana Supreme Court. So, not surprisingly, in many ways he was a product of his times and upbringing. Like nearly all of his social peers, Wisdom was an active participant in the whirl of social events that catered
to the upper crust of New Orleans society. For the entirety of his adult
life, he was a member of racially restrictive clubs and Mardi Gras organizations. He played a pivotal role in securing the Republican Party's 1952
presidential nomination for General Dwight D. Eisenhower and thereafter became the leader and public face of his state's Republican Party
until his appointment to the federal bench in 1957. During his more
than forty years of service as a member of the U.S. Fifth Circuit Court
of Appeals, Wisdom hired only one African American law clerk; he did
not hire a single female law clerk during his first seventeen years on the
bench, primarily because he believed that no woman could or should be
asked to carry one of his heavy briefcases to and from his chambers.

When President Eisenhower turned to his party leader in Louisiana
to fill a vacancy on the federal appellate court with jurisdiction over
all cases coming from the states of the Deep South, he was looking for
someone who would bring a sympathetic ear and unbiased judgment to
that court's burgeoning caseload of civil rights disputes. Wisdom did
not disappoint. As a full-time attorney and part-time law professor with
more than a quarter-century's experience, he already had earned a reputation as a thoughtful, intelligent, and creative scholar. And within the
space of only a few short years, because of his production of erudite and
highly literate opinions, founded on the pillars of precise legal analysis,
literary craftsmanship, and historical research, he became the unquestioned intellectual leader and driving force behind the court that played
the preeminent role in enforcing the U.S. Supreme Court's directive to
end racial segregation in all aspects of American society.

As the author of opinions that mandated the University of Mississippi
to admit James Meredith, the man that Wisdom labeled "the man with a
mission and with a nervous stomach," and thereby ended its century-old
policy of racial segregation; that forced the integration of public school
districts throughout the South; that eliminated longstanding arbitrary
and invidious barriers to the full and free exercise of the franchise by
African Americans; and that provided a meaningful opportunity for
women and minority group members to achieve their rightful place in
the economic order by affirming the validity of affirmative action, John
Minor Wisdom, this tradition-laden son of the Old South, became the
architect of a racially integrating New South. Additionally, when forces

in Congress sought to reshape the composition of the Fifth Circuit, he fought energetically and valiantly, though ultimately unsuccessfully, to derail this transparent effort to dilute the impact of this court's progressive handling of civil rights cases.

Wisdom did not come to the Fifth Circuit with a mission or an agenda. He never thought of himself as a reformer or as a reflexive enemy of the status quo. In fact, in many aspects of his private life he embraced and actively participated in the existing social order. But as a public man, he held dear two fundamental beliefs. As a young child, his mother had instilled in him an unshakeable commitment to the notion that everyone was entitled to be treated fairly and with respect. Moreover, as someone who came of age during the Depression and experienced firsthand the often brutal impact of the exercise of unchecked power by Louisiana governor and later U.S. senator Huey Long, Wisdom became convinced that the full blessings of democracy could not be enjoyed in the absence of a political system marked by the presence of two viable and energetic political parties. So it was simply the combination of this commitment to fairness and the steadfast conviction that democracy was best served by the presence of a vibrant two-party system that explains why he strove mightily both to revive his state's dormant Republican Party and to champion the cause of civil rights.

Wisdom was a modest and typically self-deprecating man; yet his powerful intellect and uncompromising integrity catapulted him to a position of national prominence that brought him a multitude of awards and honors from legions of admirers. But it also made him the easy target of a cascade of venom-laced criticism from those whose positions and ideologies were threatened by the social changes that flowed from his judicial opinions. Like a few of his judicial colleagues, Wisdom refused to be deterred from pursuing his sworn allegiance to the principles of fairness and democracy. This is the story of how and why he followed that path.

CHAMPION *of* CIVIL RIGHTS

1

A PRIVILEGED SON OF THE SOUTH

Wisdom. Could any judge hope for a more felicitous patronymic? Even more than Learned Hand, this name appears to predestine its owner for the contemplative, justice-dispensing life of a jurist. Yet aside from his surname, little in John Minor Wisdom's background or family history foreshadowed the path-breaking contributions he would make to the development of American law. From an early age, this gregarious, self-effacing, and scrupulously fair-minded man also displayed the characteristics of knowledge, judgment, and insight that Webster proclaims to be the benchmarks of wisdom. But his upbringing made Wisdom an unlikely candidate for the role of civil rights champion. Who could have anticipated that this scion of southern society would become not only the prime architect of a revitalized Republican Party in Louisiana, but, more important, the universally acclaimed author of tradition-shattering and precedent-making judicial opinions that would forever reshape the contours of civil liberties in the United States? How and why this son of a New Orleans cotton broker came to play such a critical role in the modern American civil rights revolution is as essential a part of his story as the accomplishments themselves.

Family history is perhaps more important in the South than in any other region in the country. Many southerners view lineage as a prominent index of social status and a reliable predictor of vocation and character. They tend to reject Ralph Waldo Emerson's claim that "men resemble their contemporaries even more than their progenitors."[1] Yet occasionally an individual will confound this stereotype by ignoring settled expectations and carving his own unique path.

John Minor Wisdom was one of those individuals. A descendant of the Minors of Virginia, a venerable line composed primarily of members of the landed aristocracy, he emerged as one of the most progressive and influential federal judges of the twentieth century. Over his forty-two-year career as a member of the U.S. Fifth Circuit Court of Appeals, he wrote scores of opinions that powerfully changed the landscape of American jurisprudence. Rulings that he authored in school desegregation and voting rights cases opened the doors of equal opportunity to women and members of racial minority groups that had been shut for decades. By insisting that all individuals, regardless of circumstance of birth or condition of existence, were entitled to a fair shake by their government and their neighbors, Wisdom gave meaning to the theretofore unrealized promise of equal rights contained in the U.S. Constitution. And although he is properly recognized most widely for his role in promoting the cause of civil rights, his influence extends far beyond that realm, into such diverse areas as criminal, tax, trust, railroad reorganization, and maritime law.

To begin to understand how far the seed fell from its ancestral tree, however, to appreciate the distance traveled by this son of the Old South, a man born of privilege and steeped in the genteel traditions of an intricate and deeply rooted social order, one must return to the mid-seventeenth century, when Wisdom's ancestors first planted their roots in American soil.

Until the English Parliament passed the Navigation Acts of the 1650s and 1660s and confined the export of colonial American goods to England, shippers from several European nations carried on a substantial amount of commerce with the colonies.[2] One of these adventurous merchants was Maindort Doodes, a wealthy ship owner from Holland who left his homeland on a Dutch sailing ship in the 1650s and settled

1. Ralph Waldo Emerson, "Uses of Great Men," in *Representative Men* (New York: 1850).

2. The Navigation Acts, a series of statutes passed by the English Parliament between 1651 and 1663, required all products from America, Asia, and Africa to be exported to England and its possessions and prohibited all foreign ships from participating in the trade between England and its colonies.

in Norfolk, Virginia. Doodes and his wife, Mary, arrived with their son and daughter, who were also named Maindort and Mary.

After the family moved westward along the mouth of the James River to what later became Nansemond County, Doodes changed his pre-name to Minor, reversed the order of his names, and began to refer to himself as Doodes Minor. Over the next eight generations, the Mi-nors of Virginia would become extremely wealthy landholders who lived comfortably among the social elite of rural Virginia. But not every mem-ber of those early generations of Minors was content to maintain his or her traditional, privileged plantation existence, or to remain steadfast to the existing political, social, and economic order. A few, like their twentieth-century descendant, were bent on charting a different course.

For example, nearly a century before John Wisdom would dismantle a racially discriminatory voting scheme in Louisiana with the power of his reason and the stroke of his pen, Virginia Louisa Minor, one of the sixth generation of U.S.-born Minors and a great-granddaughter of the Minor who had amassed the family's vast real estate holdings in Virginia, founded the women's suffrage movement in Missouri in 1867. Seven years later, the Supreme Court unanimously denied her request to be permitted to vote in Virginia, rejecting her claim that women enjoyed a constitutional right to the franchise, a ruling that re-mained undisturbed until the adoption of the Nineteenth Amendment in 1920.[3] Reflecting that same uncommon rejection of many core val-ues held dear by their social peers, Virginia's cousin, University of Vir-ginia professor John Barbee Minor, the author of *Minor's Institutes of Common and Statute Law*, a multivolume treatise on contemporary ju-risprudence, founded and supervised an antebellum Sunday school for slave children.[4] Seven decades later, the owners of a thirty-thousand-acre plantation in Mathews, Louisiana, built one of the first schools for black children in that state on their property. Their daughter, Bonnie, subsequently moved to New Orleans, where she met and married the great-great-grandson of Virginia Minor's cousin Thomas—John Minor Wisdom.

In 1675, less than four years after Maindort Doodes had immigrated to Virginia, Abner Wisdom was born in England near the Welsh bor-

---

3. *Minor v. Happersett*, 88 U.S. (21 Wallace) 162 (1874).

4. "Necrology, John Barbee Minor," *Virginia Magazine of History and Biography* 3 (January 1896): xiv.

der. When his sons immigrated to America, settling in Kentucky, they and their offspring, like the Minors, prospered mightily in their new homeland. One of Abner's grandsons, Tavner Wisdom, became one of the South's largest tobacco and cotton dealers. And his son, John Buford Wisdom, continued to grow the family business when he moved to Spotsylvania County, Virginia. His son, in turn, the first John Minor Wisdom, initially followed his grandfather and father into the cotton and tobacco commission business, but thereafter decided to seek his fortune in the larger markets of New Orleans. He had not been in the Crescent City more than a few months before he joined Hewett-Norton & Co., the largest cotton and tobacco commission house in the South. On February 11, 1854, he and his wife, Maria, celebrated the birth of their first child, Mortimer, whose second-born son was John Minor Wisdom.[5]

At the age of fourteen, too young to fight in the Civil War, Mortimer Wisdom became one of the youngest students at Washington College. A glass-framed certificate that Mortimer received for being the top student in history and political economics was displayed prominently in his son's judicial chambers. Among his most prized possessions, John Wisdom took great satisfaction in pointing out to visitors the faded signature of the then-president of Washington College, General Robert E. Lee, a man Mortimer Wisdom, and his son, admired and deeply respected.[6]

John Wisdom's mother was Mortimer Wisdom's third wife. Mortimer's

5. Like her husband, Maria Winn Bell Wisdom came from a family whose wealth was derived from the mercantile trade. However, she also had some interesting relatives that made a mark in the artistic community. Her niece, Cora Witherspoon, enjoyed a moderately successful career as a character actress in Hollywood, appearing in several well-known films alongside some of the most famous actors of her time. Among her screen credits are the classic The Bank Dick, in which she co-starred with W. C. Fields; Libeled Lady, starring Jean Harlow, William Powell, Spencer Tracy, and Myrna Loy; Quality Street, a 1937 film featuring Katherine Hepburn and Franchot Tone; and Dark Victory, the 1939 melodrama in which Cora appeared with Bette Davis, Humphrey Bogart, and Ronald Reagan. "Pictures from the Past," New Orleans Times-Picayune, November 15, 1998, E-10, col. 1. And one of Maria's brothers, William Alexander Bell, married the former Mathilde Musson, a first cousin of the famous French painter, Edgar Degas. Mathilde's sister, Estelle, married Degas's brother, Rene, who was also her first cousin. A portrait of Estelle by Edgar Degas hangs in the New Orleans Museum of Art as a tangible reminder of the Degas connections to New Orleans and the Musson and Wisdom families.

6. Some published histories of the South repeat the story that Mortimer Wisdom was one of the pallbearers at General Lee's funeral. See, for example, The Story of Louisiana, vol. II (1960), 243. However, John never heard his father speak of it and had never seen any evidence of his father's alleged participation in the event. If Mortimer played any part at all in the funeral procession, it

first wife, Rebecca de Mendez Kruttschnitt, was the daughter of the German consul at New Orleans and the sister of Ernest Benjamin Kruttschnitt, a chairman of the Louisiana State Democratic Central Committee and president of the Constitutional Convention that framed the Louisiana Constitution of 1898. She also was the niece of famed attorney, scholar, statesman, and "Brains of the Confederacy" Judah P. Benjamin.[7] Tragically, less than a year after their marriage, Rebecca died in childbirth along with their baby. Two years later, Mortimer married Martha ("Mattie") Somerville Noble, the daughter of a New York merchant. But for the second time, Mortimer's marriage was cut short by his wife's premature death. Mattie died in 1889, only ten years after the marriage, leaving Mortimer with three young children.

At the age of forty-four, Mortimer took his third wife, a thirty-year-old attorney's daughter named Adelaide Labatt. The couple had three sons, the second of whom they named after Mortimer's father, John Minor Wisdom. Like her husband, Adelaide Labatt came from a family with deep roots in the American terrain. She too could trace her lineage back to the Revolutionary era. But part of the heritage that she brought to this marriage was of a distinctly different flavor than that contributed by Mortimer Wisdom.

In sharp contrast to the Episcopalian traditions shared by the Virginia-bred Minors and the planters and merchants of the Wisdom clan, the Labatts were part of one of the oldest Jewish families in the South. The branches of their family tree contained, among others, Judah P. Benjamin, perhaps the most influential Jewish southerner of the Civil War era; Henry Hyams, the first Jewish lieutenant governor in American history; Abraham Cohen Labatt, co-founder, in Charleston, of the first Reform synagogue in the United States and of the first synagogue on the

---

was probably as an honorary pall bearer in a student procession, since he was a student at Washington College when the general died.

7. Judah Philip Benjamin, the brother of Rebecca's mother, Penina Benjamin Kruttschnitt, was a U.S. senator from Louisiana from 1853 until the state seceded from the Union in 1861. A brilliant attorney, he turned down an appointment to the Supreme Court during his Senate term. When Louisiana joined the Confederacy, Benjamin became attorney general in Confederate president Jefferson Davis's cabinet. During the Civil War, Benjamin served successively as secretary of war and secretary of state. In 1831, after Davis was captured, Benjamin fled to Great Britain with a price on his head. He eventually became one of that country's leading members of the bar. In 1868, his classic treatise, *On the Law of Sale of Personal Property*, was published. The following year, Benjamin was named a queen's counsel.

West Coast; and his son David Cohen Labatt, recipient of the first diploma in law conferred by the forerunner of what is now the Tulane Law School who gained widespread recognition for his groundbreaking work in lawsuits filed on behalf of ex-slaves against their former masters.[8]

Although Article 1 of Louisiana's Black Code (*Code Noir*) of 1724 mandated the expulsion of all Jews from the colony, by the post–Civil War period, the more than two thousand Jewish citizens of New Orleans were more integrated into the city's political, social, and civic scenes than they were in most other major American cities of that era.[9] Social prestige in the Creole and Yankee societies in pre-twentieth-century New Orleans was much more attuned to affluence or longevity in the community than to religion. Even the city's most prestigious social clubs admitted Jewish members. And though both of these organizations subsequently adopted a tacit policy of excluding Jews from membership (including the years in which John Minor Wisdom was an active member), David Labatt and Judah Benjamin were among the many Jewish members of the Boston Club. Jews also participated in the whirl of New Orleans society. In 1877, David Labatt's sister Caroline reigned as the Queen of Carnival and Louis J. Salomon was, in 1872, the city's first Rex, King of Carnival.[10]

When David Labatt married Elizabeth House, an Episcopalian from Philadelphia, the couple decided to expose some of their eight offspring

---

8. See *Biographical and Historical Memoirs of Louisiana* (Baton Rouge: 1892), vol. 1, chapter XXIV, 521; "Flashback: New Orleans a Century Ago," *New Orleans Times-Picayune*, June 15, 1948; Nathan Glazer, *American Judaism*, 2d ed. (Chicago: 1989), 35–36; "He Died at Ninety-Seven: 'Father' Abraham Cohen Labatt Has Been Gathered to His Fathers," *Galveston News*, August 17, 1899, 10; *The Universal Jewish Encyclopedia* (New York: 1944), 497. When New Orleans fell under the control of the Federal forces under General Butler, David Labatt refused to take an oath of allegiance to the Union and, consequently, was banished from the city with his family and an allotment of ten days' rations. The family ended up in Wilmington, North Carolina, where Labatt rejoined the Confederate forces with whom he had served as a member of the Fifth Louisiana volunteers until he resigned for reasons of ill health. Shortly before the end of the Civil War, Labatt was taken prisoner by General Rutherford B. Hayes's troops. After his parole, he returned to New Orleans with his family and resumed the practice of law. It was during this period that he became involved with the legal consequences of emancipation. *Biographical and Historical Memoirs of Louisiana* (Baton Rouge: 1892), vol. 1, chapter XXIV, 522.

9. John Wilds, Charles L. Dufour, and Walter G. Cowan, *Louisiana Yesterday and Today: A Historical Guide to the State* (Baton Rouge: 1996), 109–113; Bertram Wallace Korn, *The Early Jews of New Orleans* (Baton Rouge: 1969), 227 ("There was probably less prejudice against Jews in New Orleans during the ante-bellum period than in any other important city in the country").

10. Salomon was also the last Jewish monarch of New Orleans' Mardi Gras celebration.

to his Jewish heritage and others to her Christian faith. One of their four daughters, Adelaide, was among the children who accompanied their mother to church and who were raised as Episcopalians. So when Adelaide married Mortimer Wisdom, their three sons, William, John Minor, and Norton, were neither exposed to nor influenced by their Jewish heritage. And though he chose to build a law firm with a law school classmate who happened to be Jewish, Wisdom traveled throughout his adult life in a social circle that was composed nearly exclusively of non-Jews. In fact, his Jewish lineage was surely unknown to most of his acquaintances. And though he never sought to hide or disguise this aspect of his background, he rarely discussed it simply because it was a matter of no interest or consequence to him. Since neither of his parents had been raised in the Jewish faith, this aspect of the family history played no role in his upbringing and had no impact in shaping his beliefs or value system.

Adelaide and Mortimer Wisdom's first son, William, was born at the turn of the century. On May 17, 1905, Adelaide gave birth to the couple's second son, John Minor, and he was followed, two years later, by Norton. Though each of the boys eventually pursued different career paths, they were the products of a shared heritage. They had been born into a family that had enjoyed financial prosperity and social position in the United States for more than two centuries. More than that, they were the product of three distinct branches of a deeply rooted family tree. They were the tenth generation of a Dutch family whose progeny, the Minors, had built a fortune cultivating their fertile Virginia lands. The brothers also were the seventh generation of a British merchant family, the Wisdoms, whose descendants had prospered in the cotton trade. And they were the sixth-generation descendants of Western European Jews who produced a line of successful merchants and lawyers.

Yet despite their divergent backgrounds, the members of the Minor, Wisdom, and Labatt families shared a common bond. They all had achieved positions of economic security and social prominence in their respective communities. As a result, the three sons of Mortimer and Adelaide Wisdom, the twentieth-century heirs to this combined legacy, were in the fortunate position of being able to make their own assault on the incipient century as members of their city's socially elite, privileged class. And being a member of a "good" family was particularly important in a city such as New Orleans, where social position dictated so many of life's opportunities.

One reasonably could expect a product of this advantaged environ-ment to be content to enjoy the fruits of his predecessors' labors and to embrace the social order that fostered the attainment of that bounty. That certainly had been the case with most of John Minor Wisdom's ancestors. With a few notable exceptions, generations of his predeces-sors had subscribed to the conservative ideology adopted by most other wealthy, landowning members of the southern aristocracy whose privi-leged existence depended upon the preservation of the status quo.

Yet there had been occasional displays of a more independent and visionary strain in the family lineage. John Wisdom III, the brother of John Minor Wisdom's great-great-grandfather, had been an outspoken opponent of slavery during the post-Revolutionary period and John III's niece, Virginia Louise Minor, had spearheaded the woman's suffrage movement shortly after the conclusion of the Civil War. Their moral compasses pointed them in a different direction than the one taken by most of their peers and relations. Adhering to traditions and conform-ing to the status quo was impossible for them without first scrutinizing the impact that these forces had on the disadvantaged and more vul-nerable members of society. But their stories were never a part of what-ever family lore Mortimer and Adelaide transmitted to their three sons. William, John, and Norton grew up in a household with parents who were firmly entrenched in New Orleans' rigid, highly developed social network and who raised their sons to have a strong sense of their po-sition in society and the obligations that this entailed. How, then, did a son of this socially prominent family develop such a passionate con-cern for the interests of those whose life experiences were so foreign to his own? The answer lies, at least in part, in the combination of lessons learned from a mother he adored and insights absorbed from the richly diverse set of books that he devoured throughout his college career.

2

FROM BIRTH TO BONNIE
TO THE BRANCH, 1905–1946

For the first fourteen years of his life, John Minor Wisdom lived in a roomy, three-story wood-frame house on Calhoun Street. Only a block and a half off one of New Orleans' most fashionable arteries, mansion-lined St. Charles Avenue, the Wisdom home was built with New Orleans' lengthy and sultry summers in mind.[1] And though it may not have been the largest or the most magnificent residence in this tony locale, the family's lifestyle conformed to the standards expected of members of their social class and economic position.

Despite the setbacks caused by Mortimer's financially disastrous decision to leave the insurance business for the cotton trade, the family was able to maintain its accustomed lifestyle until his death on May 16, 1919, the day preceding John's fourteenth birthday. They were able to retain, for example, the cook, laundress, and butler that Mortimer initially hired during his salad days with the insurance firm.[2] Of all these employees, however, the one most dear to John was Sarah Murphy, the beloved Irish "nurse" who lived with the family and raised him and his two brothers.

1. John Minor Wisdom, interview by Joel Wm. Friedman, October 18, 1995, transcript, New Orleans, La., 3–4.

2. J. M. Wisdom interview [Friedman], October 28, 1993, 72, 75.

"We called her Mammy," Wisdom recounted, "even though she was Irish and white." Yet despite their lifelong devotion to their Irish nurse, the Wisdom brothers, particularly John and his younger sibling, Norton, did not share her, or their parents', religious proclivities. From his earliest days, John had little interest in religion. His parents were active members of their Episcopal church who regularly attended Sunday services and expected and insisted that their sons go to Sunday school. And although John dutifully heeded his parents' request, he did so solely out of obedience. He would have much preferred to spend the time playing any of a variety of sports. And throughout his adult life, Wisdom harbored an indifference, if not a cynical distrust, toward organized religion. Though he recognized that others found comfort in prayer and adherence to religious dogma, faith and belief were inconsistent with his insistence on proof and verification. Moreover, his confidence in his own judgment also deterred Wisdom from conforming to any set of organizational dictates. Consequently, religion played no role in shaping any of his personal or professional decisions.

From the time that he was old enough to throw a ball, sports were a focal point of his early life. Despite always being one of the shortest, lightest, and least athletically gifted boys on the team, Wisdom relished playing football and baseball with the neighborhood kids on a vacant lot down the street from his home or climbing the fence with his cousin Charles "Pie" Dufour (who later earned fame as a local newspaper columnist and author of several books on Louisiana and New Orleans history) to sneak into Tulane football games.

But his ardor for sports never interfered with Wisdom's two other passions—his academic pursuits and the Boy Scouts. Scouting appealed to two of his keenest interests: his love of the outdoors and his passion for learning. Developing and mastering the wide array of skills and knowledge necessary to earn merit badges was a challenge that he embraced with great enthusiasm. More important, perhaps, the fundamental moral and civic lessons he absorbed during his years as a scout came to occupy a central place in his character and clearly influenced his vision of the world and of his place in it.

Wisdom attacked scouting with the same measure of dedication and energy that he directed to all of his endeavors. He methodically mastered the various skills and acquired all the information needed to obtain dozens of merit badges. Over the next several years, he advanced from grade to grade until he reached the ultimate level of Eagle Scout.

By the time he left the Boy Scouts, he had earned more merit badges than any other Eagle Scout in the entire state of Louisiana.[3] Becoming an Eagle Scout, however, provided Wisdom with much more than the wealth of skills and information associated with his countless badges; he internalized the Scout code of honor and fairness. The obligations to help others and to compete according to the rules of fair play and sportsmanship were concepts that resonated within him, would leave a lasting mark on his personal development, and ultimately would find their way into his judicial philosophy, particularly as reflected in his decisions in civil rights cases.

In the 1910s, it was common practice for graduates of public elementary schools in New Orleans to enroll in one of the city's many private high schools. Long before some parents utilized them as a means of avoiding the racially integrated public schools, private institutions, particularly parochial schools, were a mainstay of the city's secondary school offerings. In 1918, John's parents enrolled him at the Isadore Newman Manual Training School, an institution originally established to provide vocational and academic training to Jewish orphans that had expanded and, by that time, earned a city-wide reputation for scholastic excellence.

Wisdom was a year younger than most of his classmates because he had skipped the fifth grade. And despite standing only a few inches above five feet in height and weighing less than a hundred pounds, he was eager to earn a place on his high school football team. He was determined to make the squad and believed that if he practiced long and hard enough, he could overcome his physical limitations. He was the prototypical undersized athlete; short on natural ability and physical attributes, but long on desire and drive. In some small way, his quest for a spot on the Manual varsity football team displayed a character trait that would become a hallmark of his adult life. His willingness to set a goal, to dedicate himself to its pursuit, and to focus his talents and abilities on accomplishing the objective would be repeated throughout his adult life as he moved from the athletic to the political and juridical arenas.

Wisdom's penchant for perseverance came principally from one source. Circumstances, particularly her husband's death, had compelled Adelaide Wisdom to raise her three sons on a tight budget; and the boys, especially John, seemed to draw closer to her during this difficult

3. Jack Bass, *Unlikely Heroes* (New York: 1981), 46–47.

period. Throughout her sons' childhood and adolescence, Adelaide continually stressed the value of character, the importance of proper behavior in the presence of strangers, and the necessity for, and virtues of, hard work.

Adelaide instilled in all three of her sons the notion that everyone was entitled to be treated fairly and with dignity, regardless of their personal circumstances or station in life. She did this not as a matter of noblesse oblige or of religious duty, but out of her own set of moral convictions. Adelaide did not want her boys to feel any sense of entitlement to their particular lifestyle or to think ill of others whose lives followed another orbit. Throughout their childhood, Adelaide stressed that it was incumbent upon her sons to be honorable and contributing members of society and that this involved treating everyone with respect. Moreover, if and when they were in a position to do anything about it, they should strive to ensure that everyone was given a fair shake. The passion and consistency with which Adelaide delivered this life message had a deep and lasting impact. John took it to heart, never forgetting what his mother had stressed. Throughout his adult life, he sought to live up to his mother's example even when it put him at loggerheads with many of his friends and colleagues on one of the most controversial issues of the day. Thus, while most other men of his background and social position were unsympathetic to the civic claims of minority group members, Wisdom was compelled by virtue of his unshakeable devotion to fairness to pursue a different course. His innate sense of fairness led him to conclude, passionately and without apology, that historic victims of bias and mistreatment were entitled to have the full force of the federal government protect their interests. And when presented with the opportunity to do so, Wisdom committed to doing everything in the legitimate exercise of his power to achieve that outcome. And so this son of privilege led a small group of his judicial colleagues on the path of protecting society's most vulnerable members by authoring some of the most powerful and momentous civil rights decisions of the twentieth century.

The value of perseverance was another lesson John took to heart and it held him in good stead throughout his life, including with respect to his pursuit of a place on his high school's football squad. Although a freak accident suffered in a neighborhood pickup football game prevented him from earning his varsity letter, the school principal awarded Wisdom that sought-after distinction sixty-five years after his graduation during a ceremony at which he was honored as his high school's outstanding alumnus.[4]

From his first days at Manual, Wisdom demonstrated a keen interest in reading history-related books and magazines, particularly those that dealt with the great wars of ancient and modern world history. His growing appetite for books was nourished by his liberal use of his father's extensive private library, which Mortimer Wisdom periodically supplemented with books specially ordered from England for John. This passion for history never abated and would come to play a significant role in the composition of many of his most important judicial opinions.

John's focus in history, sports, and scouting was encouraged by both of his parents. Yet as a member of a socially prominent family in New Orleans, he also was expected to adhere to a particular code of conduct that included a highly structured set of social obligations. His mother Adelaide had been raised to believe that it was essential to maintain one's social standing and she expected no less of her own family. Even after her husband's death, Adelaide was able to marshal her limited resources to ensure that her family fulfilled the lifestyle expectations imposed by her society peers. And as the boys entered adulthood, they were invited to participate in the mandated societal right of passage embodied in the exclusive, private side of the public celebration of the city's premier annual event—Mardi Gras.

From the time he was old enough to catch the coveted "throws" that float riders shower upon the teeming throngs massed along St. Charles Avenue and Canal Street, Wisdom loved to view the parades that highlight New Orleans' annual Mardi Gras revelry. When he was a boy, several of the Carnival organizations ("krewes," as they are known in New Orleans) sponsored night parades. To provide illumination for the crowds that lined the sidewalks and neutral ground along the parade route, each of the mule-drawn floats was preceded by a group of white-clad and hooded black men carrying torches, or flambeaux.[5] These flambeaux carriers developed a distinctive part-strutting, part-dancing gait, and although the flambeau itself has evolved from the original candle-lit paper lantern hung from a pole to the modern-day kerosene-lighted torch, the carrier's traditional walk has remained virtually unchanged for more than a century.[6] Also unchanged, however, is the sad

4. J. M. Wisdom interview [Friedman], October 28, 1993, 12.
5. Perry Young, *Carnival and Mardi Gras in New Orleans* (New Orleans: 1939), 26.
6. Reid Mitchell, *All on a Mardi Gras Day* (Cambridge, Mass.: 1995), 23.

fact that carrying a flambeau is the only part that African Americans are permitted to play in the parades sponsored by some of these krewes.

To receive an offer of membership in krewes such as Momus, Comus, Rex, or Proteus has always been a highly visible symbol of acceptance into the tightly controlled and highly restrictive uppermost rung of New Orleans' social ladder. By his mid-twenties, Wisdom had been invited by each of these krewes to join their ranks. Like his father and grandfather before him, he recognized this as an important rite of passage and he accepted each invitation. It would have been unthinkable for a young man of his station and position in society to do otherwise. Moreover, he keenly desired to be a member of these krewes and, in his early years, particularly reveled in the opportunity to be the target, rather than the source, of New Orleans' traditional "Throw me something, mister!" parade cry.

Although Wisdom eventually resigned from two krewes, Rex and Proteus, when the parade schedule became too strenuous, he never relinquished his membership in the krewes of Comus and Momus or in the Boston Club, the private social club affiliated with the Rex organization. During this entire period, it was a highly unguarded secret that the krewes of Comus and Momus did not admit Jewish members, and that African Americans were excluded from Comus (Wisdom's eldest daughter, Kit, was anointed queen of this extremely elite krewe during one Mardi Gras season), Momus, Proteus, and the Boston Club.[7] Nevertheless, the maintenance of these policies never caused Wisdom to consider resigning from any of these organizations. Even at the height of his public visibility, when he was writing path-breaking opinions that mandated the termination of decades of public segregation in voting, employment, and education, Wisdom maintained that there was a place within a pluralistic society for truly private pockets of exclusion. "There is something to be said," he consistently maintained, "for a place where a group of one-legged, red-haired Scots can gather together, aside from the rest of the world."[8] Although his unflinching adherence as to this matter surprised, and disappointed, some of his most ardent admirers, Wisdom never tried to hide these organizational memberships or his multiple reasons for retaining them.

First and foremost among these explanations was the fact that he sim-

7. Kathleen ("Kit") Wisdom, interview by Joel Wm. Friedman, December 29, 1993, New Orleans, La., 22.

8. J. M. Wisdom interview [Friedman], October 28, 1993, 61–62.

ply enjoyed spending time, and, particularly, playing bridge, with his friends. "The people I see in these clubs are guys that I went to school with and have known all my life," Wisdom once explained.[9] There, he could spend part of the afternoon competing against lifelong bridge buddies, or let his hair down with old friends, free from public scrutiny. "If I wanted to go to the Louisiana Club and take a few drinks in the middle of the day without somebody raising an eyebrow, I could do it, can still do it."[10] He also appreciated the opportunity to relax in an environment that permitted "absolute freedom of conversation" for those of his friends who, unlike him, did savor "the freedom of men's conversation, which is maybe a cut above locker room conversation, but not that many cuts above."[11]

Beyond enjoying the pleasure of his friends' company, to have stayed in such a club for decades and then to have resigned after he was offered a public position would have been, in Wisdom's mind, sheer hypocrisy. If being a member of the club did not offend his beliefs before joining the bench, he saw no reason to adapt a different attitude purely for public consumption. He also was unpersuaded by the legal argument that these restrictive clubs served the civic and business interests of their members and, as such, should be ineligible for the exemption afforded to private clubs by most antidiscrimination ordinances and statutes. He remained convinced that at least the Boston and Louisiana Clubs were truly private.[12]

Finally, Wisdom was resolute in his conviction that his membership in these restrictive clubs never affected his judicial judgment. Nevertheless, while the record supports this claim, he grudgingly admitted that the appearances created by membership in such organizations could reasonably lead someone else seeking high public office to eliminate such an affiliation. But at the end of the day, he never wavered from either his own determination not to resign or his candid, bluntly honest explanation for that decision. "I didn't resign in 1957 [the year of his judicial appointment], and I've been a member too long now to worry about it. Besides, everybody knows where I stand and I can't change the opinion of the members of the club to which I belong who disagree with me."[13]

9. Bass, *Unlikely Heroes*, 46.
10. J. M. Wisdom interview [Friedman], October 28, 1993, 61.
11. Ibid.
12. Ibid., 59–60.
13. Ibid., 65.

Wisdom's unyielding approach to this sensitive issue also reflects a strongly stubborn streak in his personality. "I've been a member of the Louisiana Club for sixty-two years," he explained on one of the innumerable occasions when the issue was raised with him, "and the Boston Club longer than that. It doesn't affect my opinions, and . . . hell. To hell with it, I'm not gonna change at this point."[14] And though he did not resign any of his memberships after being nominated to the federal bench in 1957, he did cease riding in all Mardi Gras parades at that time, but only because of his respect for the federal judiciary and his adamancy about not casting any possible disrepute upon that institution. "It wouldn't do," he believed, "to have a federal judge fall off the float. He could fall off the float and be cold sober, but who would believe that? And it would certainly have been a terrible reflection on the federal judiciary for a federal judge to fall off a float!"[15]

In the late summer of 1922, just a few months after his seventeenth birthday, Wisdom left New Orleans to begin his college studies at Washington & Lee University. His father, who had attended the school while Robert E. Lee was its president, was an active alumnus who sat on the university's board of trustees. Because of this role, Mortimer and Adelaide Wisdom frequently hosted visiting university officials and alumni at their home.[16] Yet despite his deeply felt commitment to his alma mater, Mortimer never pushed any of his sons to follow in his collegiate footsteps, "although he assumed," John acknowledged, "that I would go there."[17] For John's part, however, "it never occurred to me to go anywhere else."[18] His older brother, William, continuing what was becoming a family tradition, had graduated from W&L in 1921. So when John was ready to make his selection, "it was natural for me to want to go there."[19]

The school's all-male student body also helped to ease the social adjustment for this reserved seventeen-year-old.[20] But unlike his extroverted, more socially adept older brother, John tended to avoid most of

---

14. Ibid., 66.

15. Ibid., 53.

16. J. M. Wisdom interview [Friedman], September 30, 1994, 15.

17. J. M. Wisdom interview [Friedman], October 28, 1993, 80.

18. Ibid., 76.

19. Ibid., 80.

20. Geoff O'Connell, "Wisdom and Courage," New Orleans Magazine 16, no. 9 (June 1982): 51.

the school's social events, preferring to spend his free time reading. He rarely attended the parties his classmates arranged with the students at three of the state's nearby female institutions and never had a serious girlfriend. Neither did he take part in fraternity life, which, in a small college town like Lexington, Virginia, was the focal point of campus social life. Nevertheless, Wisdom did not find much difficulty in filling whatever void might have been created by the absence of an active social life. He was more than happy to pass the time reading and discovering and pursuing the university's broad array of academic offerings.

During his freshman year, Wisdom developed an interest in historical geology. In fact, he was such an excellent student in his history and geology (and, later, English) courses that the school awarded him a full scholarship for his final two years. By the end of his first year, however, he had found a new calling. He decided that he wanted to become a literary critic. This caused him to shift his attention to the English department, where he enrolled in every available English course and in the school's only offering on the Anglo-Saxon language.

Wisdom's collegiate studies, particularly his concentration on history and literature, played a critically formative role in his career. It was here that he began to develop a love for the written language and a careful attention to the nuances of expression. And this keen focus on precision of language would serve him well over the succeeding half-century. It unquestionably added power and persuasiveness to the hundreds of judicial opinions he wrote during his forty-year judicial career, even if it did, on occasion, rankle the egos of some of his law clerks. For decades, one of the rituals associated with each new clerk's entrance into the chambers was a briefing by an outgoing clerk on Judge Wisdom's writing style. Each year, on their first day on the job, the new clerks received a single-spaced five-page list of grammatical and stylistic do's and don'ts penned by the judge, called "Wisdom's Idiosyncrasies." Judge Wisdom took pride in the authorship of his opinions and insisted that his clerks scrupulously adhere to his carefully crafted guidelines, many of which were predicated upon his two foundational principles: "Be brief" and "Simple is better."

It was also during this period of separation from his childhood friends and family that Wisdom was able to observe and internalize different perspectives on life from those shared by his more tradition-bound, well-bred New Orleans peers. But this evolution came mostly from books rather than from exposure to a new set of friends and colleagues. "I think from my reading," he observed, "I tended to be more liberal than my friends."[21] So, in addition to the dedication to fairness that effectively had been wired into his DNA, the love of history and wide-ranging insights that he developed from feeding his insatiable appetite for books are reflected in both the style and substance of his most celebrated judicial opinions.

By the end of his college career, Wisdom had resolved to pursue a career in literary criticism. So he applied for, and was admitted to the graduate program at Harvard University with the intention of obtaining a master of arts, and thereafter, a doctoral degree in English. "But when I got there, I ran up against an inflexible rule that no one could receive a postgraduate degree in English unless the applicant had Latin or Greek."[22] Despite his insistence that he had never been informed of this requirement prior to being admitted, his plea for an exemption was denied, although the university allowed him to stay in residence as a non-degree student, with permission to audit any of Harvard's rich variety of courses. Having already settled in Boston and having agreed to share a room with a childhood pal from New Orleans who was just starting at Harvard Law School, Wisdom accepted this offer and remained in Cambridge for the 1925–1926 school year. The decision altered the course of his life.

Liberated from the strictures of the degree-granting program, Wisdom was free to pick and choose from the multitudinous offerings of Harvard's diverse faculties. He also had access to the university's massive library collection, which was more than sufficient to sate even his abundant appetite. He initially attended lectures by several of Harvard's English literature scholars.[23] But as the academic year progressed, he sensed that it would be difficult for him to make a living as a professional writer. While he reevaluated his career options, he also spent time with his roommate and his roommate's friends, nearly all of whom were law students. Intrigued by the snippets of their inevitably law-related conversations, Wisdom decided to sit in on a law class or two. It was enough to encourage him to forgo his original career plans.

Once he decided to enter the legal profession, the choice of a law school was simple. Even the lure of Harvard's nonpareil faculty could not withstand the call of his native New Orleans. "I wanted to be a law-

21. Ibid., 55.
22. J. M. Wisdom interview [Friedman], September 30, 1994, 29.
23. Ibid., 33.

yer in New Orleans because New York and other places did not interest me. My roots were in New Orleans and my parents' friends were in
New Orleans, and I could see a better, brighter future in New Orleans
than I could in New York."[24] Wisdom could have matriculated at Harvard and then returned home to practice law. But he never seriously
contemplated that option. Louisiana was the only state in the nation
whose legal heritage derives from continental civil law rather than British common law. In order to be prepared to practice in this unique jurisdiction, Wisdom recalled, "it was the general opinion that young [Loui-
siana] men who went away to law school at Harvard or Columbia, or
other places, usually came back and took a year of study at Tulane" to
familiarize themselves with the local jurisprudence. This sort of patchwork, last-minute approach to anything, however, was not his style. If
law was to be his life's work, it was not enough for him merely to dip his
feet in the waters; he needed to immerse himself fully in the civil law.
"I thought I might as well go to Tulane in the first place," Wisdom explained, "and really learn civil law."[25] So rather than stay in Cambridge,
he decided to attend the school that was the traditional choice for most
New Orleans males of his social position. It was also the school that had
awarded its first law degree to Wisdom's maternal grandfather, David
Cohen Labatt. In June 1925, full of enthusiasm and eager to begin this
new endeavor, Wisdom returned to New Orleans to study at Tulane
Law School.[26]

In the fall of 1926, the entering class at Tulane Law School was composed primarily of the sons of the state's socially elite and professional
classes. Although the school's first female law graduate, Bettie Run-
nels, had received her degree in 1898, few women had attended Tulane's law school prior to the 1930s.[27] Wisdom's class, like nearly all of
its predecessors, was composed entirely of men. In addition, all but two
of his twenty-five classmates came from Louisiana, and neither the student from Texas nor the classmate from Ohio stayed long enough to
graduate.

Early Thursday morning on September 23, 1926, Wisdom attended

24. Ibid., 34–35.
25. Ibid., 34.
26. For an extended narration of the history of Tulane Law School, see Joel Wm. Friedman, *A
Look Back at the Tulane Law School of John Minor Wisdom's Era*, 70 TUL. L. REV. 2091 (1996).
27. "Tulane Graduates," *New Orleans Times-Democrat*, May 24, 1898, 3.

his first law school class. Seated next to him was another New Orleanian. The pair had never met; their widely divergent backgrounds and the city's rigid social order would have made much social interaction highly unlikely. Whereas Wisdom could trace his family's roots in the United States to the middle of the seventeenth century, Saul Sokolsky was the son of Jewish immigrants who had escaped from Poland in 1902. In contrast to the privileged upbringing Wisdom had enjoyed, Sokolsky was a street-smart kid from a poor, working-class section of the city. The pair shook hands and exchanged introductions moments before the instructor began his initial lecture, commencing a close friendship that lasted for more than seventy years and formed the basis of a thirty-year professional partnership that terminated only when Wisdom left private practice for the federal bench.

Throughout his three years at Tulane Law School, Wisdom demonstrated an intellectual prowess and affinity for the profession that set him apart from his peers. He had benefited tremendously from the education he had received at Washington & Lee as well as from his brief stint at Harvard. But it was at Tulane Law School that he found his niche and distinguished himself by his academic performance.

After his first year of study, Wisdom stood at the top of his class, a position he never relinquished during his law school career. He was the only first-year student to earn a position on the dean's honors list.[28] He also was one of three students chosen by the dean to run the school's Moot Court program and to edit the *Tulane Law Review,* a student- and alumni-edited scholarly journal.[29] And at the graduation ceremony, despite the time commitment that he devoted to his duties at both the Moot Court and *Law Review,* he was awarded the Faculty Medal, the signal honor bestowed upon the student who graduated with the highest overall grade-point average.

Wisdom's dedication to his studies and to his other law school responsibilities did not, however, prevent him from continuing to indulge in two of his favorite diversions—sports and betting. He was particularly partial to playing the betting sheets that required participants to pick the winners in a collection of ten college football games. And though his wagers were always small, he approached this task, as all others, with his customary zeal and discipline. Each fall he would spend

28. Bulletin of the Tulane University of Louisiana, College of Law, January 1, 1928, 20.
29. J. M. Wisdom interview [Friedman], November 5, 1993, 4.

hours in the public library poring over out-of-town newspapers to uncover some crucial tidbit of information about a player's injury or lack of game availability that might give him an edge on the competition and increase his winning percentage. "And I got to be pretty good at it," Wisdom proudly recalled, "almost like a professional handicapper!"[30]

In light of his youthful, innocent flirtation with sports gambling, it is not surprising that Wisdom approached a case that arose early on in his judicial career[31] with particular relish. Four professional gamblers from Miami pled guilty in 1959 to evading income taxes imposed on gambling earnings. After accepting their plea, the trial judge offered the defendants the choice of jail time or probation on the condition that they give up gambling for good. After choosing the probation option, the defendants appealed the trial judge's decision to the Fifth Circuit, alleging that the judge had exceeded his authority by attaching the no-gambling rider as a condition of probation.

In his one-page opinion for the appellate court rejecting their appeal, Wisdom chided the defendants for being willing to accept probation "while seeking to welch on its price."[32] Although he appreciated the fact that the gamblers were "anxious to pursue their chosen profession," Wisdom insisted that they had "got in it of their own doing, elected to stay in it of their own free will, and the misgivings they now have should have occurred to them before they agreed to probation on the trial judge's terms."[33] After all, he concluded, these gamblers, above others, should have realized that a deal is a deal.

For the sixteen members of Tulane Law's graduating class, the summer of 1929 was not the most propitious time to enter the job market. The country was in the waning moments of the post–World War I economic boom and was riding the tail of an ephemeral "Hoover bull market" that would linger only for the first six months of his new administration. By October, the national mania for investing in the stock market was transformed into an equally desperate wave of panic selling as fortunes and lives went into a freefall on "Black Tuesday," October 29. Nevertheless, because of his stellar performance at Tulane Law School, Wisdom was

30. J. M. Wisdom interview [Friedman], October 28, 1993, 23–24.

31. *Barnhill v. U.S.*, 279 F.2d 105 (5th Cir.1960), cert. denied, 364 U.S. 824, 5 L.Ed. 2d 53, 81 S.Ct. 60 (1960).

32. *Barnhill v. U.S.*, 279 F.2d at 106.

33. 279 F.2d at 106.

much in demand, having retained offers from several of the city's most prominent law firms.[34] But he had a different plan in mind.

During the summer of 1929, after they completed the state bar exam, Wisdom and his friend and classmate Saul Sokolsky agreed to form a law partnership that would last for twenty-eight years. During their three years together at Tulane, the unlikely pair had become fast friends and shared a deep, mutual admiration and respect for each other's talents and character. Practicing law together appealed to both of them and each took pride in the fact that "we never did sign any partnership agreement. We just shook hands and that was it."[35]

Choosing a name for the firm was as uncomplicated a matter as their initial decision to join forces. Wisdom and Sokolsky never had worried about the commercial viability of a partnership pairing the son of an upper-class, socially elite southern family with someone from an immigrant, working-class Jewish background. Neither did they spend any time negotiating over the ordering of the firm's name. Wisdom may have assumed that his name would come first because of his superior performance in law school and Sokolsky may have believed that the cache attached to Wisdom's family name would assist in attracting clients. Yet when it came time to make the decision, "there was simply no argument about it at all. We didn't flip a coin," Wisdom recounted, matter-of-factly, "and we didn't argue about it. It was simply understood that it would be 'Wisdom and Sokolsky.'"[36]

The two friends and partners proudly informed anyone who would listen that they had never had a disagreement during the entirety of their professional relationship. When Wisdom was installed as a federal judge in 1957, he gave his partner a photo taken at the swearing-in ceremony upon which he penned the dedication: "A great lawyer, partner and friend for thirty years. Now we're about to have our first argument."

Despite the Depression-era financial challenges confronting their incipient joint enterprise, and decades before most attorneys came to recognize their obligation to provide free service to indigents *pro bono publico* (for the public good), Wisdom & Sokolsky's very first client was taken on a non-fee-producing basis. The case touched a raw nerve in Wisdom; it involved the sort of injustice that he could not abide. A

34. J. M. Wisdom interview [Friedman], November 5, 1993, 17–19.
35. Ibid., 26.
36. Ibid.

friend of his cook, an African American, was accused of stealing some railroad ties and was tried in Plaquemines Parish. Wisdom recalled that "they were not easy on blacks then and they didn't get a fair shake as a rule." Yet though the newly minted attorney could hardly afford it, Wisdom's abiding belief in the imperative of fair treatment, particularly when the government was involved, compelled him to represent his employee's impoverished friend at no charge.[37]

After a difficult first year or two, the firm began to prosper. Wisdom began to develop a reputation as an expert in trust law and the partners slowly gravitated toward an informal division of labor. Wisdom was the acknowledged superior writer. Accordingly, on matters that went to litigation, he would draft the briefs and other court documents, while Sokolsky handled the courtroom appearances. "Saul was a very good litigator," Wisdom explained, "and he was very friendly with all the judges, so he was a good person to have in court because of that fact." But within a short time after his admission to the bar, Sokolsky became increasingly annoyed at the inability of most judges and jurors to pronounce his name. So after a couple of years, Sokolsky changed his name to Stone. And the choice turned out to have an unintended mercantile benefit. Both partners came to believe that the fortuitous combination of their two last names generated an aura of confidence in the minds of potential clients. As Wisdom relayed, "Wisdom and Stone sounded like a good solid firm."[38]

The pair worked long hours to build up their practice. Nevertheless, Wisdom found the time to develop another interest. He began to consider the possibility of getting married. And the object of his intentions was, like him—if not more so—a child of the privileged class of Louisiana society.

Like her husband-to-be, Bonnie Mathews (born Charles Stewart Mathews, she was called Bonnie from early childhood as in "Bonnie Prince Charlie") was the child of an elderly father and the descendant of a very wealthy family whose southern roots predated the Revolution-

37. "So I took the case and I would go down to interview him and bring cigarettes and cakes or cookies. . . . He promised that he would work for me whenever I wanted him and he was going to give me I don't know how many thousands of dollars worth of work. Anyway, I got him off and that was the last I ever saw of him. He completely forgot about all those promises. He disappeared! I guess he was glad to get out of Plaquemines." J. M. Wisdom interview [Friedman], November 5, 1993, 28.

38. Ibid., 23.

ary War. Her most noteworthy predecessor, great-grandfather George Mathews, was one of Louisiana's first jurists. Like Bonnie's future husband, George Mathews was devoted passionately to Louisiana's civil law system, irrevocably committed to the principle of equal justice under law, and, in the words of one historian, "a very great judge who played a large part in the legal life of Louisiana."[39]

Appointed to the Louisiana Supreme Court by the state's first elected governor, William C. C. Claiborne, Mathews is best remembered for one historic two-paragraph opinion. In the early 1830s, a Louisiana family by the name of Marot went to France with their young slave girl, Josephine. When the Marots arrived home in Louisiana, Josephine's mother, Marie Louise, sued to obtain a declaration of her daughter's emancipation as a result of being transported to a country that did not recognize the institution of slavery. In a brief but poignant opinion penned in a dramatic and lyrical style that could easily have come from the pen of his great-granddaughter's husband, Justice Mathews, speaking for the Louisiana Supreme Court, declared that "being free for one moment in France, it was not in the power of her former owner to reduce her again to slavery."[40] Twenty-one years later, this opinion was relied upon by U.S. Supreme Court Justice John McLean, who dissented from the Court's infamous ruling in the *Dred Scott* case that a black slave was the legal equivalent of a piece of property, and as such, could be transported by his owner from a southern state into a territory that forbade slavery without losing his slave status.[41]

Among the many landholdings acquired by George Mathews from the profits reaped from several extremely lucrative investments were sugar-rich properties, including the Georgia Plantation, located along the Bayou Lafourche in Louisiana just seventy miles south of New Orleans. By the time Bonnie was born, the plantation had grown to more than thirty thousand acres and the town in which it was located had been named Mathews, in honor of its founding family. Home-schooled until age ten, Bonnie moved from the Georgia Plantation to New Orleans to attend a small private school that catered to the children of well-heeled families. While a student at Sweet Briar College Bonnie fre-

39. Henry Plauché Dart, "Mazureau's Oration on Mathews," *Louisiana Historical Quarterly* 4 (April 1921): 151.
40. *Marie Louise, free woman of color v. Marot,* 9 La. 474 (1836).
41. *Dred Scott v. Sanford,* 60 U.S. (19 How.) 393 (1857).

quently returned home to participate in the whirl of social events that were a traditional part of the life of young women in her social circle. "In New Orleans," Bonnie explained, "if you moved in a certain sphere, you were eventually bound to meet practically everybody else going around in that sphere." Among the many young men that moved in that sphere was John Wisdom. "We'd known each other quite casually for quite a long time before we became the least bit interested in each other. It was not love at first sight."[42] On October 24, 1931, John and Bonnie were wed in the Trinity Episcopal Church, the same church in which John's parents had been married and where he had, albeit reluctantly, attended Sunday school as a child.

Throughout the 1930s, Wisdom devoted himself to building up his law practice. But like most able-bodied men of his generation, he placed both his private life and his career on hold as a direct consequence of unanticipated events that occurred barely six miles off the southern coast of the Hawaiian island of Oahu on December 7, 1941. Even though he was nearly thirty-seven years old, he voluntarily enlisted in the air force only days after the Japanese attack on Pearl Harbor. Commissioned as a captain and assigned to the intelligence division, Wisdom was a member of the inaugural class of the air force's Combat Intelligence School, where he specialized in the planning and evaluation of strategic bombing operations.

Many graduates of the Combat Intelligence School were sent overseas as intelligence officers for combat units. Wisdom, however, was transferred to the Pentagon, where he was assigned to a strategic bombing team tasked with preparing a response in case the Germans decided to bomb South America.

Living in Washington was a wonderful experience for the Wisdoms. There was plenty of time and opportunity for Wisdom to attend to the needs of his two young children, John, Jr., and Kit (his younger daughter, Penelope, was born after the family's return to New Orleans), bicycle riding in nearby Rock Creek Park being a particular favorite activity of his five-year-old daughter.[43] The air force placed the family in very comfortable quarters in a local hotel, whose residents included the Duke and Duchess of Windsor. And though some of Wisdom's superior offi-

42. B. M. Wisdom by Joel Wm. Friedman, New Orleans, La., June 30, 1994, 14.
43. Kathleen ("Kit") Wisdom interview [Friedman], December 29, 1993, 29.

cers visited him in the hope of seeing the British exiles, who lived on the same floor as the Wisdoms, to John, "they never were very exciting."[44]

Apart from the pleasures associated with living in Washington, Wisdom's military experience was a significant disappointment. The work "was not fascinating by any means, and not what I thought combat intelligence would me." Preparing contingency plans in the event of a German bombing of eastern Brazil "was, to my mind—and it appeared to me to be so then—a waste, a considerable waste of energy. The likelihood of the Germans ever attempting to cross from Dakar to Belém seemed to me so improbable."[45] Yet even though his months with the tactical bombing squad did not live up to expectations, one incident did occur during this period to break the routine and create more than a bit of momentary excitement.

In the midst of his research on potential German bombing sites in South America, Wisdom was instructed to devise plans for an Allied invasion of Europe. He confected two alternative strategies: a strike through southern Italy and a landing at Normandy. As news of this junior officer's proposal filtered up the chain of command, it caught the attention of some senior air force officers, who quickly and quietly called Wisdom in for an intensive and exhaustive interrogation. The officers feared that the confidentiality of the ongoing D-Day planning process had been compromised since such a relatively low-level air force officer had secured access to the armed forces' most sensitive and highly guarded secret information. Wisdom, however, was able to convince these interrogators that his plan was the product solely of his own invention, and he was promptly dispatched to his tedious topographic study of various South American cities.

Frustrated by the tiresome tasks he was assigned and by having spent more than half of his fourteen months of active service behind a Pentagon desk instead of in the European theater, Wisdom welcomed a new and challenging assignment. As luck would have it, just as he was looking for a change of venue, the army was searching for an experienced attorney to fill a vacancy in one of its legal offices.

The inelegantly titled Legal Branch of the Contract Division of the Office of the Under Secretary of War was staffed by an extraordinary group of marvelously gifted attorneys. The Legal Branch, as it became

---

44. J. M. Wisdom interview [Friedman], November 12, 1993, 10.
45. Ibid., 11.

known, was founded in March 1941 by the under secretary of war, Judge Robert P. Patterson. Patterson, a World War I veteran and recipient of the Distinguished Service Cross, had been a U.S. district judge in Manhattan before being promoted to the U.S. Second Circuit Court of Appeals, where he served with legendary Judges Learned and August Hand. Judge Patterson chose William L. Marbury, an attorney from Baltimore, to serve as the Legal Branch's first chief and tasked the Legal Branch with devising, implementing, and monitoring the army's massive body of procurement policies.[46]

But it was not the quality or diversity of the Legal Branch's work that meant the most to Wisdom. By far, the most enduring impact of this experience was the lifelong relationships that he forged with this remarkably talented collection of lawyers. During his tenure, the Legal Branch produced "two Justices of the Supreme Judicial Court of Massachusetts, a Judge of the U.S. Court of Claims, a Governor of Indiana, an Under Secretary of the Treasury, an Assistant Secretary of State, a member of the National Labor Relations Board, the dean of a law school, several law professors, a general counsel of the Internal Revenue Service, an Insurance Commissioner of the State of New York," and, of course, a judge of the U.S. Fifth Circuit Court of Appeals.[47]

Major Robert Ammi Cutter, the Legal Branch's deputy chief, was an attorney from Boston who subsequently enjoyed a celebrated sixteen-year tenure as an associate justice on the Supreme Judicial Court of Massachusetts. And when Cutter retired from that court in 1972, his seat was filled by Harvard Law School Professor Benjamin Kaplan, who thirty years earlier had been recruited by Cutter to work at the Legal Branch. Cutter also brought in Baltimore lawyer Robert Bowie, who later served as assistant secretary of state for policy planning, and Cleveland lawyer Horace Chapman ("Chappie") Rose, a former law clerk to Supreme Court Justice Oliver Wendell Holmes who eventually served as under secretary of the Treasury Department and advised President Richard Nixon in connection with the Watergate scandal. They were joined by Texas attorney Dillon Anderson, who later served as special assistant to President Eisenhower for national security affairs, where he was one of Ike's closest advisors.

Nearly all of the members of the Legal Branch, other than Wis-

46. William L. Marbury, *In the Catbird Seat* (Baltimore: 1988), 155.
47. Ibid., 158.

dom and Anderson, were Harvard-trained men who hailed from north of the Mason-Dixon Line. Outside of his year at Harvard, this was the first time in Wisdom's life that he had been exposed to so many Eastern-educated peers. Some have speculated that this leavening experience may help to explain how Judge Wisdom developed a perspective on certain issues, such as civil rights, that was not shared by most New Orleanians of his age, educational background, and social and economic class. Wisdom would be the first to admit that he held all of his Legal Branch colleagues in the highest regard, that he maintained a close friendship with many of them over the succeeding several decades, and that the constant challenge of keeping up with these keen minds certainly expanded his own intellectual boundaries. But beyond that, he rejected, probably correctly, any attempt to link his experiences at the Legal Branch to any particular facet of his subsequent developed judicial philosophy. For the core values that found expression in his precedent-shattering (and precedent-creating) opinions on civil rights had been ingrained into Wisdom long before his army service. The lessons of fairness and fair dealing that he absorbed both from his mother and through his experiences as an Eagle Scout, as well as the social consciousness that he developed after years of voracious reading, had long since taken root and were the true wellspring from which the bedrock principles underlying his judicial decision-making flowed.[48] Moreover, as he remarked to an interviewer with respect to his Legal Branch colleagues, "as a matter of fact, many of those persons were not liberal at all."[49]

Wisdom stayed at the Legal Branch for only a year. Initially assigned to contractual matters, he soon found his niche in the Legal Branch's property division, where he became something of an expert in the handling and disposal of the army's surplus property. His acknowledged command of that subject landed him his next assignment, to serve on the team assigned to canvas the services' $8 billion reserves of surplus property on army bases throughout the world. In the course of this assignment, Wisdom stopped in Tokyo to inventory the army's cache of supplies in Japan's capital city. While there, he lunched with the Supreme Commander of the Allied Powers in Japan, General Douglas MacArthur, who presented Wisdom and the other army officers in at-

48. See generally Geoff O'Connell, "Judge John Minor Wisdom: His Trailblazing Decisions Made History," *New Orleans Magazine* (June 1982): 58–59.
49. Ibid., 55.

tendance with authentic samurai swords.[50] This would not be a Wisdom's only encounter with this larger-than-life figure of American history. Six years later, unbeknownst to MacArthur, while walking down a hallway in Chicago's Hilton Hotel to visit a friend of hers, John's wife Bonnie inadvertently passed by the general's room and overheard him rehearsing the acceptance speech he hoped to make at the 1952 Republican nominating convention for the presidency of the United States. But the Republicans ultimately tapped MacArthur's colleague and rival, Dwight Eisenhower, for the top spot on their national ticket, and so Bonnie and the others who had crowded around her in the hall were the only audience ever to hear the general's oration.[51]

In recognition of his service, the air force awarded Wisdom the Legion of Merit. So decorated, he returned in 1946 to civilian life. Although remaining in Washington was an option, he was, to his roots, a New Orleanian, and, according to his daughter Kit, "that was where he wanted to make his mark."[52] So the family returned home to New Orleans and Wisdom resumed his law partnership with Saul Stone.

50. J. M. Wisdom interview [Friedman], December 10, 1993, 30.
51. Ibid., 25–27.
52. Kathleen ("Kit") Wisdom interview [Friedman], December 29, 1993, 10. See also John Minor Wisdom interview by Fred Graham, March 7, 1981, New Orleans, La., 8.

3

AT THE BAR, 1948–1953

After nearly two decades of representing a variety of business and other clients, the firm of Wisdom & Stone was retained by a local supermarket owner whose fight against the price-fixing practices employed by national liquor distributors would take him and his attorneys all the way to the U.S. Supreme Court and would represent John Minor Wisdom's most noteworthy achievement as a member of the bar.

In 1948, John G. Schwegmann, Jr., began receiving threats from liquor distributors who disapproved of his policy of charging less than the liquor manufacturers' listed retail prices at the various locations of the supermarket chain that bore his name. Schwegmann and his two brothers had built a one-store operation into a chain of supermarkets, all of which featured a wide range of products, including liquor, sold at cut-rate prices.[1]

As far back as 1916, although predominantly in the 1930s, liquor manufacturers established minimum price schedules for the resale of their products.[2] Typically, these tariffs were enforced through contracts entered into between the distributors and their wholesaler or retail establishment clients. Retailers who signed these contracts agreed not to

1. Ronette King, "It Would Have Been Insane for Me to Stay and Bleed to Death," *New Orleans Times-Picayune*, March 2, 1997, Section F, 1–2.
2. Comment, *The Schwegmann Case and Fair Trade: An Obituary?* 61 YALE L.J. 381 (1952).

sell the manufacturer's line at less than the minimum scheduled price. Moreover, like many other states, Louisiana had a Fair Trade Law that prohibited any vendor from selling at less than the producer's stipulated price even if that vendor had not signed the distributor's price maintenance contract. And the federal Sherman Antitrust Act expressly permitted the enforcement of this type of state law.[3]

In 1949, two liquor distributors sued Schwegmann's to stop it from selling their products at cut-rate prices. Wisdom's response was brief and straightforward: holding a vendor to the minimum price terms of a contract that it had not signed constituted price-fixing in violation of the federal antitrust laws.[4] The case was assigned to U.S. district judge J. Skelly Wright, with whose name Wisdom's eventually would become forever linked in the annals of American civil rights law. But in 1949, Wisdom was simply an attorney pleading his case before the trial judge.

Judge Wright explicitly rejected Wisdom's argument, ruling that the Louisiana law required even non-signers to adhere to the distributors' contractually designated minimum price schedules and that enforcement of this state statute was permitted under federal antitrust law.[5] Wisdom promptly appealed Wright's decrees to the U.S. Fifth Circuit Court of Appeals, but failed to convince a majority of that court as well.[6] Seven months later, the U.S. Supreme Court agreed to hear the case. Wisdom, Saul Stone, and a young associate toiled for weeks over the written brief they would submit to the Court. With Wisdom playing the leading role, the trio worked together, drafting and redrafting the brief until the ninety-four-page document satisfied Wisdom's rigorous scrutiny.

The brief reflected Wisdom's penchant for precise argument and historical perspective. But it also was peppered with several instances of

3. Act of August 17, 1937, 50 Stat. 693, 15 U.S.C. 1 (1937).

4. Answer to Complaint, *Calvert Distillers Corp. v. Schwegmann Brothers*, Civil Action No. 2607, United States District Court for the Eastern District of Louisiana, filed December 12, 1949; Answer to Complaint, *Seagram Distillers Corp. v. Schwegmann Brothers*, Civil Action No. 2608, United States District Court for the Eastern District of Louisiana, filed December 12, 1949.

5. Findings of Fact and Conclusions of Law, *Calvert Distillers Corp. v. Schwegmann Brothers*, Civil Action No. 2607, United States District Court for the Eastern District of Louisiana, filed January 10, 1950; Findings of Fact and Conclusions of Law, *Seagram Distillers Corp. v. Schwegmann Brothers*, Civil Action No. 2608, United States District Court for the Eastern District of Louisiana, filed January 10, 1950.

6. *Schwegmann Brothers v. Calvert Distillers Corp.*, 184 F.2d 11 (5th Cir.1950).

the pungent and sometimes caustic Louisiana-flavored rhetoric that subsequently permeated scores of opinions that flowed from his judicial pen. Wisdom wanted each member of the Supreme Court to understand that this case demanded more than a legal technician's attention to some mundane issue of law. If he could focus their attention on the impact of the distributors' price-fixing practices on ordinary citizens, Wisdom hoped to convince the justices that his position involved more than an esoteric interpretation of some arcane provision of federal law. To this end, the brief declared that although "this case involves the price of a bottle of whisky; the principle involved affects the price of food, drugs, clothing and other necessities of life . . . [and] the decision will have an immediate and continuing effect on 140 million consumers in forty-five 'fair-trade' states who today are paying more for the goods they buy than they would pay for the goods in a free, competitive market."[7] Wisdom also made it clear that he was not talking about price-fixing in some abstract, artificial sense. "Someone sitting in New York or Montreal," he wrote, "fixes the prices to be charged by Schwegmann Bros. on St. Claude Street in New Orleans or by some little country store, say at Bayou Terre Aux Boeufs."[8]

The brief also reflected his wit and delight in using literary references for emphasis. Rather than simply declaring that the statute should be interpreted literally, Wisdom offered, in New Orleans parlance, some *lagniappe* explanation for his basic proposition that minimum prices could not be imposed on unwilling, non-contracting resalers. "*Contractual* price-fixing no more includes *non-contractual* price-fixing than 'navigable' includes 'non-navigable' or 'negotiable' includes 'non-negotiable.' Such verbal license may be fitting to Humpty Dumpty. It should not be imputed to the Congress of the United States. . . . That is a liberty with words that might be acceptable in *Through the Looking Glass*—but not in the Sherman Act."[9]

The completion and submission of the brief did not mean, however, that their labors were over. Wisdom and his partner still had to prepare themselves for the oral argument, their one opportunity to plead their case directly to the High Court's nine justices. Each side had been allotted one hour to present its case, and Wisdom and Stone agreed that each of them would handle a separate portion of the argument. Stone's

7. Brief for the Petitioners filed in *Schwegmann Brothers v. Calvert Distillers Corp.*, at 11.
8. Ibid., 4.
9. Ibid., 8, 26.

job was to present the factual background, while Wisdom would address the legal issues raised in their appeal. Oral argument was scheduled for Monday, April 9, 1951, and Wisdom squeezed every moment out of the next three weeks to hone and refine his presentation. "I remember, I stayed up late [on Sunday night]. I knew every case on the subject, upside down, and backwards and forwards. I could answer any question on any case and I made a point of citing favorable remarks to our side of the case by each of the Justices who recognized his words coming back at him."[10]

Once their case was called, Stone presented his analysis of the underlying facts and then turned the lectern over to Wisdom. Just moments earlier, Wisdom had decided to abandon his materials at the counsel table and to make his entire argument without a single glance at his notes or other documents. While this might have been a risky strategy for many attorneys, Wisdom didn't see it that way. He preferred not to interrupt the flow of his argument by pausing to refer to a book or note; he calculated that any such interlude would prove to be more of a distraction than an asset. Besides, he later remarked, "it was silly to bring up these things which I knew by heart anyway."[11]

When Wisdom had completed his argument, the lateness of the hour prompted Chief Justice Vinson to postpone the distributors' presentation until noon the next day. When the argument recommenced, the attorney who had tried the case on behalf of the distributors before Skelly Wright and who had handled the appeal in front of the Fifth Circuit Court of Appeals was not present. Instead, the crucial task of presenting the distributors' argument to the Court had been assigned to Monte Lemann, a man whom Wisdom revered as "probably the finest lawyer in the South and one of the finest in the country."[12]

Unbeknownst to Wisdom, who had been sitting in his hotel room rehearsing and recrafting his presentation the night before the argument, Lemann had passed part of that same evening dining with a close friend and former classmate from Harvard Law School. Ordinarily, Lemann's dinner plans would have held no interest to Wisdom. On this occasion, however, it happened that Lemann's dinner partner was none other than Supreme Court Justice Felix Frankfurter! Yet even after he learned of their rendezvous, Wisdom never criticized Lemann for what,

10. J. M. Wisdom interview [Friedman], November 5, 1993, 60–61.
11. Ibid., 64.
12. Ibid., 53.

in today's appearance-obsessed climate, might be considered inappropriate conduct. "I didn't think anything of it then," he reminisced, "and I wouldn't think anything of it now, because Monte was highly ethical, of high principle. And I'm sure that Frankfurter didn't think anything of it."[13]

As it turned out, neither Lemann nor Wisdom had long to wait for the Supreme Court's decision. On May 21, the Court announced its decision. By a 6–3 margin, the Court, in an opinion authored by Justice William O. Douglas, agreed with Wisdom that the federal antitrust law did not authorize the enforcement of a price maintenance contract against any retailer who had not signed it.[14] Lemann's dinner partner, Frankfurter, wrote a dissenting opinion in which he agreed with his former classmate that Congress intended to permit states to bind both signatories and non-signatories to the terms of these price maintenance agreements.[15]

Years later, Douglas and Wisdom developed a warm, personal friendship. These two naturally gregarious men enjoyed each other's company as well as a more-than-passing acquaintance with an assortment of alcoholic beverages. When Douglas came to New Orleans to receive an award from the law school at Loyola University, "we had a party at the house," Wisdom revealed, "that began after the lecture and lasted well into the wee hours. And I was drinking and everybody else was drinking. But the next morning I said to Bonnie, 'You know, it's remarkable that Douglas was drinking water most of the time.' She said, 'Don't be foolish. That wasn't water—that was vodka!' I always liked Douglas."[16]

The Court's announcement of its opinion in the Schwegmann case did not pass unnoticed by the national and local media. The next morning, every wire service and major newspaper in the country reported this monumental defeat for the liquor industry. Most editorial writers lauded the ruling as a triumph for consumers and free trade and as a proper abandonment of a superannuated Depression-era contrivance.[17] In fact, the decision sounded the death-knell for state fair trade laws.

13. Ibid., 22.

14. *Schwegmann Bros. v. Calvert Distillers Corp.*, 341 U.S. 384, 71 S.Ct. 745, 95 L.Ed. 1035 (1951).

15. *Schwegmann Bros. v. Calvert Distillers Corp.*, 341 U.S. 384, 397, 71 S.Ct. 745, 752, 95 L.Ed. 1035 (1951) (Frankfurter, J., dissenting).

16. J. M. Wisdom interview [Friedman], November 5, 1993, 60.

17. See Editorial, "High Court Ruling Aids Consumers," *New Orleans Item*, May 24, 1951, 18, col. 1; Editorial, "Free Trade," *New Orleans State*, May 22, 1951, 18, col. 2; Editorial, "Noteworthy Decision," *New Orleans Times-Picayune*, May 22, 1951, 6, col. 1.

And when the *Wall Street Journal* ran a special series in 1989 highlighting the "milestones of American business history" in commemoration of its centennial year, the Supreme Court's ruling in *Schwegmann Brothers* was singled out as the most important event of 1951.[18]

This celebrated victory not only vindicated John Schwegmann's merchandising philosophy, it was a bonanza to the fortunes of the law firm of Wisdom & Stone. The notoriety generated by their participation in the case brought not only lots of new clients, but also a much higher level of public visibility than either Wisdom or Stone previously had enjoyed. But since Wisdom had written the brief and had carried the brunt of the legal argument before the Supreme Court, and because he already had begun to develop a nationwide network of relationships through his political activities on behalf of the local and national Republican Party, Wisdom garnered the lion's share of attention. "Eventually," he recollected, "I was making talks all over the United States."[19]

The publicity that came Wisdom's way did not, however, always work to his or the law firm's advantage. Just as the habitual afternoon downpours of a New Orleans summer entice hordes of cockroaches out of their breeding grounds seeking respite from the day's oppressively hot temperatures, the spotlight that illuminated Wisdom after his litigative coup attracted unsavory as well as desirable clients. Additionally, his emergence in the early 1950s as the leader of his state's Republican Party further enhanced his national profile.[20] Consequently, until he assumed the bench in 1957, Wisdom was an increasingly inviting target for political and business opportunists. His reaction to these attacks upon his integrity or reputation reflected the approach he had taken to all challenges since childhood. From his days as an Eagle Scout, once he decided to engage in an activity, he focused on that event with laser-beam intensity. He had only one speed—full throttle. Nothing was held back and he responded to every obstacle in his path with a tenacious, fighting spirit that, in most circumstances, served him well. One such occasion involved a client from the Cajun part of his state whose business brought Wisdom more public attention than he possibly could have anticipated.

In May 1953, Alphe E. Broussard, an entrepreneur from Lafayette, Louisiana, purchased sixty-five head of Charolais cattle in Mexico for importation to the United States. Charolais are a breed of large white

18. "Centennial Journal: 100 Years in Business," *Wall Street Journal,* July 24, 1989, B1.

19. J. M. Wisdom interview [Friedman], November 5, 1993, 59.

20. Wisdom's political activities are the subject of chapters 4 and 5.

cattle that are highly prized for their beef. In the mid-1940s, an outbreak of hoof and mouth disease in Mexico caused the Mexican and American governments to enter into a treaty banning the importation of Charolais cattle into the United States from any area of Mexico that was certified to be infected with the disease.

By 1952, Pueblo was the only area in Mexico that remained infected with hoof-and-mouth disease. But Broussard's Charolais came from Pueblo and he transported the herd across the Rio Grande to a location in the northwest corner of Louisiana outside of Shreveport without authorization from either the Mexican or American authorities. After complaints by other ranchers and veterinarians were filed with the U.S. Department of Agriculture, Broussard was arrested. Shortly thereafter, however, he was released on a $2,000 bond and no further proceedings were initiated. The entire incident went largely unnoticed until it became the subject of an article four months later by Drew Pearson, one of the nation's most widely read and highly respected political reporter-commentators.

In his *Washington Post*-based and nationally syndicated column of October 19, 1953, Pearson charged that Broussard had escaped prosecution by the federal authorities because he "was smart enough to retain John Wisdom, Ike's best friend in Louisiana . . . and one of the ablest and most charming attorneys in the South."[21] A more direct volley followed this honey-worded salvo as Pearson directly charged Wisdom with representing a cattle smuggler whom he had shielded from prosecution by exercising his political clout to convince the U.S. attorney in Shreveport, T. Fitzhugh Wilson, and the collector of customs in New Orleans, Theodore Lyons, to look the other way in his client's case.

"I hit the ceiling," Wisdom recalled, "when I saw the column and I hesitated as to what to do."[22] By the next morning, however, he had decided to issue a press release to respond to Pearson's charges. The statement, which appeared on the front page of that day's edition of the *New Orleans Item* (Pearson's column was printed on page 2), denied Pearson's charges and asserted that Wisdom had advised Broussard to cooperate fully with the government from the moment he was retained as Broussard's counsel. It also stated that since the cattle had crossed the border

21. Drew Pearson, "Cattle Smuggling Arouses Ire," *Washington Post*, October 19, 1953; Drew Pearson, "Cattle Smuggling Arouses Ire," *New Orleans Item*, October 19, 1953, 2.

22. J. M. Wisdom interview [Friedman], November 5, 1993, 43.

in Texas, any prosecution would be pursued in that jurisdiction rather than in Shreveport.[23]

But Wisdom also resolved that it was not enough for him to set the public record straight; he concluded that he needed to confront Pearson directly. "I had business in Washington at that time and invited him to have lunch with me. I told him the full story . . . and he said 'I'll do something about this. I'll write another column in about a few days or so and I'll retract it.'"[24]

But even after Shreveport's U.S. attorney, Fitzhugh Wilson, wrote to Pearson stating that had not become aware of Wisdom's association with Broussard until after the matter had been transferred to Texas at the direction of the U.S. Department of Justice, and Theodore Lyons, the New Orleans collector of customs, issued a public statement denying any attempt by Wisdom to influence his conduct, Wisdom was unwilling to let the matter rest.[25] He took great pride in his professional reputation and was determined never to permit any challenge to his character and good name to go unanswered. So he followed up his luncheon meeting with Pearson with a telegraph to the journalist. "In view of the facts set forth in the Wilson and Lyons statements," he wrote, "I was astounded that you did not negate the insinuation that I exercised influence in the Broussard case. You've already done me irreparable harm. The story will continue to harm me more than you realize in the community, in my profession and in other endeavors. I appeal to your fair-mindedness which condemns guilty by association to correct this grievous wrong."[26]

Two days later, Pearson telegrammed Wisdom, assuring him that a "story which I think you'll like appears in column late this week."[27] And sure enough, in his Friday column, Pearson conceded that the delay in prosecuting Broussard was attributable to the expanded investigative efforts of U.S. Customs officials and "not any intervention by John Minor Wisdom, attorney for Broussard. . . . No political pull has had any effect in this now famous cattle smuggling case [and] it is also apparent that Wisdom did not seek to exercise political pressure."[28] Forty

23. "Wisdom Answers Pearson Attack," *New Orleans Item,* October 19, 1953, 1.

24. J. M. Wisdom interview [Friedman], November 5, 1993, 43–44.

25. Letter from T. Fitzhugh Wilson to Drew Pearson, October 20, 1953.

26. Telegram from John M. Wisdom to Drew Pearson, October 26, 1953.

27. Telegram from Drew Pearson to John M. Wisdom, October 28, 1953.

28. Drew Pearson, "No 'Pull' by Wisdom in Cattle Case," *Washington Post,* October 30, 1953.

years later, Wisdom's satisfaction from this vindication of his honor had not dimmed. "I guess," he proudly proclaimed, "I'm one of the few people in the United States who ever got close to an apology from Drew Pearson."[29]

Charolais cattle was not, however, the only subject over which Wisdom and Pearson would lock horns, although on this other occasion Pearson stuck to his guns. From 1947 until 1955, the City of New Orleans had lobbied and negotiated with the federal government over the construction of a new post office. In July 1953, frustrated by the delay in securing the services of an architect for this undertaking, New Orleans mayor deLesseps S. ("Chep") Morrison asked Wisdom to use his influence to expedite the process.[30] This assignment brought Wisdom into contact with Peter Strobel, the General Services Administration (GSA) official primarily responsible for awarding non-defense-related government construction contracts and for hiring the architects for these projects.

In the fall of 1955, Pearson charged Strobel with recommending some of his former clients as architects on a $50 million construction project to build a new Central Intelligence Administration (CIA) headquarters. In a subsequent column, Pearson wrote that Strobel had selected the architect for the $11 million post office project in Louisiana that Wisdom, the "No. 1 Republican kingpin of Louisiana," had recommended. According to Pearson, Wisdom "was quite blunt in asking at least one architect how much he would contribute to the Republican Party out of the $200,000 architect's fee for designing the post office."[31]

Once again, Wisdom's public reply was immediate and unequivocal. "The statement in Mr. Pearson's column," he announced, "is completely false. On the contrary, bad as we need money for the Republican Party in Louisiana, I have rejected offers of contributions from architects who wish me to recommend them for the post office job. Probably the source of Mr. Pearson's misinformation is one of these gentlemen whose political contributions I turned down."[32] Wisdom also dispatched a simi-

29. J. M. Wisdom interview [Friedman], November 5, 1993, 39.

30. Letter from Mayor deLesseps S. Morrison to John M. Wisdom, July 9, 1953.

31. Drew Pearson, "Who's to Design Post Office Here—and Why?" *New Orleans Item*, October 26, 1955, 18, col. 3.

32. "'False,' Wisdom Says," *New Orleans Item*, October 26, 1955, 18, col. 4.

larly worded telegram to Pearson, but the famed columnist chose not to reply and the matter disappeared from public view.

The fact that such a visible pundit as Pearson would focus several of his nationally syndicated columns on Wisdom was but one reflection of Wisdom's preeminent role in Republican Party matters in Louisiana. It was also commonplace for New Orleans carriage drivers on their tours of the city's residential Garden District to inform their customers that they were passing the home of "Louisiana's Mr. Republican" and "Ike's best friend in Louisiana" when they drove past the Wisdom residence on First Street. And when Dwight Eisenhower needed to fill a position on an innovative, but extremely sensitive committee shortly after assuming the presidency in 1953, he turned to his Louisiana ally. At the time, however, Wisdom never imagined how this seemingly mundane appointment would turn into a highly controversial assignment.

At the beginning of his third term in 1941, President Franklin Roosevelt had signed an executive order requiring nearly all government contracts to include a clause forbidding contractors to discriminate against employees and job applicants on the basis of race, color, national origin, or religion. But several years thereafter, a commission empanelled by President Harry Truman to investigate wartime allegations of fraud in federal contracting reported that Roosevelt's nondiscrimination mandate frequently had been ignored over the intervening twelve years.

Four days after taking office, Eisenhower received the final version of the Truman Committee report describing the inadequacy of the federal government's antidiscrimination policy. During his 1952 campaign for the presidency, Eisenhower consistently had opposed the enactment of a federal antidiscrimination statute. He believed that promulgating an Executive Order, rather than enacting additional federal legislation, would most effectively promote the cause of equal employment opportunity in the private sector.[33] So on August 15, 1953, President Eisenhower issued Executive Order 10479, which established a President's Committee on Government Contracts. Although the committee was not delegated any enforcement authority, Eisenhower envisioned that this blue ribbon committee, chaired by his vice president, Richard Nixon, would

33. Hodding Carter, "Eisenhower's Program for Economic Equality," *Reader's Digest*, September 1956.

promote equal employment opportunity in the private sector by exhorting companies that did business with the federal government to abide by contractual agreements to implement nondiscriminatory employment policies.

This fourteen-member group was to be comprised of six high-ranking federal employees and eight private citizens. When asked by his staff whether he had anyone in mind for the eight nongovernmental slots, Eisenhower came up with two names. One was the owner of a major corporation. As for the other, Eisenhower gave Maxwell Rabb, the assistant to Chief of Staff Sherman Adams and the person assigned the task of serving as the committee's liaison to the White House, clear marching orders: "John Minor Wisdom. You get him because now it's a presidential commission. It's not going to be any good unless we get somebody that has what it takes."[34]

One of Rabb's first tasks in connection with the committee was to make sure that Wisdom would accept the presidential appointment. On Saturday morning, August 15, Rabb asked one of the White House operators to get Wisdom on the phone. "They finally found him," Rabb recalled, "shopping in a supermarket. He was shopping in Schwegmann's."[35] Wisdom accepted the job on the spot.

The conversation was necessarily brief and, at its conclusion, Wisdom was under the clear impression that the president had tapped him for work focusing on the negotiation and enforcement of government contracts. Such an assignment seemed natural to him, particularly in light of the expertise he had developed as a contract procurement officer during his army service.[36] Within a few hours, however, apprehension had replaced enthusiasm. A reporter contacted Wisdom at home for a reaction to the White House press release announcing his appointment to this presidential commission. Only then did Wisdom discover that this Contract Compliance Committee was designed to enforce the antidiscrimination provisions contained in government contracts and that he and his colleagues would be expected to assume a publicly visible role to promote the president's civil rights agenda.

Later that afternoon, Wisdom penned a short note to Rabb, revealing his misconception of the committee's mandate and expressing some serious misgivings. "I am sure that someone from the South was needed,

34. Maxwell M. Rabb, interview by Joel Wm. Friedman, February 1, 1996, New York, N.Y., 26.
35. Ibid., 26–27.
36. Wisdom's army career is discussed *infra*.

and that someone in a hurry. You can well understand, however," he confided to Rabb, "that on this committee a Southern Republican's lot is not a happy one. Notwithstanding—I enlisted to serve the President for the duration. Rest assured that I shall give my best in a manner that will, I hope, justify whatever confidence may have been placed in me."[37] In a similarly worded note to Sherman Adams, Wisdom expressed his additional fear that "membership on this Committee may destroy my usefulness in helping to organize support in the deep south for the President and for an active Republican party."[38]

Notwithstanding these initial concerns, Wisdom pursued this task with his characteristic verve and intensity for nearly four years. In this capacity, he traveled across the country, but particularly throughout the South, speaking at conferences to spread the word of the committee's mission, to encourage representatives from business and labor groups to jump on the nondiscrimination bandwagon, and to offer specific advice on how to promote equality of employment opportunity.

His service on the President's Contract Compliance Committee provided Wisdom with the opportunity to focus an increasing amount of his attention on issues that were growing more interesting and important to him. As a product of New Orleans' segregated public and private educational system, Wisdom never went to school with a black child. Neither did he have any contact with African Americans at Washington & Lee or at Tulane Law School. In fact, like most children of prosperous New Orleans families, his only regularized contact with African Americans was with the domestic workers who raised him and cared for all the members of his immediate family and with whom he had developed close and loving relationships. "We were always very close to all the servants, black and white, and [my mother] would have washed out my mouth with soap if I'd ever use the term 'nigger' or even 'Negro.'"[39] Consequently, like most of his social peers, Wisdom never had any significant interaction with members of the black community in New Orleans until well into his adulthood.

Yet even when he became an adult, Wisdom's initial contacts with African Americans were intermittent. His law firm had few African American clients and no blacks populated his social circles. But as he became increasingly involved in local Republican Party affairs, he de-

37. Letter to Maxwell Rabb from John Minor Wisdom, August 15, 1953.
38. Letter to Sherman Adams from John Minor Wisdom, August 15, 1953.
39. J. M. Wisdom interview [Friedman], September 30, 1994, 2-3.

veloped a keener understanding of the reality confronting the general black population.

Wisdom's response to the social and political manifestations of racial bias that pervaded his home state, including his and Bonnie's intense effort to recruit and help register African American voters, was shaped both by the dedication to fair play that had been instilled into him from childhood and his desire to augment the membership rolls of the political party whose fortunes he was committed to reviving. This bone-deep commitment to playing a useful role in promoting the fair treatment of all individuals also led him to accept appointment to the board of directors of the Urban League of New Orleans.

The experience Wisdom acquired in helping to resolve specific controversies as a member of the President's Contract Compliance Committee also helped him to develop conciliatory techniques to improve the status of race relations. The combination of these experiences, in turn, would hold Wisdom in good stead when he confronted these very sensitive issues as a federal judge. But before Wisdom could or would begin his judicial career, he would make his mark in local and national politics by engineering the resuscitation of Louisiana's Republican Party and helping to secure his party's 1952 presidential nomination for General Dwight Eisenhower.

4

BATTLING THE BOSSES
CREATING A TWO-PARTY SYSTEM IN LOUISIANA

The decision to join or otherwise identify with a political party can be influenced by any of a multitude of factors. Some individuals become Democrats or Republicans simply because their parents are members of that party, or because they grew up in an environment where one party was routinely praised and the other disparaged. For others, the choice may be based upon their affinity for the Democratic Party platform or the Republicans' ideological orientation. Still others may be attracted by a charismatic leader or group of leaders associated with one party or the other. None of these factors, however, accounted for John Minor Wisdom's decision to align himself with the Republican Party. In fact, his father had been an active member of Louisiana's Democratic Party. But family tradition also played no role in his decision to promote the development of a Republican Party in his home state. Rather, his motivation was his absolutely unshakeable conviction that a healthy democratic system demanded the existence of two vital, rival political parties. So beginning in the late 1940s Wisdom dedicated himself to the resuscitation of the Republican Party as a means of bringing two-party politics back to Louisiana. What Wisdom already knew, and others would soon discover, however, was that his most formidable opposition would come from within the very ranks of the party he sought to revive.

The history of the national political parties in Louisiana is a tale of nearly perpetual Democratic Party domination from Reconstruction through the middle of the twentieth century. During this period of Democratic hegemony, the southern version of the party of Lincoln wavered "somewhat between an esoteric cult on the order of a lodge and a conspiracy for plunder in accord with the accepted customs of our politics."[1] Membership in the Democratic Party had become close to a tradition in most southern families, transmitted instinctively across generational lines like church membership or loyalty to the home state university's football team. Particularly in the rural areas and among the well-established families in the urban centers of the South, registered Republicans were as scarce as hen's teeth.

From its founding in 1865 until 1898, the Louisiana Republican Party did function as an active challenger to the majority Democratic Party. But when black voters, the mainstay of its registrant corps, were disenfranchised by the 1898 Louisiana Constitution, the party fell into disarray. By the 1920s, its membership had been depleted to the point where the organization became vulnerable to the contrivances of a small group intent on transforming the party into an organ devoted primarily to political patronage and plunder. For the next three decades, the changing cast of characters who sat atop the Republican pyramid all clung tenaciously to one overarching article of faith. Each successive cadre of party bosses was intent on discouraging any and every effort to expand party membership. To perpetuate their coveted power to dispense patronage and to retain their control over the other boons of party rule, it was essential to frustrate any and every attempt at increasing the size of the party rolls.[2] So instead of serving as a buffer against the exercise and potential abuse of power by the ruling Democrats, the Republican Party served almost exclusively as a conduit for federal pa-

1. V. O. Key, Jr., *Southern Politics in State and Nation* (New York: 1949), 277.

2. Ibid., 277, 292. ("Southern Republican leaders are usually pictured as vultures awaiting the day when the party wins the nation and they can distribute patronage in the South. Meantime, they exert themselves only to keep the party weak in the South in order that there will be few faithful to reward.") See also Joseph Alsop and Stewart Alsop, "Taft Can't Split South," *New Orleans Item*, March 13, 1952, 16, col. 4.

tronage distribution in those years in which a Republican resided in the White House. It was precisely this absence of a two-party system in his home state that fueled Wisdom's drive to breathe life into the political corpse that the Republican Party of Louisiana had become.[3]

Wisdom's concern over the state of governmental affairs in Louisiana, however, originated long before he actively entered the political arena. From the beginning of his final year at Tulane Law School in the fall of 1928 through the early years of his career at the bar, the Louisiana political landscape had been dominated by Governor and, later, Senator Huey P. Long. Long's unfettered ability to exert nearly dictatorial control over the affairs of state government, and the ruthlessness with which he exercised his dominion, profoundly contradicted every political impulse in Wisdom's body. Long's callous pursuit of self-interest and reckless disregard of the concerns of those who did not bear slavish allegiance to him was the antithesis of Wisdom's fundamental commitment to fair play.[4]

Wisdom's virulent opposition to Long, however, did not rest merely on some abstract, ideological plane. He had experienced firsthand the brutal force of the fist within Long's populist glove. One of his earliest encounters with the Kingfish occurred in 1932, the year Long relinquished the governorship to become a U.S. senator. During the election campaign to select his successor, Long boasted that his preferred candidate, O. K. Allen, would not only win the election, but would do so in the first primary without the need for a runoff. And to back up his claim, Long offered to take on all bets against Allen by posting $40,000 with a local newspaper, the *New Orleans Item,* on Saturday morning, January 16.

The temptation was too strong for Wisdom to withstand. He fancied himself as something of an amateur handicapper in politics as well as in football. Buoyed by confidence in his odds-making abilities, rather than

3. "I chose the Republican Party because I felt that the lack of a two party system was a main reason for the development of our demagogues. The rise of demagogues in the Deep South states, such as Louisiana, was directly attributable to the absence of a party out of power to act as a check on the abuses of power by the party in power." J. M. Wisdom interview [Friedman], June 22, 1993, 1.

4. "We thought that Huey Long was a danger to the community; a danger to the state. And he was. Huey Long was an incipient Mussolini [and] a real danger to [President Franklin D.] Roosevelt for that matter." J. M. Wisdom interview [Friedman], November 5, 1993, 73.

by any desire to make a political statement, he went down to the news-paper office that Saturday afternoon and plunked down $15.[5] By the end of the day, it appeared that he was the only person who would take up Long's offer. The senator, however, was livid that anyone would have the temerity to meet his challenge and insisted on discovering the iden-tity of this insolent skeptic. After learning that Wisdom was the brazen gambler, Long called the paper's publisher and demanded that he pub-lish something that would ridicule Wisdom.[6] But the publisher was a friend of the Wisdoms and refused to accede to Long's demand.[7]

Wisdom had dodged this salvo, but in the process had made a for-midable enemy of someone with both a long memory and an extensive arsenal of weapons at his command. Months later, the State of Louisi-ana offered to take out an insurance policy underwritten by the firm where Wisdom's older brother, William B., worked as advertising man-ager. Senator Long tried to arrange for the agreement to require the firm to discharge Wisdom. This maneuver failed, but the incident il-lustrated Long's emblematic determination to pursue even petty adver-saries. It also reinforced John Wisdom's conviction that Long had to be stopped. Yet Wisdom also recognized that Long's position was unassail-able as long as his Democratic Party retained its monopolistic hold over the state's political system.

A flourishing democracy—which, for Wisdom, meant the toppling of Long—was simply incompatible with a one-party political system. Without a second party to act as a buffer against the misuse of power by the incumbents, no state, including Louisiana, could expect to insu-late itself against abuses of authority by Long and his successors. So Wis-dom committed himself to resurrecting the state's Republican Party, an organization that had been converted from a proponent of public policy to a purveyor of private patronage and privilege. And though the state Republican Party did not promote any political agenda, Wisdom's deci-sion to join the Grand Old Party (GOP) was in no way related to any af-finity on his party toward the national party's platform. He did not be-come a Republican, in other words, in order to pursue any particular political ideology or agenda. He simply wanted to ensure that the gover-nance of his state would not be subject to single-party control.

Neither was Wisdom's enlistment in the GOP a function of familial

5. B. Wisdom interview [Friedman], June 30, 1994, 25.

6. Ibid., 26.

7. Ibid.

tradition. To the contrary, his father, Mortimer, had been actively involved in the Democratic Party for the entirety of his adult life. Mortimer could not abide the Radical Republicans who controlled the New
Orleans city government during Reconstruction and he genuinely subscribed to the policies of the Democratic Party. Initially content to engaging in behind-the-scenes activity that kept him out of the public eye,
Mortimer ultimately found himself thrust into the eye of one of the
state's countless political storms.

In 1908, Governor Newton C. Blanchard appointed Mortimer Wisdom to replace the incumbent state registrar of voters, Jere M. Gleason,
whom Blanchard had dismissed, purportedly for engaging in a pattern
of fraudulent activities, including a consistent failure to purge the rolls
of the names of dead and unlawfully registered individuals.[8] It also was
true, however, that Wisdom was a vocal supporter of Blanchard's hand-
picked successor, while Gleason supported the rival gubernatorial candidate.[9] Once Blanchard's decision to replace Gleason was announced,
the registrar brought suit in state court to bar Wisdom from taking office. And though the jury ultimately found that Blanchard was authorized to remove his political appointee, it also determined that Wisdom was ineligible to assume the office of registrar because he had been
a candidate for membership on the Democratic Party's State Central
Committee when Blanchard appointed him. As a result, Wisdom was
denied the opportunity to hold public office and walked away from the
experience having felt used by Blanchard.[10]

Nevertheless, Mortimer rarely shared his feelings of disappointment
with the rest of his family. His middle son John was less than three years
old at the time, and was incapable of comprehending the significance of
these events. And since Mortimer died before John's thirteenth birthday, the pair never had any opportunity to seriously discuss this matter. Consequently, this event never caused John to harbor any ill will
toward the Democratic Party. But neither did his father's ideological allegiance with the Democrats deter John from vigorously promoting the
fortunes of the Republican Party. Thus, neither family traditions nor
political ideology played any meaningful role in John's decision to join
with the Republicans. His agenda was focused on a single objective—

8. "Comedy in Situation Locally," *New Orleans Item*, January 12, 1908.

9. J. M. Wisdom interview [Friedman], October 28, 1993, 37.

10. "Wisdom Is Enjoined," [*New Orleans*] *Times Democrat*, January 12, 1908; "The Gleason Verdict," *Times-Democrat*, April 11, 1908.

to promote democracy by ending Long and the Democratic Party's unilateral control over state government, a situation that that had been fostered and nurtured by the absence of any viable political alternative.

In the fall of 1865, a group of white abolitionists in Louisiana combined with a small number of ex-slaves to establish a Republican Party in Louisiana.[11] The party initially was so successful in recruiting new members from the readily available class of ex-slaves (over fifty thousand blacks registered to vote in 1867) that by 1868 Republicans were able to elect one of their own, Henry Clay Warmoth, as governor. But by 1872, control over the party had shifted from free men of color (*gens du couleur libre*) and ex-slaves to the northern carpetbaggers who had migrated to New Orleans after the city's fall to the Union forces in 1862. Yet as quickly as the Republicans had seized power, they lost it. The end of Reconstruction in 1876 marked the return of the Democrats to control in Louisiana, a position they would not relinquish for nearly a hundred years.[12]

The Republican Party's loss of political clout in Louisiana was accompanied by the crumbling of its organizational structure. Nearly all of the ward clubs, as well as the parish and district committees, either disbanded or ceased functioning.[13] Those voters who remained in the party eventually divided along racial lines, with two segregated blocs engaged in a political tug-of-war for party dominance over the next forty years. White members created a "Lilywhite Republican" faction unwilling to join forces with the group dominated by the party's black members that was unofficially labeled by the local media as the "Black and Tans." But when the Louisiana Constitution was amended in 1898 to limit the franchise to property owners or the sons of property owners, black enrollment plunged, and by 1923 only 598 African Americans remained on the rolls in Louisiana, effectively eliminating the Black and Tans as a viable force within the state party.[14]

As the Lilywhites became the dominant force in the state party, a

11. Philip D. Uzee, "Republican Politics in Louisiana, 1877–1900" (unpublished PhD dissertation, Louisiana State University, 1959), 14–15.

12. Wilds, Dufour, and Cowan, *Louisiana Yesterday and Today: A Historical Guide to the State* (Baton Rouge: 1996), 58–60; Wilds, "New Orleans: Election Day, 1876," *New Orleans States-Item*, November 2, 1976, Section B, 1, col. 1.

13. Uzee, "Republican Politics in Louisiana, 1877–1900," 36.

14. Frederick J. Dumas, "The Black and Tan Faction of the Republican Party in Louisiana, 1908 to 1936" (unpublished MA thesis, Xavier University, New Orleans, 1943), 14; Alden L. Powell and Emmett Asseff, *Registration of Voters in Louisiana* (1951), 5.

series of aspirants competed for its leadership. But by the end of the 1920s, a young attorney from New Orleans, John E. Jackson, had solidified his position with the Lilywhites. In 1934, already the elected chairman of the Louisiana Republican Party's Central Committee, Jackson was named the state's national committeeman.[15] Two years later, the Louisiana attorney general issued an opinion recognizing Jackson's Lilywhite group as the official Louisiana Republican Party, which sounded the death knell of the Black and Tans, sparked a defection of the few remaining black Republicans to the historically segregated Democratic Party, and solidified Jackson's position as the undisputed boss of state Republican Party bosses. For the next dozen years, Jackson dominated every phase of party activity and exercised virtually uncontested control over the distribution of federal patronage positions. No one was interested in or capable of asserting even the most modest challenge to Jackson's reign until 1948.[16] It was only then that Jackson finally met his match—a small but persistent group of insurgents led by another attorney from New Orleans, John Minor Wisdom.

Jackson and his now-entrenched leadership cadre actively discouraged any attempt to bolster the size of their party roster. After all, the fewer the number of party members, the easier it was for the incumbent leadership to retain control of the party apparatus. For example, the party rarely, if ever, put forward candidates for most local contests. This made the Democratic primary tantamount to a general election in these local races. Consequently, voters otherwise prepared to vote for the Republican candidate for the presidency or other national office, but who also wanted to have a voice in local elections, felt compelled to register with the party that represented the only political game in town.[17] Thus, by 1952, the number of registered Republicans in the state had shrunk to barely 1,500 from more than 5,000 in the 1920s. New Orleans accounted for only 309 registered Republicans in 1950 and in many of the outlying parishes Republicans had become extinct, except, as Wisdom whimsically observed in 1951, for perhaps "two, three or four zombies or corpses waiting for the resurrection."[18]

15. Thomas Sancton, "Fur Flies Over Taft and Ike," *New Orleans Item*, April 20, 1952, 22, col. 1.

16. In 1940, James C. Woods, a wealthy oilman, did lead a feeble effort to overthrow Jackson, but the attempted revolt was unsuccessful.

17. Stella Z. Theodoulou, *The Louisiana Republican Party, 1948–1984: The Building of a State Political Party* (New Orleans: 1985), 4.

18. Letter to George Healy from John M. Wisdom, June 21, 1951.

Jackson's use of the Louisiana Republican organization as a personal patronage dispensing mechanism was anathema to Wisdom's vision of the role of a political party. He intensely believed that the existence of two independent, competitive parties was an essential component of a healthy, vital democracy. It was not enough, in his view, that Louisiana's highly factionalized Democratic Party could be counted on to offer a variety of candidates in most local races. Unlike many of his contemporaries, Wisdom did not view this intra-party competition as the functional equivalent of a two-party system. "People have said that Louisiana had a two party system in that they had the Longs and the anti-Longs. But that, of course, is really a very short-sighted approach to the problem because you're not going to have Longs and anti-Longs forever. . . . The only real solution is an active two party system."[19] But in order to resuscitate the functionally moribund Republican Party in his state, Wisdom had to release it from the chokehold of its theretofore-unchallenged commander-in-chief John E. Jackson.

In July 1948, a small group of Republicans from New Orleans who were determined to unseat Jackson and to establish a bona fide two-party system in the state scheduled a meeting with a local attorney who they believed could mobilize public support and who would be willing, as well as able, to conceive, coordinate, and implement a bold strategy to take on the entrenched old guard—and win.[20] After a brief discussion centering on the deplorable current state of the party and the possibility of converting it into an active organization that could be a source of pride rather than shame, Wisdom accepted the delegation's offer to become the leader of their movement and to head their newly formed "Republican Club of Louisiana," which he quickly renamed the "New Republican Leadership." This decision set in motion a series of events that eventually would recast the state party, play a decisive role in the selection of the Republican Party's 1952 presidential nominee, and lead ultimately to the appointment of a federal judge who would play an indispensable role in the desegregation of American society and leave an indelible imprint on civil rights and other areas of American law.

From the outset, Wisdom determined that the only way to disentangle the party from Jackson's tenacious grasp was to mount a direct and coordinated challenge to all of Jackson's various power bases. The

19. J. M. Wisdom interview [Friedman], June 22, 1994, 2.
20. Paul T. David, Malcolm Moos, and Ralph M Goldman, *Presidential Nominating Politics in 1952: The South* (Baltimore: 1954), 267.

prime source of Jackson's dominion was his membership on the Republican National Committee and his unrivaled control of the party's State Central Committee, which occupied the top rung on the state party hierarchy and functioned as its executive arm. Anyone who controlled membership on the Central Committee, therefore, had effective command over the entire party apparatus. So the State Central Committee would be the first battleground in the battle to depose Jackson.

In October 1951, Wisdom's New Republicans put forward their own candidates for twelve of the seventeen spots on the State Central Committee allocated to Orleans Parish—the first time in a dozen years that anyone had opposed the nominees backed by Jackson.[21] For the ensuing three months, the 1,500 registered Republican voters in the dozen battleground wards in Orleans Parish were the targets of a zealous door-to-door canvassing effort and a blitz of radio, television, newspaper, and mail messages.[22] When the dust settled, Wisdom and his New Republicans had accomplished a near sweep, winning eleven of the contested Central Committee contests. The Jacksonites' lone victory occurred in the Twelfth Ward, Jackson's home district. The New Republicans also achieved a commensurate level of success at the local level, winning seventeen of the twenty seats on the party's Orleans Parish Executive Committee and electing Wisdom as parish executive committee chairman.[23]

All in all, Wisdom and his band had reason to rejoice over their first major triumph against the Old Guard. They now controlled an important arm of the state party apparatus and Wisdom was the leader of a vocal minority faction on the all-important State Central Committee. Moreover, their decisive victory demonstrated to Louisiana Republicans that Wisdom and the New Republican leadership were a force to be reckoned with. Nevertheless, as Wisdom fully appreciated, it was only a toehold. The parish committee's ability to undertake meaningful reform of party processes remained subject to the overarching con-

21. L. Vaughan Howard and David R. Deener, *Presidential Politics in Louisiana, 1952* (New Orleans: 1954), 12. Each of the seventeen wards in Orleans Parish was allotted one seat on the Central Committee. But not only did this ward representative serve on the Central Committee, he or she was responsible for calling that ward's mass meeting and serving as its temporary chairman. See also David, Moos, and Goldman, *Presidential Nominating Politics in 1952: The South*, 268.

22. Howard and Deener, *Presidential Politics in Louisiana, 1952*, 13.

23. "Wisdom Elected by Republicans," *New Orleans Times-Picayune*, March 4, 1952, 5, col. 3; "Wisdom Is Elected Chairman of GOP Parish Committee," *New Orleans Item*, March 3, 1952, 1, col. 5.

trol of the Central Committee, over which Jackson continued to hold the reins. And though Wisdom's New Republicans had garnered eleven seats on the Central Committee, the fact remained that Jackson still controlled the rest of the fifty-eight filled slots on the committee.[24] Consequently, despite the losses suffered in Orleans Parish, the Central Committee remained firmly under Jackson's control.

Nevertheless, Jackson and his followers were unwilling to tolerate even this relatively trifling encroachment into their theretofore exclusive domain. Jackson immediately asked the Central Committee to invalidate the Wisdom group's election victory. And with a substantial majority of its members under his control, the resolution to invalidate the election results easily passed and the Central Committee refused to seat the eleven New Republicans from Orleans Parish.[25] Deprived of their election victory, the New Republicans sought and obtained relief from the courts. They brought suit in a state trial court in Baton Rouge, where they convinced the trial judge to issue an order compelling the Central Committee to recognize their victories and seat the eleven duly elected members.[26] The only recourse available to Wisdom and his colleagues was to seek vindication of their position from either a court of law or, occasionally, the court of public opinion.

With these hard-earned election victories under their belt, the New Republicans turned their attention to electing a pro-Eisenhower slate of delegates to the party's national nominating convention in Chicago. Wisdom was quite familiar with the complicated, multi-tiered process for selecting these delegates and recognized that he was in for an uphill struggle. Since the selection system was, in large part, a creature of the state party hierarchy that remained under Jackson's dominion, the incumbents started this contest with a built-in advantage. Wisdom also knew that Jackson would never feel constrained by the parliamentary, evidentiary, and other procedural rules that he and his New Republicans were intent on observing. To the contrary, the Old Guard's response to the New Republicans' initial election victory was replicated throughout the election campaign. Time after time, backroom maneuvers were employed to frustrate ballot box victories. So Wisdom entered this electoral engagement fully cognizant of the need for a battle plan

24. David, Moos, and Goldman, *Presidential Nominating Politics in 1952: The South*, 269.

25. Howard and Deener, *Presidential Politics in Louisiana, 1952*, 14.

26. The ruling was upheld by the Louisiana First Circuit Court of Appeals. *Allen v. Republican State Central Committee of Louisiana*, 57 So.2d 248, 249 (La.App.1st Cir.1952).

that could avoid the many land mines strewn along the road to Chicago, the site of the Republican Party's 1952 presidential nominating convention.

Delegates to presidential nominating conventions typically are selected in each state's presidential primary election. But in states where a primary is not held, national party rules dictate that the overwhelming majority of the state's delegation be selected at conventions held in each of its congressional districts. The remaining delegates-at-large are elected at a single statewide convention. Since Louisiana did not hold presidential primaries in 1952, all fifteen of its delegates to the Republican national convention were chosen via this convention route.[27] But party rules did not prescribe the manner in which delegates to the district and statewide conventions were chosen. In Louisiana, the tradition was to select the convention delegates at local mass meetings, often called caucuses in other states. With the exception of Orleans, the state's largest parish, one mass meeting was held in each parish.[28] In Orleans Parish, which encompassed the city of New Orleans, separate mass meetings were held in each of its seventeen local wards.[29]

Thus, to control the selection of both district and at-large delegates to the national nominating convention, one had to command a majority of the delegates to the district- and statewide conventions. And since the delegates to these local and statewide conventions were chosen at the mass meetings, both Wisdom and Jackson knew full well that they needed to focus their attention on these local meetings to ensure that the Louisiana contingent to the national nominating convention would vote in favor of their preferred presidential candidate.

Although the Jackson and Wisdom camps shared this common objective, their implementing strategies varied dramatically. Jackson was a lawyer by training but a politician by profession, the preeminent insider possessing all the bounties of incumbency. He viewed the mass meetings (and the district and state conventions that followed) as little

27. Since more than ten thousand Republican votes had been cast in the 1948 presidential election in Louisiana's First, Second, and Third Congressional Districts, each of these districts was entitled to send two "district delegates" to the 1952 national nominating convention. The other five districts were allotted one delegate apiece, making a total of eleven district delegates. The remaining four slots in the fifteen-party delegation were assigned by party rules to delegates-at-large chosen at the party's statewide convention.

28. A parish is the Louisiana equivalent of a county.

29. Eight of the wards were located in the First Congressional District and nine in the Second District.

more than a bothersome prerequisite to preserving his most prized possession—the power to distribute federal patronage posts. To perpetuate his position at the top of the political pyramid, he needed to promote the candidacy of the party's presidential nominee while simultaneously minimizing the number of local party faithful who might assert their own claim to the federal jobs that would accompany a successful election effort.

Wisdom, on the other hand, was first and foremost an attorney, an insurgent outsider in the political arena whose experience and expertise had been shaped in the courthouse rather than the clubhouse. But despite his comparatively limited experience in the rough and tumble of local politics, he had built up a network of relationships with many city leaders as a result of his own civic and social activities. He was prepared to go toe to toe with Jackson, even in the face of the enormous built-in competitive advantages Jackson enjoyed by virtue of his control over the state Central Committee. Wisdom was confident that he could recruit plenty of new members to his party, and through superior organization and preparation, defeat Jackson in a fair political fight. And he also insisted that everyone on their team adhere strictly to a high standard of fairness, honesty, and decency. Political campaigning was, to Wisdom, no different in this regard than practicing law. Each had to be undertaken according to one's personal code of honor and sense of fair play or it was not worth the candle.

Jackson, conversely, could not be bothered by such naïve and irrelevant considerations. These idealistic concerns played no part in his game plan. To him, politics was a high-stakes game and he was a skilled player who was prepared to do whatever it took to win. In this contest, however, he violated a cardinal rule of the game—he underestimated his opponent. To this established, comfortably ensconced party boss, Wisdom was barely more than an annoyance, an idealistic, irksome upstart who wasn't savvy enough to realize that he could not hope to stand up to Jackson's raw political power. "We're throwing a little procedure at Wisdom," snickered a Jackson lieutenant. "He's a good boy. But he's an amateur. Those amateurs get angry when they can't get their way. I'm not angry."[30]

As Jackson would soon discover, to his everlasting regret, Wisdom

---

30. Thomas Sancton, "Louisiana's Republican Party: Admits Patronage Is Issue," *New Orleans Item*, April 29, 1952, 1, col. 3.

was no amateur. And he certainly was not about to be bamboozled or intimidated by Jackson's procedural maneuvers. But more important, politics was not a game to Wisdom; it was a mechanism for transforming ideology into reality. For Wisdom, the base reality was that a functioning two-party system was an indispensable component of a robust democracy. Of course, Wisdom also believed that the nation would be better served by General Dwight D. Eisenhower of Kansas than by John E. Jackson's preferred candidate, Senator Robert A. Taft of Ohio.

Wisdom's unquestioned preference for Ike was not, unlike many other Eisenhower supporters, part and parcel of any irrevocable antipathy toward Senator Taft. To the contrary, back in 1949, Wisdom had labored diligently for Taft's reelection to the U.S. Senate. In a letter he sent to Taft, Wisdom expressed his conviction "that your reelection transcends state and party lines . . . and is of paramount importance to the country as a whole."[31] By 1952, however, Wisdom had grown increasingly dissatisfied with Taft's isolationist views. His wartime experience had convinced him that America needed to play a prominent role in global politics. And Eisenhower, he believed, would bring a more global perspective to American foreign policy than his rival from Ohio. Wisdom also intuited that as a newcomer to Republican Party politics, Eisenhower offered the best opportunity for bringing about a rethinking of the old attitudes that had contributed to keeping the party small in southern states and out of the White House.[32] Without question, however, Wisdom's affection for and belief in Eisenhower was never as important a motivating force for him as his commitment to the development of a two-party system in Louisiana. Every decision he made, every plan and strategy he devised, was formulated with that primary mission in mind.

Wisdom anticipated that Jackson would utilize the advantages of incumbency to manipulate the results at the mass meetings and the district conventions and that the New Republicans' pro-Eisenhower slate would not be recognized as the state's official delegation to the national convention without a fight. From the outset, Wisdom appreciated that he would have to take his fight ultimately to the floor of the national convention in the form of an official challenge to the Jackson-dominated, pro-Taft delegation.

31. Letter to Robert A. Taft from John M. Wisdom, September 3, 1949.
32. J. M. Wisdom interview [Friedman], June 22, 1994, 24.

Wisdom also had a pretty good idea of the tactics Jackson would employ to ensure the recognition of a pro-Taft slate of delegates to the party's national nominating convention. He predicted to the leader of the pro-Eisenhower forces in Georgia, Elbert Tuttle, that in those parishes and wards where Jackson's supporters were in the minority, the Old Guard leader would have his minions meet in rump sessions outside the confines of the official mass meeting to choose pro-Taft delegates to the district and state conventions. These Taft "delegates," Wisdom also forecast, would then join with pro-Taft delegates lawfully elected from the northern Louisiana parishes (where the New Republicans could not mount a serious challenge) to form a majority of voters at the district and state conventions to elect a slate of pro-Taft delegates to the national convention.[33] And that is precisely what happened.

To beat Jackson at this game, Wisdom confected a two-part strategy. First and most obviously, the New Republicans needed to secure electoral victories at the mass meetings and, later, at the district and state conventions. But second, and equally important, they would have to accurately and comprehensively document an incontrovertible record of their success to support the challenge they inevitably would be required to mount against the Jackson slate at the national convention. Each meeting's proceedings would have to be recorded and notarized. The New Republicans would need irrefutable evidence that they had complied in every respect with the letter and spirit of the governing political rules. They also would need conclusive proof of the manner by which Jackson and his followers had attempted to subvert the party rules and overturn the will of the majority of voters. In short, the Wisdom team would have to treat this electoral battle like a massive piece of litigation. Jackson's defeat would hinge on Wisdom's ability to utilize the same organizational, tactical, and oratorical skills that he had exercised less than a year earlier, when he and Saul Stone convinced the U.S. Supreme Court to break up a price-fixing scheme by interstate liquor distributors.[34]

With his lawyer's affinity for detail, his professional dedication to orderly process, and one eye focused always on the ultimate appellate tribunal—the national nominating convention—Wisdom directed his campaign team to adhere to a consistent strategy designed to provide

33. Telegram to Elbert Tuttle from John M. Wisdom, April 10, 1952.

34. Wisdom's victory in *Schwegmann Bros. v. Calvert Distillers*, 341 U.S. 384 (1951) is detailed in chapter 3, *supra*.

them with the kind of documentation and foundation that every good trial lawyer strove to produce for the benefit of an anticipated appeal. All New Republican volunteers were instructed to come to every mass meeting equipped with the registrar of voters' certified list of eligible, registered voters and to secure the registrar's signature on that list by the close of business on the day of each mass meeting. Wisdom also made sure that at least one New Republican attendee at every mass meeting prepared notes of the meeting and then verified the accuracy of the contents of those notes before a notary public. Everything was geared toward producing a voluminous and unimpeachable record attesting to the validity of their election victories and documenting the undemocratic tactics employed by the Jackson camp at the mass meetings.

Jackson, meanwhile, was content to rely on his time-tested political might to secure a favorable result at the mass meetings. If and when it came time to present his case to the national convention, he would disdain the need for evidence and coherent argument; he simply would lob longwinded, rambling, unsubstantiated broadsides on his challengers and present self-indulgent testimonials to his own veracity.

Since little or no Republican Party machinery existed in many of the precincts and wards outside of the Crescent City, most of the very contentious and acrimonious confrontations between these two combatants occurred on Wisdom and Jackson's home turf—New Orleans. The campaign to win votes at the mass meetings held throughout Orleans Parish pitted a devoted and well-organized, though somewhat inexperienced and occasionally naïve, group of reformers against an entrenched group of shrewd political operatives.

The initial round in the convention delegate bout was fought in early April 1952, when seventeen mass meetings were conducted at a variety of locations throughout Orleans Parish. Most were held on private property, usually in a home, yard, or garage; some were held in or around churches.[35] Each involved, to different degrees, a face-off between Jackson's veteran Old Guard and Wisdom's upstart New Republicans. On rare occasion, the session went off without a hitch. Most of the meetings, however, were marked by vehement, usually vitriolic, and occasionally even violent confrontations between the two camps. And though the particulars varied from scene to scene, a clear-cut and manifest pattern emerged.

35. Howard and Deener, *Presidential Politics in Louisiana, 1952*, 16.

At most of these sites, because Wisdom's partisans constituted the clear preponderance of voters, Jackson attempted to circumvent the will of the majority by manipulating, disregarding, or simply flaunting the governing rules. In those wards where the small number of registered Republicans made it difficult for either camp to predict in advance which of them would possess a majority at the mass meeting, Jackson supporters would only remain in attendance until it became evident that they were clearly outnumbered. At that point, under the guise of a multiplicity of implausible excuses, they would retreat to the confines of a rump session and select their own district or state convention delegates. At other meetings, Jackson followers transformed a voting minority into a narrow election victory either by disqualifying pro-Eisenhower voters or allowing unregistered, ineligible Taft supporters to vote. And in yet other wards, the Jacksonites shunned the official meeting altogether, preferring to rump and select their delegates in a more congenial atmosphere, undistracted by any opposition slate.

The elections at the mass meetings were held for the sole purpose of electing delegates to congressional district-wide conventions where these individuals would elect a specified number of delegates to represent Louisiana's Republican Party at the party's national presidential nominating convention. Because Orleans Parish overlapped into both the First and Second Congressional Districts, the delegates elected at some ward mass meetings were assigned to the First District convention while others attended the Second District convention. In open defiance of unambiguous national Republican Party rules, Jackson, through the Central Committee that he controlled, arranged for the convention in each of these two districts to be held at unscheduled times to ensure the absence of the New Republicans' pro-Eisenhower delegates and, therefore, guarantee the election of Taft supporters to represent the district at the national nominating convention. In response, the New Republicans held "their" district convention at which pro-Eisenhower delegates were elected, ensuring that a fight over these competing delegates' eligibility would have to be resolved at the national convention itself.

Similarly, seven of the eleven delegates that emerged from the district conventions held outside of Orleans Parish also became the subject of a challenge at the Republican Party's national convention. The only convention delegates that went unchallenged came from the state's Fourth and Fifth Congressional Districts (each of which was allotted one national convention delegate) in northern Louisiana, where Wisdom conceded that Senator Taft had overwhelming support, and the Third Congressional District, where Jackson did not challenge the New Republicans' success in obtaining that district's two national convention delegates.

But in addition to the delegates chosen at the various district conventions, Louisiana also was entitled to send four at-large delegates to the national convention. By party rule, these delegates were elected at a single statewide convention. After a lengthy and raucous session held at the Alexandria City Hall, the delegates initially elected four Eisenhower delegates-at-large.[36] But half an hour later, after the New Republican delegates had boarded their buses for the ride back to New Orleans, the Jackson contingent reconvened the meeting and proceeded to elect four Taft supporters as the state's at-large delegates.[37]

Jackson's coordinated plan to ramrod the state convention and to quash any trace of Eisenhower support in Louisiana's delegation to the national convention did not go unnoticed by the local media. A series of articles in the *New Orleans Item* took sharp aim at the "steamroller" tactics that had been employed to steal delegates from the Eisenhower camp. "Observers who have watched this process," the reporter observed, "know that a 15-member pro-Taft delegation has not been elected in Louisiana in any framework of American 'fair play' or all the other ideals and traditions of democracy and popular government. If a 15-member pro-Taft delegation is seated, Eisenhower will be deprived of from 10 to 13 delegates which regular meetings and parliamentary process would have given him."[38] The controversy also attracted the attention of observers from outside the Pelican State. Famed political commentator Joseph Alsop wrote a blistering column in which he wryly observed that as a result of Wisdom's "eccentric passion for a genuine two-party system in the South," he not only "impertinently intervened . . . in the selection of delegates to the Republican National Convention," but actually soundly defeated Jackson in six of the state's eight congressional districts. Alsop concluded with this stinging evaluation of Jackson's stratagems: "Jackson responded like the brave fellow he is.

36. Roy Steinfort, "Two Sets of GOP Delegates Named," *New Orleans Times-Picayune*, April 24, 1952, 20, col. 1.

37. Thomas Sancton, "La. Taft-Ike Battle Heads for Chicago," *New Orleans Item*, April 24, 1952, 3, col. 1; "GOP Fight to Go into Convention," *New Orleans Item*, April 21, 1952, 5, col. 5.

38. Thomas Sancton, "State Taftite Pros 'Rob' Ike in La.," *New Orleans Item*, May 2, 1952, 5, col. 4.

He used his remaining control of the State Republican Committee in the Texas manner. He ignored the ballots of the pro-Eisenhower Wisdomites. He nullified their undoubted legal victories. And he rigged the State convention, by seating his own minority instead of the Wisdomite majority, to send a solid pro-Taft delegation to Chicago. No impartial observer here doubts that this pro-Taft Louisiana delegation is a simple product of John E. Jackson's force or character. Even John E. himself does not really bother to argue that he had the majority of Republican voters on his side."[39]

Although this public recognition offered some meager consolation to the Wisdom camp and provided additional fuel to the fire they were trying to light under the public, Wisdom fully recognized that his biggest challenge lay ahead. Seven of his state's eleven district delegate slots and all four of the at-large delegate positions would have to be fought for at the national convention in Chicago. But he faced a daunting challenge. Not only would he have to establish the validity of his faction's claim to these delegates, he would first have to convince the national party leaders to assert jurisdiction over this question and not merely defer to the decision of the state's Jackson-dominated Central Committee. If Wisdom could not persuade these national leaders to divest Jackson's Old Guard of the power to issue the final word over a challenge to its theretofore unfettered dominion over delegate selection, the die would be cast.

The Call for the 1952 convention and the Rules of the 1948 Convention, however, contained what appeared to be contradictory language concerning the assignment of jurisdiction over delegate challenges. Rule 4(b) of the 1948 Convention Rules and paragraph (c) of the section of the 1952 Call entitled "Filing of Credentials and Contests"[40] stated that "only contests affecting delegates at large shall be presented to the national convention." But Rule 4(a) of the 1948 Convention contained language suggesting that the National Committee retained jurisdiction over all (that is, district as well as at-large) delegate contests reported to its secretary.[41] Since district delegates accounted for eleven of the state's

<hr />

39. Joseph Alsop, "Matter of Fact," *Washington Post*, June 2, 1952.

40. This provision was taken *in haec verba* from Rule 4(b) of the 1944 Convention Rules.

41. "Where more than the authorized number of Delegates from any State . . . are reported to the Secretary of the National Committee, a contest shall be deemed to exist and the Secretary shall notify the several claimants so reported, and shall submit all such credentials and claims to the whole Committee for decision as to which claimants reported shall be placed upon the temporary roll of the Convention."

fifteen convention seats, seven of which Wisdom intended to contest, it was imperative that any national party review not be limited to the four at-large contests.

This language of Rule 4(b) gravely concerned Wisdom. But "as any lawyer can," he acknowledged, "we were able to devise arguments in support of the Convention taking jurisdiction."[42] Wisdom's first gambit was to lodge a challenge with the Republican National Committee. But the National Committee declined to resolve the disputes, choosing instead to remand them to the State Central Committee.[43]

Naturally, Wisdom harbored no illusions of prevailing before the Jackson-dominated Central Committee. The meeting at Shreveport's City Hall was a bruising session that lasted for over seven hours.[44] The ensuing pattern was as consistent as it was predictable; the committee patiently listened to all of Wisdom's arguments and evidence. And even though the final result was never in doubt, Wisdom and his colleagues diligently interrogated witnesses and submitted documentary evidence to build up the kind of record Wisdom knew his side would need in order to have any hope of prevailing in front of their true target audience—the delegates to the Chicago convention. Finally, one by one, district by district, the Central Committee disqualified all seven Eisenhower delegates and certified every competing Taft delegate. They also disqualified the two pro-Eisenhower delegates elected at the Third District convention, even though Jackson had not challenged these delegates![45]

Since the only unchallenged delegates were the pair of Taft supporters who had been elected at the Fourth and Fifth Congressional District conventions without opposition, the rulings by the Central Committee meant that the Jackson delegation now claimed all eleven district delegates. In addition, since the National Committee also had rejected Wisdom's challenge to all four delegates-at-large, Jackson now commanded the entirety of the Louisiana delegation. At least Jackson thought he did. But Wisdom had vowed to bring this fight all the way to the national convention and he did not intend to renege on that commitment.

42. Unaddressed copy of letter from John Minor Wisdom dated April 19, 1952.

43. David, Moos, and Goldman, *Presidential Nominating Politics in 1952: The South*, 272; Howard and Deener, *Presidential Politics in Louisiana, 1952*, 31.

44. Thomas Sancton, "La. Taft-Ike Fight Bound for Chicago," *New Orleans Item*, June 23, 1952, 4, col. 3.

45. Howard and Deener, *Presidential Politics in Louisiana, 1952*, 31; David, Moos, and Goldman, *Presidential Nominating Politics in 1952: The South*, 273.

He had to persuade either the national party leaders or, if necessary, the convention delegates themselves, that the members of his delegation were the fairly elected representatives of the Republican voters in Louisiana.

Wisdom's first step after the Shreveport debacle was to meet with General Eisenhower, who happened to be in Dallas to confer with leaders of the Texas and Louisiana delegations. After reporting to Eisenhower on the results of the Shreveport meeting, Wisdom previewed his strategy to a group of reporters covering the meeting. "The General now is very deeply incensed by the tactics employed by the Jackson faction," he told them. "There will be and can be no compromise on a moral outrage. This fight goes to Chicago. The General is depending on the consciences of 1200 delegates who meet there."[46]

And so the battle was joined. For the first time in modern Louisiana history, under Wisdom's leadership, there was a real chance of ending decades of the Old Guard's unopposed, autocratic domination of a patronage dispenser that had masqueraded for generations as a political party. Wisdom would bring his fight to the convention and try to appeal to the moral sense of the delegates. Yet as events unfolded and the national convention drew nearer, there was a growing sense throughout the country that not only was the future of Louisiana's Republican Party on the line, but that these fifteen votes from the Bayou State might hold the key to the presidential nomination itself. It was on to Chicago!

46. Sancton, "La. Taft-Ike Fight Bound for Chicago," *New Orleans Item*, June 23, 1952, 4, col. 3.

5

THE 1952 CONVENTION
VICTORIES FOR EISENHOWER AND
A TWO-PARTY SYSTEM IN LOUISIANA

At the same time that John Minor Wisdom was struggling to unseat John E. Jackson and rebuild Louisiana's Republican Party, another southern attorney, Elbert Parr Tuttle of Atlanta, was spearheading a movement to reform and broaden the base of the Republican Party organization in Georgia. And when Wisdom asked Senator Henry Cabot Lodge in the winter of 1951 to recommend someone who had experience in a delegate challenge and who might be able to advise him in his nascent Eisenhower effort in Louisiana, Lodge immediately tendered the name of Tuttle.

Wisdom took Lodge's advice to heart, called Tuttle, and Tuttle instantly agreed to take a Sunday train to New Orleans so that the two could compare notes. Tuttle was well acquainted with the problems that Wisdom was confronting in Louisiana. The Georgia Republican Party was run by a small clique of "Post Office Republicans," the term used to describe those who became Republicans "because they hoped that a republican President would be elected so that they could name all the Postmasters as well as everybody that worked at the post office, the district attorney and the marshals."[1] Wisdom and Tuttle spent much of

1. Transcript of interview of Elbert Parr Tuttle by Joel Wm. Friedman, Atlanta, Ga., February 22, 1993, 8.

the day in the garden of Wisdom's magnificent Garden District home. Within a few hours, the two had forged a bond of personal friendship and professional admiration that would last for more than forty years.

"Of course I fell in love with the Wisdoms the minute I met them," Tuttle recalled.[2] The two men commiserated over the common obstacles that lay in each of their paths and exchanged ideas about how to overcome these hindrances and to promote the hoped-for candidacy of General Eisenhower. And while this initial meeting created a tremendous sense of camaraderie between these two established attorneys, it also had a much more profound impact on the future of their party and the nation. For the strategies exchanged during this initial encounter laid the groundwork for a grassroots movement that eventually reshaped the southern Republican Party and played a pivotal role in Eisenhower's capture of the Republican Party's presidential nomination.

In the summer of 1952, the epicenter of the political world was located three and a half miles to the southwest of the Chicago loop. Here, on the easternmost edge of the city's south side—surrounded by mammoth stockyards, steel mills, and diverse ethnic neighborhoods populated by thriving Irish, Greek, Slavic, and Italian communities—lay the Chicago Convention Building and International Amphitheatre, the site chosen by both political parties to host their 1952 presidential nominating conventions. This marked the thirteenth time that the Party of Lincoln chose to gather in Carl Sandburg's "City of the Big Shoulders," including the turbulent session in 1912 when Theodore Roosevelt and President William Howard Taft locked horns in a delegate fight eerily premonitory of the contest that ensnared that president's son exactly four decades later.[3]

For nearly a week prior to the arrival of most of the attendees, long before they would begin the official business of choosing a candidate and adopting a platform, several critically important committees were busily at work. In clandestine caucuses and casual corridor conferences held throughout the massive Conrad Hilton Hotel, as well as in stuffy, smoky salons and bustling ballrooms teeming with reporters eager for any hint of an impending breakthrough, the committee members spent grueling days examining evidence and witnesses and engaging in end-

2. Ibid., 7.
3. *World Affairs*, 12 Facts on File 213,216 (1952).

less and spirited debates. Nearly all of this intensive activity centered on a trio of disputes that most insiders realized certainly would affect, and might even resolve, the increasingly bitter battle between the two contenders for the presidential nomination, Senator Robert Alphonso Taft and General Dwight David Eisenhower.

This was only the second time in its hundred-year history that the GOP convention experienced a floor fight over the seating of groups of delegates. The previous occasion, separated by two score years from the current controversy, was strikingly similar in some ways to its latter-day counterpart. This earlier contest pitted the Bull Moose supporters of Theodore Roosevelt against followers of the incumbent president, William Howard Taft. And just as in 1952, one of the focal points of the antecedent struggle was the seating of contested delegates from the country's southern states. In 1912, President Taft's delegates prevailed in their challenge, and he garnered the party's nomination. But the dispute proved costly for the Republicans in the end, as the divisions it engendered led directly to the Progressive Party revolt of Theodore Roosevelt and contributed significantly to Taft's defeat in the general election at the hands of his Democratic challenger, Woodrow Wilson.[4] Clearly, President Taft's son, Robert, hoped for a more successful outcome in 1952.

Herbert Brownell was keenly aware of this slice of party history. Several weeks before the convention began, he had begun to devise a strategy designed to garner the nomination for his candidate, General Eisenhower. Brownell was a former chairman of the party's National Committee and had been the campaign manager for Tom Dewey's presidential campaigns of 1944 and 1948. Widely respected among party professionals as a campaign strategist, in the Eisenhower campaign Brownell was primarily responsible for fashioning and implementing a plan to collect and retain a majority of the convention delegates. After meeting with delegations from states across the country, it became evident to Brownell that Eisenhower would have to overcome the significant lead that Taft already had amassed as a result of his unquestioned national stature and the campaign that his followers had mounted since the early months of 1950.[5] By the middle of June 1952, just a few weeks

4. "G.O.P. Delegate Contests Going On for Century," *Chicago Sunday Tribune,* July 6, 1952, 12, col. 4.

5. See John Robert Greene, *The Crusade: The Presidential Election of 1952* (Lanham, Md.: 1985), 73.

before the opening of the convention, the Associated Press was reporting that Taft controlled 458 delegates to Eisenhower's 402, with 604
needed to secure the nomination. By the eve of the convention, Taft's
count had increased to 504, just 100 short of a majority.[6]

It was common knowledge among political operatives and other serious campaign watchers that serious challenges were likely to be mounted
against the delegates chosen to represent several southern states, particularly those from Georgia, Texas, and Louisiana. Brownell, who possessed a keen ability to count noses, sensed that the contest for delegates between the two major candidates would be quite close—probably
within sixty or seventy votes—and that the balance of power at the
convention could rest in the hands of the delegates from these three
southern states—all of whose traditional leaders were solidly in the
Taft camp.[7]

The authority to decide delegate contests resided, in the first instance, with two of the party's most powerful committees—the National Committee and the Credentials Committee; both of which also
were dominated by Taft supporters. With little hope of convincing either of these groups, Brownell had to bank on convincing sufficient
number of delegates to overturn the judgment of their most respected
and influential committees. Moreover, this task was complicated by the
party rule authorizing contested delegates to vote on all seating controversies, including their own.

The success of this strategy depended heavily on the talents and abilities of the Eisenhower leaders in the three key southern states. Eisenhower partisans in these states would have to come to the convention,
not only with clean hands, but with a truckload of ammunition. Unless
they could document their claims to delegate status and repudiate each
and every attempt by the Taft forces to retain their seats at the convention, the effort would fail and the nomination would be lost.

The Republican National Committee was scheduled to begin its deliberations on the delegate challenges on June 13, a full month before the
convention's official July 14 opening day.[8] Although initially opposed

---

6. David Halberstam, *The Fifties* (New York: 1993), 211.

7. Herbert Brownell and John P. Burke, *Advising Ike: The Memoirs of Attorney General Herbert Brownell* (Lawrence, Kans.: 1993), 114.

8. W. H. Lawrence, "Both G.O.P. Camps Bar Compromise on Delegate Issue," *New York Times*, July 1, 1952, 17, col. 3.

to allowing live television and radio coverage, the party leaders eventually yielded, in part, to public pressure and agreed to permit full media access—television, radio, and newsreel—to some of the proceedings.[9] Although the National Committee's deliberations would continue to be shielded from media exposure, the Credentials Committee's hearings would be fully accessible to the public. As a result of this decision, for the first time in American history, between sixty and seventy million citizens all across the nation were able to view firsthand the workings of a national political convention.

But the public would have to wait for its bird's-eye view until the National Committee had rendered its decision on the delegate contests. After summarily rejecting the challenge to the Taft-dominated delegation from Florida, and then voting to seat the Georgia delegation pledged to cast all of its seventeen votes for Senator Taft, the National Committee focused on the Louisiana contest.[10]

Wisdom fully appreciated the extent to which the forces arrayed in support of Senator Taft would fight to seat every delegate favorable to their cause. His experiences at the Louisiana State convention and with the State Central Committee had dispelled any illusion that his opponents would submit docilely to the justice of his cause. To the contrary, the Jacksonites came to Chicago brimming with confidence and secure in the conviction that their controlling position in the party hierarchy was unassailable. Several of them even went so far as to issue public pronouncements boasting about the inevitability of their triumph and deriding the fortunes of their misguided opposition. "Jackson has a big national name," his aide Van Buren Harris had gloated. "He's known at these national conventions, been a delegate five times. Do you think a credentials committee at a convention examines these disputes?— 'Okay, buddy, tell your story. That's all. Okay, thank you, next case.' That's what Wisdom will get at the national convention."[11] Baton Rouge attorney and Taft backer Brittmar Landry similarly prophesied that Wisdom "will get nowhere at Chicago."[12]

9. W. H. Lawrence, "G.O.P. Chiefs Bar Delegate Hearings to TV and Radio," New York Times, July 2, 1952, 1, col. 1. See also Brownell and Burke, Advising Ike: The Memoirs of Attorney General Herbert Brownell, 115.

10. W. H. Lawrence, "Kansas Vote Goes to Ike in Lone Victory," Atlanta Constitution, July 3, 1952, 1, col. 8.

11. Sancton, "Admits Patronage Is Issue," New Orleans Item, 5.

12. Ibid.

John and Bonnie Wisdom had departed New Orleans for Chicago about two weeks prior to the opening of the convention. At the same time, a young attorney from New York named Jack Wells also arrived in Chicago. Wells, along with William Rogers, had been tabbed by Brownell to be the national campaign's liaison with the Texas and Louisiana delegations. They were members of a group of Republican attorneys in New York who had worked with Brownell in the Dewey campaigns of 1944 and 1948.[13] Wells and Wisdom had a good working relationship, but there was little for Wells to do prior to Wisdom's arrival in Chicago. The Louisiana statutes and regulations governing the selection of delegates were so complex, and Wisdom had displayed such a mastery of the process, that neither Rogers nor Wells played any meaningful role in the efforts Wisdom had spearheaded in Louisiana prior to the national convention. Wells, however, did play a key role in Wisdom's final preparation for his arguments to the National and Credentials Committee members and to the convention delegates.

In advance of his arrival in Chicago, Wisdom had prepared a lengthy, extensively annotated brief for distribution to every committee member and convention delegate. Nevertheless, there was still additional work to be done to be fully prepared for his anticipated appearances in the National and Credentials Committee meeting rooms and on the convention floor. Wells and Wisdom prepared a condensed version of the massive convention brief that they entitled *The Louisiana Story*.[14] Wells also suggested that the impact of Wisdom's presentation would be enhanced by the use of large visual aids to direct the committee members' attention to facts and figures that were critical to Wisdom's argument. So the pair began working sixteen- to eighteen-hour days, busily preparing and arranging for the printing and reproduction of large, square charts and other exhibits that measured between five and six feet in height. These visual aids had to be large enough for the committee members to see clearly from a distance, because Wisdom intended to refer to them throughout his presentation to depict in very graphic fashion precisely what had occurred at each local ward and district meeting in the course of the delegate selection process in Louisiana.

Once the abridged brief and the visual aids were prepared, the next step was to rehearse the entire presentation, including the opening and

13. Transcript of interview of Herbert Brownell, Jr., by Joel Wm. Friedman, New Orleans, La., April 7, 1994, 12, 15, 16.

14. J. M. Wisdom interview [Friedman], July 5, 1994, 4–10.

closing statements and examination of witnesses who had been brought to Chicago a few days before their scheduled appearance before the National Committee.

The National Committee heard the Louisiana challenge on Thursday morning, July 3. According to the agreement worked out several days earlier with its chairman, Guy Gabrielson, each side was allotted ninety minutes to present its case.[15] Wisdom's strategy was straightforward. He would prove that the New Republican leadership movement in Louisiana had operated within the rules and had soundly defeated the Jackson faction in the January primary and in the April mass meetings. Pro-Eisenhower delegates had prevailed in six of the state's eight congressional districts, which accounted for nine convention delegates. Additionally, the Eisenhower-backing New Republicans were entitled to all four of the delegate-at-large slots. As promised, however, Wisdom would not challenge the pair of delegates elected from the Fourth and Fifth Districts, where the New Republicans had not mounted any opposition to the Old Guard's pro-Taft slate.

Wisdom approached this appearance just as he had handled so many court trials in New Orleans. He came to the hearing room accompanied by mounds of copies of his 104-page brief, twenty-five exhibits, and a truckload of affidavits. This was not a time for overblown political speeches. Time was limited; Wisdom's opening and closing statements had been pared down to the essentials after endless stopwatch-focused rehearsals. Each witness's examination also had been timed to the second so that the entire case would fit within the allotted ninety minutes.

Direct and to the point, Wisdom opened his presentation with a clear and emphatic statement of his baseline position. The Louisiana dispute was "not just another southern contest."[16] It was, he emphasized, a challenge that placed the party's democratic ideals on the line. The entire party was on trial before a jury of 160 million Americans. Wisdom urged the committee members to compare the "shoddy tactics" of the Jacksonite contenders, designed "to defeat the will of the vot-

15. W. H. Lawrence, "Taft Forces Seat 16 More Delegates; Eisenhower Gets 3," *New York Times*, July 4, 1952, 1, col. 8; 9, col. 5. Wisdom chose to reserve fifteen of his allotted ninety minutes for rebuttal. Republican National Committee Chicago Convention, 1952: Hearing on Contests 177 (July 3, 1952) [hereinafter National Committee Hearing] (unpublished transcript on file with author); "Rival Louisiana Groups Battle for Recognition," *Times-Picayune*, July 9, 1952, 1, col. 8.

16. National Committee Hearing, 179.

ers" and "work a fraud on the National Committee," with the actions of his group, all of which had been in strict compliance with Louisiana law and the rules of the Republican Party. Through a series of witnesses, Wisdom established that although his group had fairly elected a majority of the delegates to the state convention, a "kangaroo court" state Credentials Committee had replaced them with Jackson's pro-Taft cohorts.[17]

After Wisdom completed his initial presentation (having reserved fifteen of his ninety minutes for rebuttal), Jackson took center stage. He relied solely on a perfunctorily delivered lecture, rarely looking up at the committee members as he read from a long, handwritten memorandum. He presented no witnesses and submitted no briefs or documentation of any kind to the committee.[18] To Jackson, the entire matter was nothing more than a purely local dispute between politically motivated rivals. He did not need to respond to the issues on the merits because, Jackson blindly assumed, nobody would be interested in the merits. It would simply be a question of politics as usual. And when a committee member questioned whether Jackson's delegation reflected the will of the majority of Louisiana Republicans, a defensive Jackson offered a characteristically nonresponsive retort. "There are all kinds of majorities. You wouldn't count the heads of a mob when you were about to be attacked. You wouldn't just say 'I give up, I surrender,' because there were a lot of people in the mob."[19] The New Republicans' claims, Jackson insisted, represented nothing more than a self-serving grab for power. His was the only lawfully recognized Republican Party organization in the state because it had always been the official party organization. The New Republicans, on the other hand, "had made alliances with the Democrats, persuaded many of them to change their registration to vote Republican and [were] attempting to usurp the authority of the regular organization."[20]

Reporters fortunate enough to cram into the packed hearing room were treated to a display of oratorical flourishes rarely, if ever, heard in the traditional humdrum of convention preliminaries. They reveled

17. Ibid., 180, 182, 223.

18. "Victory for Ike and Louisiana," *New Orleans Item*, July 10, 1952, 14, col. 1.

19. Richard B. Stone, "Birth of a Party: How Louisiana's New Republicans Beat the Bosses," *Harvard Review* (Winter 1963): 55, 59.

20. Lawrence, "Taft Forces Seat 16 More Delegates; Eisenhower Gets 3," *New York Times*, July 4, 1952, 9, col. 5.

in Jackson's contorted explanation of why several veterans of his delegations to prior conventions had chosen to switch to the Wisdom faction in 1952. Men like New Iberia sugar planter Paulin Duhe, he replied, were merely seeking "the sophistry of dreams . . . the fruits of political ambitions . . . not devotion to political duty, but diversion, pleasure, and recreation in the assembly of their friends gathered." Wisdom, of course, was not to be outdone. Pencils flew in the hands of the enthralled reporters as he complained, "We have had hayrides in Louisiana. But now we are being taken for a steamroller ride the like of which has not been seen before."[21]

By the time that Jackson and Wisdom had completed their presentations and responded to all of the members' questions, the committee had been in session for more than four hours. Yet after listening to hours of arguments and hearing testimony from many witnesses, committee chair Guy Gabrielson ruled that since Louisiana's State Central Committee already had upheld the legitimacy of Jackson's claim to the district delegate seats from all but the Third District (Jackson had not asserted an express challenge to those seats before the State Central Committee), Wisdom's challenge to all of these slots was out of order. This ruling immediately was sustained by a voice vote of the full committee.[22] Thus, of all the district elected delegates, the eligibility of only the pair representing Louisiana's Third Congressional District was subject to committee review. By a vote of 61–41, the National Committee declared that these two delegate slots properly belonged to General Eisenhower.[23] That left only the question of the competing claims to the state's four delegates-at-large. Here, the committee sided with the Jacksonites, voting 58–42 to seat the Old Guard's four at-large delegates.[24]

Within minutes of the announcement of the National Committee's decision, Wisdom and Jackson were surrounded by a barrage of newsreel and television reporters in a corridor outside the hearing room.[25] In his first television interview of the convention and in front of a nation-

21. Sancton, "Warnings of Past Haunt GOP Convention Leaders," *New Orleans Item*, July 6, 1952, 1, col. 2; 12, col. 4.

22. Lawrence, "Taft Forces Seat 16 More Delegates; Eisenhower Gets 3," *New York Times*, July 4, 1952, 1, col. 8.

23. National Committee Hearing, 313.

24. Edgar Poe, "Taft Supporters Win Most La.-Miss. Republican Seats," *Times-Picayune*, July 4, 1952, 1, col. 4.

25. Sancton, "Warnings of Past Haunt GOP Convention Leaders," *New Orleans Item*, July 6, 1952, 1, col. 2; 12, col. 3.

wide audience, Wisdom, visibly angry and growing angrier by the minute, shouted, "It's a day of infamy! The Republican National Committee was tried and found guilty."[26] Similarly dismissing the committee's patronizing decision to recognize two of his thirteen delegates, Wisdom added, "They just threw a bone to a dog." Jackson, naturally, was not about to permit Wisdom to monopolize the attention of the television audience. He made light of Wisdom's charges by suggesting that his livid reaction was to be expected of someone who has just lost his case. "When a lawyer loses a case," Jackson smirked, "he can appeal or cuss the court. Mr. Wisdom has chosen to cuss the court."[27] Wisdom snapped back. "We have not lost this case. We have won this case before the American people and they're the real judges. It is now apparent why the committee was afraid to have TV cameras and radio broadcast at the hearings. They had already planned to steal these delegations for Taft. The Republican Party is now on trial before 160 million Americans."[28]

Speaking to the press was an essential component of Wisdom's overall strategy. He hoped that the reportage would create a groundswell of public support that would impede the ability of the entrenched party leadership to continue to adhere to the political status quo. And after his performance at the National Committee, the strategy appeared to be working. As one correspondent from the St. Louis Post-Dispatch observed, "shortly after the Louisiana steal, there were signs that some of the delegates were disturbed by these pressure tactics. Eisenhower supporters were making the most of their reverses in the committee. They were taking their case to the television cameras outside the hearing room."[29] Another reporter noted that "even cynical political correspondents wondered, before the vote was cast, whether the committee would have the gall to hand the delegates to Jackson. They were agreed [that] the decision represented ruthless machine politics at its worst."[30]

The positive press that Wisdom began to generate did not, however, have any immediate impact upon the National Committee. A few hours after handing most of the Louisiana delegation to Senator Taft,

26. "State Ike Faction Bitter over Decision," New Orleans Item, July 4, 1952, 1, col. 2.
27. Sancton, "Warnings of Past Haunt GOP Convention Leaders," New Orleans Item, July 6, 1952, 1, col. 2; 12, col. 3.
28. "State Ike Faction Bitter over Decision," New Orleans Item, July 4, 1952, 1, col. 2.
29. "Victory for Ike and Louisiana," New Orleans Item, July 10, 1952, 10, col. 1.
30. Ibid.

the National Committee turned away the challenge to the five-member Taft delegation from Mississippi. Nevertheless, these two predictable setbacks did not deter Wisdom. A couple of days after his defeat at the hands of the National Committee, he and Jack Porter, an Eisenhower leader from Houston, were the featured speakers at a "Dixie indignation rally," where he regaled the crowd with "the complete lowdown on the 'big swindle' in Louisiana."[31] "It is now evident," Wisdom exclaimed, "that the Taft forces are rattled. They don't know how high to gear the steamroller that is already rolling. They have made a lot of people mad, including a good many Republicans who ordinarily might have gone along with them."[32]

On July 7, four days after the National Committee's tumultuous hearings on the Louisiana contest, more than 1,200 delegates responded to the call to order as the official proceedings of the convention commenced. While most of the convention delegates were involved in the flurry of opening day activities in the Grand Ballroom at the Hilton Hotel, in the ornate setting of the Gold Room of the Congress Hotel the Credentials Committee was holding its initial meeting.[33]

Back at the Hilton Hotel, Wisdom sat at the desk in his suite several floors above the convention din, poring over the papers and charts that he intended to use that evening when he appeared before the Credentials Committee.[34] The committee was composed of one representative from each of the forty-eight states and the five territories. And with the election of former Oklahoma congressman and Taft backer Ross Rizley as its chairman, most observers presumed that Taft held sway with a majority of the committee's fifty-three members.

The Credentials Committee's proceedings more closely resembled a retrial than an appeal of the rulings by the National Committee. And since Chairman Rizley had instructed both sides to confine themselves to the case that had been presented to the National Committee, Wisdom concentrated on honing and refining his argument and presentation of witnesses in the hope, though not the expectation, of achieving victory in front of this new tribunal.

The Credentials Committee did not begin its consideration of the

31. "Wisdom to Blast at 'Big Swindle,'" *Times-Picayune*, July 5, 1952, 2, col. 3.

32. Norman Walker, "Both Louisiana Groups Protest," *Times-Picayune*, July 6, 1952, 19, col. 5.

33. Lawrence, "Delegate Test On," *New York Times*, July 9, 1952, 1, col. 8; 12, col. 2.

34. Walker, "Louisiana Rivals Awaiting Result," *Times-Picayune*, July 8, 1952, 8, col. 2.

Louisiana controversy until the late evening hours of July 8 because it had spent the earlier part of that day resolving the contest over the composition of the Georgia delegation. The Georgia contest, an all-afternoon slugfest marked by "charges and counter-charges of thievery,"[35] had resulted in another victory for the pro-Taft forces. The Credentials Committee voted 30–21 to uphold the National Committee's decision.[36] The vote was misleading, however, in some regards. Each state, regardless of size, was entitled to a single representative on the Credentials Committee. The members who had voted in favor of the Eisenhower delegation came from states that held 646 convention votes. And 646 was substantially more than a majority of both the 1,206 delegates that would vote on the presidential nomination and the 1,138 uncontested delegates that were authorized to vote on any delegate challenge that came to the floor of the convention for resolution. So even though Senator Taft was able to muster the support of a majority of the committee members to seat his Georgia delegation, Wisdom had reason to be cautiously optimistic about an ultimately favorable result on the convention floor.

The Credentials Committee's hearing on the Louisiana delegation began at 9:30 on Tuesday evening, July 8, in the Congress Hotel's rococo Gold Room.[37] Once again, Wisdom chastised the Jackson forces for their illegal tactics and their continual use of rump meetings to thwart the true wishes of a majority of the voters at district meetings. These rump sessions, he exclaimed, were worse than a kangaroo court. "A decent, respectable kangaroo wouldn't be caught dead in such meetings."[38]

Wisdom's carefully chosen words, delivered in a calculatedly deliberate, New Orleans–accented cadence, were clearly directed not only at the members of the committee but also at the much larger television audience that was, in some respects, a more important jury panel. "We are not supplicants asking for favors," he insisted. "We are the legal delegates. This is not just another southern contest. The hope of the Republican Party for future growth in the South will rest on your deci-

---

35. Lawrence, "Delegate Test On," *New York Times,* July 9, 1952, 1, col. 8; 12, col. 3.

36. M. L. St. John, "Tucker Camp Asks Decision from Floor," *Atlanta Constitution,* July 9, 1952, 1, col. 8.

37. Rose McKee, "Puerto Rico 3 Lift Ohioan's Bag to 42," *Atlanta Constitution,* July 9, 1952, 1, col. 4.

38. "National Affairs," *Time,* July 21, 1952, 15, col. 3.

sion and so also will the integrity and moral soundness of the Republican Party."[39]

Jackson belittled Wisdom's accusations, characterizing them as merely another attempt to unseat democratically elected delegates in order to garner personal political clout. He also claimed that the Wisdom faction included Democrats who had violated state law by participating in GOP meetings less than six months after switching party affiliation.[40] To support this contention, Jackson offered only his personal view that these voters had acted in contravention of the relevant law, admitting, in response to questions by committee members, that he could not cite a single Louisiana court decision that supported such a conclusion. Wisdom, on the other hand, did not rely on personal opinion. Instead, he proffered an official statement from Louisiana's attorney general declaring that recently registered Republicans were not barred by the statute from participating in party caucuses and conventions.[41]

The members of the committee listened attentively to the arguments made by both sides. Despite the lateness of the hour, they continued to pepper both camps with questions for several hours. Finally, long past midnight, Chairman Rizley called a halt to the proceedings, adjourning the session until 8:00 that morning without taking a vote. Although some insisted that the lateness of the hour compelled this decision, one reporter suggested that Rizley declared the recess "to let the effect of Wisdom's hard-hitting arguments cool off."[42]

As it turned out, however, the brief morning respite did little to stem the rising tide of opinion that Wisdom had whipped up in his favor. This shift of momentum also did not escape the attention of some of the more perceptive, experienced Taft hands. So in a last-gasp effort to turn a potentially embarrassing defeat into a gracious compromise, Ohio congressman and national committeeman Clarence Brown asked his colleague from Massachusetts, Representative John Heselton, to meet him in a nearby kitchen for some old-fashioned horse trading. Standing under a sign that read "Keep It Clean," Brown proposed that the Taft supporters on the Credentials Committee would vote in favor of Wisdom's delegation from Louisiana if Eisenhower would recognize twenty-

39. Sancton, "Wisdom Scores in Fight," *New Orleans Item*, July 9, 1952, 1, col. 6; 5, col. 3.

40. "Rival Louisiana Groups Battle for Recognition," *Times-Picayune*, July 9, 1952, 1, col. 8.

41. "Jackson's Defeat," *Times-Picayune*, July 10, 1952, 10, col. 2.

42. Sancton, "Wisdom Scores in Fight," *New Orleans Item*, July 9, 1952, 1, col. 5.

two Taft members of Texas's thirty-eight-member delegation.[43] Congressman Heselton, however, had been carefully prepped for the meeting by fellow Bay Stater Henry Cabot Lodge. Lodge, who had accepted Herb Brownell's offer to become chairman of, and chief public spokesman for the Eisenhower campaign, had instructed Heselton to reject any and all offers of compromise. The no-compromise policy proved to be a winning strategy.

To the astonishment of many and the consternation of some, the Taft campaign yielded on Louisiana in an apparent bid for psychological advantage in the now-inevitable convention floor tussle. Whether it was a strategic retreat or a reaction to the nose count that revealed that an all-out fight over the Louisiana delegates would be lost on the convention floor and that any further attempt to challenge Wisdom's delegation would be both futile and counterproductive,[44] the members of the Credentials Committee voted unanimously to seat all thirteen of Wisdom's New Republican members of the fifteen-member Louisiana delegation. The unanimous verdict overturned the week-old ruling by the National Committee to seat only two Louisiana backers of the candidate from Abilene.

Media pundits immediately explained this unforeseen turn of events as a ploy by the Taft managers to convince the convention delegates to uphold the Credentials Committee's favorable decisions in the Georgia and Texas contests. By demonstrating their candidate's willingness to compromise as well as his desire for party harmony, the Taft handlers hoped to minimize the damage generated by the committee vote and to encourage the convention delegates to engage in a bit of political horse trading.[45]

A newspaper journalist from New Orleans, however, offered an alternate analysis. He reported that the Rhode Island representative on the committee had insisted during the deliberations that "the Louisiana Taft delegation is a stolen delegation" and had asked his colleagues, "is the Republican Party going to swallow it?"[46] Moreover, the reporter concluded, it was Wisdom's patient, but hard-driving presentation that had convinced the Ocean State's representative to the committee of the justness of his cause. "It had the touch of the [Tulane] law school . . .

43. "National Affairs," *Time*, July 21, 1952, 15, col. 3.

44. Felix Belair, Jr., "Taft Aides Yield Louisiana Votes," *New York Times*, July 10, 1952, 17, col. 1.

45. See Lawrence, "Lodge Is Confident," *New York Times*, July 10, 1952, 1, col. 8; 12, col. 1.

46. Sancton, "Here's How La. Ikemen Won Case," *New Orleans Item*, July 12, 1952, 10, col. 1.

And some of the older, self-respecting lawyers on the Taft majority of the Committee just couldn't go against Wisdom's witnesses and evidence."[47] Similarly, another committee member was quoted as advising his counterparts "I wouldn't be frank with you if I didn't tell you that if I had substantial doubt on a question of fact or law in any of these cases that were determinative of the result, I would be inclined to give the benefit of that doubt to the Taft side. But in my judgment, members of the Committee, there is neither question of law nor question of fact that throws any substantial doubt on what we ought to do in this case."[48]

When another pair of Taft supporters informed Chairman Rizley that they also could not ignore the overwhelming case tendered by Wisdom, the Taft managers realized that they had lost their voting majority on the committee. Thus, as the Rhode Island member opined, "when [the Taft majority] saw that they would be beat[en], they did the strategical thing; they made the vote unanimous."[49]

Whatever the motivation behind the Taft campaign's final maneuverings, by relinquishing his claim to the Louisiana delegation, Senator Taft effectively abandoned Jackson—the state's "Mr. Republican" for nearly thirty years—and ensured the election of Wisdom as the next national committeeman from Louisiana.[50]

Bedlam erupted in the Credentials Committee hearing room immediately after the representative from the Virgin Islands cast the fiftieth and final vote in support of Louisiana's Eisenhower delegation. Well-wishers from every corner of the room swarmed around Wisdom in an enthusiastic display of emotion and support. In a matter of seconds, he was overwhelmed by back-slapping, hand-shaking admirers, many of whom were weeping openly. Some of the more athletic Louisianians eschewed the stairways and leapt over the railing from their perch on the balcony to the floor below in order to join the celebration. The throng became so thick so quickly that the short and slight attorney was unable to escape the embrace of the jubilant mass and move from his counsel table to offer a conciliatory word to his crestfallen rival.[51]

47. Ibid.

48. Richard B. Stone, "Birth of a Party: How Louisiana's New Republicans Beat the Bosses," *Harvard Review* (Winter 1963): 55, 61.

49. Sancton, "Here's How La. Ikemen Won Case," *New Orleans Item*, July 12, 1952, 10, col. 1.

50. James A. Hagerty, "Eisenhower Camp Bars Texas 'Deal,'" *New York Times*, July 10, 1952, 13, col. 3.

51. Belair, "Taft Backer Heads Credentials Body," *New York Times*, July 8, 1952, 19, col. 3.

The next day, the thirteen members of the newly recognized Louisiana delegation caucused and ended Jackson's eighteen-year reign as national committeeman by electing Wisdom as the state party's new leader. Two dissenting votes were cast by the delegation's remaining pair of unchallenged Taft delegates from the state's northern parishes.[52] A few hours after the Credentials Committee rendered its decision, Wisdom and the dozen other New Republican delegates made their triumphant entrance onto the convention floor.

Party rules required the presence of a minority report from the Credentials Committee in order to bring an appeal.[53] Consequently, the Credentials Committee's unanimous vote in the Louisiana contest precluded the Jackson forces from bringing an appeal of that decision to the convention floor. But the Taft forces, notwithstanding their public declarations of fealty to party unity, had no intention of relinquishing their claim to the Texas delegation. And when the Taft-controlled National Committee voted, as anticipated, to award twenty-two delegates of the state's thirty-eight delegates to Senator Taft, they did so by a divided 27–24 vote, thereby setting the stage for an all-out battle over the Texas delegation on the convention floor.

Senator Taft quickly hailed the National Committee ruling on the Texas delegation as placing nomination "almost in the bag for me."[54] But Wisdom's thoroughly documented and largely unrefuted claim that Taft's surrogates in Louisiana had attempted to steal the election from the lawfully elected delegates was having a very positive effect. The delegates were becoming increasingly cynical about the bona fides of the Taft campaign. The nomination was turning into a moral referendum. And it was the evidence presented by Wisdom that had created this wellspring of doubt over the tactics employed by the Taft campaign in the two states whose delegations were still in play. It was now time for the convention delegates to cast the deciding vote on the composition of the delegations from Texas and Georgia.

The Georgia contest was first on the conventioneer's agenda and the report of the Credentials Committee sparked a lengthy and frequently vituperative exchange. By the time the strife-racked convention was prepared to vote, it was nearly midnight and the exhausted, grim-faced dele-

52. "Eisenhower Backers Win," *New York Times*, July 11, 1952, 9, col. 4.
53. "Pro-IKE Delegates From Texas, Georgia Seated By Convention," *Times-Picayune*, July 10, 1952, 2, col. 7.
54. Lawrence, "Lodge is Confident," *New York Times*, July 10, 1952, 1, col. 8.

gates, looking more like sober waiters at the end of a Mardi Gras ball than invitees to a soiree, voted 607–531 to overturn the decision of the Credentials Committee. The vote unseated the 17 pro-Taft delegates from Georgia and replaced them with a delegation that favored Eisenhower by a 14-to-3 margin.[55] The convention had just dealt a powerful and potentially lethal blow to Taft's hopes for the nomination.[56] As the Eisenhower partisans reveled in this dramatic victory, even the most ardent Taftite had to concede that the vote had decelerated, if not derailed, the Taft steamroller and had tilted the scales heavily toward the now-likely nomination of Eisenhower.[57]

In the wake of their defeat in the Georgia contest and in the sober recognition that they did not have the votes to prevail, the Taft managers abandoned their pursuit of the Texas delegation and permitted a pro-Eisenhower Texas slate divided 33–5 to be seated by acclamation.[58] This put Eisenhower ahead in the delegate count for the first time and gave tremendous impetus to the now seemingly unstoppable Eisenhower bandwagon.

Wisdom sat back in his chair in the Louisiana delegation with a broad smile on his face, buoyed by the realization that all of his weeks and months of tireless effort were finally paying off. His demonstration to the nation of how the Old Guard had systematically overridden and ignored the democratic aspirations of the majority of loyal Republican voters in Louisiana had inspired his fellow delegates to throw the rascals out and usher in a new era of Republican politics. Not only had he ousted Jackson and provided Eisenhower with thirteen votes from Louisiana, but he had set the stage for the delivery of the Texas and Georgia delegations into the Eisenhower column. And the combined forty-two votes represented by these three states provided Eisenhower with his eventual margin of victory.

At 11:49 a.m., convention secretary Mrs. Charles P. Howard of Massachusetts began the call of the states, commencing with Alabama, which split its votes 9 to 5 in favor of Taft. When she called on Louisiana,

55. M. L. St. John, "Bitter Vote of 607–531 Tops Ohioan," *Atlanta Constitution*, July 10, 1952, 1, col. 8.

56. "Pro-IKE Delegates from Texas, Georgia Seated by Convention," *Times Picayune*, July 10, 1952, 1, col. 8.

57. Ralph McGill, "Ga. Pivots GOP Swing to General," *Atlanta Constitution*, July 10, 1952, 1, col. 4.

58. Lawrence, "Lodge Is Confident," *New York Times*, July 10, 1952, 1, col. 8.

the state's newly elected national committeeman, John Wisdom, surrounded by a throng of exhausted but exhilarated friends, proudly announced that his state cast 13 "hard earned votes" for General Eisenhower and 2 for Senator Taft.[59] By the end of the first roll call of the
states, Eisenhower had amassed 595 votes, only 9 short of the required
majority of 604. When "favorite son" candidate former Minnesota governor Harold Stassen released his 28 delegates from their pledge to
support him on the first ballot, Eisenhower's total count rose to 614,
10 above the necessary majority.[60] But though Stassen's decision provided the final votes to push Eisenhower over the top, Eisenhower and
Herbert Brownell both knew that without Wisdom's leadership, the pivotal southern states would have remained in Bob Taft's pocket and the
senator, rather than General Eisenhower, would now be mulling over a
short list of names for a running mate.

Once their nominee made his vice presidential preference known,
it took the convention delegates less than half an hour to affirm it.
Richard Nixon's name was placed in nomination and was declared the
winner by acclamation.[61] This was the signal for a brief demonstration in support of the nominee. Among the demonstrators was Wisdom, who had grabbed his state's standard and joined the march down
the aisles[62] in support of the man who years later would deny him the
only possibility he ever had to be promoted to a seat on the U.S. Supreme Court.

Wisdom had vaulted into a powerful leadership position within the
Republican Party. For the first time in modern Louisiana history, there
was real hope that leadership of the state GOP would rest in the hands
of someone who was committed to building a political force that would
compete, on local and national levels, with the Democratic opposition.
Yet as he boarded the train for New Orleans, Wisdom knew that his vision of a true two-party system in Louisiana was not yet a reality. Much
of the most difficult work lay ahead of him. But for the immediate fu-

59. Edgar Poe, "Louisiana Vote Unanimous for Ike after Shift by Two," *Times-Picayune*, July 12,
1952, 4, col. 1.

60. Arthur Krock, "Minnesota a Kingmaker," *New York Times*, July 12, 1952, 8, col. 6; "How
Minnesota's Switch Was Revealed to Martin," *New York Times*, July 12, 1952, 10, col. 3; ibid.;
Lawrence, "Restoring Party's Unity Deemed the First Task," *Atlanta Constitution*, July 12, 1952,
1, col. 3.

61. Lawrence, "Revised Vote 845," *New York Times*, July 12, 1952, 1, col. 8; 7, col. 4.

62. "Wisdom Carries Banner for Nixon," *Times-Picayune*, July 12, 1952, 5, col. 4.

ture, his primary assignment was to elect the man whose nomination he had been so instrumental in securing.

Unfortunately for Wisdom, the combination of a decades-long, traditional allegiance to the Democratic Party and a deeply divided local Republican Party was too much to overcome. Even so, and despite the fact that the New Republicans did not have the resources to place poll watchers at voting locations in many parishes,[63] Ike lost Louisiana to Adlai Stevenson by only 38,000 votes. Thanks to the ceaseless efforts spearheaded by Wisdom and his New Republican leadership team, Eisenhower received 47.1 percent of the total state vote—the largest number of votes received, to that time, by any Republican presidential candidate in Louisiana history. Wisdom may not have been able to deliver the state's electoral votes into the Eisenhower column, but he had generated a base of support that would provide a solid foundation for the development of a strong, cohesive political organization. Finally, after more than ninety years of electoral inertia, the Republican Party could honestly point to the existence of a viable entity in Louisiana.

In his new roles as national committeeman and leader of the state party, Wisdom was at the center of nearly every federal appointment or project affecting Louisiana, including, he loved to recount, "the Postmaster at Rabbit Island, which was accessible only by boat!"[64] He also was becoming widely regarded by the public at large as the state's key link to the Eisenhower administration. Carriage drivers who escorted the throngs of tourists interested in viewing the exquisite homes located in the city's famed Garden District residential area invariably informed their charges that they were passing the home of "Louisiana's Mr. Republican" or "Ike's best friend in Louisiana" as they drove by the Wisdoms' impressive Greek Revival residence on First Street.

Although overseeing federal patronage appointments was a critical part of his job as national committeeman, Wisdom held as his primary objective the expansion of the Republican Party's political base. After all, Eisenhower's election, while important, had never been Wisdom's political end game. As he had reminded the convention delegates

63. The value of having poll watchers present to guard against or to report voting irregularities was vividly highlighted to Bonnie Wisdom by one of the state's chief engineers. In response to her inquiry about the voting machines' susceptibility to tampering, the engineer replied, "Lady, with a bobby pin I can make them sing."

64. J. M. Wisdom [Friedman], November 5, 1993, 41.

in Chicago, he and the other New Republican reformers "were in this fight primarily for a two-party system, and secondarily for [their] candidate, General Eisenhower."[65] This goal, however, could not be reached solely on the back of an aggressive membership drive. The legislative deck was stacked too strongly against such an effort. Recruiting any meaningful number of active party members depended upon the adoption and implementation of a series of statutory changes designed to remove the roadblocks that continued to frustrate efforts to bolster the party's membership rolls.

The most obvious and imperative target for legislative reform was the statutory provision that restricted party committee participation to individuals with five years of prior continuous party affiliation. Another obstacle to party registration efforts was the prevailing system in which each party held a separate primary election, with voting limited to members of that party. Under that scheme, in Wisdom's judgment, there was little, if any, incentive for Democrats to shift parties since the Democratic primary historically had been tantamount to a general election in most local and statewide races. By staying where they were, registered Democrats could continue to vote for the Republican presidential candidate in the general election while retaining their ability to participate in the only meaningful contest for local officeholders by voting in the Democratic primary. What was needed, in Wisdom's view, was an open primary system in which all candidates for an office competed in a single election open to all registered voters, regardless of party affiliation. This change would not only encourage the development of a two-party system, Wisdom adjudged, but would also be more efficient, less time consuming, and less costly than the extant multi-primary scheme.

For two years, Wisdom struggled to reform a political structure that had been erected and maintained for the express purpose of thwarting the development of a true two-party system in his state. By the end of that period, however, his efforts had met only with mixed success. In 1954, the Louisiana legislature amended the election law to reduce the five-year period to two years for membership on the state Central Committee and to six months for service on parish committees.[66] But he

65. Sancton, "New La. GOP Heads Gird for New Fights," *New Orleans Item*, July 11, 1952, 4, col. 7; 22, col. 7.
66. See 1954 La. Acts 373 (amending LA. REV. STAT. ANN. §18:290 [West 1950]). This provision was amended in 1976 to delegate authority to set qualifications for members of the central and parish committees to each political party. LA. REV. STAT. ANN. §§18:444(A) (West 1979).

could not convince the legislature to reform the dual-primary system. The bill that he drafted to replace closed primaries with open ones was introduced into the legislative session, but died in committee. Eventually, however, Wisdom's vision was translated into reality. In 1975, nearly two decades after he had left the political arena and had assumed his place on the Fifth Circuit Court of Appeals, the Louisiana legislature passed an open primary law.[67]

Wisdom's campaign to promote the development of a two-party system in Louisiana also took him outside of the state. His prominent role in the 1952 convention had made him a highly sought-after speaker in Republican Party circles throughout the South and he was eager to export his strategy for party reform to other states in his region. On one such occasion, he was thrust into the center of a decades-old controversy in neighboring Mississippi, a state with a Republican history that paralleled, in many ways, the Louisiana experience. In one very important regard, however, the conflict in Mississippi involved an issue that Wisdom had never faced in Louisiana. In the Magnolia State, the Old Guard, do-nothing "regular" Republican organization was headed by an African American and traditionally had sent racially mixed delegations to the party's national convention. The reform-minded insurgent group, on the other hand, consistently and affirmatively had maintained an exclusively white membership. This political conflict put Wisdom in a difficult situation, forced to choose between an all-white reform party and a racially integrated, do-nothing group led by the Republican Party's only African American national committeeman.

As far back as the late 1920s, Mississippi's Republican Party had been cleaved along racial lines. Just as in Louisiana, Black and Tan and Lily-white factions fought for recognition as the state's official Republican organization. The Mississippi party also shared another insalubrious characteristic with its Louisiana counterpart. One leader had dominated the Black and Tans since 1924. Perry W. Howard, an African American attorney from Jackson, wielded absolute authority over nearly every aspect of Republican Party activity, even though he actually had left Mississippi in 1921 to reside full-time in Washington, D.C., when he was appointed special assistant to the U.S. attorney general.[68] But in 1928, a schism developed in the party, which led to the founding of a break-

---

67. LA. REV. STAT. ANN. §18:401(B) (West 1979).

68. David, Moos, and Goldman, *Presidential Nominating Politics in 1952: The South*, 219.

away group. This organization's official name was the "Independent Republican Party of Mississippi," but it quickly was labeled by the press as the "Lilywhites." From 1928 through 1952, the two rival groups functioned as the equivalent of two separate Republican parties, sponsoring separate slates of national nominating convention delegates.

In 1952, the Republican National Committee voted to seat Howard's biracial, Taft-supporting Black and Tan delegation at its presidential nominating convention. And even though Howard packed the losing horse in the race for the presidential nomination, he succeeded in retaining his position as state national committeeman and anticipated dispensing the patronage fruits produced by Eisenhower's victory. Other emerging southern leaders of the party, however, including Wisdom, wanted Howard out. To them, Howard was not only a Taft supporter; he was one of the oldest of the Old Guard Republicans who consistently had blocked their attempts to breathe life into the party and to bring two-party politics to the South. They preferred to reward the Citizens for Eisenhower leaders, commonly known as "Eisencrats," even if they were not registered Republicans.

In mid-November 1952, a deal was brokered between Mississippi's rival Republican factions that established a coalition committee to handle patronage matters. Howard traveled to New Orleans on November 27 to lobby his fellow national committeeman. Wisdom apparently did not tell Howard what he wanted to hear, because Howard followed up their meeting the next day with a letter in which he implored Wisdom to "kindly remember that after 20 years of blood, sweat, sacrifice and tears, we have come back into our political estate" and urged him not to "attempt to throw out of the window the 'Old Dog Tray.'"[69]

Wisdom did not respond to the letter. Instead, he quietly convinced the Eisenhower administration to give lip service to Howard but to route nearly all patronage decisions through E. O. Spencer, a Democrat who had worked hard for Eisenhower in the general election. On March 30, 1953, Wisdom went to Jackson, Mississippi, to supervise the organization of a Mississippi Eisenhower Advisory Committee under Spencer's chairmanship.[70] The committee contained representatives from the Lilywhite/Mississippi Republican Party, as well as another all-white

69. Letter to John M. Wisdom from Perry W. Howard, November 28, 1952.
70. Letter to Leonard W. Hall from E. O. Spencer, January 25, 1954.

Republican group, Mississippians for Eisenhower, that enthusiastically had supported Eisenhower during the 1952 campaign. Conspicuously absent from the joint committee roster, however, was any member of Howard's Black and Tans. And despite entreaties from Leonard Wood Hall, the Republican Party's new National Committee chairman, Spencer, steadfastly refused to have anything to do with Howard.[71]

This uneasy relationship continued throughout the next three years, with Howard retaining his spot on the National Committee while Spencer was consulted on patronage issues. On March 22, 1956, Mississippi's Lilywhite Republicans held their annual convention at the Hinds County Courthouse in Jackson, intent on formulating a strategy that would convince the national party chieftains to remove Howard as national committeeman. Fortuitously, their convention's keynote speaker, John Wisdom, came equipped with the game plan to accomplish precisely their goal.[72] He urged them to replace their tread-worn leaders with younger, more aggressive faces who would more actively promote the party's interests by offering voters in their state a serious alternative to the Democratic Party.[73] They embraced his game plan. They named Spencer as their choice to replace Howard as national committeeman. By the end of the day, Spencer announced that he was now a "fullfledged Republican."[74] That evening, Wisdom cabled National Committee Chairman Leonard Hall from Jackson with the news that "we kindled a flame today that will not be extinguished at San Francisco." Ever the odds-maker, Wisdom also prognosticated that Howard would not "have the nerve to oppose this new group."[75]

On this rare occasion, however, Wisdom's prediction was off the mark. Howard arrived at San Francisco's cavernous Cow Palace for the Republican Party's twenty-sixth national convention as the head of a fifteen-person Black and Tan delegation ready to take on the by-now customary challenge of his Lilywhite rivals. The Mississippi delegate con-

71. Letter to Leonard W. Hall from E. O. Spencer, January 25, 1954.

72. "Wisdom to Keynote GOP Confab Today," *Jackson Clarion-Ledger*, March 22, 1956, 16, col. 6.

73. "Lily White GOP Hears Address by Spencer, Wisdom," *Jackson Clarion-Ledger*, March 23, 1956, 1, col. 6.

74. Harold Foreman, "Ex-Democrats Take Over Top Spots in State GOP; Spencer Gets No. 1 Spot," *Jackson Daily News*, March 23, 1956, 1, col. 3; Robert Webb, "Spencer Leads GOP in State," *Jackson State Times*, March 23, 1956, 1, col. 4.

75. Telegram to Leonard W. Hall from John M. Wisdom, Jackson, Mississippi, March 22, 1956, 8:00 p.m.

test was a rare source of contention in an otherwise lackluster assembly that one journalist characterized as "one of the most whoopless conventions in history."[76]

Though Howard had easily vanquished every previous challenge to his dominion over the Mississippi delegation, this one was different. This time, his opponents were aided by the presence of an experienced and successful advocate on their team. With Wisdom assisting in the preparation and presentation of their case,[77] the Lilywhites finally achieved a measure of recognition from the national party. Late in the day on Tuesday, August 14, the Committee on Contests voted unanimously to split recognition between the two factions, awarding a majority of eight seats to Howard and allotting the remaining seven spots to Spencer's Lilywhite Republicans.[78] On its face, the committee's actions preserved the Black and Tan majority and, thereby, permitted Howard to retain his post as national committeeman.[79] But since Chairman Hall, and several other National Committee members, secretly wanted to oust Howard from his role as Mississippi's party chief, with Wisdom's assistance they cut a deal with the Lilywhite faction that accomplished that objective while eschewing a public hearing or a floor fight over the Contest Committee's ruling.

First, the National Committee announced its decision to approve the Contest Committee's decision to split the Mississippi delegation. Wisdom, party chairman Len Hall, Spencer, and seven other members of Spencer's Lilywhite party then signed a document that was placed in a sealed envelope and entrusted solely to Wisdom's guardianship. The instrument guaranteed recognition to the Spencer-led Lilywhite group in exchange for its promise not to appeal the National Committee's decision. It also stated that the chairman of the National Committee would recognize the Executive Committee of Spencer's faction as the sole body authorized to represent the national party in Mississippi and that the Lilywhite's chairman, twenty-six-year-old Wirt Yerger, Jr., would be listed

76. Doc Quigg, "Grand Old Party Launches Convention with Dull Thud," *Jackson State Times,* August 20, 1956, A-6, col. 4.

77. "Citizens Group Will Back Ike," *Times-Picayune,* July 15, 1956.

78. Gene Wirth, "Spencer GOP Group Loses in Contest to Obtain Seating," *Jackson Clarion-Ledger,* August 15, 1956, 1, col. 1.

79. In fact, four members (three delegates and an alternate) of the Spencer-Yerger faction split with their colleagues and chose to sit with the Howard contingent rather than occupy some special balcony seats that had been set aside for the seven newly recognized Lilywhite delegates. Robert Webb, "Spencer Deplores Bust-Up," *Jackson State Times,* August 22, 1956, A-7, col. 4.

as the state chairman of Mississippi in all publications and releases and would be the only person invited to any meeting of Republican state chairmen. Most significant, it provided that all policy matters affecting Mississippi thereafter would be handled by the Lilywhites. Finally, the agreement also guaranteed recognition at the 1960 national convention to all delegates elected by the Lilywhites. And although the document did not refer explicitly to patronage, or the post of national committee-man, it clearly paved the way for the removal of all decision-making and patronage-dispensing authority from the Black and Tans.[80]

The fact that he was enabling Mississippi Republicans to replace a racially mixed party headed by an African American with a segregated, all-white party did not deter Wisdom. For better or worse, naïvely or insensitively, he simply never saw the choice in racial terms. To him, Howard's racial identity was an irrelevancy. Howard was an absentee potentate who deliberately had constricted the size of the Mississippi Republican Party for decades to perpetuate his remote control over the party apparatus and its patronage opportunities. Wisdom's focus was on finding and cultivating Mississippi Republicans who would be committed to creating a functioning party that would remove the state from one-party control. And though Wisdom had devoted a significant amount of his time to recruiting African Americans to register to vote in Louisiana, and to register as Republicans, this effort was undertaken primarily as a strategy to expand his party's membership rolls rather than as part of a comprehensive mission to reform the political status of African Americans. It was not that Wisdom did not believe that African Americans were entitled to unfettered exercise to the franchise. He believed fervently, as his mother had taught him, that all persons, including African Americans, were of equal dignity and should be treated fairly and with equal respect. And this meant that they should be entitled to go to public schools alongside white children, to vote under the same conditions applied to white citizens, and to enjoy all other civil rights on a par with whites. Nevertheless, his primary focus at this time was on developing a strong and effective political party and this is what motivated him to worked tirelessly at increasing black voter registration.

In Mississippi in 1956, on the other hand, Wisdom concluded, the

80. Wirth, "Perry Howard Reign as State GOP Boss May Be Near End," *Jackson Clarion-Ledger*, August 16, 1956, 1, col. 1; Spencer, "Howard Faction Bout Unsettled Despite Compromise," *Jackson State Times*, August 16, 1956, B-8, col. 1; Webb, "Spencer Deplores Bust-Up," *Jackson State Times*, August 22, 1956, A-7, col. 4.

political reality was that any viable Republican Party in the Magnolia State was going to be all-white. Consequently, in pursuit of his primary objective, he cast his lot with a segregated group that provided the best chance of establishing and maintaining a functioning party organization that would promote the cause of two-party politics in Mississippi.

Back home in Louisiana, Wisdom, by 1956, had solidified his position as leader of the state's Republican Party. Now known to many as Louisiana's new "Mr. Republican," he no longer had to deal with broadsides aimed at him from within the party ranks and could concentrate on building party registration and promoting the reelection candidacy of Dwight Eisenhower. On Election Day 1956, a hopeful, if not confident Wisdom went on television and predicted that Ike would carry the state by forty thousand votes.[81] Several hours later, the vote tabulations confirmed his startlingly accurate prognostication. With a united party behind him and combining its existing strength in the urban industrial parishes of the state with a renewed appeal to African American voters, the Wisdom-led Republican Party carried the state for President Eisenhower by 40,550 votes.

For the first time since Rutherford B. Hayes's victory in 1876, Louisiana's electoral votes were delivered to the Republican candidate. Two weeks later, on the night of November 20, Wisdom proudly read the contents of a five-page telegram he had received that morning to the jubilant celebrants at his post-election victory party. The "Dear John" cable congratulated Wisdom and his Louisiana colleagues on ending four decades of one-party voting in their state and acknowledged that "Louisiana leads the nation in percentage of increase over 1952 in Republican voting." The author also expressed his "grateful thanks for a job splendidly done" and his hope that this would be a victory that they would "always pleasantly remember." As Wisdom reached the end of the text, he paused, and then, his normally raspy voice now filled with emotion, dramatically proclaimed the last three words—"Dwight D. Eisenhower."

81. Letter to John M. Wisdom from Alfred Whitney "Brother" Brown, November 13, 1956; "Republicans Hail Vote in Louisiana," New York Times, November 8, 1956.

6

ASSUMING THE BENCH
NOMINATION AND CONFIRMATION

With an incumbent President Dwight D. Eisenhower appreciative of the role John Minor Wisdom had played in helping secure both his presidential nomination and, to a lesser degree, his election victory in 1952, and with friends and close working associates, such as Attorney General Herb Brownell, White House chief of staff Sherman Adams, Deputy Attorney Bill Rogers, and National Security Council chief Dillon Anderson, holding positions of power and influence, Wisdom's name frequently surfaced when vacancies occurred in important federal law enforcement posts. Typically, the impetus for such consideration came from one or more of his many admirers. It has frequently, and correctly, been reported, for example, that he turned down a judicial appointment two years before his eventual nomination to the Fifth Circuit Court of Appeals. On two other occasions, however, Wisdom was unsuccessful in obtaining a position that he not only coveted, but actively pursued. Finally, however, in 1957, President Eisenhower offered him a federal judicial post. And although he did have to endure and respond to some token opposition from a small band of his political enemies, the president's confidence in Wisdom was fully vindicated when the members of the U.S. Senate voted unanimously to confirm his appointment to the Fifth Circuit bench.

*   *   *

The U.S. solicitor general, an officeholder largely unknown to the general public, is extremely important and prestigious in the legal community. Described as "the highest government official who acts primarily as a lawyer," the solicitor general is appointed by the president and bears the responsibility of representing the federal government in front of the U.S. Supreme Court.[1] The solicitor general determines not only which cases the government will ask the Supreme Court to review, but also what legal position the government will pursue in those suits. Moreover, because the Supreme Court frequently requests the solicitor general to submit briefs offering the government's position on difficult legal questions arising in cases in which the federal government is not a party, this officer often is referred to as the High Court's "tenth justice."

On December 2, 1952, during his last full month in the White House, President Harry S. Truman decided to name a permanent replacement to fill the vacancy in the solicitor general's office that had been occupied on a temporary basis by Acting Solicitor General Robert Stern after Philip B. Perlman's resignation in mid-August of that year. Truman's choice, thirty-six-year-old Walter Cummings, Jr., resigned three months later, ending the shortest tenure in the history of the office. Determined to clean up the "mess in Washington" that included scandals surrounding several posts within the Department of Justice, Herbert Brownell, who had been appointed U.S. attorney general upon Eisenhower's assumption of the presidency, approached the task of recommending a successor for Solicitor General Cummings with dispatch.[2]

One of the attorneys to whom Brownell, and Eisenhower, frequently turned for advice on appointment matters was Dillon Anderson. Anderson was a partner in the Houston law firm of Baker & Botts whose career had been linked to Wisdom's since 1944, when Anderson's departure from the War Department's Legal Branch created the vacancy that Wisdom filled. But it was not until the two were thrown together during Eisenhower's drive for the 1952 Republican presidential nomination that they developed a close friendship based on deep, mutual admiration. Anderson was intimately involved in an effort in Texas to replace a pro-Taft slate of delegates with those committed to General

---

1. Joan Biskupic and Elder Witt, *Guide to the United States Supreme Court*, 3d ed. (Washington, D.C.: 1997), 831–832.

2. Although he denied it, Cummings is alleged to have obtained the appointment because his father, a Chicago banker, had guaranteed several of President Truman's 1948 campaign loans. Lincoln Caplan, *The Tenth Justice: The Solicitor General and the Rule of Law* (New York: 1987), 14.

Eisenhower that mirrored the course Wisdom was pursuing in Louisiana. Throughout that period, the pair conferred frequently on tactical issues and Anderson modeled his own presentation strategy after the litigation-oriented approach Wisdom employed in his delegate challenge before the National and Credentials Committees.[3]

Following Eisenhower's inauguration, Wisdom let it be known to his Texas friend that he would not object if Anderson recommended him to Brownell to fill the solicitor general post. Unfortunately for Wisdom, however, this was one appointment about which Brownell did not seek counsel. On April 20, 1953, Wisdom received a brief letter from Anderson. "Brownell has apparently drawn an iron curtain around himself and his thinking on the subject of the office of the Solicitor General," he reported. "I put out several lines on your behalf . . . and I have touched base on the telephone when the occasion permitted," Anderson assured Wisdom. In addition, Anderson emphasized, "I have made it amply clear that I am not interested any more in any connection or capacity except on behalf of Wisdom for the job."[4] Ten months later, President Eisenhower nominated Simon Sobeloff, a prominent civil rights attorney from Maryland, for the post.[5]

Within a year, however, Wisdom's name resurfaced before Brownell, this time in connection with an important vacancy in the federal judicial. From 1942 until 1954, the Fifth Circuit Court of Appeals consisted of six judges. At the time, it was customary for each one of these slots to be allocated to one of the six states located within the circuit.[6] But on February 10, 1954, in response to the court's expanding docket, Congress passed a statute authorizing a seventh seat for the court. This naturally became the object of competition between the circuit's six constituent states, each of which had ambitions to double its representation on this federal tribunal of next-to-last resort. Texas seemed to have the strongest claim since its population was more than twice the size of that of the next largest state in the circuit. Eisenhower ultimately chose to

3. J. M. Wisdom [Friedman], July 5, 1994, 11–12.

4. Letter to John Minor Wisdom from Dillon Anderson, April 20, 1953.

5. Sobeloff served for nearly two and a half years, until President Eisenhower nominated him for a seat on the U.S. Fourth Circuit Court of Appeals, where he sat with distinction from 1956 until his death in 1973. Judge Sobeloff played a crucially important role in Wisdom's decade-long effort to forestall the subdivision of the Fifth Circuit. The story of the splitting of the Fifth Circuit is the subject of chapter 15.

6. Harvey Couch, A History of the Fifth Circuit, 1891–1981 (Washington, D.C.: 1984), 67.

nominate a Georgian to the coveted opening, but only five months after Congress had created the extra slot.

More than four months before the president's choice was announced,
however, Attorney General Brownell asked Wisdom to come to Washington to discuss an important matter. Wisdom knew full well about
the vacancy and was certain that Brownell's invitation involved more
than a social call. He also believed, however, that if he refused the
offer, Brownell would turn next to the recently named general counsel of the Treasury Department—Wisdom's close friend and colleague
Elbert Tuttle of Atlanta. So when he arrived in Washington, Wisdom
made a point of meeting with Tuttle prior to discussing the matter with
Brownell.[7]

During their conversation, Tuttle informed Wisdom that he was reluctant to resign from the Treasury Department. Tuttle had only recently accepted this appointment, and he felt committed to remaining on the job for at least a decent interval. Wisdom empathized with
his friend's situation, since he similarly felt obliged to abide by his com-
mitments to his private law practice and to his position as national
committeeman.

Wisdom repeated these misgivings to Brownell, who nevertheless offered, and urged him to accept, the nomination.[8] But notwithstanding
Brownell's assurances that Wisdom "could have had it on a silver plat-
ter" (the Texas Republican leadership already had informed Brownell
that they would relinquish their claim to the slot if it were awarded
to their Louisiana comrade-in-arms), Wisdom asked the attorney general to withdraw his name from consideration with the understanding
that this would not preclude reconsideration on either of their parts if
and when a future vacancy arose.[9] This "soul-searching" decision, however, was not without its price.[10] Less than a year later, Wisdom experienced the political reality that opportunity does not always ring twice.

On July 7, 1954, the judgeship was offered, as Wisdom anticipated,
to Tuttle. Tuttle accepted the nomination, won quick and easy confirmation, and assumed his place on the bench on August 4. Although
Wisdom eventually was nominated to sit on that same circuit court, he

7. Transcript of interview of John Minor Wisdom by Dori Dressander, New Orleans, La., December 10, 1978, 1–2; J. M. Wisdom interview [Graham], March 7, 1981, 26.

8. Sancton, "Wisdom Refuses Judgeship," New Orleans Item, February 28, 1954, 1, col. 4.

9. Ibid.

10. Ibid.

forever remained in a junior position to Tuttle on the court's seniority ladder. The most tangible impact of Tuttle's greater seniority was felt when Richard T. Rives of Alabama stepped down as chief judge of the Fifth Circuit in December 1960. Since that position automatically was assigned to the most senior active member of the court, it was Tuttle, and not Wisdom, who filled that singularly influential post during the heyday of the court's role as the preeminent judicial guardian and enforcer of civil rights. Wisdom, however, never regretted either his decision to stay in private practice or the effect that decision had on the leadership of his court. Quite the contrary. "I feel it was an act of God," he modestly revealed to one reporter. "Tuttle had the administrative ability that I have never felt I had and he had great qualities of leadership. He had been a combat general and so he had commanded respect and understood discipline. Elbert was really a superb Chief Judge."[11]

Barely six months after Tuttle joined the court, the other Georgian on the Fifth Circuit, Robert L. Russell (who had voted in Wisdom's favor in the Schwegmann antitrust case), succumbed to a lengthy illness and passed away on January 18, 1955. Texans, who had seen their dream of a second seat on the court evaporate with the appointment of Tuttle, were quick to reassert their claim. Their favored candidate was John R. Brown, a Nebraska native who had become one of Houston's leading admiralty lawyers. But Brown was not the only interested candidate. The Republican Party's national committeeman from Louisiana now was ready and anxious to be considered for an appellate judgeship.

On February 8, 1955, precisely three weeks after Judge Russell's death and less than a year after declining Brownell's original offer of a Fifth Circuit seat, Wisdom wrote letters expressing his interest in the vacancy to both Brownell and White House Chief of Staff Sherman Adams. He reminded Brownell of how when he had stepped aside in favor of Tuttle he had asked Brownell not to count him out from consideration in connection with a subsequent vacancy. And though Wisdom recognized "that the eyes of Texas are upon you," he also opined that neither Brown "nor any other lawyer in Texas has a comparable claim." And so he asked Brownell to discuss the matter with the president. "I should like to take it up directly with the President," he acknowledged, "but I would not do so without first receiving your complete clearance—if not your blessing."[12] His note to Adams similarly reiterated his conviction

11. J. M. Wisdom interview [Graham], March 7, 1981, 27-28.
12. Letter to Herbert Brownell from John Minor Wisdom, February 8, 1955.

"that there is not any lawyer in Texas who has worked as hard as I have for the President and for the Republican Party. Professionally, I am willing to match my qualifications against Brown's or any other aspirant from Texas."[13]

Brownell's reply was immediate, short, and succinct, though less than sweet music to Wisdom's ears. "I understand your position," Brownell acknowledged with his usual measure of forthrightness leavened with tact, "and I trust you understand mine." He advised Wisdom that Eisenhower believed that "the Texas commitment . . . was made sometime before we learned of your interest in the matter." In concluding, Brownell reminded Wisdom "how hard I tried to get you to take the position for which Elbert Tuttle was later selected."[14] Five months later, President Eisenhower honored the Texas commitment. John Brown was sworn in, at age forty-five, the youngest person ever named to the Fifth Circuit.[15] It would be another year and a half before retirement yielded a new vacancy on that court.

Wayne G. Borah, like Wisdom, was the son of a prominent New Orleans family, pursued his undergraduate studies at Washington & Lee University, attended law school in Louisiana (although Borah matriculated at Louisiana State University rather than Tulane), entered private practice in New Orleans, and interrupted his career to serve as a military officer during wartime (World War I, in Borah's case).[16] Named by President Calvin Coolidge in 1928 to fill the vacancy on the New Orleans federal district court occasioned by the death of Louis Burns, Borah served with distinction on the trial bench for over two decades until he was promoted by President Harry S. Truman.[17] In 1949, Truman nominated Borah to replace the recently deceased Judge Elmo Pearce Lee, Sr., on the Fifth Circuit Court of Appeals, a post Borah held until his retirement on December 31, 1956.

Within a few weeks after Judge Borah publicly revealed his decision to leave the bench, the list of consensus front-runners to succeed him quickly narrowed down to two names.[18] The unquestioned lead Repub-

13. Letter to Sherman Adams from John Minor Wisdom, February 8, 1955.
14. Letter to John Minor Wisdom from Herbert Brownell, February 21, 1955.
15. Harvey Couch, A History of the Fifth Circuit, 1891–1981 (New Orleans: 1984), 92.
16. Judge Borah reigned as Rex, King of Carnival, for Mardi Gras 1946 in New Orleans.
17. Sancton, "Tiny Group Could Influence Issues," New Orleans Item, April 27, 1952, 6.
18. "Mention 2 As Borah's Successor," New Orleans Item, February 4, 1957, 1, col. 8.

lican candidate for the $25,000 life-tenured job was John Wisdom.[19] And once his name became publicly linked with the Borah seat, Wisdom was flooded by expressions of encouragement from friends, supporters, and colleagues. One interesting exception, however, came from an unexpected source. On December 28, 1956, just a few days before Borah's resignation became effective, John Brown, the Texan who received the Fifth Circuit slot that Wisdom had sought in 1955, sent Wisdom a short typewritten note. The message, typed on a 3 x 5 inch note pad containing Brown's official letterhead, stated that Brown would be in New Orleans on court business during the week of January 5, 1957, and asked Wisdom to either drop by his chambers or join him for dinner "for a little personal chat."

Wisdom was so taken aback by their subsequent conversation that, upon returning to his office, he retrieved Brown's note and penned a short notation to the bottom of the note that, like all his correspondence, he retained in one of a voluminous set of files. "He wanted me not to serve on the court. Said that he found it an unsatisfactory experience. Very strange!"[20] Although Wisdom never discussed that matter again with Brown, he presumed that the sentiments expressed on the note had been the product only of Brown's initial unhappiness as a member of the court.

Despite the increasing attention that was coming his way, Wisdom went to great lengths in mid-December 1956 to inform the press that he had not received any prior notice of Borah's intentions and that he was not prepared to declare his interest in the position.[21] Nevertheless, on the day after Borah's pronouncement, Thomas Sancton, New Orleans' preeminent political commentator, reported that informed Republican sources had told him that Wisdom "could get the appointment if he sought it."[22] This prediction, it quickly became apparent, was premature. Wisdom was going to face competition for this position, and from an estimable opponent—a former Louisiana governor who was intent on making a determined run for the appointment.

Robert F. Kennon, the former mayor of Minden, the seat of Webster Parish in the northwest corner of the state, had held several local and statewide elective offices before capturing the governorship of Louisi-

19. John Minor Wisdom, *In Memorium: One of a Kind*, 71 TEXAS L. REV. 913, 914 (1993).

20. Note to John Minor Wisdom from John R. Brown, December 28, 1956.

21. "Borah to Retire as Federal Judge," *New Orleans Item*, December 13, 1956, 1, col. 4.

22. Sancton, "Speculate on New Judge," *New Orleans Item*, December 14, 1956, 1, col. 6.

ana in 1952. A typically conservative southern Democrat, Kennon was a staunch segregationist who fought against the corrupt practices and demagoguery of the Long faction of his local Democratic Party as well as the liberal values of the national Democratic Party.[23] Within six months of his election as governor, Kennon endorsed Republican Dwight Eisenhower's 1952 presidential candidacy, the first southern Democratic governor to do so. Ironically, it was Wisdom, albeit in a rather unorthodox way, who had played the pivotal role in securing Kennon's support for Ike's candidacy.

During the 1952 campaign, Wisdom determined that it would be awkward for both of them if the recently elected Democratic governor was seen meeting with the opposition party leader about the upcoming presidential campaign. Kennon similarly was reluctant to discuss the matter with Wisdom in public view. Nevertheless, he was willing to chat with Wisdom about supporting Ike. So the two agreed to meet in the back of a small cemetery located near the capitol building in Baton Rouge. There, under the shroud of secrecy provided by these grave surroundings, Wisdom sought to convince the governor that it would be extremely useful for Kennon to have a supporter in the White House.

Kennon agreed to support Eisenhower, and assumed that the White House would reciprocate his demonstration of support. In addition, during the first years of his term as governor, Kennon had developed a close relationship with the then–New Hampshire governor and now–chief of staff to President Eisenhower, Sherman Adams.[24] This important connection to the White House inner sanctum, combined with the political capital he had earned by breaking with his party and supporting candidate Eisenhower, made Kennon a formidable candidate for this plum judicial post in 1957.

This was not, however, the first occasion on which Kennon and Wisdom had squared off against one another in connection with a federal judicial appointment. Four years earlier, Kennon had sought to convince President Eisenhower to appoint his executive counsel, Wilburn Lunn, to a vacancy on the federal district court in Shreveport. Wisdom had opposed Lunn and had succeeded in convincing the president to tap Wisdom's preferred candidate, Democrat Ben Dawkins, Jr. But this

23. William C. Havard and Robert J. Steamer, "Louisiana Secedes: Collapse of a Compromise," *Massachusetts Review* 1 (October 1959): 134.

24. Transcript of interview of John Minor Wisdom by Jeffrey Young, New Orleans, La., February 22, 1991.

time, Kennon was in the race for himself, and as early as December 13, the date of Borah's resignation announcement, one local New Orleans newspaper handicapped the race, predicting that Kennon had "the inside track on the appointment."[25]

This forecast proved to be both inaccurate and premature. Wisdom had built up a solid professional reputation in the state, and even most of his political adversaries recognized his legal abilities and acknowledged his intellectual and personal integrity. Kennon, on the other hand, during his tenure on both the Louisiana Second Circuit Court of Appeals and the Louisiana Supreme Court, repeatedly had been found in violation of the American Bar Association's Canons of Judicial Ethics by running for political office while remaining on the bench.[26]

On Fat Tuesday, March 5, 1957, while most New Orleans were caught up in the revelry that envelops the city during its Mardi Gras celebration, Wisdom issued a press release confirming that Attorney General Brownell had recommended to President Eisenhower that he be nominated for the vacant Fifth Circuit position, the traditional precursor to the actual nomination.[27] According to Brownell, President Eisenhower was anxious to use this judicial appointment to signal his commitment to respond forcefully and visibly to the efforts of most southern U.S. senators to encourage massive resistance to the enforcement of the Supreme Court's desegregation opinion in *Brown v. Board of Education*.

Less than one year earlier, on March 12, 1956, Senator Walter F. George of Georgia and Representative Howard Smith of Virginia had introduced a document, officially entitled the "Declaration of Constitutional Principles," in both houses of Congress. It had been signed by all but three U.S. senators from the eleven southern states (Estes Kefauver and Albert Gore of Tennessee and Lyndon B. Johnson of Texas were the principled holdouts) and nearly eighty members of the House of Representatives, including the entire Louisiana contingent. This document, commonly referred to as the "Southern Manifesto," condemned the Supreme Court's opinion in *Brown* as both a departure from well-settled "separate but equal" doctrine and an encroachment on authority over local matters reserved to the states by the Tenth Amendment. It encour-

25. "Borah Resigns Place on Bench," *New Orleans States*, December 13, 1956, 1, col. 1.

26. Editorial, "More Experienced Judges Are Needed," *Shreveport Times*, March 17, 1957, B-2, col. 2.

27. "Wisdom Named for Court Post," *New Orleans Item*, March 5, 1957, 2, col. 5; "John M. Wisdom Is Recommended for Appeal Court," *New Orleans Times-Picayune*, March 5, 1957, 1, col. 8.

aged southern states to resist forced integration by lawful means and pledged that the signatories would use "all lawful means" to overturn the decision and to prevent integration.[28]

"We selected Wisdom over Governor Kennon of Louisiana," Brownell related, "[because Kennon was] a staunch segregationist."[29] And though Wisdom had never taken any vocal public position on segregation prior to assuming the bench, Brownell was thoroughly familiar with Wisdom's efforts to register African Americans to vote in Louisiana. He also knew of Wisdom's devotion to fair play and equality of treatment well enough to presume that Wisdom would work diligently to promote and enforce the Supreme Court's determination that racial segregation constituted a denial of the fundamental constitutional right to equal protection under the laws. He was, as it turned out, correct on both counts.

The local press now presumed that this contest was over and that Wisdom's path to confirmation would be free of further obstacles. In fact, within two days after Wisdom's issuance of his press release, several newspapers began speculating on his successor as Republican national committeeman.[30] And when President Eisenhower officially nominated Wisdom on March 14, sending his name to the Senate for its consent, one New Orleans newspaper declared that, "barring unexpected complications, confirmation is expected within a week or 10 days."[31] Another journal opined that "approval by the Senate is expected to be a formality."[32] Once again, however, the media's prognostications were wide of the mark. Wisdom, meanwhile, remained sanguine about the ultimate result of the process, even though he had to wait more than three months for a Senate vote on his nomination.

From the moment that Wisdom's name was transmitted by President

28. Alvin Shuster, "96 in Congress Open Drive to Upset Integration Ruling," *New York Times*, March 12, 1956, 1, col. 2; "96 Dixie Solons Sign Declaration," *New Orleans Item*, March 12, 1956, 3, col. 2.

29. Brownell and Burke, *Advising Ike: The Memories of Attorney General Herbert Brownell*, 182.

30. See Iris Turner, "Open Race Looms for Wisdom's Job," *New Orleans States*, March 7, 1957, 1, col. 1; Bill Reed, "GOP Eyes Possible Wisdom Successors," *New Orleans Item*, March 15, 1957, 1, col. 5.

31. "Eisenhower Names Louisianan Judge," *New York Times*, March 15, 1957, 15, col. 1; Reed, "GOP Eyes Possible Wisdom Successors," *New Orleans Item*, March 15, 1957, 1, col. 5.

32. William Madden, "Wisdom Favors Judell as State GOP Leader," *New Orleans States*, March 15, 1957, 5, col. 3.

Eisenhower to the Senate for confirmation, a small cabal of rabid segregationists and, as Wisdom described them, "kooks who had supported John E. Jackson" against Wisdom's New Republican challenge to Jackson's entrenched leadership of the state Republican Party, banded together to oppose his appointment.[33] Through a calculated public relations campaign, this group of no more than a dozen individuals claimed that Wisdom's lack of judicial experience and training, and the commission of a series of alleged improprieties in his role as Republican national committeeman, rendered him unfit for appointment to the federal bench.[34] Yet though they were given several opportunities to make their case, none of these concerned citizens could offer any evidence to support their bold assertions.

Though he was irked by having to respond to what he deemed baseless charges about his competence and bad-faith challenges to his integrity, Wisdom never shrank from his conviction that the nomination would receive quick and favorable action by the Senate. And his optimism was reinforced when he learned that he was not only the consensus choice of Republican partisans, but that his nomination would be supported by one of his state's two Democratic national committeemen. Committeeman Camille Gravel was able to persuade the state's two Democratic senators, Allen J. Ellender and Russell B. Long (Huey's son), not to exercise the powerful right of "Senatorial courtesy" to veto the judicial appointment of an individual that any senator found to be "personally objectionable."[35]

Although Senator Ellender staunchly opposed the integrationist philosophy embodied in the Supreme Court's opinion in *Brown*, and had some reason to believe that Wisdom's philosophy on this and related matters might not be compatible with his own, he also took a limited view of the Senate's advise and consent role concerning judicial appointments. He firmly believed that he was obliged to defer to the president's

33. J. M. Wisdom interview [Young], February 22, 1991; Robert Pugh, *An Interview with the Honorable John Minor Wisdom*, 39 LA. B.J. 254, 259 (1991).

34. See "Chandler Urges Protest to Wisdom on Bench," *Shreveport Journal*, April 8, 1957, 1, col. 5 (reporting that Robert Chandler, chairman of Louisiana's States Rights Party, urged all fellow travelers to make their objections to Wisdom's nomination known to Senators Ellender and Long by bombarding them with letters and telegrams).

35. J. W. Peltason, *Fifty-Eight Lonely Men: Southern Federal Judges and School Desegregation* (Urbana: 1971), 27; Frank T. Read and Lucy S. McGough, *Let Them Be Judged: The Judicial Integration of the Deep South* (Metuchen, N.J.: 1978), 55.

choice as long as the president's candidate was objectively qualified for the post. Consequently, Ellender had voted to confirm all but two judicial appointments during his two decades in the Senate.[36]

Russell Long's agreement not to stake out a position opposing the Wisdom nomination did not prevent him, however, from requesting that the Senate Judiciary Committee hold a hearing to investigate charges against Wisdom that were circulating around his state. Long emphasized, however, that notwithstanding the presence of "some objections" to Wisdom's appointment within Louisiana, he intended to vote in favor of the nomination unless evidence was unearthed that confirmed these allegations.[37] But to avoid any appearance of prejudgment or unwillingness to keep an open mind, rather than out of any concern over Wisdom's qualifications, Senator Long requested that his Senate colleagues go through the motions of holding what he, and the other Senate members, expected to be nothing more than a *pro forma* hearing.

Not long thereafter, a three-member Special Subcommittee on Nominations of the Senate Judiciary Committee was impaneled to hold hearings on Wisdom's nomination. Whether by design or chance, the composition of this panel had a southern and decidedly conservative bias. The chairman of the Senate Judiciary Committee, Senator James O. Eastland of Mississippi, one of Congress's most strident and powerful segregationists, appointed himself as subcommittee chairman. The other Democrat on the subcommittee, Olin D. Johnston of South Carolina, was similarly inclined on civil rights issues. The lone Republican of the trio was Indiana's William E. Jenner, another fiercely conservative legislator.

At precisely 2:05 on the afternoon of April 29, 1957, Chairman Eastland raised his gavel and convened the subcommittee hearing on the confirmation of Wisdom's nomination to the U.S. Fifth Circuit Court of Appeals. Senator Ellender opened the proceedings by offering a brief statement as to why he did not intend, at that moment, to voice a position on Wisdom's nomination. Ellender had solicited the opinion of every member of the Louisiana Bar Association and had received replies from eighty-eight of the 138 attorneys to whom he had written. Nearly three-quarters of these eighty-eight, Ellender reported, ex-

36. Liva Baker, *The Second Battle of New Orleans* (New Orleans: 1996), 288.
37. "Late Items," *New Orleans Item*, April 4, 1957, 1, col. 7.

pressed support for the nominee, while six individuals opposed Wisdom's appointment.[38]

Despite the overwhelmingly favorable response he received from members of the bar, Senator Ellender preferred to focus on the reservations raised by the nominee's few opponents. Much of the protest over this judicial appointment, Ellender explained, revolved around Wisdom's involvement with the New Orleans Urban League and its activities in support of school desegregation. A typical example, Ellender noted, was a telegram that he had received from the Claiborne Parish Bar Association in which its president stated that his group had met in special session and had voted to ask the Senate to investigate whether Wisdom's membership in the Urban League rendered him unqualified to impartially judge cases "arising in connection with the laws and customs of the several states."[39] Ellender concluded his opening remarks by stating that he had provided Chairman Eastland with a list of questions to be propounded to the nominee. These questions, he asserted, would address all of the objections raised against Wisdom's confirmation. With that, Ellender departed and Senator Eastland called on the first witness, Dr. Emmett L. Irwin of New Orleans.

Irwin was chairman of the Citizens Council of New Orleans, a group dedicated to thwarting the desegregation of public facilities in the post–*Brown v. Board of Education* era. Irwin, along with former Council Chairman and state legislator Willie Rainach, was a key player in the Louisiana legislature's unremitting efforts to thwart the implementation of *Brown*'s desegregation mandate in that state. The Citizens Council had reason to be particularly interested in this judicial appointment. The Fifth Circuit had appellate authority over the decisions rendered by U.S. district judge Skelly Wright of New Orleans, including those that ordered the desegregation of the New Orleans public school system. With Circuit Judges Tuttle, Brown, and Rives clearly aligned on the side of enforcing the Supreme Court's ruling in *Brown*, the occupant of this seat

38. The remaining eighteen attorneys voiced no opinion on the matter. "Report of Proceedings," Special Subcommittee on Nominations of the Committee on the Judiciary: Nomination of John Minor Wisdom of Louisiana to Be United States Circuit Judge of the Fifth Circuit, April 29, 1957, 3.

39. "Report of Proceedings," Special Subcommittee on Nominations of the Committee on the Judiciary: Nomination of John Minor Wisdom of Louisiana to Be United States Circuit Judge of the Fifth Circuit, April 29, 1957, 6.

would play a pivotal role in the ultimate resolution of Louisiana's states' rights–based challenge to the federal government's authority to desegregate its public institutions.

In a letter written to Senator Eastland two weeks after the announcement of Wisdom's appointment, Irwin had insisted that Wisdom was unfit for membership on this appellate court because he lacked judicial training and experience. Irwin also maintained that Wisdom's membership in the Urban League prevented him from rendering an unbiased judgment in segregation-related cases.[40] After repeating these concerns to the subcommittee, Irwin levied four additional charges against Wisdom.

First, he cited the four-year-old Drew Pearson column linking Wisdom to an alleged smuggler of Charolais cattle, although Irwin admitted that he did not possess any evidence that Wisdom actually had exercised improper influence in the case. Second, he stated that he had heard from other individuals that as state Republican chieftain, Wisdom had demanded that postal workers shift their registration to the Republican Party as a prerequisite for obtaining any promotion. Once again, however, Irwin denied any firsthand information about the veracity of these rumors. His third accusation centered on the Pearson column alleging that Wisdom had demanded a 15 percent kickback from architects bidding on a post office construction project. But when Senator Eastland asked if Irwin possessed any evidence of Wisdom's involvement in kickbacks, the witness quickly retreated and replied that he was not charging Wisdom with anything, but merely was repeating what he had read in a newspaper article about the incident. Irwin's fourth and final claim was that Bonnie Wisdom had accepted free passage to France on a steamship owned by Lykes Steamship Company, a New Orleans firm that did business with the government.[41]

The subcommittee then heard briefly from Robert Chandler, a Shreveport attorney who chaired Louisiana's States Rights Party, and William Dane, a burly former lieutenant to John E. Jackson, both of whom repeated some of the objections that had been levied by Irwin.[42] They were followed to the witness table by Cecil Pettepher, one of Wis-

40. "Segregationist Claims Wisdom Unqualified," *New Orleans States*, March 25, 1957, 6, col. 3.

41. "Report of Proceedings," Special Subcommittee on Nominations of the Committee on the Judiciary: Nomination of John Minor Wisdom of Louisiana to Be United States Circuit Judge of the Fifth Circuit, April 29, 1957, 10–29.

42. Ibid., 33–34.

dom's former clients. Pettepher charged that Wisdom had not properly represented his son after he had hired Wisdom to bring a lawsuit challenging the state law that required all candidates for membership on state Republican Party committees to have been registered members of that party for five years. Pettepher informed the subcommittee that he had complained about Wisdom's conduct to the Louisiana Supreme Court Committee on Professional Ethics and Grievances, but then admitted that the committee had dismissed his complaint. Finally, Pettepher avowed that he had seen Wisdom in public places on several occasions, including Mardi Gras Day, in "an intoxicated condition" and that on one of the instances, it seemed to him that Mr. and Mrs. Wisdom had just had a "scuffle or some misunderstanding."[43]

The final two witnesses, New Orleanian Harry McCall and Payne Breazeale of Baton Rouge, were attorneys who had known Wisdom professionally and personally for several decades. They lauded Wisdom's integrity, legal ability, and civic commitment, and reported that he enjoyed an outstanding reputation among the lawyers and other citizens of his state.[44]

It was now time for Wisdom to take the oath and testify. Until the day of his arrival in Washington, he had not been provided with any notice of which, if any, witnesses would testify in favor or in opposition to his nomination. On the day before his hearing, however, he had been given the names of four individuals from Louisiana who would be appearing before the subcommittee. By this time, he could easily anticipate the tenor of their testimony and was anxious and ready to respond. That evening, Wisdom prepared a nineteen-page typed statement ribboned with those handwritten annotations, additions, deletions, and other editorial changes that he appended up to the moment he arrived at the Senate Office Building. The document was drafted in the form of an opening statement, but Wisdom never was accorded the opportunity to deliver these remarks in anything close to their original form. For during the entirety of Wisdom's thirty-minute presentation, Senator Eastland maintained a tight rein on the conduct of the hearing by peppering the nominee with a series of prepared questions. Nevertheless, as a seasoned appellate attorney, Wisdom was able to interweave the substance of his prepared comments into his answers to Eastland's interrogatories.

43. Ibid., 44–47.
44. Ibid., 49–54.

Following some routine questions concerning Wisdom's personal history, Eastland asked the nominee to explain the facts surrounding his wife's receipt of free passage to France from the Lykes Brothers steamship company. Beyond noting that the president of Lykes, Solon Turman, had been the couple's friend for more than twenty-five years, and that it was not uncommon for Lykes to provide individuals with free passage on its freighters, Wisdom maintained that the gift "didn't mean anything to me and it didn't mean anything to Lykes." Moreover, he averred, he had never sought favors for Lykes from the government and "I never asked a favor of Lykes for the government."[45]

Eastland then turned to the charge that Wisdom had limited Post Office promotions to Democrats who shifted their registration to the Republican Party. Wisdom admitted making recommendations to the postmaster of New Orleans for the promotion of postal workers, and acknowledged that some applicants did shift their registration to the Republican Party because they perceived that doing so might enhance their prospects for advancement. But he emphatically denied ever requesting that any civil servant change his registration and noted that the postmaster himself was a Democrat.[46]

The focus of the inquiry then shifted to Wisdom's representation of Alphe E. Broussard in the highly publicized case involving the transporting of Charolais cattle from Mexico into the United States. Wisdom informed Senator Eastland that he had advised his client to plead guilty to the criminal charge and to "make a clean breast of it."[47] He also assured Eastland that he had not attempted to exert "the slightest political influence or pressure"[48] in the case. Furthermore, Wisdom reminded Eastland, the case ultimately was brought by the Justice Department in Texas, not in Louisiana, and that he had received a full retraction from Pearson of the suggestion in his column that Wisdom improperly had exerted political muscle in the case.

Wisdom had been particularly peeved by the suggestion that he had solicited and accepted kickbacks from architects competing for assignment to a Post Office construction project and wanted to make sure that he provided the subcommittee with his understanding of the facts. He emphatically denied ever asking for or receiving a kickback of any

45. Ibid., 60.
46. Ibid., 61.
47. Ibid., 62.
48. Ibid., 63.

amount from an architect or anyone else in Louisiana who solicited business from the federal government. Wisdom freely admitted that he had recommended the three architects who were chosen for the project, but explained that he had received no fee from the successful competitors and had "scrupulously refrained from asking them for any contributions" to the Republican Party.[49]

Wisdom's response to the oft-stated concern over his membership in the New Orleans chapter of the Urban League might surprise those familiar with the leadership role he later played from the bench in civil rights, and particularly school desegregation, cases. Instead of forcefully and proudly defending his membership in this organization, Wisdom sought to defuse the allegation by minimizing the Urban League's activist role. He told the subcommittee that the Urban League relied solely on mediation, conciliation, and persuasion techniques, and not on pressure, litigation, or legislative lobbying to accomplish its goal of improving the state of race relations. Moreover, he added, the New Orleans branch was not involved in school integration efforts.[50] Wisdom took a similar approach to the allegation that he also was a member of the National Association for the Advancement of Colored People (NAACP). He insisted that this charge was "absolutely irresponsible because the slightest inquiry or investigation would have determined otherwise."[51] And a few days later, in a letter to Senator Ellender, Wisdom proclaimed that "I am not now, nor have I ever been a member of a Fair Employment Practices Commission or the N.A.A.C.P."[52]

Finally, Wisdom concluded his subcommittee testimony with a vigorous denial of Pettepher's charges that he had been intoxicated during Mardi Gras and had engaged in a "scuffle" with Mrs. Wisdom. He told the subcommittee that while he did take a drink or two on Mardi Gras, he drank in moderation. And as to the scuffle, "we have been very happily married for 25 years, 26 years," Wisdom wryly noted, and "we expect to stay married, without scuffling."[53] With that, the hearing ended, precisely two hours after it had commenced.

49. Ibid., 68.

50. Ibid., 72–73.

51. Telegram to Charles L. Bennett from John M. Wisdom, April 11, 1957.

52. Letter to Allen J. Ellender from John M. Wisdom, April 15, 1957.

53. "Report of Proceedings," Special Subcommittee on Nominations of the Committee on the Judiciary: Nomination of John Minor Wisdom of Louisiana to Be United States Circuit Judge of the Fifth Circuit, April 29, 1957, 75.

There has been some speculation about the role played by Senator Eastland in Wisdom's confirmation process. An unapologetic segregationist who subsequently would lead the charge to dismantle the Fifth Circuit in direct response to Wisdom-authored civil rights opinions, Eastland was in a position to deal a powerful, if not fatal, blow to Wisdom's chances at confirmation. But it turned out that Wisdom had little to worry about from Eastland.

Some have suggested that Wisdom was aided in obtaining Eastland's endorsement through the good offices of an arch-conservative sitting member of the Fifth Circuit Court and Eastland's fellow Mississippian, Judge Benjamin F. Cameron. Cameron did indeed support Wisdom's nomination. In a letter to Deputy Attorney General William Rogers recommending Wisdom for the vacancy on the Fifth Circuit, Cameron labeled Wisdom "the best qualified" candidate for the job.[54] Moreover, Cameron's support alone was sufficient to convince a local Jackson, Mississippi, newspaper to support Wisdom's appointment.[55] And it also is true that when Judge Edwin Ruthven Holmes, a former federal district judge from Mississippi, had retired from the Fifth Circuit in 1954, Wisdom had suggested to his friend Attorney General Brownell that Cameron was the best of the available Republican jurists in the state to fill this vacancy. "We just wanted to get an honest man who would have some reputation in the community," Wisdom explained many years later, "so his appointment would reflect credit on the [Eisenhower] Administration. There were no Republicans of any reputation in Mississippi at that time, certainly none with Cameron's reputation for being a good, honest lawyer."[56] Three years later, according to legend, Wisdom asked Cameron to return the favor by interceding on his behalf with Senator Eastland and assuring Eastland that Wisdom's position on civil rights cases would mirror his own.[57]

Wisdom, however, always vehemently denied any such linkage be-

54. Letter to William P. Rogers from Ben C. Cameron, February 23, 1957, 1; Editorial, "Judge Cameron Best Recommendation of John M. Wisdom for Circuit Court," *Jackson State Times*, May 7, 1957, A-10, col. 1.

55. Editorial, "Judge Cameron Best Recommendation of John M. Wisdom for Circuit Court," *Jackson State Times*, May 7, 1957, A-10, col. 1.

56. J. M. Wisdom interview [Young], February 22, 1991. Wisdom is also reported to have transmitted his favorable opinion of Cameron to Brownell at the urging of Wisdom's friend Blanc Monroe, who was, at the time, the chief counsel for the Southern Railroad. Anne S. Emanuel, *Forming the Historic Fifth Circuit: The Eisenhower Years*, TEXAS FORUM ON CIV. LIB. & CIV. R. 233 (2002).

57. Read and McGough, *Let Them Be Judged: The Judicial Integration of the Deep South*, 55–56.

tween his earlier support for Cameron's appointment and Eastland's favorable treatment of Wisdom's own confirmation. He always maintained that "I never told Cameron to pass the word to Eastland that he doesn't have anything to worry about. I never talked to Ben or asked him to talk with Eastland. Plus, it would never occur to me to say that. I don't know if Cameron helped me out. I have no notion what he did."[58] Moreover, Wisdom was able to propose an equally plausible, and much simpler and more obvious explanation for Eastland's lack of opposition. "Eastland and I," Wisdom suggested, "had far more in common than that which divided us. Remember that we were both Southerners from the same social and economic class and that I was precisely the kind of guy he was comfortable dealing with. Besides, with the exception of my membership in the Urban League and service on the President's Committee on Government Contracts,[59] I had not developed any public position on controversial civil rights issues such as school segregation." Consequently, Wisdom maintained, "Eastland had no reason to be concerned about me."[60]

Senator Eastland's actions throughout the confirmation process support Wisdom's analysis of the situation. Despite the fact that Eastland grilled Wisdom on the issues that had been presented to him by Senator Ellender, the chairman never adopted an aggressively hostile position toward the nominee. Neither did he ever validate the veracity of the charges or otherwise exhibit the slightest antipathy toward Wisdom, personally or professionally. In fact, one newspaperman observed that Eastland "seemed satisfied" with Wisdom's answers to his questions.[61] And immediately after the hearing, Wisdom told that same reporter that, in his judgment, Senator Eastland had conducted the hearing "in a most fair and judicial way."[62] But the most telling incident occurred just at the completion of Wisdom's testimony. As he was about to exit the committee room, the senior senator from Mississippi walked over to the nominee "and took me to one end of the room and said—not in

58. J. M. Wisdom [Graham], March 7, 1981, 32–33.

59. Wisdom might have downplayed the importance of this assignment, but it did rankle those who believed it essential to nominate pro-segregationists to the federal courts. See Editorial, "Any Questions, Senators?" *Shreveport Journal*, March 10, 1957, B-2, col. 1.

60. J. M. Wisdom [Friedman], July 16, 1998, 1–2.

61. Paul Wooton, "Wisdom Replies Seem to Please," *New Orleans Times-Picayune*, April 30, 1957, 1; J. W. Peltason, *Fifty Eight Lonely Men: Southern Federal Judges and School Desegregation*, 28.

62. Wooton, "Wisdom Replies Seem to Please," *New Orleans Times-Picayune*, April 30, 1957, 2, col. 5.

a whisper, but virtually a whisper because nobody else could hear it— 'Don't worry about this, John. I'm going to send an investigator down there to New Orleans. But he'll come back and clear you. You'll be cleared.'"[63] And true to his word, that is exactly what Eastland did and that is precisely what happened.

Nevertheless, a little more than one week after the conclusion of the subcommittee hearing, Senator Eastland dispatched Robert B. Young, counsel to the Senate Judiciary Committee, to New Orleans to further investigate the charges that had been raised by witnesses at Wisdom's confirmation hearing. But "I knew from Eastland," Wisdom explained with a huge grin on his face, "that he did this just for appearances. He wanted to give this small band of my political opponents every opportunity to voice their concerns and to appear to be fully airing every objection to my candidacy. But he and I knew there was nothing to it."[64]

Early Saturday morning on May 11, 1957, Judiciary Committee counsel Young solicited additional testimony from a group of witnesses in the office of Dr. Emmett Irwin. The witnesses had been organized by Irwin for the purpose of expressing their opposition to Wisdom's appointment. Wisdom was never informed of the precise date or location of the hearing, nor invited to appear, to confront these witnesses, or to respond to their statements. But based on Eastland's assurances, he did not take them seriously.

Irwin repeated the same unsubstantiated charges that he had asserted at the subcommittee hearing. When pressed by Counsel Young, Irwin admitted (as he had in Washington) that he did not possess any direct evidence of wrongdoing on Wisdom's part with respect to any of these matters. He insisted, nevertheless, that it was important for the Senate committee to be aware of these hearsay allegations. Pettepher followed with a restatement of his brief against Wisdom, all of which centered in Wisdom's alleged failure to follow through on his promise to file suit on behalf of Pettepher's son.

The next witness was Violet Allen, a woman who had worked tirelessly for years with Wisdom to help defeat John E. Jackson's stranglehold over the state Republican Party. Allen had been unable to attend the subcommittee hearing in Washington two weeks earlier, and so she

63. J. M. Wisdom interview [Friedman], July 16, 1998, 1–2. See also J. M. Wisdom interview [Young], February 22, 1991.

64. J. M. Wisdom interview [Friedman], July 16, 1998, 1–2.

took this opportunity to corroborate Pettepher's story. When he learned that she would testify against his appointment, Wisdom initially was surprised. Allen was as passionately anti-Jackson as Wisdom, and had joined with him to unseat the Republican Old Guard in their state. So it was difficult for Wisdom to imagine why Allen suddenly would join his, and her, political opponents in attacking his competence and integrity. Years later, Wisdom learned that Allen never had forgiven him for refusing to name her as Louisiana's Republican Party national committeewoman after their victory at the 1952 national convention. He understood and sympathized with her disappointment since there was no question that Allen's work on behalf of the party made her as deserving a choice as anyone else. But she, like him, was from New Orleans and Wisdom had concluded it was essential to acknowledge the significant contribution made by workers from the northern part of the state. So for that reason, and that reason alone, Wisdom had picked Mrs. Andrew Jackson Hodges, Jr., of Shreveport over Mrs. Allen to be the national committeewoman.

The final witness, Steve Quarles, a postal worker from New Orleans, concluded the nearly three-hour session. Quarles reported that though he did not possess any personal information about the matter, it was widespread gossip within the post office that promotions were restricted to members of the Republican Party. Then, after admitting that he did not know whether Wisdom had anything to do with such a practice, Quarles opined that it was likely that Wisdom knew about and approved this policy.[65]

By the middle of the next week, word of the committee counsel's investigation had reached the press. Several local New Orleans newspapers contacted Young and reported his observation that none of the interviewed witnesses had provided any firsthand information at the secret session and that all of their complaints against Wisdom had been based solely on hearsay.[66] Nevertheless, Senator Eastland directed his counsel to return to New Orleans for a second round of interviews the following Tuesday, May 21. This meeting was held in the Roosevelt Ho-

---

65. "Report of Proceedings," Special Subcommittee on Nominations of the Committee on the Judiciary: Nomination of John Minor Wisdom of Louisiana, to Be United States Circuit Judge of the Fifth Circuit, Executive Session—Staff Meeting, May 11, 1957, New Orleans, La., 2–6, 8–12, 14, 16, 18, 21, 25, 29, 30, 35, 37, 51–52, 58.

66. See "Wisdom Charges Hearsay—Prober," *New Orleans States*, May 15, 1957, 1, col. 6.

tel and lasted for a day and a half. Once again, Wisdom was not invited to the meeting and was denied the opportunity either to cross-examine the witnesses or to respond directly to their allegations.

This two-day proceeding involved little more than rehashing of the unsubstantiated charges that previously had been leveled against Wisdom.[67] Upon returning to Washington, Young briefed Louisiana Senator Russell Long on the two sets of hearings he had conducted in New Orleans. On June 17, Long announced that the Senate's investigator had found no support for any of the charges asserted against Wisdom and, therefore, that he intended to vote to confirm Wisdom's nomination.[68] Long's colleague, Allen Ellender, however, remained noncommittal, and declared that he would defer reaching any conclusion until he had read Young's official report.[69]

One week later, on the morning of Monday, June 24, the members of the Senate Judiciary Committee voted unanimously to approve Wisdom's nomination.[70] That Wednesday, nearly three and a half months after President Eisenhower had nominated Wisdom to a seat on the U.S. Fifth Circuit Court of Appeals, his appointment was confirmed on the floor of the Senate by another unanimous vote.[71] On July 13, in the courtroom of U.S. district judge J. Skelly Wright (who sent a short note to Wisdom acknowledging that that, "other than myself, there is no one that I would prefer to see on the Fifth Circuit"), and with his son, wife, and oldest daughter Penny looking on, Wisdom took the oath of office from his former law partner, Saul Stone, and commenced a career that would span five decades and would place him in the pantheon of this country's greatest and most influential appellate jurists.[72]

Among the many expressions of congratulation and welcome he re-

67. "Report of Proceedings," Special Subcommittee on Nominations of the Committee on the Judiciary: Nomination of John Minor Wisdom of Louisiana, to Be United States Circuit Judge of the Fifth Circuit, Executive Session—Staff Meeting, May 21, 1957, New Orleans, La., 2–4, 8, 16, 22, 23, 27, 29–34.

68. "Long Agrees to Wisdom's Confirmation," *New Orleans States*, June 18, 1957, 6, col. 1; "Not Opposed to Wisdom, Says Long," *New Orleans Times-Picayune*, June 18, 1957.

69. "Not Opposed to Wisdom, Says Long," *New Orleans Item*, June 18, 1957, 1, col. 4; "Long Agrees to Wisdom's Confirmation," *New Orleans States*, June 18, 1957, 6, col. 3.

70. "Okay Wisdom in Committee," *New Orleans Item*, June 24, 1957, 1, col. 2; "Senate Unit OKs Wisdom Nomination," *New Orleans States*, June 24, 1957, 1, col. 1.

71. "Wisdom Given OK by Senate," *New Orleans Item*, June 16, 1957, 1, col. 1; "Confirm Wisdom as Federal Judge," *New Orleans States*, June 26, 1957, 1, col. 2.

72. Baker, *The Second Battle of New Orleans*, 117.

ceived was a brief letter from his friend and now colleague, Judge John Brown of Houston, Texas. Neither its author nor its grateful recipient could ever have imagined the ironic significance of one particular portion of the courtly Houstonian's well-meaning missive. "I found no difficulties," Brown reported, "which exceeded those which a competent lawyer has to meet daily. But if occasionally there are little stumbling blocks or if the mechanics which we have set up seem to offer obstacles, let me know if I can be of any help."[73] In about six years, Brown would find himself at the eye of a storm swirling around some of his responses to "obstacles" generated by a variety of the court's "mechanics." And it would be Wisdom who would come to the aid of his more senior colleague in the gravest crisis that had ever confronted their court.

73. Letter from Judge John R. Brown to Judge John M. Wisdom, July 22, 1957.

7

THE FIFTH CIRCUIT'S EMERGING
INTELLECTUAL LEADER, 1957–1966

In 1950, two African Americans, Clifton Alton Poret and Edgar Labat, the latter a hospital orderly with no prior arrest record, were apprehended and charged with rape. Nearly two years after the incident, these two defendants asked the trial judge to dismiss the indictments against them, claiming that the systematic exclusion of African Americans at all stages of the indictment and jury selection process violated their constitutional rights to due process and equal protection under the law. But the trial judge refused to consider the merits of their arguments, ruling simply that the motions had been filed too late under the governing Louisiana law. The case then went to trial before an all-white jury, which, on May 23, 1953, convicted and sentenced the pair to death by electrocution. Both the Louisiana and the U.S. Supreme Court upheld both the conviction and the trial judge's ruling on the defendants' constitutional challenge to the indictment.[1]

Nearly two years after the U.S. Supreme Court's ruling, the defendants applied to the federal district court in New Orleans for a writ of habeas corpus. After a criminal defendant's appeals are exhausted and his conviction becomes final, he can file a petition for a writ of ha-

---

1. *State of Louisiana v. Labat*, 226 La. 201, 75 So.2d 333 (1954); *Michel v. State of Louisiana*, 350 U.S. 91, 76 S.Ct. 158, 100 L.Ed. 83 (1955).

beas corpus in a federal district court alleging that the conviction was obtained in violation of his federal statutory or constitutional rights. Labat and Poret claimed that their rape convictions had been based on the perjured testimony of a witness who had been coerced by the police into offering false testimony purpose. But their application was rejected the very next day by U.S. district judge J. Skelly Wright of New Orleans because the defendants had not asserted this constitutional claim before the state courts.[2] Now sitting on death row subject to a date with the executioner the following week, the defendants desperately needed to secure a stay of the order of execution, and quickly, to have any hope of preserving their chance to return to state court to assert their perjury-based challenge. And that stay would have to come through an appeal of Judge Wright's decision to the U.S. Fifth Circuit Court of Appeals.

So Labat and Poret's attorneys hustled later that afternoon to the chambers of the one Fifth Circuit judge who was based in New Orleans.[3] They appeared before John Minor Wisdom to ask the court's newest member to issue a temporary stay of execution as his first judicial act. For a judge who had been sworn in barely two months earlier, and whose practice as a member of the bar had been limited exclusively to civil cases, it was a sobering moment, one he would never forget. "That was a hell of a thing to be confronted with as your first official act," Wisdom recalled. "The warden had kept the line open and I telephoned the warden and told him I had stayed the execution until a panel of the court should meet and act on it."[4]

Later that same evening, after conferring with his most senior colleague, Judge Richard Rives of Montgomery, Alabama, Wisdom extended his stay for ten days, a decision that reflected the type of pragmatic reflection that would come to be a hallmark of his jurisprudence. With execution staring Poret and Labat in the face, to deny the writ until the defendants properly had pursued their claim in state court, Wisdom calculated, "would necessitate their resurrection."[5] The ruling,

2. Letter to Judges Richard T. Rives and Elbert P. Tuttle from Judge John M. Wisdom, September 21, 1957.

3. See Letter to Judges Richard T. Rives and Elbert P. Tuttle from Judge John M. Wisdom, September 21, 1957.

4. J. M. Wisdom interview [Graham], March 7, 1981, 47.

5. See Letter to Judges Richard T. Rives and Elbert P. Tuttle from Judge John M. Wisdom, September 21, 1957.

however, did not mark the end of Wisdom's involvement with Labat and Poret.

After a series of procedural maneuvers, Labat and Poret's attorneys ultimately succeeded in persuading the U.S. Supreme Court to direct the federal district court in New Orleans to rule on whether African Americans had been systematically excluded from sitting on the petit jury panel in violation of the U.S. Constitution.[6] On October 8, 1964, fourteen years after the rape allegedly had occurred, District Judge Gordon West of New Orleans ruled against the defendants, finding that African Americans had not been targeted explicitly by Louisiana law for exclusion from jury duty.[7] Labat and Poret appealed that decision to the Fifth Circuit, where it was consolidated with six other cases that also challenged the alleged exclusion of African Americans from criminal juries and heard by the entire court sitting *en banc*, that is, with the participation of every active member of the court, rather than, as was typically the case, by a panel of only three judges.[8] Chief Judge Tuttle assigned Wisdom the task of writing the opinion in a case that would resolve a major constitutional challenge to Louisiana's petit jury selection system. He did not shrink from the challenge.

Wisdom's opinion for the majority of the *en banc* court in *Labat* is a classic example of the interweaving of literary references, historical perspectives, painstaking legal research, lyrical prose, and a passionate dedication to fairness into the dissection of a complicated and controversial issue that would become the hallmarks of a "Wisdom opinion." His treatise-like historical explication of the constitutional prohibition against racial discrimination in jury service dating from the Magna Carta opened, however, with a very non-treatise-like quotation from Shakespeare's *Measure for Measure*: "The law hath not been dead, though it hath slept." He introduced this theme in the opening sentence of the opinion, where he lamented the protracted history of the case: "'Death' for thirteen years has kept close tab on Edgar Labat and Clifton Poret."[9] Nevertheless, Wisdom continued, despite the "twists and turns of their

6. *U.S. ex rel. Poret v. Sigler*, 361 U.S. 375, 80 S.Ct. 404, 4 L.Ed.2d 380 (1960).

7. *U.S. ex rel. Poret and Labat v. Sigler*, 234 F.Supp. 171 (E.D.La.1964).

8. *Labat v. Bennett*, 365 F.2d 698 (5th Cir.1966).

9. 365 F.2d at 701. Not to be undone, Judge Gewin turned to *Henry VI*, Part I, for inspiration at the commencement of his dissenting opinion. There, he bemoaned the fact that this case had been lost in the "nice, sharp quillets of the law." Shakespeare, *King Henry VI*, Part I, Act II, Scene IV, quoted at 365 F.2d 729 (Gewin, J., dissenting).

convoluted legal proceeding," the defendants' motion was "clear enough to a Louisiana lawyer. . . . The vice permeates the entire jury system; the motion attacks the system."[10]

For Wisdom, this case involved more than just a question of fairness. It raised two potentially conflicting principles that were of paramount importance to him and that featured prominently in many of his most significant and celebrated opinions—the scope of federal constitutional rights, and the contours of federalism, the doctrine dealing with the interplay between America's federal and state government systems.[11] A defendant's constitutional right to challenge her or his state court conviction in federal court through the filing of a habeas corpus petition was, to Wisdom, as precious as it was venerable. At the same time, however, he worried that any federal court interference with a state's criminal proceedings would "strain federal-state relations by lessening the finality of state criminal judgments."[12] Nonetheless, after balancing these competing considerations, and offering an exhaustive narration of the history of the habeas writ in American jurisprudence, Wisdom concluded that the concern was trumped by the overarching need to ensure that claimed deprivations of federal constitutional rights of personal liberty be accorded the "fullest opportunity for federal judicial review."[13]

So turning to the merits of Labat and Poret's claim, Wisdom rejected District Judge West's determination that since the exclusion of African Americans from petit juries in Louisiana was not the result of overt, intentional discrimination, Labat and Poret's constitutional challenge failed on its merits. He was, at his core, a pragmatist, one who not willing to ignore a set of disturbing facts that stared him square in the face.

Although the Louisiana statutes controlling jury selection did not re-

10. 365 F.2d at 702.

11. Wisdom did not restrict the expression of his views on federalism to his judicial opinions found on the pages of the Federal Reporter series. He further developed and refined his perspective on the proper allocation of authority between the federal and state sovereigns in a collection of law reviews. See Wisdom, *The Frictionmaking, Exacerbating Political Role of Federal Courts*, 21 Sw. L.J. 411 (1967); Wisdom, *The Ever-Whirling Wheels of American Federalism*, 59 Notre Dame L. Rev. 1063 (1984); Wisdom, *A Southern Judge Looks at Civil Rights*, 43 F.R.D. 453 (1967); Wisdom, *A Federal Judge in the Deep South: Random Observations*, 35 S.C. L. Rev. 503 (1984); Wisdom, *Rethinking Injunctions* (Book Review), 89 Yale L.J. 825 (1980).

12. 365 F.2d at 707.

13. 365 F.2d at 707.

quire the exclusion of persons on the basis of race, the impact of the state's jury selection policy was undeniable. "In Orleans Parish," Wisdom reported, "there has never been a Negro jury commissioner. And the [Orleans Parish Jury] Commission [that selected the names from which prospective jurors were chosen] has never employed a Negro."[14] Furthermore, even though African Americans constituted about 32 percent of Orleans Parish residents as of the time of Labat and Poret's trial, Wisdom noted that "no Negro had ever served on a petit jury in a criminal case in Orleans Parish."[15] Moreover, during the year of the defendants' trial, African Americans comprised only 3 percent of the membership of the petit jury venires from which jurors were selected. These were statistics that Wisdom could and would not ignore. He was unwilling to countenance the state's facile explanation that the systematic exclusion of African Americans from jury service resulted not from invidious racial discrimination, but, rather, solely from a "benign practice" designed to insulate manual laborers and other daily wage earners from the economic hardship caused by uncompensated jury service. "A benign and theoretically neutral principle," he wrote, "loses its aura of sanctity when it fails to function neutrally."[16]

These cold, hard political realities could not be overlooked and Wisdom said so in characteristically blunt, unambiguous, and pointed language. "The system was neutral, principled and foolproof: No Negro ever sat on a grand jury or a trial jury in Orleans Parish."[17] The exceedingly disproportionate disqualification of black potential jurors through the statute's facially race-neutral exclusion for daily wage earners "amounted to a deliberate decision to continue the systematic limitation of Negroes on the venires . . . [and produced] the end effect of totally excluding Negroes from the . . . system."[18] Accordingly, he declared that the state's jury selection procedures were unconstitutional, and ordered the district judge to issue a writ of habeas corpus releasing Labat and Poret from custody, subject to re-indictment and retrial by the state. After a retrial, Labat and Poret were sentenced to precisely the length of time they had served on death row with credit for that time

14. 365 F.2d at 713.
15. 365 F.2d at 716.
16. 365 F.2d at 724.
17. 365 F.2d at 725.
18. 365 F.2d at 715–716.

served.[19] The Supreme Court declined to review the Fifth Circuit's decision, which meant that Wisdom's opinion was the final word on the unconstitutionality of Louisiana's petit jury selection procedure.[20]

The opinion was widely praised by Wisdom's colleagues. Judge Dick Rives called it "masterful,"[21] and John Brown sent a letter to all of the court's active circuit judges sharing his reaction to another "one of your monumental works: I feel as did the Indian looking out at the mushroom cloud of the first atomic explosion at Alamogordo. Sighing, he uttered, 'I wish I had said that.'"[22] District Judge Joseph Lord of Philadelphia sent a note congratulating Wisdom on his "monumental opinion" that "certainly ties the law in this area into a neat and understandable bundle."[23]

But Wisdom's opinion was not only notable for its effective use of literary allusions and historical analysis. This decision played an influential role in shaping the Supreme Court's jurisprudence in several areas. Most directly, Wisdom's assertion in *Labat* that the integrity of the jury's fact-finding function depended upon the assembling of jury panels that represented a cross section of the community subsequently was adopted by the Supreme Court.[24] Additionally, *Labat* was a precursor to Wisdom's groundbreaking voting rights opinion in *U.S. v. Louisiana*, which itself was the analytical forerunner of a line of Supreme Court decisions holding that a plaintiff could establish unconstitutional discrimination by proving the discriminatory impact of a facially neutral policy.

Four years after writing *Labat*, Wisdom authored another opinion that demonstrated his technique of interweaving historical and legal analysis. After Carlos Garza De Luna was convicted of federal drug offenses, he appealed his conviction on the ground that his co-defendant's attorney had commented to the jury on De Luna's failure to testify on his own behalf. In *De Luna v. U.S.*, Wisdom wrote the first federal appellate court opinion recognizing that a criminal defendant's Fifth Amendment right against compelled self-incrimination included the right to be

19. Burton H. Wolfe, *Pileup on Death Row* (Garden City, N.Y.: 1973), 296–297; Hugo Adam Bedau and Michael L. Radelet, *Miscarriages of Justice in Potentially Capital Cases* 40 STAN. L. REV. 21 (1987), 135–136.

20. *Bennett v. Labat*, 386 U.S. 991 (Mem.), 87 S.Ct. 1303, 18 L.Ed.2d 334 (1967).

21. Letter to John M. Wisdom from Richard T. Rives, July 1, 1966.

22. Letter to John M. Wisdom from John R. Brown, July 5, 1966.

23. Letter to John M. Wisdom from Joseph S. Lord, III, November 14, 1966.

24. *Peters v. Kiff*, 407 U.S. 493, 92 S.Ct. 2163, 33 L.Ed.2d 83 (1972).

free from prejudicial references to his or her invocation of that right, including those made by a co-defendant's attorney.[25] The utility of the right to remain silent, Wisdom declared, necessarily implied the right to assert that right free from adverse comment and harmful presumptions. And he supported this conclusion with an exhaustively footnoted homage to the Fifth Amendment that described in detail the historical pedigree and development of the right of silence in Anglo-American jurisprudence.[26]

Nevertheless, Wisdom's insistence on preserving fairness in the administration of criminal justice was not a one-way street. When a federal prosecutor re-indicted and obtained a conviction against Daniel Robinson for possession of bootleg whisky after a federal district judge had dismissed the original indictment, Robinson appealed his conviction on the ground that the prosecution's only recourse to the dismissal was to appeal that decision and not re-indict him for the same offense. Wisdom disagreed.[27] Since the dismissal of the first indictment was not based on the merits of the charges against Robinson, re-indictment did not violate Robinson's constitutional right to be free from double jeopardy. "The avoidance of a miscarriage of justice," Wisdom explained, "cuts both ways. It would be a miscarriage of justice in this case to hold that the [defendant] may escape a second indictment when dismissal of the first indictment was based on . . . a misunderstanding of the facts having to do not with the . . . guilt or innocence of the accused."[28]

Ensuring fairness to all participants in the criminal justice system neither began nor ended, however, with Wisdom's opinions in *Labat* or *Robinson*. His very first written opinion similarly demonstrates his unbending commitment to fairness. At the same time, however, it reflected either inexperience with or insensitivity to manifestations of entrenched racial prejudice.

A. Z. Handford, an African American who had been convicted in Georgia of the illegal possession of bootleg whiskey, challenged his conviction on the basis of the statement in the federal prosecutor's closing argument to the jury that too many of his friends and his friends' chil-

25. 308 F.2d 140 (5th Cir.1962).

26. A similarly detailed historical treatment, this time of the law concerning libel and slander, can be found in Wisdom's oft-cited opinion in *Belli v. Orlando Daily Newspapers, Inc.*, 389 F.2d 579 (5th Cir.1968), cert. denied, 393 U.S. 825, 89 S.Ct. 88, 21L.Ed.2d 96 (1968).

27. *Robinson v. U.S.*, 284 F.2d 775 (5th Cir.1960).

28. 284 F.2d at 776–777.

dren had been run over on the public highways. Since this case had nothing to do with vehicular accidents or highway safety, Wisdom announced in this 1957 opinion that the prosecutor's comments were not only irrelevant but highly prejudicial to the jury's ability to arrive at a fair determination of Handford's guilt or innocence.[29] But what particularly incensed Wisdom was the fact that these remarks were made by a government attorney charged with the obligation to refrain from improper trial tactics. "A United States district attorney," he explained, "carries a double burden. He owes an obligation to the government . . . to conduct his case zealously. But he . . . also . . . is the representative of a government dedicated to fairness and equal justice to all and, in this respect, he owes a heavy obligation to the accused. Such representation imposes an overriding obligation of fairness. . . . In this case zeal outran fairness."[30] The panel unanimously decided to vacate the conviction and grant a new trial.

The three-member panel that decided this appeal consisted of Wisdom and two of his senior colleagues, venerable Chief Judge Joe Hutcheson and Judge Elbert Tuttle. Lurking in the background of this case was an issue that barely found its way into the text of the court's opinion, but which reflected an uncharacteristic lack of sensitivity to racial matters by Wisdom and Tuttle. Originally, Wisdom and Tuttle had intended to vote to affirm the conviction. In the initial draft of his opinion, Wisdom expressed his belief that several references to the defendant and others as "niggers" by both a witness and the prosecutor did not warrant overturning the conviction. Although he believed that the trial judge should have prevented the constant recitation of that odious term, Wisdom nevertheless concluded that "since there was no pitting of one race against the other, but merely a prosecution of this one Negro for a violation of the Internal Revenue laws, I do not think the remarks influenced the jurors nor were the remarks inflammatory nor prejudicial."[31] This draft made no reference to the prosecutor's discussion of the effects of drunk driving.

Tuttle also circulated a memorandum in which, like Wisdom, he concluded that the references to "nigger" did not justify a conviction. Although Tuttle characterized the use of this term as "uncouth and irrelevant," he concluded that "the fact that it was not really prejudicial to

29. *Handford v. U.S.*, 249 F.2d 295 (5th Cir.1957).

30. 249 F.2d at 296.

31. Draft memorandum by Judge John Minor Wisdom in *Handford v. U.S.*, at 3.

the defendant can be assumed from the fact that his own counsel, in cross examining the sheriff, asked him 'And how many niggers were standing around there at the time?'"[32] On the other hand, Chief Judge Hutcheson wanted to reverse the conviction from the outset, believing that "the defendant has been convicted mainly because he was a Negro."[33] Eventually, Hutcheson convinced Wisdom and Tuttle to vote to overturn the conviction. But they based their conclusion solely on the basis of the prosecutor's prejudicial references to driving accidents. The final, official opinion of the court retained Wisdom's earlier stated view that any potential racial prejudice caused by the use of "nigger" by the witness and prosecuting attorney was cured by the trial judge's instruction to the jury that race should play no part in its decision-making process. When compared with his rulings less than a decade later in a case like Labat, however, this opinion reflects, at a minimum, Wisdom's initial inexperience in dealing with entrenched racial prejudices.

Wisdom's reliance on his broad knowledge of history to resolve a legal dispute, coupled with his unwavering commitment to fairness as a guiding principle in his decision-making, is vividly evident in another of his early opinions. A defendant convicted of marijuana smuggling maintained that the trial judge had failed to alert the jury to the credibility concerns associated with trial testimony offered by the defendant's alleged accomplice. In Phelps v. U.S.,[34] the court overturned a marijuana smuggling conviction. In overturning the conviction, Wisdom explained why the trial judge had erred in concluding that this witness was not an accomplice by citing historical references that few, if any of his colleagues, could have mustered. "From Crown political prosecutions and before," he detailed, "to recent prison camp inquisitions, a long history of human frailty and governmental overreaching for conviction justifies distrust in accomplice testimony. Cobham's misplaced hope for immunity that helped send Raleigh to the Tower is on the same level with the hope of some narcotic peddler or some other poor wretch to save his skin by laying the entire blame on a friend or close associate."[35] Not long after the opinion was published, Wisdom received a brief note from his good friend and colleague, Judge John Brown, who praised the opinion as "wonderful" and as demonstrating "a real under-

32. Draft memorandum by Judge Elbert P. Tuttle in Handford v. U.S.
33. Tentative Draft memorandum by Judge John Minor Wisdom in Handford v. U.S., at 3.
34. 252 F.2d 49, 52 (5th Cir.1958).
35. 252 F.2d at 52.

standing, a great capacity for writing, and a live appreciation of the importance of history." Brown also offered his junior colleague this advice: "Do not let anyone change your style. Do not let anyone make you get somber or funereal."[36]

This was high praise and valued advice in Wisdom's eyes since Brown already enjoyed a reputation as a wordsmith. Brown, like Wisdom, took pride and pleasure in displaying his facility for coining colorful phrases. So much so, that even Brown's own law clerks referred to the "Browning" of an opinion.[37] But Brown's flamboyant tendency to overwork and sometimes even mix metaphors was incompatible with Wisdom's more exacting stylistic and grammatical standards. For example, Brown, Rives, and Wisdom sat together on a case that raised the question of the extent to which the appellate court should be bound by a trial judge's particular factual determination.[38] Brown wrote the opinion for the unanimous court and explained that the trial judge's findings "come here well armed with the buckler and shield of Federal Rule of Civil Procedure 52(a)." And though Wisdom agreed with the substance of the remark, he later cited this as a dramatic example of Brown's exaggerated style. After all, he insisted, "you are not 'armed' with a buckler. A buckler defends you. It is not a weapon."[39]

Wisdom unhesitatingly followed his colleague Brown's advice, and in 1959, his third year on the bench, released an opinion that displayed both his obvious delight in, and facility for, crafting language that framed and resolved thorny issues with grace, precision, clarity, and consummate wit. Although the case raised a highly technical question within the specialized field of admiralty law, Wisdom's opinion is universally regarded as both a technical and artistic masterpiece.

An employee who had been injured while working on a drilling platform in the middle of the Gulf of Mexico filed suit to recover damages for his injuries, medical expenses, and lost wages in federal court under a federal statute, the Jones Act, which provides the right of a "seaman" to bring a negligence claim if he is injured while working on a "vessel." But since the Jones Act did not define either "seaman" or "vessel," the court had to determine whether this law applied to Mr. Robison, an oil field worker who had been hired to do manual labor as a driller's helper

36. Letter from Judge John R. Brown to Judge John Minor Wisdom, February 19, 1958.
37. Bass, *Unlikely Heroes*, 105.
38. *Horton v. U.S. Steel Corp*, 286 F.2d 710 (5th Cir.1961).
39. J. M. Wisdom interview [Graham], March 7, 1981, 83–84.

(also called a "roughneck") on an offshore drilling platform that rested firmly on the floor of the Gulf of Mexico.

This seemingly esoteric matter was actually an issue of great moment to the entire maritime industry. For if this injured offshore worker was found *not* to be a Jones Act "seaman" on a "vessel," his only recourse would be to file a claim against his employer under general maritime law, where the proof requirements were significantly more onerous than those governing Jones Act cases. Thus, the stakes were high for both the worker and the ship owners and their insurers. Moreover, the stack of judicial opinions that previously had grappled with this murky problem in the forty years since the passage of the Jones Act in 1920 had only muddied the waters for those seeking interpretive clarity. As Judge Wisdom colorfully explained, "the reach of the Jones Act is a peril of the sea that could hardly have been dreamt of by the landlubbers in the oil business."[40]

Wisdom began his opinion in strict adherence to the first two of a list of stylistic commandments codified in a writing primer he had devised for his law clerks. Rule One of "Wisdom's Idiosyncrasies" instructed his clerks to "try to state the key question in the first sentence." And according to Rule Two, they were to "put the sex appeal in the first sentence and last sentence of each opinion." The opening sentence of *Robison* not only met both of these standards, it did so in a way that also distilled a complex controversy to its core element: "This case propounds a riddle. When is a roughneck a seaman?"[41] But to fully resolve this controversy, the court also needed to address the ancillary question of under what circumstances the determination of "seaman" status was to be resolved by either the trial judge or the jury. And if the court's resolution of both of these questions was to be provide clear guidance to other courts, jurors, and litigants in the thousands of future Jones Act cases in which this issue would surely arise, it had to be couched in precise, yet understandable terms.

Wisdom answered these interconnected questions by exhaustively cataloguing, analyzing, and synthesizing the existing jurisprudence in a way that, according to his friend and Fifth Circuit colleague Alvin Rubin, demonstrated "Wisdom's profound study of admiralty law as well as his felicity of language and eloquent style."[42] Similarly, in a letter to

40. *Offshore Co. v. Robison*, 266 F.2d 769, 771 (5th Cir.1959).
41. 266 F.2d at 771.
42. Alvin B. Rubin, *"John Is Every Inch a Sailor,"* 60 Tul. L. Rev. 256, 259 (1985).

Wisdom, Judge Rives, a member of the panel in *Robison,* predicted that "a thorough opinion like this will help the lawyers keep their thinking straight, and may lighten our labors in future like cases. The distinction [between issues that should be resolved by either the court or the jury] is so fine that it is almost invisible, but this opinion furnishes the microscope through which it may be discerned."[43] The formula that Wisdom confected to guide courts and juries in this critical undertaking was precise, comprehensive, and, equally important, comprehensible and accessible.[44] The most telling testament to the value of Wisdom's contribution is that his analysis has been relied upon by courts and juries in hundreds of subsequent cases and by attorneys in thousands of unlitigated or voluntary settled controversies.[45]

As a result of his training at Tulane Law School and his nearly thirty years of experience as a member of the Louisiana bar and adjunct professor at his alma mater, Wisdom had become steeped in the heritage and content of Louisiana's unique, European-derived civil code and was committed to preserving his state's civil law traditions. In cases that required the interpretation and application of Louisiana law, Wisdom was able to draw heavily from the contents of the impressive collection of civil law texts and manuscripts that lined both his bookcase shelves and the portable wooden cart customarily located directly adjacent to his oversized desk. And in a tax case involving Louisiana's community property regime, Wisdom not only displayed his capacity for detailed, historical analysis and his devotion to Louisiana's civil law origins; he showcased his facility for fashioning an ingenious solution to a seemingly intractable problem, particularly when creativity was essential to arriving at a just and fair result.

One of the foundational principles of Louisiana community property law is that wages earned during the life of the community by either spouse are deemed community income and, therefore, each spouse has a one-half ownership interest in any earnings acquired by the other

43. Letter from Judge Richard T. Rives to Judge John Minor Wisdom, April 15, 1959.

44. "There is an evidentiary basis for a Jones Act case to go to the jury: (1) if there is evidence that the injured workman was assigned permanently to a vessel (including special purpose structures not usually employed as a means of transport by water but designed to float on water) or performed a substantial part of his work on the vessel; and (2) if the capacity in which he was employed or the duties which he performed contributed to the function of the vessel or to the accomplishment of its mission, or to the operation or welfare of the vessel in terms of its maintenance during its movement or during anchorage for its future trips." 266 F.2d at 779.

45. Alvin B. Rubin, "*John Is Every Inch a Sailor,*" 60 TUL. L. REV. 256, 257 (1985).

spouse during the marriage. The flip side of this, however, is that since the non-earning spouse owns half of such income, that spouse could be subject to federal income tax on his or her share of the community income.

That was precisely the position adopted by the Internal Revenue Service (IRS). In two consolidated cases, the IRS sought to collect unpaid income taxes from a pair of wives on one half of the unreported earnings of their tax-evading husbands. In both cases, the husbands and wives had lived separately and the husbands had kept the wives completely in the dark with respect to what their earnings were and how they were spent. As Judge Wisdom more elegantly and sympathetically explained, these wives were "impoverished victims of their husbands' profligacy. The IRS has stripped clean one of the wives. The other is about to be stripped clean." He also reluctantly admitted, however, that "this horrendous result flows from Louisiana law, not from federal tax law."[46]

The rationality of the IRS's position, if not its compassion, could not be gainsaid. The wives had formal legal ownership of half of the income and therefore were subject to federal taxation. "There is no doubt," Wisdom observed, "that a Louisiana court would hold that each taxpayer owned one-half of the community property, including the husband's earnings." Furthermore, he conceded, "we must apply Louisiana law as we find it."[47] On the other hand, the case veritably cried out for a solution that would avoid the inequity produced by exalting form over substance. For, as Wisdom noted, one of the two wives "lived in grinding poverty, often with the utilities cut off, sometimes with not enough to eat."[48]

Wisdom made no attempt to hide his concern and compassion. "Ground down but attempting to keep her head up, she worked sporadically."[49] At the same time, however, he remained unwilling to "permit a hard case to induce us to make bad law."[50] So instead of betraying his commitment to the rule of law, Wisdom devised a theory that not only would do justice, but also would not do violence to the Louisiana Civil Code, would be reconcilable with the Internal Revenue Code, and

46. *Bagur v. C.I.R.*, 603 F.2d 491, 494 (5th Cir.1979).
47. 603 F.2d at 499.
48. 603 F.2d at 495.
49. 603 F.2d at 495.
50. 603 F.2d at 494.

would remain faithful to the principles of Louisiana community property doctrine formulated by the Louisiana state courts. He creatively reasoned that if, as alleged, the husbands had absconded with their wives' share of these earnings, they had effectively stolen this money from their wives. This, in turn, meant that the wives could offset the reportable income with the deduction allowed for such uncompensated losses. Writing the opinion for a unanimous panel, Wisdom ordered the case remanded for a determination of whether the husbands had misappropriated their wives' shares of the earnings.

Nearly a quarter of a century later, Supreme Court justice Ruth Bader Ginsberg told a law school audience that this opinion "represents for me Judge Wisdom at his best."[51] And in 1980, just months after the release of Wisdom's opinion, Congress took note of this problem and amended the Internal Revenue Code to create an exception to its normal treatment of community income.[52]

Wisdom did not have to wait very long after assuming his seat on the Fifth Circuit before he was assigned to write the opinion in an important civil rights case, the subject area with which his name would be forever linked. In the summer of 1959, with just two years of judicial experience under his belt, Wisdom sat on the first of many voting rights cases that would find their way to his court. The case of *Gomillion v. Lightfoot*,[53] or at least Wisdom's participation in it, pitted two principles to which this judge held great fealty against one another. And his decision to rule in favor of one at the expense of the other was a source of regret and disappointment that lingered with Wisdom for the remainder of his judicial career. "My concurring opinion in that case," Wisdom acknowledged near the end of his life, "was painful for me to write, and it was probably my worst opinion."[54]

Although African Americans historically had constituted about 80

51. Ruth Bader Ginsburg, text of Judge Robert A. Ainsworth, Jr., Memorial Lecture: *Four Louisiana Giants in the Law*, Loyola University New Orleans School of Law, February 4, 2002, at http://www.supremecourtus.gov/publicinfo/speeches/sp_02-04-02.html.

52. Section 66(c) of the Internal Revenue Code now provides that if one spouse doesn't know about, and has no reason to know of, the existence of some community income, and it would be inequitable to subject that "innocent" spouse to tax liability for his or her share of that community income, then the innocent spouse is relieved of that tax liability. P.L. 105–206, §3201(b), 26 U.S.C. §66(c)) (1980).

53. 270 F.2d 594 (5th Cir.1959), rev'd, 364 U.S. 339, 81 S.Ct. 125, 5 L.Ed.2d 110 (1960).

54. John Minor Wisdom, *In Memoriam: One of a Kind*, 71 Tex. L. Rev. 913, 916 (1993).

percent of the general population of Tuskegee, Alabama, it was not until after World War II that they began to register to vote in significant numbers. By the mid-1950s, however, it became apparent that African Americans soon would constitute a voting majority in the home of the Tuskegee Institute.

In July 1957, the Alabama legislature passed, unanimously and without debate, a reapportionment statute that reconfigured the shape of Tuskegee's boundaries from a square to "a curious twenty-eight-sided figure resembling a stylized sea horse."[55] The undeniable effect of this gerrymander mirrored its openly acknowledged purpose. According to its sponsor, the redistricting act was designed to remove Tuskegee Institute and the residences of all but four or five of the city's four hundred registered African American voters from the municipality.[56] At the same time, the newly drawn boundaries retained the residences of all of the city's approximately six hundred white voters. This resulted, as intended, in elimination of the black residents' right to vote in Tuskegee municipal elections (although they remained eligible to vote in county and statewide races as well as in federal elections), thereby preserving a white voting majority in Tuskegee municipal elections. This legislative action, however, prompted an organized response from the city's African American community.

Charles Gomillion was a burly man in his fifties who had been born and raised in Johnston, South Carolina. Gomillion had moved to Alabama in the fall of 1928 when he joined the Tuskegee faculty. Within a few years, Gomillion had assumed a position of leadership in the local black community's campaign for equal voting rights. Later, as president of the Tuskegee Civil Association (TCA), the city's leading African American civic organization, Gomillion became the recognized leader of Tuskegee's African American community.

Led by Gomillion, a group of African American residents of Tuskegee filed suit against Philip M. Lightfoot, the mayor of Tuskegee, and several other city and county officials. They alleged that by depriving them of the right to vote in Tuskegee municipal elections, the state reappointment statute deprived them of their rights under the Fourteenth

55. Bernard Taper, Reporter at Large, "Gomillion Versus Lightfoot I—Waiting," *The New Yorker,* June 10, 1961.

56. Brief of the United States as Amicus Curiae before the U.S. Supreme Court in *Gomillion v. Lightfoot,* 3n3.

and Fifteenth Amendments of the U.S. Constitution.[57] The case involved a clash between one principle that occupied a deep-seated and
irrevocable place in Wisdom's personal belief system and another that
lay at the core of his developing judicial philosophy.

On one hand, Wisdom was unwavering in his devotion to preserving and protecting that most precious and fundamental of all individu-
ally held political rights—the franchise. As part of his strategy to revive Louisiana's languid Republican Party, Wisdom actively supervised
and personally participated in efforts to expand the availability of the
vote for black citizens. At the same time, however, he was resolutely
committed to maintaining an appropriate balance between the powers exercised by the federal and state governments in America's federalist system. But he was unable to envision a resolution of the conflict
in *Gomillion* that could accommodate both of these salient objectives.
Forced to choose, Wisdom sided with Alabama's federalism-based argument and became the swing vote in a split-panel decision that ultimately rejected the plaintiffs' constitutional challenge to the redistricting statute.

From the outset of their deliberations, the three judges assigned to
decide this case were painfully aware of its momentous import. Early
in the deliberative process, Judge Warren Le Roy Jones of Jacksonville,
Florida, the member charged with writing the opinion, confided to Wisdom that "this case is certain to be reviewed by the Supreme Court and
it is not unlikely that it will be reversed."[58] So Jones asked for his junior
colleague's assistance in drafting an opinion that would "clearly and
logically" set forth their views.[59] Jones's prediction proved to be right on
the money. For the first time in its history, the Supreme Court agreed
to hear a case involving racial gerrymandering.

The issues presented by *Gomillion* were clear, even if their resolution
was not. The state legislature had enacted a statute redrawing the city's
boundaries, a traditional and commonplace exercise of legislative authority that rearranged the composition of the electorate for municipal elections. The plaintiffs claimed that by eliminating nearly all black

57. Robert J. Norrell, *Reaping the Whirlwind: The Civil Rights Movement in Tuskegee* (New York:
1985), 95; Taper, A Reporter at Large: "Gomillion Versus Lightfoot II—An Eminently Realistic
Body of Men," *The New Yorker*, June 17, 1961.

58. Letter to Judge John Minor Wisdom from Judge Warren J. Jones, July 7, 1959.

59. Letter to Judge John Minor Wisdom from Judge Warren J. Jones, July 7, 1959.

voters from the city limits while retaining all existing white residents, the statute disenfranchised black citizens in violation of the Fourteenth and Fifteenth Amendments. The State of Alabama, on the other hand, insisted that establishing municipal boundaries fell within the plenary, unreviewable authority of the state legislature and argued that the Supreme Court consistently had refused to intervene in such "political" matters.

Although Jones wrote the opinion for the majority in which Wisdom fully concurred, "the gravity of the issue, the gulf between the majority and dissenting opinions, and a few sharp quillets in the dissent [by John Brown]" impelled Wisdom to write a concurring opinion to more fully articulate his views on the application of the doctrine of judicial abstention to "political" cases.[60]

Wisdom could not discern any reasonable and justifiable basis upon which to distinguish gerrymandering that disenfranchised individuals on the basis of race from the well-established and historically legitimated practice of redrawing political borders in order to advantage the ruling political party. Furthermore, since the Supreme Court steadfastly had refused to intervene in cases involving the right of state legislatures to establish local political boundaries, Wisdom concluded that the same hands-off policy should apply even when the motive and/or ineluctable effect of such action was to disenfranchise individuals on the basis of their race. In his characteristically straightforward yet eloquent style, Wisdom insisted that he could "see no difference between partially disenfranchising Negroes and partially disenfranchising Republicans, Democrats, Italians, Poles, Mexican-Americans, Catholics, blue-stocking voters, industrial workers, urban citizens, or other groups who are euchered out of their full suffrage because their bloc voting is predictable."[61]

Wisdom also agreed with Jones that even if a federal court could interject itself into this controversy by exercising its undeniable authority to review the constitutionality of state legislation, the unconstitutionality of the statute would have to be demonstrated on its face and not through an assessment of either the legislature's motivation or the statute's impact on members of the affected racial group. For Wisdom, the fact that the redistricting act did not make any explicit reference to

60. 270 F.2d 599 (Wisdom, J., concurring).
61. 270 F.2d at 612 (Wisdom, J., concurring).

race foreclosed further analysis of either the subjective motivation of its enactors or its actual exclusionary impact on black voter eligibility in Tuskegee.

Even though he admitted to his law clerk that Brown's dissent in *Gomillion* would probably convince the Supreme Court both to hear the case and to reverse the Fifth Circuit's opinion, Wisdom was unmoved by the argument that formed the core of his friend's dissenting opinion.[62] In Brown's view, any statute that totally disenfranchised individuals on the sole basis of their race was sufficiently distinguishable from other forms of total or partial disenfranchisement to require, let alone permit, the federal courts to evaluate the constitutionality of that enactment by treating its impact on the disenfranchised race as demonstrative of its discriminatory purpose.

When the case was appealed, Wisdom's prognostication proved correct on both counts. The Supreme Court granted the plaintiffs' petition for review, agreed with Judge Brown's analysis, and held that a statute's discriminatory effect could be the basis of a finding of discriminatory intent, at least where no rational, nondiscriminatory motivation could be found for the action that produced that inescapable result.[63] Moreover, the Supreme Court's opinion in *Gomillion* provided the logical underpinning for several subsequent opinions dealing with the means by which a plaintiff could prove that a racially neutral act was motivated by a discriminatory purpose.[64]

Wisdom frequently referred to his opinion in *Gomillion* as his most painful memory of judicial service. He freely and frankly admitted that he had overreacted to a skepticism that he had developed in law school over judicial intermeddling into purely "political" matters that were better left to the legislative and executive branches.[65] His professors at Tulane Law School, he invariably explained, had "brainwashed" the

---

62. Transcript of interview of U.S. District Judge Martin L.C. Feldman by Joel Wm. Friedman, New Orleans, La., November 22, 2002, at 8.

63. *Gomillion v. Lightfoot*, 364 U.S. 339, 347, 81 S.Ct. 125, 130, 5 l.Ed.2d 110 (1960).

64. See *Personnel Administrator of Massachusetts v. Feeney*, 442 U.S. 256, 99 S.Ct. 2282, 60 L.Ed.2d 870 (1979); *Village of Arlington Heights v. Metropolitan Housing Development Corp.*, 429 U.S. 252, 97 S.Ct. 555, 50 L.Ed.2d 450 (1977). See generally Erwin Chemerinsky, *Constitutional Law: Principles and Policies* (New York: 1997), 568–569.

65. See Bass, *Unlikely Heroes*, 100; Jack Bass, *Taming The Storm* (New York: 1993), 147–178; Philip P. Frickey, *Judge Wisdom and Voting Rights: The Judicial Artist as Scholar and Pragmatist*, 60 TUL. L. REV. 276 (1985); Geoff O'Connell, "Judge John Minor Wisdom: His Trailblazing Decisions Made History," *New Orleans Magazine*, June 1982, 50.

students with the prevailing legal philosophy that judges were neither competent nor authorized to second guess the decisions of legislators on "political" matters such as apportionment.[66]

Thus, to Wisdom's eternal consternation, it was Brown, rather than he, who in *Gomillion* crafted a novel legal theory that eventually was adopted by the Supreme Court as part of its constitutional law jurisprudence. Nevertheless, Wisdom's level of intellectual honesty was such that given the subsequent opportunity to discard his original view and acknowledge that discriminatory effects could demonstrate the presence of discriminatory motivation, he did so. And the evolutionary process that led him to that ultimate position is best reflected in a pair of employment discrimination cases, the first of which was decided nearly eight months before *Gomillion*.

The employees at all the steel mills operated by the Sheffield Division of Armco Steel Corp. were represented by the United Steelworkers union. Over the years, the union and employer executed collective bargaining agreements that, among other things, divided all departments into two lines of progression, one line for skilled jobs and one line for unskilled jobs. Each line organized the jobs within the skilled or unskilled category into a hierarchy with the lowest job on each line requiring the least amount of skill, experience, and ability. The knowledge and experience obtained in performing each job on the progression ladder job were relevant to a worker's ability to successfully perform the next highest job. Prior to 1956, all of these contracts also provided that the skilled progression lines jobs could be filled only by white employees. But the agreement executed in 1956, employees in the unskilled progression line were permitted, for the first time, to bid on the lowest-ranked job in the skilled progression line. This meant that any black worker who wanted to obtain a job in the skilled line of progression had to start at the bottom of that ladder, regardless of either his or her position on the unskilled ladder or level of seniority with the company. And for those African American employees who held a high-level position on the unskilled ladder, transferring to the other progression line entailed, at least initially, a wage cut. Later that year, a group of African American employees at Sheffield's Houston mill sued the company and their union to challenge the legality of the 1956 agreement.

Writing for a unanimous panel that included Chief Judge Hutcheson

---

66. John Minor Wisdom, *In Memoriam: One of a Kind*, 71 Tex. L. Rev. 913, 917 (1993).

and Judge Rives in *Whitfield v. United Steelworkers of America*, Wisdom ruled against the workers.[67] He concluded that employees in the unskilled line could, and should, not expect to transfer to mid-level jobs in the skilled progression line since their employment in the unskilled jobs did not provide them with the training necessary to qualify them for these intermediate-level positions. He also reasoned that although this restricted transfer opportunity would require black workers to absorb an immediate pay cut, the payoff would ultimately come in the form of promotion and higher pay as they progressed up the skilled job chain.[68]

Wisdom was not unaware of the fact that many senior African American employees did not have the skills necessary to perform mid-level skilled jobs precisely and only because of the company's pre-1956 policy of excluding African Americans from all skilled jobs.[69] Nonetheless, he determined that this unfortunate consequence "was a product of the past" and that "we cannot turn back the clock."[70] Wisdom remained convinced that with employers only just beginning to make the transition from a racially biased to an equal opportunity workplace, it was "impossible to place negro incumbents holding . . . unskilled jobs, on an absolutely equal footing with white incumbents in skilled jobs."[71] Rather, he counseled, "time and tolerance, patience and forbearance, compromise and accommodation [would be] needed in solving a problem rooted deeply in custom." In his judgment, this union and this company had worked together in good faith toward a fair solution of a formidable and highly sensitive problem. "Angels," he observed, "could do no more."[72] A decade later, however, Wisdom reformulated his views on the meaning of unlawful discrimination in another case involving a facially nondiscriminatory employment practice that was alleged to operate to the disadvantage of prior victims of racial discrimination.

Bogalusa, Louisiana, a city in Washington Parish located seventy miles north of New Orleans and just west of the Pearl River near the Mississippi border, was the home of a huge paper mill operated by

67. 263 F.2d 546 (5th Cir.1959), cert. denied, 360 U.S. 902, 79 S.Ct. 1285, 3 L.Ed.2d 1254 (1959).
68. 163 F.2d at 550.
69. 163 F.2d at 551.
70. 163 F.2d at 551.
71. 163 F.2d at 550.
72. 163 F.2d at 551.

Crown Zellerbach Corporation. By the middle of the 1960s, Bogalusa had become known as much for its climate of racial hostility and violence as for its logging and papermaking prowess. It was home to the most powerful and active Ku Klux Klan organization in the state (at least a hundred of whose approximately eight hundred members were Crown Zellerbach employees) and was the site of frequent lynchings. Not coincidentally, a few years after winning a precedent-creating civil rights lawsuit against the Bogalusa chapter of the Klan (in which Wisdom wrote the opinion for the court), the U.S. Department of Justice sued Bogalusa's most important and influential employer to enforce the antidiscrimination mandate of the recently enacted Civil Rights Act of 1964.[73]

Crown Zellerbach created job progression lines with each department at the mill. Prior to 1964, the progression lines within each department were racially segregated, with the more desirable and higher-paying jobs organized on a line that was reserved for white employees. With few exceptions, the lowest-paying job on the "white" line paid more than the highest-rated job on the "black" progression line. After the enactment of the 1964 Civil Rights Act, the company merged the progression lines, but ranked jobs within each line according to the rate of pay. This meant that almost all of the jobs that previously had been available to African American employees were at the bottom of the progression ladder. Moreover, the agreement also provided that promotion to the next highest job on the line was based on seniority on the present job, rather than seniority with the company as a whole. Consequently, since African American workers had no seniority in jobs previously restricted to white workers, they could not compete for anything other than entry-level jobs on the previously all-white progression line, even when they had significantly more total years of service at the Bogalusa mill than their white competitors.

When the Justice Department and a group of African American employees sued Crown Zellerbach, alleging that the progression line system was in violation of Title VII of the 1964 Civil Rights Act, which prohibits employers from discriminating on the basis of race, the company insisted that it had ceased discriminating when, after the enactment of the 1964 Act, it merged the racially segregated lines of progres-

---

73. *U.S. v. Original Knights of the Ku Klux Klan*, 250 F.Supp. 330 (E.D.La.1965). Wisdom's opinion in this case is discussed in detail in chapter 12, *infra*. See Adam Fairclough, *Race and Democracy: The Civil Rights Struggle in Louisiana, 1915–1972* (Athens, Ga.: 1995), 345–350.

sion, thereby eliminating all explicit racial classifications. The plaintiffs, on the other hand, argued that the current system perpetuated the effects of the company's pre-1964 use of racially segregated job progression lines. Black employees hired under the old system would forever be penalized when competing against white employees for high-level jobs since the job-based seniority system allocated rewards based on something they previously had been denied—job seniority on formerly white-only jobs.

District Judge Frederick J. R. Heebe of New Orleans agreed with the government and ordered the company thereafter to base promotions up the ladder exclusively on a candidate's total number of years of seniority in the mill whenever when one of the competing employees was a black worker hired prior to 1966.[74] The appeal was heard by a Fifth Circuit panel composed of Wisdom and two Floridians, Circuit Judge David Dyer of Miami and District Judge Ben Krentzman of Tampa. As the senior member of the trio, Wisdom assigned himself the job of writing the opinion for the unanimous panel in *Local 189, United Papermakers and Paperworkers, AFL-CIO v. U.S.*[75]

The fundamental question in *Local 189*, as in *Whitfield*, was whether a job seniority–based system that applied to all workers regardless of race nevertheless was unlawfully discriminatory because of its contemporary impact on black workers. But Wisdom seized upon a crucial factual difference in the two cases to justify a different legal result. The white and black job progression lines in *Local 189* were not, as in *Whitfield*, divided solely along skilled and unskilled lines. An African American employee holding an intermediate-level job on the black progression line was not, therefore, necessarily unqualified for an intermediate-level job on the white line. Consequently, since no legitimate business reason justified Crown Zellerbach's reliance on job-based seniority for promotion up the progression ladder, its continued use of this admittedly facially race-neutral policy was unlawful because it perpetuated the consequences of the company's prior lawful acts of racial discrimination.

This conclusion, however, did not completely resolve this controversy. It was one thing to determine that reliance on job seniority, given the company's prior history of racial exclusion, violated Title VII. It was

74. *U.S. v. Local 189, United Papermakers and Paperworkers, AFL-CIO*, 282 F.Supp. 39 (E.D.La.1968).

75. 416 F.2d 980 (5th Cir.1969), cert. denied, 397 U.S. 919, 90 S.Ct. 926, 25 L.Ed.2d 100 (1970).

another to confect an effective remedy that would not amount to the kind of reverse discrimination that would violate the language and spirit of the federal antidiscrimination law.

The task of determining just how far a federal court could go in remedying prior acts of discrimination was just beginning to confront the judiciary in the mid-1960s. And it would continue, over the ensuing four decades, to occupy a central place in a highly charged and divisive national debate over whether, or to what degree, affirmative action was an appropriate response to the legacy of this country's history of racial prejudice. As Wisdom succinctly explained in *Local 189*: "The crux of the problem is how far the employer must go to undo the effects of past discrimination."[76] His answer to this question would be relied upon by the Supreme Court ten years later as the theoretical underpinning of its decisions that set forth the boundaries of lawful affirmative action in employment.[77]

Wisdom's approach was to focus prospectively—to prevent further perpetuation of the effects of the company's racist past—rather than to look back and disrupt settled expectations by vacating previously made promotion decisions. He could not subscribe to the "freedom now" theory that sought to purge all of the remnants of prior discrimination by replacing incumbent white employees with black workers in those jobs that, in the absence of the past racial exclusion, would have been awarded to African American workers on the basis of their overall mill seniority.[78] At the same time, however, maintaining the status quo by requiring only that the company adhere thereafter to a strictly race-blind seniority system ignored the legitimate claims of the present victims of that prior discrimination. In place of either of these alternatives, Wisdom chose to adopt the "rightful place" remedy that had been imposed by District Judge Heebe. Wisdom ordered the union and employer to award vacant jobs on the basis of plant seniority whenever one of the candidates was an African American worker who had been hired prior to the elimination of the segregated job progression lines.[79] The

76. 416 F.2d at 998.

77. *United Steelworkers of America v. Weber*, 433 U.S. 193, 99 S.Ct. 2721, 61 l.Ed.2d 480 (1979). The Supreme Court's decision in *Weber*, as well as Wisdom's dissenting opinion for the Fifth Circuit in that case, are described at length in chapter 14.

78. 416 f.2d at 988.

79. A few years later, the African American employees of Scott Paper Company's pulp and paper mill in Mobile, Alabama, challenged the company's reliance on educational and aptitude test-

concept, in both name and effect, appealed to Wisdom's sense of fairness. Black employees would now get a fair shake without imposing an unfair burden on either the company or the white employees who had been the beneficiaries of the previous regime.

Two weeks after the Fifth Circuit panel issued its judgment in *Local 189*, the union petitioned the entire Fifth Circuit to consider rehearing the case *en banc*. This ordinarily perfunctory procedure, however, took an unusual turn. These developments outraged Wisdom and impelled him to engage in a rare, but not unprecedented, outburst of hubris against a couple of his judicial brethren as well as the attorneys who, he believed, had challenged his three most cherished attributes—his intelligence, judgment, and integrity.

Among the reasons listed in support of the union's request for reconsideration was its claim that in his opinion for the court, Wisdom had included footnote references to a law review article that had been published after the panel had heard the parties' oral argument. It is, of course, commonplace for judges (or their law clerks) to undertake their own research after hearing argument in a case and to cite sources and authorities in their opinions that are not provided to them by the parties to the case. In this instance, however, the authors of the law review article in question were lawyers representing some of the African American plaintiffs in the case. The union maintained that by citing and relying on an article written by opposing counsel without offering it any opportunity to respond to its contents, Wisdom's panel had relied on an *ex parte* communication in violation of the union's constitutional right to due process of law.[80]

It did not take long for the judicial fur to begin to fly. Three days after the petition had been filed and circulated to all active members of

---

ing requirements, as well as seniority, for all transfers from previously all-black lines of progression to previously all-white lines of progression. Drawing heavily on the analysis developed in his *Local 189* opinion Wisdom wrote a forty-page decision for the unanimous panel in *Watkins v. Scott Paper Co.*, 530 F.2d 1159 (5th Cir.1976). The court struck down these policies on the ground that they unlawfully perpetuated the effects of the company's prior history of racial discrimination. And, as in *Local 189*, Wisdom and his colleagues compelled the company to undertake a series of remedial responses designed to place these victims of racial discrimination in their "rightful place."

80. An *ex parte* communication occurs when a judge has some case-related discussion with only one party to the case in the absence of, and without notice to, the opposing side. While there are exceptions to the rule, this one-sided opportunity to influence the court ordinarily is prohibited as being procedurally unfair to the excluded party.

the Fifth Circuit, Judge Griffin Bell sent a short note to Wisdom. Bell, a native Georgian who would later leave the court to become U.S. attorney general under President Jimmy Carter, had been appointed to the Fifth Circuit by President John F. Kennedy after a distinguished career as an attorney in Atlanta and a stint as chief of staff to Georgia governor Ernest Vandiver. Bell and Wisdom frequently clashed over internal court matters, and over the course of their joint service on the court Wisdom grew increasingly disenchanted with Bell on both a personal and a professional level.

Wisdom's relationship with Bell, however, had not started out badly. To the contrary, barely a month after Bell had received his permanent appointment to the Fifth Circuit,[81] Wisdom felt compelled to write a dissenting opinion in a case in which Bell had written for the majority. Sensitive to the feelings of a very junior colleague, Wisdom made a point of enclosing a note of explanation with his proposed opinion. "I have been on the Court such a short time," Wisdom wrote, "compared with some of our fellow judges, that I can still remember the shock I had when I received the first dissents to my opinions. I have tried my level best, therefore, to see these cases your way. After a good deal of struggling with myself, however, I find that I cannot go along with your unquestionably able, persuasive, and carefully prepared opinion."[82]

For whatever reason, Bell chose to couch his note to Wisdom concerning the petition for en banc rehearing (which he copied to all the other active members of the court) in polite, yet forceful terms. He began collegially enough by emphasizing that he did not disagree with the merits of Wisdom's decision in the case. Bell then voiced his concern, however, with "what appears to be a serious point in [the union's] charge that your panel relied on a post-argument Harvard Law Review article by counsel for the opposite party in rendering the decision." And he ended the brief missive by asking Wisdom to "enlighten us regarding the union's charge" since he understood "how they may felt that they have been mistreated."[83]

A few days later, John Brown echoed Bell's sentiments in a letter to Wisdom and the other judges, although in a more conciliatory tone. Brown agreed with Bell not only as to the substantive correctness of

81. Bell initially received a recess appointment to the Fifth Circuit by President Kennedy on October 5, 1962. The Senate confirmed his permanent appointment on February 9, 1962.

82. Letter to Griffin B. Bell from John M. Wisdom, March 27, 1969.

83. Letter to John M. Wisdom from Griffin B. Bell, August 14, 1969.

Wisdom's judgment, but also as to the perception that may have been created by Wisdom's citations to the law review article. He attempted to soft-pedal his criticism, however, by explaining why he was suggesting that the union attorneys be given thirty to fifty days to file a supplemental brief commenting on the materials referred to in Wisdom's opinion. "I do this as a matter of just good administration," Brown explained, "because I do not regard this as a denial of due process."[84] In fact, he added, he expected that the union attorneys would not be able to contradict the arguments contained in the law review article and that "this would enable you to make note of it in some brief *per curiam* order denying the petition for rehearing." Moreover, Brown concluded, "your opinion is too good, the result too right to allow your disposition to be even possibly diverted for a moment by a thing which can be so readily adjusted."[85]

Brown's placatory effort to leaven the critical tone of Bell's letter did not, unfortunately, produce its hoped-for effect on Wisdom. Within a few days of receiving Brown's note, Wisdom sent a blistering response to both Brown and Bell, as well as a copy to all the active circuit judges. After sarcastically suggesting that "perhaps in the interest of institutionalizing a court as large as ours, each of us should regard himself as a monitor over the opinion-writing process," Wisdom added that "perhaps, too, we should be tolerant of mis-monitoring," But, he icily charged, "you both failed to examine the factual basis necessary for monitorial jurisdiction. The lawyers for the movants were as careless as you two judges."[86]

Anyone who had read the opinion with care, Wisdom insisted, would have observed that it relied not on the law review article in question, but upon a student-authored publication. The allegedly offending law review article, Wisdom explained, was nothing more than a rehash of the authors' brief to the court that raised no new arguments. Moreover, not only were none of his three citations to that article used to support or otherwise refer to any disputed issue in the case, "to make sure that *careful* readers would be on their guard, I took the unusual precaution," he advised, to mention in one of the footnotes that the authors of one of the articles cited in the opinion were of counsel in the case before the court. "In short," Wisdom vituperatively counseled his colleagues,

84. Letter to John M. Wisdom from John R. Brown, August 18, 1969.
85. Letter to John M. Wisdom from John R. Brown, August 18, 1969.
86. Letter to John R. Brown and Griffin B. Bell from John M. Wisdom, August 25, 1979.

"look before you leap into dictation. If you had read with both eyes the footnotes . . . —as any good monitor would have done—you would have known that the movants' complaint was frivolous. A telephone call would have saved a lot of trouble."[87]

Neither Brown nor Bell rose to the bait, preferring instead to send Wisdom very cordial replies disclaiming any intent to be a "monitor," explaining why they did not telephone him directly with their concern, and concluding that the matter was not important enough to justify voting to grant the request for a rehearing.[88] Judge Brown, however, could not resist the temptation to needle his good friend. In his letter, Brown explained that he chose not to telephone Wisdom about the issue because "you were not in your office and I assumed you were busy telling people how to be Judges and hence good monitors."[89]

Wisdom also made sure, however, that the attorneys who had placed the tempest in this teapot also received an earful. He wrote to each of the union's attorneys informing them that they had "erred egregiously" in asserting that the court had relied on the law review article written by opposing counsel and reiterating his disclaimer of having cited the article with approval on a disputed legal issue as well as his characterization of the article as a "bland rehash" of the briefs.[90] A little more than two weeks later, on October 1, the storm subsided when the court denied the request for rehearing.

This heated exchange with Bell and, to a lesser degree, with Brown, was neither the first nor the last internal squabble in which Wisdom was more than a willing participant. A similar contretemps had flared up between Wisdom and Judge Walter Pettus Gewin three years earlier, a dispute that arose in connection with Gewin's dissenting opinion in *Labat,* the case in which Wisdom's opinion for a majority of the *en banc* court struck down Louisiana's racially discriminatory jury selection system. Gewin, who had left a successful law practice in Alabama to accept an appointment to the Fifth Circuit from President John F. Kennedy in

87. Letter to John R. Brown and Griffin B. Bell from John M. Wisdom, August 25, 1979.

88. Letter to John M. Wisdom from Griffin B. Bell, September 8, 1969; Letter to John M. Wisdom from John R. Brown, August 26, 1969 (documents on file with author).

89. Letter to John M. Wisdom from John R. Brown, August 26, 1969 (documents on file with author).

90. Letter to Warren Woods, Betty S. Murphy, C. Paul Barker and Jerry L. Gardner from John M. Wisdom, September 15, 1969.

1961, was an unassuming man who did not share Wisdom's belief that the judiciary could and should take an active, affirmative part in attacking societal problems such as racial discrimination.[91]

The initial sentence of Gewin's dissenting opinion in *Labat*, which described the case as involving "one of the most heinous crimes ever committed in the rich and varied history of New Orleans,"[92] probably was not designed to appeal to either Wisdom's fastidiousness in historical analysis or his local civic pride. And it went downhill from there. Upon "careful analysis" of Wisdom's opinion, Gewin concluded that there had been a "serious misconception of the issues we are called upon to decide, a misinterpretation or disregard of certain salient facts and a lack of understanding of the prior decisions in the case."[93] As far as Gewin was concerned, the only issue that was properly before the Fifth Circuit was whether there had been a deliberate and intentional policy of excluding individuals on the basis of race in the selection of petit jury panels. The majority's foray into the constitutionality of a selection process based on "chiefly theoretical, statistical proof"[94] of the actual impact of its policies on the demographics of grand jury composition exceeded the bounds of the court's appellate jurisdiction.[95]

Attached to a copy of the proposed dissent that Gewin sent to all the active members of the court was a cover letter in which he explained that he felt compelled to part company with the majority because of his deep conviction that the "Court is about to make a serious mistake."[96] Wisdom responded straightaway with a detailed six-page reply, a copy of which he also relayed to every active member of the court. His letter opened with a temperate, judicious explanation of his differences with Gewin, stating that his "general reaction to Judge Gewin's dissent is, first, simply that he reads the facts differently from the way I read them and, second, he takes a narrower view of the issues."[97] Continuing in that same tone, Wisdom also rejected Gewin's claim that he had failed to address the central issue in the case, that is, the alleged exclusion of

91. See Couch, *A History of the Fifth Circuit, 1891–1981*, 114.
92. *Labat v. Bennett*, 365 F.2d 698, 729 (Gewin, J., dissenting).
93. 365 F.2d at 729.
94. 365 F.2d at 738.
95. 365 F.2d at 730–731.
96. Letter to All Active Judges of the Fifth Circuit from Walter P. Gewin, July 13, 1966.
97. Letter to All Active Judges of the Fifth Circuit from John M. Wisdom, July 19, 1966.

African Americans from petit juries. Wisdom informed his colleagues that "most of the facts . . . referred to in my opinion relate to the petit jury venires and their sources."[98] He further insisted that Gewin had erred in failing to recognize that a presumption of intentional exclusion could be generated by evidence of the total absence of African Americans from all petit and grand juries and the disproportionately small number of black citizens serving on the venires.

Gewin was now ready to give as good as he had received. "If Judge Wisdom would enjoy writing another letter like the one he wrote on July 19, 1966," Gewin's rejoinder commenced, "he is respectfully advised that my other cheek is already turned. He knows the attitude and motives which prompted the expressions contained in his letter, and only he knows whether the tone and spirit of them make him comfortable."[99]

Gewin's letter served only to further infuriate an already incensed Wisdom. This sarcastic response by Gewin, on top of the very pointed manner in which his dissent had criticized Wisdom's analysis of both the factual record and the preexisting jurisprudence, was more than Wisdom could tolerate as a matter of collegial discourse. This had escalated into an *ad hominum* attack. Wisdom instantly dashed off a response to his colleagues. "I thought *I* turned the other cheek. I am not thin-skinned, but when I read Judge Gewin's dissent I was shocked at its offensive tone and the bluntness of its reflections upon my judicial integrity and ability. After a night's sleep, I tore up my first letter, decided to pass the matter off lightly, and wrote what I regard as a soft answer."[100] Yet ever the politician, Wisdom closed by insisting that "as far as I am concerned, the incident is closed without any residue of rancor." Nevertheless, he just could not resist taking one more shot at Gewin. "I attribute Judge Gewin's overlooking the beam in his eye to the fervor of his almost evangelical convictions in this case."[101]

Within a few years after taking the bench, Wisdom's opinions so impressed his colleagues for their erudition, eloquence, and creativity that he quickly earned a level of respect disproportionate to his years of ser-

98. Letter to All Active Judges of the Fifth Circuit from John M. Wisdom, July 19, 1966.
99. Letter to All Active Judges of the Fifth Circuit from Walter P. Gewin, July 26, 1966, at 1.
100. Letter to All Active Judges of the Fifth Circuit from John M. Wisdom, July 28, 1966, at 1.
101. Letter to All Active Judges of the Fifth Circuit from John M. Wisdom, July 28, 1966, at 2.

vice. Naturally, however, he was not always able to convince at least one other member of the three court panels in which the court typically sat to join with him in the resolution of a case. To the contrary, Wisdom frequently was the dissenting member in both memorable and mundane cases.

Wisdom's first significant dissenting opinion was written in a case that, ironically, placed him in the position of protecting the right of Louisiana's registrars of voters, a group whose obfuscatory and blatantly racist tactics he had battled for years in working to help register black voters in his home state. In *Larche v. Hannah,* sixty-seven African American voters in Shreveport had complained to the U.S. Commission on Civil Rights that they had been prevented from voting on account of their race by several state registrars of voters.[102] As party of its investigation, the commission ordered the registrars in sixteen Louisiana parishes to appear and to produce their voting and registration records. The registrars responded by filing an action in federal court to prevent the commission from conducting that inquiry. They argued that by not informing them of the nature of the charges leveled against them or of the identity of those asserting the complaints prior to the hearing, the commission had deprived them of their constitutional rights to due process and to confront and cross-examine their accusers.

Writing for the majority, District Judge Edwin F. "Chug" Hunter of Lake Charles sidestepped the constitutional issue, concluding that since the statute that created the commission had not expressly authorized the commission to promulgate rules that would preclude confrontation and cross-examination, the commission lacked the statutory authority to deprive the registrars of these "traditional rights."[103] Wisdom, on the other hand, chose to meet the constitutional issue head-on in his dissenting opinion. He concluded that a lower level of procedural protection was required in an investigative, as opposed to an adjudicative, proceeding.[104] As long as a witness to the investigative hearing was afforded her or his constitutional right against self-incrimination, the availability of all the other traditional due process protections in the subsequent adjudicative proceeding was sufficient to meet the constitutional requirements of fairness. Within a year, the Supreme Court re-

102. 177 F.Supp. 816 (W.D.La.1959).
103. 177 F.Supp. at 824.
104. 177 F.Supp. at 831 (Wisdom, J., dissenting).

versed Judge Hunter's ruling and adopted the reasoning of Wisdom's dissenting opinion *in toto*.[105]

Five years after vindicating Wisdom's dissenting position in *Larche*, the Supreme Court relied on another Wisdom dissenting opinion as the basis for its decision in *Dombrowski v. Pfister*, a highly publicized case involving the prosecution in Louisiana of a civil rights organization and some of its leaders and supporters.[106]

The Southern Conference Educational Fund (SCEF) actively pursued an anti-segregation agenda that focused primarily on achieving equality of opportunity in voting and education in Louisiana and other southern states. In October 1963, several of its leaders were arrested and jailed, their homes were subjected to nighttime raids at gunpoint, and their organization's office was ransacked by city and state police officers. Just over a month later, even though a state judge previously had vacated the arrest warrants and found the searches to be illegal, the Joint Legislative Committee on Un-American Activities of the Louisiana legislature declared that the SCEF was a communist front organization and urged the New Orleans district attorney to prosecute its leaders under Louisiana's Subversive Activities and Communist Control Law and its Communist Propaganda Control Law. The organization and its leaders responded by filing suit in federal court seeking an injunction against the threatened prosecution and a declaration that these two state statutes were unconstitutional. Since the case involved a federal constitutional challenge to a state statute, a three-judge federal district court, composed of Wisdom and District Judges Frank Ellis and Gordon West of New Orleans, was convened.

The two district judges agreed that the case should be dismissed because it was inappropriate for a federal court to intervene to quash a not-yet instituted state court criminal proceeding.[107] In the name of federalism, they concluded, the federal court should step aside and let a state court rule on the constitutionality of the statutes when and if a

105. *Hannah v. Larche*, 363 U.S. 420, 80 S.Ct. 1502, 4 L.Ed.2d 1307 (1960). Justice William O. Douglas, joined by Justice Hugo Black, dissented on the ground that by summoning someone to determine the truth of an accusation that this individual violated the federal election law, the commission was acting in lieu of a grand jury or committing magistrate, which are the only bodies that the Constitution permits to engage in the task of sifting criminal charges against people. 363 U.S. at 493, 80 S.Ct. at 1546 (Douglas, J., dissenting).

106. 380 U.S. 479, 85 S.Ct. 1116, 14 L.Ed.2d 22 (1965).

107. *Dombrowski v. Pfister*, 227 F.Supp. 556, 559, 562–563 (E.D.La.1964).

prosecution was initiated. Wisdom responded to this ruling with one of his most impassioned dissenting opinions. Although he conceded that the State of Louisiana had the right to take reasonable steps to ensure its own preservation, he believed that this was truly the motivation behind the threatened action. He offered a typically blunt, courageous, and insightful assessment of what he saw as the real stakes involved in the case. Stripping the state's case to its pretextual core, Wisdom revealed that, "under the pretext of protecting itself against subversion, [the State of Louisiana] has harassed and humiliated the plaintiffs and is about to prosecute them solely because their activities in promoting civil rights for Negroes conflict with the State's steel-hard policy of segregation."[108]

Wisdom also angrily renounced his two colleagues' invocation of federalism. By viewing this case as a threat to states' rights rather than as a menace to the citizenry's constitutional liberties, Wisdom avowed, the majority had invoked "mystical, emotion laden words" that "evoke visions of the hearth and defense of the homeland and carry the sound of bugles and the beat of drums."[109] In his judgment, the "crowning glory" of federalism was not states' rights, but the federal constitutional protection accorded every private citizen "against all wrongful governmental invasion of fundamental rights and freedoms."[110] And though it certainly was true that state judges, like their federal counterparts, were empowered to enforce federal constitutional guarantees, Wisdom would not engage in ostrich-like aversion to the reality that state judges, particularly in the South, were inclined to be unsympathetic to constitutional challenges to state law.

Where the state government's interference with the exercise of fundamental rights, he declared, occurred in an environment that was hostile to the enforcement of federal constitutional rights, federal judges, immunized from local prejudices and peer pressure by their grant of life tenure, should be expected to step in and assume the primary responsibility for safeguarding these precious liberties. In such instances, intervention by the federal courts could not be considered overreaching into matters reserved to the states. To the contrary, Wisdom declared, the exercise of authority under those circumstances "makes federalism workable."[111]

108. 227 F.Supp. at 569 (Wisdom, J., dissenting).
109. 227 F.Supp. at 570 (Wisdom, J., dissenting).
110. 227 F.Supp. at 570 (Wisdom, J., dissenting).
111. 227 F.Supp. at 571 (Wisdom, J., dissenting).

The plaintiffs appealed the dismissal of their action to the Supreme Court, which reversed the lower court's decision and adopted Wisdom's analysis, including his view that litigants could not expect a fair adjudication of the constitutional challenge by state court judges.[112]

Although these lawsuits did not become a fixture in the public consciousness until decades later, the first wave of cigarette litigation, which consisted of an unbroken series of victories for the cigarette companies, actually began in the mid-1950s.[113] But in 1963, a Wisdom-authored decision on a purely procedural point of law in one of these early cases, *R. J. Reynolds Tobacco Co. v. Hudson,*[114] helped set the stage for the reversal of that tide in favor of the plaintiffs that would occur thirty to forty years later.

Elbert Hudson had smoked a tin of Prince Albert tobacco and two packages of Camel unfiltered cigarettes every day for thirty-three years. A biopsy revealed a cancerous tumor on his larynx and vocal cords. Two days short of one year later, Hudson sued the R. J. Reynolds Tobacco Company for $250,000, claiming that smoking the defendant's products had caused the cancer. R. J. Reynolds asked the trial court to dismiss the case on the ground that this lawsuit was barred by the expiration of the applicable Louisiana statute of limitations, which provided that plaintiffs in cases like this had to file their suit within one year from the time that "damage was sustained." The tobacco company pointed to affidavits from two cancer specialists stating that Hudson's cancer had appeared months prior to his biopsy, which was more than a year before he filed this suit. Hudson, on the other hand, argued that he had not been made aware of the connection between smoking and his cancer until the time of biopsy, which occurred less than a year before the commencement of his civil action.

Since cancer, Wisdom observed, "comes like a thief in the night,"[115] the limitations period should be construed to begin from the moment the plaintiff knew or should have known that he has sustained damage, and not from the date of the act causing the damage. This generous (to the plaintiff) interpretation of the statute of limitations issue

112. *Dombrowski v. Pfister,* 380 U.S. 479, 85 S.Ct. 1116, 14 L.Ed.2d 22 (1965).

113. Mark Z. Edell, *Cigarette Litigation: The Second Wave,* 22 TORT & INS. L.J. 90 (1986).

114. 314 F.2d 776 (5th Cir.1963); James W. Henges, *Cigarettes: Defectively Designed or Just Extremely Dangerous?* 18 OKLA. CITY U. L. REV. 559, 562 (1993).

115. 314 F.2d at 779.

significantly enhanced the ability of cigarette smokers to gain access to the courts in cancer-based personal injury cases. And just as *R. J. Reynolds* blazed the trail for mass tort litigation in the cigarette industry, another Wisdom opinion eventually generated a tidal wave of asbestos litigation.

In 1973, on behalf of a unanimous panel, Wisdom wrote the first federal appellate court decision holding asbestos manufacturers strictly liable for injuries to insulation workers caused by the manufacturers' failure to warn of the dangers associated with prolonged on-the-job exposure to asbestos. His opinion in *Borel v. Fibreboard Paper Products Corp.* has been hailed as "the Magna Carta of asbestos litigation," and is widely acknowledged to have triggered the avalanche of more than 25,000 mass toxic substance lawsuits over the succeeding decade.[116]

In less than a decade of service on the Fifth Circuit, Wisdom had produced an impressive body of work noted for its erudition, precision, and stylish literacy. These opinions reflected the components of a judicial philosophy that would guide his decision-making throughout the remainder of his judicial career—an unwavering commitment to preserving those civil rights guaranteed to all citizens by the Constitution and ensuring that the law operate, in both its process and result, in a manner that accorded with his innate sense of fairness; a devotion to maintaining the constitutionally fashioned relationship between the federal and state governments; and an insistence that the courts honestly adhere to the rule of law irrespective of its consequences to the resolution of the merits of any individual dispute.

By the end of 1962, only five years removed from his appointment to the federal bench, Wisdom already had secured his undisputed position as the Fifth Circuit's resident scholar and intellectual luminary.

---

116. 493 F.2d 1076 (5th Cir.1973), cert. denied, 419 U.S. 869, 95 S.Ct. 127, 42 L.Ed.2d 107 (1974). Gary T. Schwartz, *Modern American Tort Law*, 26 GA. L. REV. 601, 667 (1992); Paul Brodeur, "Annals of Law: The Asbestos Industry on Trial II—Discovery," *The New Yorker*, June 17, 1985, 45. See also Deborah R. Hensler and Mark A. Peterson, *Understanding Mass Personal Injury Litigation: A Socio-Legal Analysis*, 59 BROOK. L. REV. 961, 1003 (1993); Michael D. Green, *The Road Less Well Traveled (and Seen): Contemporary Lawmaking in Products Liability*, 49 DEPAUL L. REV. 377, 382 (1999). John D. Rue, *Returning to the Roots of the Bramble Bush: The "But For" Test Regains Primacy in Causal Analysis in the American Law Institute's Proposed Restatement (Third) of Torts*, 71 FORDHAM L. REV. 2679, 2698 (2003). If the extent to which an opinion is cited approvingly by other courts and/or commentators is any measure of its impact, Wisdom's opus in *Borel* must be considered one of his most significant products. A 2004 Westlaw-KeyCite search revealed that this opinion has been cited in nearly a thousand judicial opinions and scholarly publications.

Within months thereafter, he, his court, and the nation, would confront the sternest test of his intellectual leadership and moral rectitude as the Fifth Circuit occupied ground zero in the country's most divisive conflict since the Civil War—the civil rights struggle of the 1960s.

8

SHOWDOWN IN MISSISSIPPI

STANDING UP FOR JAMES MEREDITH
AND TO ROSS BARNETT

Located at mile marker 160 on the Natchez Trace amid central Mississippi farmlands, the city of Kosciusko is best known for its pure drinking water. It also, however, is the birthplace of the son of a cotton and corn farmer and grandson of a slave whose persistent, courageous, and ultimately successful campaign to gain admission to the state's segregated flagship university as the result of a Fifth Circuit decision authored by John Minor Wisdom, was a defining moment in the civil rights struggle of the 1960s that forever changed the face of American society.

The sixth of ten children, James Meredith left his family's eighty-four-acre cotton and corn farm in Attala County after his high school graduation to enlist in the U.S. Air Force, where he was one of the first black soldiers to serve in the recently integrated American armed forces.[1] But the challenges and rewards of being in the vanguard of an integrated air force paled in comparison to the impact generated eleven years later when this one "man with a mission and with a nervous stom-

---

1. "Resolute Mississippian: James Howard Meredith," *New York Times*, September 21, 1962, 13, col. 1; Walter Lord, *The Past That Would Not Die* (New York: 1965), 36–37; William Doyle, *An American Insurrection: The Battle of Oxford, Mississippi, 1962* (New York: 2001), 18–20.

ach" faced off against the combined military and political might of the most segregated state in the nation and integrated its foremost public university situated in the heart of the Old Confederacy.[2]

On January 21, 1961, the day after John F. Kennedy's inauguration as the thirty-fifth president of the United States, Meredith requested an admissions application to the University of Mississippi. Ten days later, he submitted his application with an attached photograph and a cover letter explaining that he was unable to meet the requirement of furnishing the names of six alumni "because I am a Negro and all graduates of the school are white [and] I do not know any graduate personally." Instead, he offered five written testaments to his moral character from "Negro citizens of my state."[3]

Meredith's application generated a telegram from Robert B. Ellis, the registrar at Ole Miss, informing Meredith that his submission could not be considered since it had been filed after the deadline for applying for admission to the spring semester. With the assistance of a civil rights attorney in Jackson, Meredith contacted Burke Marshall, the U.S. assistant attorney general who headed the Justice Department's Civil Rights Division. Marshall communicated his department's keen interest in Meredith's situation and willingness to provide assistance.[4] Meredith also wrote to Thurgood Marshall, director of the NAACP's Legal Defense and Educational Fund, asking for legal assistance in a fight he was prepared to pursue "all the way."[5]

Marshall assigned one of his staff attorneys, Constance Baker Motley, to work with Meredith.[6] Motley, a tough-minded, deliberate, and relentless courtroom combatant, had just secured a noteworthy victory in obtaining a federal court order compelling the University of Georgia to admit its first two African American students, Charlayne Hunter and Hamilton Holmes. Motley wrote Meredith on February 16, advising him to recontact the university registrar and to request that his original application be considered a continuing application for admission at the earliest possible time, including either the summer 1961 term

2. *Meredith v. Fair*, 305 F.2d 343, 358 (5th Cir.1962). According to *Time* magazine, "of the Southern states that have avoided even token compliance with the Supreme Court's 1954 school-desegregation decision, none has thundered 'never' louder than Mississippi." "A Negro in Ole Miss," *Time*, July 6, 1962, 37.

3. James Meredith, *Three Years in Mississippi* (Bloomington: 1966), 58.

4. Ibid., 59.

5. Ibid., 56.

6. Jack Greenberg, *Crusaders in the Courts* (New York: 1994), 35.

or the succeeding 1961–1962 academic year. Meredith studiously followed Motley's advice and sent the registrar a series of three letters over a two-month period reiterating his desire to be considered for admission. Finally, on May 25, 1961, Registrar Ellis notified Meredith by letter that his application had been denied on several grounds. First, the university would not accept a transfer from an unaccredited institution such as Jackson State (where Meredith previously had been enrolled). Second, Meredith's letters of good character were not, as required, written by Ole Miss alumni. Finally, Ellis referred to other deficiencies that "I see no need for mentioning."[7]

Less than a week later, Meredith, accompanied by Connie Motley, Medgar Evers, and local attorney R. Jess Brown, drove to Meridian, Mississippi, to file his historic complaint against several University of Mississippi officials in the courthouse presided over by U.S. district judge Sidney C. Mize.[8] Meredith's suit alleged that Ole Miss had rejected his application on the basis of his race and sought an injunction ordering the university to admit him and to terminate its practice of restricting admission to white applicants.

Simultaneously with the filing of his complaint for permanent relief, Meredith filed a motion asking Judge Mize to issue a temporary injunction that, pending resolution of the case at trial, would permit his enrollment for the 1961 summer session that was scheduled to begin less than two weeks later, on June 8. In the first of a seemingly never-ending series of delays, Judge Mize did not begin to hear testimony on the request for a preliminary injunction in Biloxi until June 12, four days after the beginning of the university's summer session. Then, when the hearing was not completed at the end of that day, Judge Mize recessed the proceedings until July 10, which, he claimed, was the next available date on his crowded calendar. Meredith and his lawyers returned to Judge Mize's courtroom on July 10, only to learn that Mississippi Assistant Attorney General Dugas Shands, counsel for the university, had advised Judge Mize that he was seriously ill and that Mize had agreed to another month's delay.[9] By this time, of course, the summer session had

---

7. Meredith, *Three Years in Mississippi*, 62–65, 77.

8. Greenberg, *Crusaders in the Courts*, 319.

9. When this case reached the Fifth Circuit, Wisdom expressed his own deeply felt skepticism at the need for such a lengthy interruption, noting that "the Attorney General's Office is well-staffed" with nine lawyers, including three who were working directly with Mr. Shands on the Meredith case. *Meredith v. Fair*, 305 F.2d 343, 352 (5th Cir.1962).

nearly come to an end and any realistic chance of Meredith's attending Ole Miss that semester had evaporated.[10] The hearing finally resumed in Jackson on August 10 and concluded on August 16, just in time for Mize to render a decision before the commencement of the fall 1961 term.[11]

Throughout the proceedings before Judge Mize, the university boldly and consistently disclaimed having or applying any race-based admissions policy and denied that Meredith had been refused admission because of his race. It maintained that the decision had been based solely on Meredith's failure to submit the required five alumni recommendations and on its policy of not accepting transfers from institutions that were unaccredited by the Southern Association of Colleges and Secondary Schools. The school failed to mention that its no-transfers rule had been concocted by the Ole Miss board of trustees just days after the university received Meredith's initial application.[12]

The deadline for registering for the fall term ended on September 28. Nevertheless, Judge Mize did not render his decision until December 12, nearly four months after the hearing had concluded. By then, of course, the fall semester had slipped away and Meredith, who never stopped attending classes at Jackson State, had earned additional credits toward his degree. Endorsing the testimony offered by Registrar Ellis, Judge Mize adopted wholesale the university's contentions and denied Meredith's request for a temporary injunction, finding that although the university had been segregated prior to the Supreme Court's decision in *Brown v. Board of Education*, it had discontinued that policy after that landmark ruling. He also set the case for trial on January 15, 1962.[13]

Meredith immediately appealed Judge Mize's interim decision to the Fifth Circuit. On January 9, 1962, a panel composed of Chief Judge Tuttle and Judges Rives and Wisdom heard the appeal. Three days later, the panel released its Wisdom-authored unanimous ruling.[14] Since it was reviewing only a preliminary, pretrial decision, the issue before the appellate court was whether the trial judge's conclusions were consistent with or contradicted by the limited evidence that had been presented at the preliminary injunction hearing. Nevertheless, there was no mis-

10. Lord, *The Past That Would Not Die*, 106.

11. *Meredith v. Fair*, 199 F.Supp. 754 (S.D.Miss.1961).

12. *Meredith v. Fair*, 305 F.2d 343, 353 (5th Cir.1962). See also Doyle, *An American Insurrection: The Battle of Oxford, Mississippi, 1962*, 33.

13. *Meredith v. Fair*, 199 F.Supp. 754 (S.D.Miss.1961).

14. *Meredith v. Fair*, 298 F.2d 696 (5th Cir.1962).

taking Wisdom's disdain for the explanations offered by the university. "This case was tried below and argued here," Wisdom wrote, "in the eerie atmosphere of nevernever land."[15]

Wisdom ridiculed the university's suggestion that his court could not take judicial notice (that is, acknowledge the existence of a fact so well and widely recognized that it need not be established by independent evidence) of a "plain fact known to everyone." In response to the university's preposterous claim that Meredith was required to provide the court with the genealogical records of all Ole Miss students and alumni in order to prove that the university refused to admit nonwhite applicants for admission, Wisdom offered a simple, yet dramatic retort. "We take judicial notice," he declared, "that the state of Mississippi maintains a policy of segregation in its schools and colleges."[16]

Moving then to whether Meredith had been rejected pursuant to this general policy, Wisdom announced that the university's alumni certification policy amounted to a denial of every black applicant's constitutional right to equal protection under the laws. For even though the certificate requirement was imposed on white and black candidates alike, the obvious and intended effect of the policy, Wisdom explained, was to erect an insuperable barrier to black applicants. Nevertheless, Wisdom continued, the fact that the university had a general policy against admitting black applicants and had relied on an unconstitutional admissions requirement did not necessarily negate the existence of a nondiscriminatory justification for rejecting Meredith's application. Based on the limited evidence that had been presented at the preliminary injunction hearing, the appellate court could not determine conclusively that the trial judge had erred in his preludial finding that Meredith had failed to show that race was the reason for the denial of his admissions application. Consequently, although without ever referring to him by name, the Fifth Circuit upheld "the district judge's" denial of Meredith's request for a preliminary injunction and instructed him to conduct the trial at the earliest possible date. The university's spring term was scheduled to start on February 6 and Wisdom did not want another semester to pass by.

Wisdom's blunt and vigorous renunciation of the university's claim that it did not have a custom or policy of discriminating on the basis of race in making admissions decisions had absolutely no impact on

15. 298 F.2d at 701.
16. 298 F.2d at 701.

Sidney Mize. On February 3, 1962, after conducting a full trial, Mize reaffirmed his earlier ruling, denied all relief, and dismissed Meredith's complaint.[17] Mize ruled that the evidence uncontrovertibly established that Ole Miss had ceased to be a racially segregated institution and that Meredith had not been denied admission because of his race.

On February 10, Meredith and his NAACP attorney Constance Motley were back in court seeking temporary relief from the Fifth Circuit. Appearing once again before the Tuttle-Rives-Wisdom panel, Motley requested that the court order the university immediately and provisionally to admit Meredith for the spring semester (which had commenced on February 6) while his appeal of Judge Mize's trial judgment was pending. Otherwise, she claimed, by the time the Fifth Circuit was ready to decide his appeal, the semester would be over, Meredith would have graduated from Jackson State, and, consequently, his appeal would be dismissed as moot since he no longer would be eligible for admission as a transfer student. But in an unsigned *per curiam* opinion that Wisdom drafted, a majority of the court, with Tuttle dissenting, denied Meredith's request for temporary relief. Meredith could avoid the mootness problem, Wisdom explained, by not attending Jackson State for one term or by not taking the courses required for graduation.[18]

On June 25, the Fifth Circuit released its ruling on Meredith's appeal from Mize's final, post-trial judgment. This panel was composed of Brown, Wisdom, and District Judge Dozier A. DeVane of Tallahassee, Florida. The panel's senior, and therefore presiding member, John Brown, assigned the task of composing what everyone knew would be a history-making decision to the court's resident scholar, John Wisdom.

Wisdom wasted no time and minced no words in skewering the university, its legal posturing, and its incessant invocation of the principle of "deliberate speed."[19] To the contrary, he countered, "time is of the essence."[20] Digging deep into his bountiful quiver of stinging, sardonic rhetoric and barbed historical allusions, Wisdom blasted both Judge Mize and the Ole Miss bureaucracy. The university's open-faced insistence that it had no policy of excluding African Americans in the face of the fact that "no person known to be a Negro has ever attended the Uni-

17. *Meredith v. Fair*, 202 F.Supp. 224 (S.D.Miss.1962).
18. *Meredith v. Fair*, 305 F.2d 341 (5th Cir.1962); *Meredith v. Fair*, 305 F.2d 341, 342 (5th Cir.1962) (Tuttle, Ch.J., dissenting).
19. 305 F.2d at 352.
20. 305 F.2d at 352.

versity," he charged, "defies history and common knowledge."[21] With his own literary flair, Wisdom left absolutely no doubt as to his court's reaction to the collection of rationalizations proffered by Ole Miss. "A full review of the record leads the Court inescapably to the conclusion that from the moment the defendants discovered Meredith was a Negro they engaged in a carefully calculated campaign of delay, harassment, and masterly inactivity. It was a defense designed to discourage and to defeat by evasive tactics which would have been a credit to Quintus Fabius Maximus."[22]

Wisdom also made no effort to camouflage his and his colleagues' incredulity at Judge Mize's central finding that Ole Miss had discontinued its segregationist policies following the Supreme Court's ruling in *Brown*. "This about-face in policy, news of which may startle some people in Mississippi," Wisdom retorted, "could have been accomplished only by telepathic communication among the University's administrators."[23] One by one, Wisdom examined and disemboweled the factual predicates for Mize's startling conclusion that Ole Miss did not refuse to admit all African American applicants for admission. He announced that the university's policy against transferring credits from unaccredited universities had been discriminatorily applied and irrationally construed to bar Meredith's admission. In that connection, Wisdom noted, even though Jackson State had been admitted to membership in the relevant accrediting organization on December 16, 1961, the Ole Miss registrar could or would not reveal whether the May 25 decision to reject Meredith's application had been or would be reconsidered in light of that change in Jackson State's accreditation status. The university also refused to transfer credits that Meredith had earned at three accredited institutions while serving his country in the air force.

Wisdom further chastised Mize (although, once again, never referring to him by name but, rather, as the "trial judge," "district judge," or

21. 305 F.2d at 360.

22. 305 F.2d at 344. Born circa 275 BC, Fabius Maximus was a Roman general best known for his defeat of Hannibal in the Second Punic War. His primary strategy against Hannibal, as described in Plutarch's *Lives*, was to delay confrontation and to rely on repeated acts of harassment without ever actually joining battle. In satiric tribute to his deployment of these tactics, Fabius was called *Cunctator*, Latin for "delayer." Wisdom also knew that Fabius Maximus was the inspiration for the term *Fabian*, referring to a waiting policy, as evidenced by Wisdom's reference in *Meredith* to the University of Mississippi's "Fabian policy of planned discouragement and discrimination by delay." 305 F.2d at 346.

23. 305 F.2d at 344.

"district court") for his role in abetting the university's strategy of delay and obstruction designed to prevent Meredith, whom Wisdom admiringly described as "a man with a mission and with a nervous stomach," from obtaining a judgment prior to graduating from Jackson State.[24] Moreover, Wisdom acknowledged, "it almost worked."[25] But only "almost," at least as long as he and John Brown were in a position to prevent that unfortunate result. Fortunately for Meredith, they were and they did. The two-John majority ruled that Meredith's application had been rejected solely because of his race pursuant "to a Fabian policy of worrying the enemy into defeat while time worked for the defendants."[26] They ordered Judge Mize to issue an injunction compelling Ole Miss to admit Meredith.[27]

Wisdom's powerful opinion produced equally emphatic reactions on both ends of the ideological spectrum. His colleague, John Brown, wrote Wisdom that the opinion "demonstrates once again that the most powerful statement is a simple statement of fact. It is your capacity to see what those facts are and to portray them honestly, but vividly, that makes this opinion such a great contribution."[28]

Other responses, however, were neither so appreciative nor dispassionate. Although Wisdom, by this time, already had authored several controversial opinions, none of these cut so close to the bone for many southerners as *Meredith*. Only the depth of hostility and fervor that it generated across Dixie matched the breadth of notoriety and public scrutiny that *Meredith* received. Scores of venomous, hate-filled, and typically unsigned and handwritten letters reached Wisdom's home (his home telephone number and address were always listed in the New Orleans phonebook) and office over the weeks following the release of that

24. 305 F.2d at 358.

25. 305 F.2d at 352.

26. 305 F.2d at 343.

27. District Judge DeVane wrote a brief and very narrow dissenting opinion. In his view, Judge Mize had correctly determined that Meredith "bore all the characteristics of becoming a troublemaker if permitted to enter the University of Mississippi" and, therefore, had properly found that Meredith was denied admission on that nonracial ground. 305 F.2d 361 (DeVane, J., dissenting). Before submitting his opinion to the clerk for filing, however, DeVane sent a copy to Judges Wisdom and Brown soliciting their reactions because he was "very anxious that nothing in this dissent be offensive to either of you and if you find any part of it so, please advise me and I will correct it. Psalm 19:12 [Who can discern his errors? Acquit me of hidden faults.]." Letter to John R. Brown and John M. Wisdom from Dozier A. DeVane, June 28, 1962.

28. Letter to John M. Wisdom from John R. Brown, June 20, 1962, at 2.

ruling. In addition to the predictably sarcastic references to *Minor* Wisdom, most of these communications expressed their authors' deep commitment to the preservation of segregation, their profound hatred for nonwhites, and their revulsion toward Wisdom's traitorous, communist-inspired betrayal of southern traditions.

A letter from "Mrs. B., a friend (who was)," for example, complained that "the whole negro race is multiplying like rats—most illegitimates full of venereal disease" and that "you are destroying your own race" because "no negro is equal to a white man!"[29] And an exceedingly more vulgar note was sent from another New Orleanian to "Judge Chicken Shit Wisdom" excoriating him for choosing "to start kissing nigger asses."[30] Wisdom, however, was not terribly bothered by what he and several of his colleagues referred to as "fan mail."[31] In fact, he chose to collect all of them, inventorying them in a "Crank" file that he kept in his chambers.

Yet despite the seemingly unambiguous wording of Wisdom's opinion, Ole Miss was unwilling to let the matter die and voluntarily comply with the court's carefully prepared order. On July 18, fully in keeping with its Fabian policy of delay and harassment, the university applied to Fifth Circuit judge Ben Cameron in Meridian, Mississippi, for an ordering postponing the implementation of the panel's June 25 ruling. Cameron, the Fifth Circuit's most consistently conservative member and a persistent ideological thorn in Wisdom's and Brown's sides, agreed to issue the order that same day, even though Meredith's attorneys were not informed of the request until the following day.[32] This unprecedented act by a single appellate judge of issuing a stay in a case in which he had not participated commenced a battle royal between Cameron and his colleagues, particularly Wisdom.

Constance Baker Motley hurriedly appeared before Judges Brown, Wisdom, and DeVane with a request to dissolve Cameron's order and compel the university to abide by the court's previous directive to admit Meredith. On July 27, two days after Cameron's action, all three members of the panel, including DeVane, who had dissented from the ma-

29. Letter to John Minor Wisdom from Mrs. B., January 7, 1963.

30. Letter to John Minor Wisdom from Joe Jared, May 9, 1963.

31. Letter to John Minor Wisdom from Bryan Simpson, June 24, 1964.

32. Appellant's Motion to Recall the Mandate, Vacate the Stay of July 18, Enter an Injunction Pending Appeal, and Continue in Effect the Injunction of June 12, 1962, filed July 23, 1962, at 3–4.

jority decision ordering Meredith's admission, issued a judgment (the actual order was dated July 28) setting aside Cameron's stay and re-ordering Ole Miss to admit Meredith immediately.[33] The initial version of that judgment had been drafted by John Brown as a *per curiam* decision. But after Wisdom made extensive changes to Brown's proposed ruling, the panel agreed that it should be issued as a signed opinion bearing Wisdom's name.[34] Having previously announced, in his June 25 decision, that "time is of the essence," Wisdom now declared that "time is now of the quintessence."[35] He then proceeded to lambaste Cameron for taking action to frustrate the will of their court. "The Court is bigger than a single judge," Wisdom proclaimed.[36] Moreover, he added, "it is unthinkable that a judge who was not a member of the panel should be allowed to frustrate the mandate of the Court."[37]

This dramatic rebuke by his colleagues did nothing, however, to faze Cameron. Within twenty-four hours, he defiantly issued another stay,[38] granting a request by Charles Clark, a young Jackson attorney who had been specially appointed to assist the Mississippi attorney general in representing the university trustees (and who was nominated to a post on the Fifth Circuit seven years thereafter by President Richard M. Nixon), to issue an order reinstating his previous stay of execution in order to preserve the status quo while the university appealed the case to the U.S. Supreme Court.[39] Cameron insisted that the panel had exceeded its authority by overruling his stay. And just to make sure, the Mississippian issued a third stay order on July 31.[40]

Cameron's actions so outraged Judge Rives that he felt obliged to send a letter to all of his colleagues condemning Cameron's course of conduct. Rives had sat with Wisdom and Tuttle on the initial circuit panel that had reviewed and upheld District Judge Mize's denial of

33. *Meredith v. Fair*, 306 F.2d 374 (5th Cir.2962).

34. Draft opinion in *Meredith v. Fair*.

35. 306 F.2d at 375.

36. 306 F.2d at 376.

37. 306 F.2d at 376.

38. *Meredith v. Fair*, Order Issued on July 28, 1962 by Judge Ben Cameron Staying Execution of Fifth Circuit Judgment of July 27, 1962; Letter to All Judges of the Fifth Circuit from Edward W. Wadsworth, July 30, 1962.

39. Motion of Appellees for Additional Relief Pending Application for Writ of Certiorari, *Meredith v. Fair*, July 30, 1962.

40. Letter to Chief Judge Tuttle and Judges Hutcheson, Rives, Jones, Brown, Wisdom, Gewin, Bell and DeVane from Ben F. Cameron with attached copy of Order Granting Stay, July 31, 1962.

Meredith's request for a preliminary injunction. The fact that his court had never ruled definitively upon the authority of a single judge to issue a stay in a case in which he had not participated, Rives suggested, could be explained by the fact that such conduct was totally without precedent throughout his long tenure on the court. Moreover, Rives predicted, any such attempted action by a single member of the court would not only bring unpleasant repercussions from those judges who had been afforded the opportunity to study the record and rule on the case, but, more important, would "bring disrespect for and loss of prestige of the Court as a whole."[41]

Buoyed by the their respected colleague's declaration, Brown, Wisdom, and DeVane issued another *per curiam* opinion on August 4, vacating Cameron's two additional stays on the ground that they were "unauthorized, erroneous and improvident."[42] Judge Cameron, however, still refused to give in. On August 6, he issued yet a fourth stay, suspending the panel's August 4 judgment and reinstating his previous three stays pending final disposition of the case by the Supreme Court.[43]

At this point, Meredith's attorneys concluded that they had no alternative but to ask the Supreme Court to put a stop to Cameron's rebellion and to order their client's admission to Ole Miss. But as the Court was still in its summer recess, yet a month away from the beginning of its October term, their only option was to request action by the single justice charged with overseeing action by the Fifth Circuit—Alabamian Hugo L. Black. So they filed a motion with Justice Black to enforce the Fifth Circuit's rulings, vacate all of Judge Cameron's stays, and compel Meredith's matriculation.

On September 10, Justice Black granted Meredith's request. In a brief order, Black noted that although he was of the opinion that he was authorized to act alone in the matter, he had canvassed all eight of his brethren and they unanimously concurred in his assessment of his authority. They also agreed with his decision on the merits.[44] Three days

41. Letter to Chief Judge Tuttle and Judges Hutcheson, Cameron, Jones, Brown, Wisdom, Gewin, Bell and DeVane from Richard T. Rives, August 2, 1962, at 2.

42. *Meredith v. Fair*, Order Vacating Previous Stays Issued by Judge Cameron, August 4, 1962; Memorandum for the United States as Amicus Curiae to the Supreme Court of the United States on Motion for Vacation of Stay Orders, August, 1962, at 4.

43. Memorandum for the United States as Amicus Curiae to the Supreme Court of the United States on Motion for Vacation of Stay Orders, August, 1962, at 4.

44. *Meredith v. Fair*, 83 S.Ct. 10, 9 L.Ed.2d 43 (1962) (Black, J.).

later, District Judge Sidney Mize reluctantly issued a permanent injunction ordering Ole Miss to enroll James Meredith, thereby bringing the matter to its litigative conclusion. "This is the end of the road for the University," an exhausted but delighted Connie Motley gleefully announced to the press.[45] Or so she thought.

Ross Robert Barnett was born on January 22, 1898, in Standing Pine, a farming community in the midst of the rolling hill country of Leake County in north-central Mississippi. Like his antagonist, James Meredith, he was one of ten children of a poor farming family in rural Mississippi. But any similarity between these two sons of the South began and ended there. The youngest child of a former Confederate soldier, Barnett received his law degree from the University of Mississippi in 1926. After building up a wildly successful personal-injury trial practice in Jackson and conducting two unsuccessful campaigns for his state's highest office, Barnett was elected governor of Mississippi in November 1959. His single four-year term (his first and only stint in elective office) was devoted to honoring the single campaign theme he had announced at his inauguration: to do whatever was necessary to ensure the maintenance of a racially segregated Mississippi.[46] A fervent proponent of states' rights whom *Time* magazine labeled "as bitter a racist as inhabits the nation," Barnett achieved national notoriety as one of the most vocal and fervent leaders of the forces hell-bent on resisting any and every federal effort at desegregating public institutions.[47]

At 7:30 p.m. on September 13, 1962, just hours after District Judge Sidney Mize grudgingly ordered Ole Miss to admit Meredith, Governor Barnett took to the local television and radio airwaves to proclaim that he would do everything in his power to defy the federal court order.[48] He invoked the previously discredited doctrine of interposition as justification for his promise that "no school in our state will be integrated while I am your Governor."[49] He also announced that he was in-

45. Lord, *The Past That Would Not Die*, 137.

46. "Defiant Dixie Governor: Ross Robert Barnett," *New York Times*, September 20, 1962, 27, col. 2.

47. "Mississippi Mud," *Time*, September 7, 1959, 13.

48. Mize reportedly stated that he had issued the order only because the Fifth Circuit ordered him to do it. "Two Miss. Mix Orders Conflict," *New Orleans States-Item*, September 14, 1962, 1, col. 2; "Mississippi Board Focal Point in Meredith Battle," *New Orleans Times-Picayune*, September 16, 1962, 22, col. 5.

49. Text of Governor Ross Barnett's Proclamation to the People of Mississippi broadcast via

structing all state educational authorities to ignore the federal court orders and to continue to administer all public schools in conformity with state segregation laws, even if that meant going to jail for contempt of court.[50] Within a few hours, under the cover of early morning darkness, a dummy representing James Meredith was hanged from a lamppost in front of the student union building on the Ole Miss campus bearing a sign reading "Hail Barnett."[51] It was but a harbinger of more violent things to come.

The doctrine of interposition upon which Barnett had relied was the doctrinal justification for local resistance to the Supreme Court's 1954 public school desegregation ruling in *Brown v. Board of Education of Topeka*.[52] It was derived from the notion that the United States is a compact of states, any one of which can "interpose" its inherent sovereignty against enforcement of a federal legislative or judicial decision concerning those matters that the state believes have been reserved to state authority by the Tenth Amendment to the U.S. Constitution. Additionally, the doctrine conveniently declares that the determination of whether the challenged federal action invades state sovereignty is the province of the individual states and not the Supreme Court. And the fact that the Supreme Court had unanimously repudiated this concept in 1960, declaring it to be "without substance," did not dissuade Barnett from resurrecting it in his virtual declaration of war against the federal courts, if not against the entire federal government.[53]

With Meredith scheduled to register at Ole Miss on September 20, U.S. attorney general Robert F. Kennedy had only one week to respond to Barnett's threats. Kennedy already had assembled a team of outstanding lawyers to staff the Justice Department, and, in particular, its Civil Rights Division, the group he had assigned to represent the government's position in the Meredith case. Kennedy tapped Burke Mar-

---

TV and radio on September 13, 1962; see also Doyle, *An American Insurrection: The Battle of Oxford, Mississippi, 1962*, 65; "Two Miss. Mix Orders Conflict," *New Orleans States-Item*, September 14, 1962, 1, col. 2; "Barnett Defies Federal Court on Mississippi U. Integration," *New York Times*, September 14, 1962, 15, col. 1.

50. Meredith, *Three Years in Mississippi*, 166–167; "Barnett Defies Federal Court on Mississippi U. Integration," *New York Times*, September 14, 1962, 1, col. 1.

51. "Meredith Hanged in Effigy on Campus," *New Orleans States-Item*, September 14, 1962, 10, col. 4; "Mississippi Charts U.S. Showdown," *Atlanta Constitution*, September 15, 1962, 8, col. 4.

52. 347 U.S. 483, 488, 74 S.Ct. 686, 688, 98 L.Ed. 873 (1954).

53. *U.S. v. State of Louisiana*, 364 U.S. 500, 501, 81 S.Ct. 260, 5 L.Ed.2d 245 (1960).

shall, a brilliant, witty, and unflappable corporate attorney at one of the most prestigious law firms in Washington, D.C., to head the division and shortly after taking over the office, Marshall selected John Doar, a Republican trial attorney, as his top aide and assigned him the task of spearheading division's campaign to ensure that Meredith was admitted to Ole Miss.[54]

On September 15, just a few days after the U.S. Senate confirmed President Kennedy's nomination of NAACP general counsel Thurgood Marshall to the U.S. Second Circuit Court of Appeals, John Doar asked District Judge Mize for permission to intervene directly in the Meredith litigation for the purpose of initiating both civil and criminal contempt of court proceedings against any state official who chose to follow Barnett's direction to defy the court orders to admit Meredith. Mize denied the request on September 18. Within a few hours, St. John Barrett, a Civil Rights Division attorney, appealed that ruling before a Fifth Circuit panel composed of John Brown, John Wisdom, and Griffin B. Bell that was sitting in special session down in Hattiesburg.[55] Later that same day, the panel reversed Mize and granted the Department's request.[56]

Meanwhile, the Mississippi legislature was conspiring with the Ole Miss board of trustees to prevent Meredith from enrolling. The legislature sought to transfer authority over the registration of college students from the board to Governor Barnett while the trustees named Barnett temporary university registrar and voluntarily ceded their authority over all Meredith-related matters to him.[57] The stage was now set for the most dramatic confrontation between state and federal authorities since the Civil War.[58]

On September 20, an unmarked green-and-white border patrol car containing James Meredith, Civil Rights Division attorney St. John Barrett, and three federal marshals made the nearly hundred-mile drive from Millington Air Force Base located just north of Memphis, Tennessee, to Oxford, the site of the main campus of the University of Mis-

54. Lord, *The Past That Would Not Die*, 119–120.

55. Claude Sitton, "Gov. Barnett 'Steadfast' Against Integrating U. of Mississippi," *New York Times*, September 19, 1962, 19, col. 4.

56. W. F. Minor, "Contempt Move Way Is Clear," *New Orleans Times-Picayune*, September 19, 1962, 3, col. 1; Anthony Lewis, "Mississippi Writs Are Asked by U.S.," *New York Times*, September 21, 1962, 12, col. 7; Greenberg, *Crusaders in the Courts*, 322; Order Designating United States of America as *Amicus Curiae* in *Meredith v. Fair*, September 18, 1962.

57. Lord, *The Past That Would Not Die*, 154.

58. "The States: The Edge of Violence," *Time*, October 5, 1962, 15, col. 1.

sissippi. To shield Meredith from the mob of jeering student protesters that had begun massing in front of the pink brick Lyceum, the anticipated site of Meredith's attempt to register, the marshals swiftly ushered him to the university's remotely located and little used Continuation Center. Governor Barnett, who had been waiting in a small anteroom in that building, confronted Meredith in its auditorium. The acting registrar read a copy of his September 13 interposition proclamation to the calm, twenty-nine-year-old air force veteran and proceeded to exit the building to a roar of applause from the appreciative crowd of two thousand students now assembled outside the alumni house adjoining the Continuation Center.[59]

Later that evening, Justice Department attorneys persuaded Judge Mize to sign an order in his Meridian hotel room ordering three Ole Miss officials—the chancellor, the dean of the liberal arts college, and the registrar—to appear before him the very next day to demonstrate ("show cause") why they should not be held in contempt of court for failing to comply with his previous order to admit Meredith to their segregated institution.[60] The following day, the seventy-two-year-old jurist, himself an Ole Miss alumnus, found the three university administrators innocent of contempt.

Undeterred, the Justice Department lawyers sought a separate contempt citation from the Fifth Circuit for the failure of these three officials and the thirteen university trustees to comply with that court's July 28 order to admit Meredith.[61] The panel, composed of Judges Brown, Wisdom, and Bell, responded immediately with a show cause order requiring the university officials to appear before the entire membership of

59. Greenberg, *Crusaders in the Courts*, 323; Lord, *The Past That Would Not Die*, 153–155; W. F. Minor, "Gov. Barnett Takes Role as Registrar," *New Orleans Times-Picayune*, September 21, 1962, 1, col. 8; Claude Sitton, "Negro Rejected at Mississippi U."; "U.S. Seeks Writs," *New York Times*, September 21, 1962, 1, col. 5; Transcript of Hearing Before Fifth Circuit Court of Appeals on Order to Show Cause Why the Board of Governors and Certain University Officials Should Not Be Cited for Civil Contempt, September 24, 1962, 91 [hereinafter Contempt Hearing Transcript].

60. "Meredith Blocked at Ole Miss; Officials Cited for Contempt: Must Appear Today in Federal Court," *New Orleans Times-Picayune*, September 21, 1, col. 4; "13 on College Panel Face Meredith Case Contempt: Hearing Set Monday in Orleans," *New Orleans States-Item*, September 21, 1962, 1, col. 8; Anthony Lewis, "Mississippi—A Crucial Civil Rights Test," *New York Times*, September 23, 1962, 8, col. 1; Lord, *The Past That Would Not Die*, 156.

61. "2 Days Left for Meredith to Register at Ole Miss," *New Orleans States-Item*, September 22, 1962, 1, col. 2; "Ole Miss Case Moves to N.O.," *New Orleans Times-Picayune*, September 24, 1962, 1, col. 5; Anthony Lewis, "9 Judges to Hear Mississippi Case," *New York Times*, September 24, 1962, 1, col. 2.

the Fifth Circuit in New Orleans on the following Monday. All eyes now shifted to Room 222 in the Camp Street post office building in New Orleans where, on Monday morning, September 24, eight of the nine judges of the Fifth Circuit, sitting *en banc,* had assembled. Only Ben Cameron's illness prevented a full complement from attending. And though an appellate court sitting *en banc* rarely conducts a trial, a trial was necessary in this situation because the alleged contempt of court consisted of the defendants' refusal to comply with the Fifth Circuit's own previous order. Nonetheless, the extraordinary presence of the entire court at a proceeding involving the introduction of witness testimony manifested the judges' collective sense of the significance of the issues raised by this confrontation between the state and federal governments.

After an all-day hearing, Chief Judge Tuttle announced that his colleagues unanimously had agreed that the university trustees had willfully violated the court's prior order. But when the trustees' counsel assured the court that his clients would comply promptly and in a timely fashion with any court order, a relieved Tuttle announced that the court would not issue any contempt finding against the trustees as long as they did everything within their power to carry out the court's previous order by no later than 4:00 p.m. the following day and withdraw the authority they had delegated to Governor Barnett over Meredith's admission.[62] But the trustees did not and could not speak for Governor Barnett, who was embarking upon his most aggressively rebellious step yet to force the Justice Department's hand and to set up Wisdom and his colleagues as the ultimate arbiters of Barnett's duel with the federal government.

At the same moment that the Fifth Circuit was hearing arguments in the contempt proceeding against the university trustees, Barnett was signing an Executive Order mandating the immediate arrest of any federal officer who sought to arrest or fine any Mississippi official for defying court desegregation decrees. The governor simultaneously summoned a formidable array of state and local law enforcement personnel to Oxford to prepare for the now-unavoidable clash with federal authori-

62. Order by Fifth Circuit *en banc* in *Meredith v. Fair,* September 24, 1962; Contempt Hearing Transcript, at 225–243; Hedrick Smith, "Court Is Obeyed: College Trustees Heed 8 Judges' Demand Made at Hearing," *New York Times,* September 25, 1962, 1, col. 8; Greenberg, *Crusaders in the Courts,* 324.

ties.[63] These defiant actions, in turn, impelled the Justice Department to seek additional assistance from the Fifth Circuit, even though they knew full well that this ultimately would produce precisely the result that they had sought to avoid. Although they needed the court to prevent Barnett from carrying out his threats against the federal authorities, they also recognized that the governor would ignore such an order in precisely the same way that he had defied the court's original injunction to enroll Meredith. But such a second act of disobedience could not be ignored; the federal attorneys would have to institute a contempt proceeding against him. And this, of course, was precisely what the martyrdom-seeking demagogue wanted. At 8:30 the following morning, September 25, the wheels were put in motion. A panel composed of Judges Tuttle, Rives, and Wisdom granted the federal government's ambivalent request and issued a sweeping restraining order that enjoined all Mississippi officeholders, including Barnett, from interfering in any way with Meredith's registration.[64]

Later that afternoon, Meredith, chief U.S. marshall James McShane, and John Doar flew from New Orleans to Jackson on a federal border patrol plane to complete the registration process in the university trustees' tenth-floor headquarters.[65] But when Meredith arrived at the entry to Room 1007, he found Governor Barnett standing in front of the door, literally interposing himself between the federal officials accompanying Meredith and the university board of trustees. Then, after twice refusing to accept a copy of the Fifth Circuit's restraining order from Doar, Barnett read a proclamation declaring that he was interposing the

63. Claude Sitton, "Barnett Defiant: Threatens to Jail U.S. Aides if They Seize Officials of State," *New York Times*, September 25, 1962, 1, col. 7.

64. "U.S. Moves to Block Barnett," *New York Times*, September 25, 1962, 26, col. 4; "Obey State Laws, Says Gov. Barnett," *New Orleans States-Item*, September 25, 1962, 1, col. 8; Greenberg, *Crusaders in the Courts*, 325; Temporary Restraining Order, *Meredith v. Fair*, September 25, 1962. The following day, in Barnett's absence, his lieutenant governor, Paul B. Johnson, physically prevented Meredith and his Justice Department envoy from entering the campus. That evening the Rives-Brown-Wisdom panel also found him in contempt. Although all of the subsequent contempt actions discussed in this chapter actually involved both Barnett and Johnson, since the prime actor in this drama was Governor Barnett, the discussion of these events refers only to him.

65. According to NAACP Legal Defense Fund chief Jack Greenberg, whenever Meredith boarded this government plane, an identical aircraft also took off from the same airstrip to act as a decoy to confuse anyone who might have harbored ideas of shooting down Meredith's plane. Greenberg, *Crusaders in the Courts*, 325. See also Doyle, *An American Insurrection: The Battle of Oxford, Mississippi, 1962*, 77; Meredith, *Three Years in Mississippi*, 194.

state sovereignty of Mississippi in order to "finally deny" Meredith admission to the university.[66]

The Justice Department now had no choice but to seek a contempt citation against Barnett from the Fifth Circuit. At 8:20 p.m., less than four hours after the showdown in Jackson, a Fifth Circuit panel in New Orleans composed of Dick Rives, John Wisdom, and Walter Gewin issued an order directing Governor Barnett to appear before the entire court sitting *en banc* at 10:00 a.m. on Friday, September 28, to show why he should not be held in contempt of that court. When a telegraphed copy of the contempt summons was delivered to Barnett's Jackson office, the governor disdainfully refused to accept it. He also stationed a squadron of state troopers directly in front of his office to prevent anyone from physically serving him with the contempt summons.[67] Then he thumbed his nose directly at the Fifth Circuit by refusing to appear at the show cause hearing.

With all members but the ailing Ben Cameron present, and in the absence of any attorney representing the governor, the court heard argument from the Justice Department attorneys and Meredith's lawyers on September 28 and unanimously found Barnett in civil contempt of court for defying its previous orders mandating the Meredith's admission to Ole Miss.[68] Its brief but unequivocal order, released at 5:00 p.m.,

66. Sitton, "Meredith Rebuffed Again Despite Restraining Order," *New York Times*, September 26, 1962, 1, col. 6; "Federal Court Order and 2 Barnett Proclamations," *New York Times*, September 26, 1962, 22, col. 8; W. F. Minor, "Meredith Is Blocked Again in Mississippi," *New Orleans Times-Picayune*, September 26, 1962, 1, col. 6; 3, col. 1; Lord, *The Past That Would Not Die*, 160–162; Doyle, *An American Insurrection: The Battle of Oxford, Mississippi, 1962*, 82; Meredith, *Three Years In Mississippi*, 195–196.

67. Hedrick Smith, "Barnett Ordered to Face U.S. Court," *New York Times*, September 26, 1962, 1, col. 7; "Gov. Barnett Ordered into U.S. Court Friday," *New Orleans Times-Picayune*, September 26, 1962, 1, col. 8; "Text of Appeal Court's Order to Gov. Barnett," *New Orleans Times-Picayune*, September 26, 1962, 2, col. 3; "Barnett Rejects Notice of U.S. Court Order," *New Orleans States-Item*, September 26, 1962, at 1, col. 8; "Governor Ordered into Court Friday," *Atlanta Constitution*, September 26, 1962, 1, col. 5; "Lt. Gov. Johnson of Miss. Ordered to Appear in Court," *New Orleans Times-Picayune*, September 27, 1962, 1, col. 6; Hedrick Smith, "Barnett Eludes U.S. Effort to Serve Court Summons," *New York Times*, September 27, 1962, 1, col. 6; 28, col. 5; "Troopers Block Ole Miss Doors," *Atlanta Constitution*, September 27, 1962, 1, col. 6. The Fifth Circuit show cause order, initially issued at the request of the Justice Department, was reissued on Wednesday at the request of Meredith's attorneys. "Texts of Court of Appeals Orders Issued to Barnett," *New York Times*, September 27, 1962, 28, col. 5.

68. Cameron previously had been diagnosed with congestive heart failure and had been advised by his physician not to attend any court sittings or conferences "which would entail controversy or excitement." Figuring that this *en banc* contempt hearing on September 28 met that stan-

stated that unless Barnett purged himself of the contempt by obeying the court's antecedent directives no later than 11:00 a.m. on the following Tuesday, October 2, he would be arrested by and placed in the custody of federal authorities. The court's order also stated that criminal contempt proceedings could be asserted against the governor at a later date. Finally, five of the eight judges also concluded that Barnett should be assessed a fine of $10,000 per day until he complied with all of the court's orders and instructed all law enforcement officers under his command to do the same.[69]

The next day, Saturday, September 29, President John F. Kennedy was on the phone with Ross Barnett in a final desperate effort to put an end to this escalating constitutional crisis. But after three separate conversations over the course of the day, the president failed to obtain any assurance that Barnett would either bow to the federal court orders or assure Meredith's safety in the event he made another attempt to enroll at the university. So JFK decided to raise the ante. Just after midnight, in the White House's Indian Treaty Room, he signed Proclamation No. 3497 ordering all citizens of Mississippi to end their defiance of federal law. He also inked an implementing Executive Order placing the 11,000-strong Mississippi National Guard under federal control and authorizing the secretary of defense, Robert S. McNamara, to take any other measures, including the mobilization of the armed forces, he deemed necessary to enforce the court mandates.[70]

In the early morning hours of Sunday, September 30, as part of that initial mobilization, a battalion of nearly two hundred paratroopers from Fort Bragg, North Carolina, flew to a staging area at the Naval Air Station located eighteen miles north of Memphis. They were joined

dard, Cameron informed his colleagues that he would not be able to attend. Letter to All Judges of the Fifth Circuit from Ben C. Cameron, September 22, 1962.

69. Warren Jones, Walter Gewin, and Griffin Bell dissented from the part of the order that imposed a fine on Barnett. "Text of Court Ruling Given," *New Orleans Times-Picayune*, September 29, 1962, 13, col. 1; Hendrick Smith, "Gov. Barnett, in Contempt, Faces Arrest and Fine of $10,000 a Day Unless He Obeys U.S. By Tuesday: 8 Judges Convict," *New York Times*, September 29, 1962, 1, col. 8.

70. "Text of Kennedy Orders on Mississippi Situation," *New Orleans Times-Picayune*, October 1, 1962, 3, col. 1; "Guard Ordered to Go to Oxford," *New Orleans Times-Picayune*, October 1, 1962, 20, col. 1; "Text of Proclamation by the President," *New York Times*, October 1, 1962, 22, col. 2; "Kennedy Telegram and Executive Order," *New York Times*, October 1, 1962, 22, col. 6; Lord, *The Past That Would Not Die*, 190.

there by nearly five hundred federal marshals. At the same time, a battle group of the Second Infantry Division stationed in Fort Benning, Georgia, was placed on alert for possible assignment to Oxford. The number of army troops, federal marshals, and others poised for deployment in Oxford now had swelled to nearly six thousand and been placed under the overall command of Major General Creighton W. Abrams, the army deputy chief of staff for military operations.[71] Robert Kennedy had spoken with Barnett on four separate occasions during the course of the preceding day and evening, but, just like the president, had been unable to convince the governor to accede to the demands of the federal courts. So with an overwhelming force now at his disposal, the thirty-six-year-old attorney general finally gave the order to the military forces to enforce the court decrees.[72]

By 5:30 p.m. on Sunday, more than two thousand students were milling about the campus, many of them having recently returned from the state capital, where the university's football team had defeated the University of Kentucky on Saturday night. While the crowd waited for what everyone expected to be a dramatic confrontation, a convoy of seven olive-drab army trucks carrying 350 steel-helmeted federal marshals and other civilian federal officers (but no military troops) passed by a squadron of highway patrolmen who were anxiously standing guard at the Sorority Row entrance. Rolling past stately sorority houses, the trucks reached their destination, the white-columned Lyceum, without resistance. There, the soldiers lined up shoulder to shoulder, completely encircling the three-story administration building that housed the registrar's office.[73]

71. "JFK Gathers Forces, Issues Proclamation: Miss. Guard Federalized; Army on Move," *New Orleans Times-Picayune*, September 30, 1962, 1, col. 8; 30, col. 1; "Federal Troops Massing at a Base near Memphis," *New York Times*, September 30, 1962, 1, col. 6; Anthony Lewis, "Acts at Midnight: President Holds Talks with Gov. Barnett but to No Avail," *New York Times*, September 30, 1962, 1, col. 8; Raymond J. Crowley, "Obey Law, JFK's Appeal to Miss.," *New Orleans Times-Picayune*, October 1, 1962, 1, col. 5; "Mississippi Guard Units Ordered to Go to Ole Miss," *New Orleans Times-Picayune*, October 1, 1962, 1, col. 6; "Build-Up Mounts at Memphis Base," *New York Times*, October 1, 1962, 24, col. 5.

72. Anthony Lewis, "President Asks Mississippi to Comply with U.S. Laws," *New York Times*, October 1, 1962, 1, col. 6; 22, col. 1.

73. "Miss. Troops Fire over Oxford Mob; Meredith Is Enrolled for Classes: Nab Walker for Inciting Rebellion," *New Orleans States-Item*, October 1, 1962, 1, col. 3; 6, col. 1; "Two Are Killed, Troops Arrive; Barnett Apparently Yielding," *New Orleans Times-Picayune*, October 1, 1962, 1, col. 8; 2, col. 1; 5, col. 3; Whitey Shoemaker, "Kennedy Moves Quickly as Pleas to Barnett Fail," *New Orleans Times-Picayune*, October 1, 1962, 11, col. 1; "Report Barnett Capitulation Led U.S. to Move

Minutes before 8:00 p.m., just as President Kennedy was preparing to give a nationally televised address on the Mississippi conflict, James Meredith finally set foot on the Ole Miss campus. Accompanied by deputy U.S. attorney general Nicholas deB. Katzenbach, John Doar, and a host of other federal officials, Meredith drove from the Oxford airport in a green Plymouth sedan through the campus's little-used West Gate and arrived virtually undetected at the Baxter Hall dormitory on the northwest edge of the campus. He swiftly ascended to the second floor and entered the two-bedroom counselor's apartment that he would share temporarily with Doar. The contingent of federal marshals who would become Meredith's constant campus companions occupied the adjoining room. Meanwhile, back in Jackson, Ross Barnett was hunkered down in the Governor's Mansion while a crowd of over two thousand men, women, and children ringed the residence for the express purpose of shielding their governor from arrest.[74]

In contrast to Meredith's practically unnoticed entry, the unmistakable presence of the marshals on campus triggered an immediate and violent reaction. At 7:58 p.m., as darkness fell over the campus, a group of students driving a bulldozer that they had commandeered from the nearby construction site of a new science center, trailed by other students driving a fire truck, and yet others following behind on foot and waving Confederate flags, surged directly toward the human barricade the marshals had formed around the university's administration building. The marshals responded by unleashing a torrent of tear gas in the students' direction. About a thousand students then charged the mar-

---

Meredith onto Campus," *New Orleans States-Item,* October 1, 1962, 3, col. 5; George B. Leonard, T. George Harris, and Christopher S. Wren, "How a Secret Deal Prevented a Massacre at Ole Miss," *Look,* December 31, 1962, 24.

74. "Two Are Killed, Troops Arrive; Barnett Apparently Yielding," *New Orleans Times-Picayune,* October 1, 1962, 1, col. 8; 2, col. 1; 5, col. 3; Shoemaker, "Kennedy Moves Quickly as Pleas to Barnett Fail," *New Orleans Times-Picayune,* October 1, 1962, 11, col. 1; Anthony Lewis, "President Asks Mississippi to Comply with U.S. Laws," *New York Times,* October 1, 1962, 1, col. 6; 22, col. 1; Sitton, "Tear Gas Is Used: Mob Attacks Officers—2,500 Troops Are Sent to Oxford," *New York Times,* October 1, 1962, 1, col. 7; 23, col. 6; Thomas Buckley, "Tear Gas and Sticks Repel Wild Student Charges," *New York Times,* October 1, 1962, 23, col. 4; Hedrick Smith, "2,000 in Jackson 'Guard' Barnett," *New York Times,* October 1, 1962, 23, col. 5; McCandlish Phillips, "Campus a Bivouac as Negro Enters," *New York Times,* October 2, 1962, 1, col. 8; "Meredith Booed in Halls; 16,000 GIs Keep Peace," *Atlanta Constitution,* October 3, 1962, 1, col. 5; "The States: Through the Heavens Fall," *Time,* October 12, 1962, 19, 20; Greenberg, *Crusaders in the Courts,* 330; Lord, *The Past That Would Not Die,* 203.

shals, pelting them with bottles, rocks, and bricks. The marshals countered with another volley of tear gas, while other students sprayed the marshals with fire extinguishers, torched and vandalized military vehicles, and attacked several cameramen and reporters.

In the midst of this chaos on what became known as "Bloody Sunday," around 9:00 p.m., all of the two hundred state troopers that Governor Barnett had detailed to the campus to maintain order and to provide security for Meredith, along with the federal marshals, abruptly and inexplicably departed. The peace officers disappeared even as a thirty-year-old reporter for a French news agency was bleeding to death about 165 yards northeast of the Lyceum, alongside a women's dormitory, shot in the back by a .38 pistol from an unidentified assassin, the first casualty of the Battle of Oxford. That same evening, Ray Gunter, a twenty-three-year-old jukebox repairman from nearby Abbeville, became the rioters' second victim when he died after being shot in the forehead by a .38. The campus now had been transformed into a virtual battlefield—the central quadrangle surrounding the Lyceum not only strewn with wrecked vehicles, chunks of concrete, and scores of tear gas canisters and broken Coke bottles, but also enveloped by a stifling odor and blanketed with a thick pall of smoke, the lingering remnants of the tear gas barrage. Robert Kennedy could no longer avoid an escalated demonstration of military force. Pursuant to his order, trucks carrying nearly two hundred military policemen and five jeeps loaded with a detachment of federalized Mississippi National Guardsmen from Tupelo sped onto the campus after midnight.[75]

75. "Two Are Killed, Troops Arrive; Barnett Apparently Yielding," New Orleans Times-Picayune, October 1, 1962, 1, col. 8; 2, col. 1; 5, col. 3; Sitton, "Tear Gas Is Used: Mob Attacks Officers—2,500 Troops Are Sent to Oxford," New York Times, October 1, 1962, 1, col. 7; 23, col. 6; "French Reporter in U.S. Two Years," New York Times, October 1, 1962, 23, col. 8; Bill Shipp, "Marshal Is Wounded: Ex-General Hails Mob," Atlanta Constitution, October 1, 1962, 1, col. 7; 9, col. 1; "Miss. Troops Fire over Oxford Mob; Meredith Is Enrolled for Classes: Nab Walker for Inciting Rebellion," New Orleans States-Item, October 1, 1962, 1, col. 3; 6, col. 1; W. F. Minor, "Troops Hold Rigid Control at Oxford," New Orleans Times-Picayune, October 2, 1962, 1, col. 7; Gardner L. Bridge, "Police Pullout Blamed By RFK," New Orleans Times-Picayune, October 2, 1962, 1, col. 5; 3, col. 6; Sitton, "Shots Quell Mob: Enrolling of Meredith Ends Segregation in State Schools," New York Times, October 2, 1962, 1, col. 8; 21, col. 6; "Kennedy Is Dismayed by Killing of French Newsman during Riots," New York Times, October 2, 1962, 27, col. 5; Thomas Buckley, "Action at Oxford Is Re-created by Chief of Army Detachment," New York Times, October 4, 1962, 29, col. 1; Doyle, An American Insurrection: The Battle of Oxford, Mississippi, 1962, 138, 163; George B. Leonard, T. George Harris, and Christopher S. Wren, "How a Secret Deal Prevented a Massacre at Ole Miss," Look, December 31, 1962, 30.

Just before the federal troops arrived on campus, however, Governor Barnett released a statement from the Governor's Mansion in Jackson. As part of a pledge he had made to Attorney General Kennedy over the telephone earlier that day, Barnett promised the citizens of Mississippi that he would carry on his crusade in the courts to prevent the involuntary integration of Ole Miss. But he also acknowledged that Mississippi was powerless to withstand the onslaught from the federal government's overwhelming military forces. Accordingly, at 8:15 a.m. on Monday, October 1, University Registrar Robert Ellis formally registered James Meredith as a transfer student in the College of Liberal Arts, the first African American knowingly admitted to the university in its 114-year history. Flanked by a pair of federal marshals, the incipient political science major quickly exited the Lyceum past a throng of about fifty jeering students to attend Professor Clare L. Marquette's colonial history class that morning and a Spanish course in the afternoon.[76]

Some observers predicted that Ross Barnett's midnight announcement signaled his permanent acquiescence to Meredith's presence at the state university. Nothing could have been further from the truth. Barnett remained as intransigent as ever. On Monday evening, only hours before the Fifth Circuit's 11:00 a.m. deadline for purging himself of his contempt of court conviction, NBC broadcast across the nation a previously taped address in which Governor Barnett called for Meredith's immediate removal from the campus. He also placed all blame for the violent and bloody riots on the Ole Miss campus on President Kennedy for dispatching "inexperienced, nervous—you might say trigger-happy" federal troops to "invade" the Magnolia State.[77]

It now was up to the Fifth Circuit to decide what, if anything, to do

76. Text of Barnett Statement, *New York Times*, October 1, 1962, 23, col. 4; "Miss. Troops Fire over Oxford Mob; Meredith Is Enrolled for Classes: Nab Walker for Inciting Rebellion," *New Orleans States-Item*, October 1, 1962, 1, col. 3; "Report Barnett Capitulation Led U.S. to Move Meredith onto Campus," *New Orleans States-Item*, October 1, 1962, 3, col. 5; W. F. Minor, "Troops Hold Rigid Control at Oxford," *New Orleans Times-Picayune*, October 2, 1962, 1, col. 7; Tom Pendergast, "Meredith Has Uneventful Day in First Classes," *New Orleans Times-Picayune*, October 2, 1962, 17, col. 2; McCandlish Phillips, "Campus a Bivouac as Negro Enters," *New York Times*, October 2, 1962, 1, col. 8; 26, col. 1; Doyle, *An American Insurrection: The Battle of Oxford, Mississippi, 1962*, 257–259.

77. "President Blamed for Miss. Violence," *New Orleans Times-Picayune*, October 2, 1962, 1, col. 8; Text of Barnett Speech on Ole Miss Issue Given, *New Orleans Times-Picayune*, October 2, 1962, 14, col. 4; Hedrick Smith, "Barnett Charges Marshals Erred," *New York Times*, October 2, 1962, 1, col. 7; Text of a Statement by Gov. Barnett, *New York Times*, October 2, 1962, 25, col. 6.

to the governor. Ross Barnett had not demonstrated the slightest intention of meeting the rapidly approaching Tuesday morning deadline for purging his previous contempt. At precisely 11:00 a.m. on Tuesday, while scores of Rebel flag–waving Barnett loyalists encircled the Governor's Mansion in downtown Jackson to thwart the rumored arrest of their leader, a Fifth Circuit panel composed of Judges Rives, Wisdom, and Gewin assembled in the Federal Building on Lafayette Square in New Orleans to hear arguments in the contempt proceeding. Once again, Barnett chose not to attend, although this time he did send counsel to argue on his behalf. Presiding Judge Rives informed counsel that because five of the six other Fifth Circuit judges were hearing arguments in cases in Houston and Jacksonville, and as Judge Cameron was too ill to attend, it was impossible for an *en banc* court to be reconstituted before October 12. But he also informed the lawyers that all of the absent members other than Cameron had been polled by telephone and had agreed to delay further action in the civil contempt proceeding until they could reconvene *en banc*. In the meantime, the court issued an order vacating contempt proceedings against the university administrators and the board of trustees in light of their compliance with the court's previous orders.[78]

The court reassembled as scheduled in New Orleans on Friday, October 12. With Judge Hutcheson no longer able to actively participate in the case because of his frail health, and Ben Cameron similarly incapacitated, the *en banc* panel now had been reduced to seven judges. Once again, the defense lawyers appeared without their client, but on this occasion they did not offer any evidence relating to the governor's conduct subsequent to the issuance of the Fifth Circuit's initial civil contempt judgment. The Justice Department lawyers, on the other hand, acknowledged that Governor Barnett finally had abandoned his direct efforts at barring Meredith from enrolling at Ole Miss and that neither he nor any state agent under his control physically or otherwise prevented Meredith from entering the campus or registering as a student. Nevertheless, they

78. "Barnett Case Ruling Delayed by U.S. Court," *New Orleans Times-Picayune*, October 3, 1962, 1, col. 8; "Scores of Mississippians Guard Barnett Mansion," *New Orleans Times-Picayune*, October 3, 1962, 5, col. 6; Foster Hailey, "Barnett Contempt Case Put Off, Court Clears University's Aides; Campus Calm, 3,500 Troops Leave," *New York Times*, October 3, 1962, 1, col. 8; 29, col. 1; Texts of Court's Orders, *New York Times*, October 3, 1962, 29, col. 3; Carl P. Leubsdorf, "Governor Must Yield in 10 Days," *Atlanta Constitution*, October 3, 1962, 1, col. 8; 10, col. 1; Hearing on Return on Contempt Citations Issued against Governor Ross R. Barnett and Lieutenant Governor Paul B. Johnson, October 2, 1962.

maintained that Barnett had not fully purged himself of civil contempt because he had failed to order the police to abide by the court's order to maintain law and order around the university and to ensure that Meredith was treated like all other students. The hearing terminated with Chief Judge Tuttle informing the attorneys that a judgment would be released after all of the judges had an opportunity to read and consider the briefs filed by both sides.[79]

On the following Monday, October 15, Tuttle circulated a proposed judgment to his colleagues that adopted the Justice Department's position that Barnett had not fully purged himself of the contempt and ordered federal authorities to arrest him until he complied fully with the court's previous orders. This proposed order also, however, provided that his arrest would be delayed until October 24 to give him time to appeal this ruling to the Supreme Court.[80] But the draft elicited immediate and forceful objections from several quarters. John Brown and Dick Rives insisted that Barnett had complied with the gravamen of the court's orders by permitting Meredith to enroll and attend classes and that imposing further contempt sanctions would yield no practical value, particularly when Tuttle's proposal did not detail with specificity the precise actions that Barnett would have to take to be released from jail.[81] So Brown issued an alternative order stating that Barnett had partially purged himself of the civil contempt but mandating his arrest by federal authorities until he rescinded his proclamations, ordered all state officials to comply fully with all federal court orders, and filed a signed statement with the court promising to comply with all of its orders.[82] Warren Jones and Walter Gewin, on the other hand, urged that the undisputed fact of Meredith's registration should trump the unrepentant attitude reflected in Barnett's public declarations, and that the court should not attempt to humiliate the state's chief executive.[83]

79. "Barnett Denies Contempt Guilt; 'Conscience Clear' on Legal Duty," New York Times, October 17, 1962, 1, col. 3; 20, col. 4.

80. First Draft of Findings of Fact, Order, and Judgment on Hearing to Afford Ross R. Barnett an Opportunity to Purge Himself of Civil Contempt, Meredith v. Fair; Letter to Judges Rives, Jones, Brown, Wisdom, Gewin, and Bell from Chief Judge Elbert P. Tuttle, October 15, 1962.

81. Letter to Judges Tuttle, Jones, Wisdom, Gewin, and Bell from John R. Brown and Richard T. Rives, October 16, 1962.

82. Judge Brown's Rough Draft of Proposed Order on Hearing to Afford Ross R. Barnett an Opportunity to Purge Himself of Civil Contempt; Letter to Judges Tuttle, Rives, Jones, Wisdom, Gewin, and Bell from John R. Brown, October 17, 1962.

83. Letter to Judges Tuttle, Rives, Jones, Brown, Wisdom, and Bell from Walter P. Gewin, Oc-

Any likelihood that the court could coalesce around a compromise order and thereby avoid the convening of another *en banc* meeting vanished when Wisdom distributed a memorandum announcing that he could not join in either Tuttle's or Brown's proposal. As far as he was concerned, imprecise language contained in each of these drafts was likely to generate insuperable interpretive problems.

So the seven available judges reconvened in New Orleans on Friday, October 19. Wisdom's detailed handwritten notes of the conference reveal that the court was unable to arrive at any consensus. Each member simply reiterated his previously articulated views. Judges Tuttle, Brown, and Wisdom maintained that upholding the honor of the court and fidelity to the rule of law compelled both a finding that Barnett remained in partial civil contempt and an express listing of specific and stringent requirements of future actions on his part as a condition for his release from custody. Judges Gewin, Bell, and Jones, on the other hand, continued to argue that substantial compliance had, in fact, occurred, that achieving compliance with court orders, rather than punishment, was the objective of a civil contempt proceeding, and that no good purpose would be served by punishing or humiliating the governor by taking him into custody and requiring him either to rescind his prior proclamations or to submit a signed promise of future good behavior. And Dick Rives self-consciously admitted that he continued to "flip and flop" between the two camps.[84]

That evening, after the judges had retired to their hotel rooms, Tuttle drafted a dramatically toned-down version of his draft order. This proposal declared that since Meredith had been enrolled and was attending classes, no further sanctions would be imposed on the governor in the immediate future. Nevertheless, it also specified that the court reserved the right to take further action if warranted by the governor's future conduct, including the consideration of criminal contempt charges.[85] This compromise elicited the support of Wisdom, Brown, and Bell, which constituted a majority of four. Judges Gewin, Jones, and Rives,

---

tober 17, 1962 (with attached draft dissenting opinion); Letter to Judges Tuttle, Rives, Brown, Wisdom, Gewin, and Bell from Warren L. Jones, October 17, 1972.

84. Handwritten notes by John Minor Wisdom during Fifth Circuit conference of October 19, 1962.

85. Rough Draft of Proposed Order on Hearing to Afford Ross R. Barnett an Opportunity to Purge Himself of Civil Contempt; Letter from Chief Judge Elbert P. Tuttle to Judges Rives, Jones, Brown, Wisdom, Gewin, and Bell, October 25, 1962.

however, remained dissatisfied and tendered their own dissenting opinions.[86] Two days later, however, the world changed.

At 7:00 p.m. on Monday evening, October 22, President Kennedy delivered a televised address to the country in which he informed a startled nation of the confirmed presence of Soviet missile sites and nuclear-capable bombers in Cuba. He warned the Soviet government that any nuclear missile launched from Cuba against any nation in the Western Hemisphere would be deemed an attack upon the United States, and announced the initiation of an American naval blockade of Cuba that imposed a quarantine on all incoming offensive military equipment and that would turn back all Cuba-bound ships found to contain cargoes of offensive weapons to their port of origin.

With the country teetering on the brink of nuclear war, Tuttle dispatched a letter to his six colleagues suggesting that the court defer making or issuing any decision in the Barnett contempt case to avoid ordering the imprisonment of a governor at a time when international events required "a great degree of solidarity behind the efforts of the President."[87] Tuttle hoped, however, that when the time was ripe, an opinion could be drafted that would produce greater than a one-vote majority of the seven participating judges. So, as he often did in cases of moment, Tuttle turned to Wisdom, who readily agreed to accept this assignment.[88] But before he could share his effort with the other judges, Judge Rives threw a monkey wrench into the operation.[89]

Rives repeatedly had switched sides between the triad—Tuttle, Brown, and Wisdom—who believed that Barnett should be jailed for his continued acts of civil contempt and the trio—Gewin, Jones, and Bell—who insisted that imprisonment was unnecessary in light of Barnett's eventual acquiescence to Meredith's registration and continued presence at Ole Miss.[90] On November 5, Rives circulated an alternative solution to the Barnett controversy predicated on the notion that although

86. Letter to Elbert P. Tuttle from Richard T. Rives, October 20, 1962; Letter to Elbert P. Tuttle from John M. Wisdom, October 22, 1962; Letter to Judges Brown and Wisdom from Griffin B. Bell October 25, 1962.

87. Letter to Judges Rives, Jones, Brown, Wisdom, Gewin, and Bell from Chief Judge Elbert P. Tuttle, October 25, 1962.

88. Letter to John M. Wisdom from Elbert P. Tuttle, November 1, 1962.

89. See handwritten and typed draft opinion prepared by Judge John M. Wisdom.

90. On October 24, Rives sent a letter to the other six members of the en banc court apologizing for his indecision and announcing that the proposed dissenting opinion by Warren Jones had "brought me back around" to concluding that sanctions were not needed to secure compliance by

imprisoning the governor no longer was a practicable remedy in the civil contempt proceeding, Barnett's previous acts of defiance could support a charge of *criminal* contempt of court. He proposed that the Fifth Circuit consider issuing a criminal contempt citation and either terminate the civil proceeding or proceed jointly with both contempt citations against the governor. He conceded, however, that this would "be a serious step" and presciently observed that instituting criminal contempt proceedings would force the court to address two difficult questions. Would Barnett be entitled to a jury trial on the charges? And, if so, should such a trial be conducted by the circuit court *en banc* or by the three-member panel (Tuttle, Rives, and Wisdom) that had issued the September 25 restraining order that Barnett had disobeyed?[91]

Rives's proposal drew an instantly favorable response from everyone except Gewin. On November 15, the other six members (Judges Hutcheson and Cameron remained sidelined for health reasons) signed a decree ordering the U.S. attorney general to institute and prosecute criminal contempt proceedings against Governor Barnett. The order made no mention of the pending civil contempt charges. Tuttle pleaded strenuously with Gewin to join his other colleagues so that the court could present a unified public face on this grave matter during this trying time of national uncertainty. But Gewin could not be persuaded and insisted that the order reflect his lone dissenting vote.[92]

On December 21, in accordance with the court's judgment, the Justice Department filed an application for an order requiring Barnett to show cause why he should not be held in criminal contempt of the Fifth Circuit. As evidence of the significance attached to this proceeding by the Justice Department, this document was signed not only by John Doar, the Justice Department attorney assigned to the case, but by Attorney General Robert Kennedy and Assistant Attorney General Burke Marshall.[93]

Governor Barnett. Letter to Judges Tuttle, Jones, Brown, Wisdom, Gewin, and Bell from Richard T. Rives, October 24, 1962.

91. Letter to Elbert P. Tuttle from Richard T. Rives, November 5, 1962.

92. Letter to Judges Rives, Jones, Brown, Wisdom, Gewin, and Bell from Chief Judge Elbert P. Tuttle, November 8, 1962; Letter to Judges Rives, Jones, Brown, Wisdom, Gewin, and Bell from Chief Judge Elbert P. Tuttle, November 12, 1962; Letter to Elbert P. Tuttle from Walter P. Gewin, November 15, 1962; Order in Meredith v. Fair, November 15, 1962.

93. Application for an Order Requiring Ross R. Barnett and Paul B. Johnson, Jr., to Show Cause Why They Should Not Be Held in Criminal Contempt, December 21, 1962.

After extensive intra-circuit correspondence, every member of the court except for Judge Jones agreed that the criminal contempt proceeding should be conducted by the court *en banc,* and that both Judges Cameron and Hutcheson should be allowed to participate.[94] Cameron not only agreed, but affirmatively sought to take part in the proceedings. The court subsequently acceded to Hutcheson's request to be excused from any further role in the matter since he had become physically unable to leave Houston.[95] On January 3, 1963, the court granted the Justice Department's request and set the case for hearing in New Orleans at 9:30 a.m. on Friday, February 8.[96]

The eight-member *en banc* court heard several hours of spirited argument on February 8 and spent most of Saturday in conference to determine how they were going to proceed.[97] All but one member of the octet agreed without difficulty to deny Barnett's request to dismiss the criminal contempt proceedings. In light of Cameron's previous role in the Meredith saga—issuing four stays designed to enjoin the implementation of the court's order to admit Meredith to Ole Miss and not participating in the court's *en banc* decision to find Barnett in civil contempt—it came as no surprise that he was the solitary dissenter.

But the court was significantly less united on the question of whether Barnett was entitled to a trial by jury. On this critical matter, the court split right down the middle. Tuttle, Rives, Brown, and Wisdom were of the view that the defendants did not enjoy a right to jury trial, while Cameron, Jones, Gewin, and Bell took the opposite position. With Hutcheson not participating, the court was deadlocked. And the case could not move forward unless and until this issue was resolved. This particularly troubled Wisdom and the three other members of the Tuttle quartet, all of whom were exceedingly anxious to avoid further delay and come to closure on this important case. To break the deadlock, all eight members agreed to invoke a procedure that never had been

94. Jones believed that the contempt hearing was a new proceeding and should be assigned to a three-member panel of the court. Letter to Judges Tuttle, Hutcheson, Rives, Cameron, Brown, Wisdom, Gewin, and Bell from Warren L. Jones, January 2, 1963.

95. Letter to Judges Tuttle, Hutcheson, Rives, Jones, Brown, Wisdom, Gewin, and Bell from Ben F. Cameron, December 31, 1962; Letter to Elbert P. Tuttle from Joseph C. Hutcheson, January 2, 1963.

96. Order signed by Chief Judge Tuttle authorizing court sitting *en banc* to conduct criminal contempt proceeding in U.S. v. Barnett, January 3, 1963; Letter to E. W. Wadsworth from Elbert P. Tuttle, January 3, 1963.

97. Transcript of Hearing on Order to Show Cause, February 8, 1963.

used by the Fifth Circuit. For the first time in its history, the Fifth Circuit decided to certify a specific question of law directly to the U.S. Supreme Court for resolution.[98] The judges also resolved that each member should be given the opportunity to write an individual opinion on the jury question issue so that the Supreme Court could benefit from each of their views.[99]

Nearly a year later, on April 6, 1964, the Supreme Court delivered its answer to the question posed to it by the Fifth Circuit. By a 5-4 vote, the majority agreed with Wisdom, Brown, Tuttle, and Rives that Barnett did not possess either a constitutional or statutory right to a jury trial.[100] The ball now was back in the Fifth Circuit's court; it had to decide whether or not the governor should be prosecuted for criminal contempt.

The members of the Fifth Circuit regrouped in Atlanta on March 12, 1965, to discuss how or if they should proceed.[101] By this time, however, the court had dwindled to only seven members. Cameron had passed away in April 1964, Hutcheson had retired seven months thereafter, and their slots remained vacant until July 1965.[102] During the conference, several judges expressed the view that it was time to close the books on this case by terminating the contempt proceedings. Their remarks so disturbed Wisdom that he jotted down on one of the pages of his handwritten notes of the conference: "I'll have no part of it. For what it is worth, I hope to write a strong dissent."[103] And he did.

As expected, Judges Jones, Gewin, and Bell urged the court not to go forward with the criminal prosecution. Equally predictably, Tuttle, Brown, and Wisdom voiced their strenuous opposition to that option. The wild card, as he had been throughout the contempt phase of this

98. Letter to Judges Tuttle, Brown, and Wisdom from Richard T. Rives, February 11, 1963; Letter to Judges Tuttle, Rives, and Wisdom from John R. Brown, February 15, 1963; Letter to All Judges of the Court from Ben F. Cameron, February 16, 1963.

99. Letter to Judges Tuttle, Brown, and Wisdom from Judge Richard T. Rives, March 18, 1963.

100. *U.S. v. Barnett*, 376 U.S. 681, 84 S.Ct. 984, 12 L.Ed.2d 23 (1964).

101. Letter to All Active Judges of the Fifth Circuit from Judge Richard T. Rives, March 25, 1965.

102. Hutcheson's position remained vacant until President Lyndon B. Johnson tapped District Judge Homer Thornberry, a former congressman from Austin, for promotion. Johnson also nominated the successor to Ben Cameron's post. His choice was James P. Coleman, one of the attorneys who had represented Ross Barnett in his criminal contempt hearing before the Fifth Circuit and who had immediately preceded Barnett as governor of Mississippi.

103. Wisdom's holographic notes of Fifth Circuit conference in *U.S. v. Barnett*, March 12, 1965.

controversy, was Rives. Rives, who had admitted to ambivalence on the value and desirability of pursuing these contempt proceedings, finally determined that prosecuting Barnett no longer would serve any useful purpose. So on May 5, by a 4–3 margin, the Fifth Circuit voted to terminate the still-pending civil contempt proceedings and to dismiss the criminal contempt charges against Barnett.[104] The unsigned majority opinion, written by the swing vote, Rives, declared that in light of Barnett's substantial compliance with the order to admit Meredith, as well as the distinct unlikelihood that any other person would thereafter commit a similar act of contempt, the prosecution of the criminal contempt proceedings was both unnecessary and not in the public interest.[105]

Wisdom, Tuttle, and Brown each wrote separate dissenting opinions, but neither Tuttle's nor Brown's opinion contained the eloquence and passion that flew from Wisdom's pen. Wisdom complained that adopting the majority's reasoning necessitated "a precision in crystal-gazing and clairvoyant timing that permits no latitude for cloud or haze on the crystal ball."[106] He decried the majority's reliance on their own unsubstantiated assessment of the public interest as well as their uninformed calculation of the probability that a conviction would deter others from similar misconduct. In so doing, Wisdom charged, the majority was attempting to dispense justice in a subjective, arbitrary, hit or miss manner reminiscent of a French monarch or, "coming closer to home, like the Law West of the Pecos." Deeply pained by malevolent response to Meredith's entry onto the Ole Miss campus on September 30, a day he called "the worst of many bad days in the Deep South," he was unmoved by the fact that Barnett had not personally taken part in that violent chain of events. "No one can say," he opined, "that the rioting and insurrection that took place September 30, 1962, in Oxford, Mississippi, and the death and disorder that have occurred in many other places in the South since that insurrection, were not due, at least in part, to the imprimatur the Governor of Mississippi placed on lawless defiance of the federal courts."[107]

To this born-and-bred southerner, the misconduct of Barnett, "The Man in High Office Who Defied the Nation," ran far deeper than contempt of court. The governor's defiance of federal authority under

104. *U.S. v. Barnett*, 346 F.2d 99 (5th Cir.1965).
105. Letter to Richard T. Rives from Warren L. Jones, March 16, 1965.
106. *U.S. v. Barnett*, 346 F.2d 104, 105 (Wisdom, J., dissenting).
107. 346 F.2d at 106.

the guise of the "political poppycock" known as the doctrine of interposition constituted "the contempt of a Governor of a State against the Nation."[108] As such, Wisdom concluded, it posed a serious threat to the Republic's constitutionally created federalist form of government, a public wrong of such enormity that its perpetrator had to be called to account.

The conclusion of the lengthy, contentious, and divisive Meredith and Barnett saga, coupled with the death of Cameron, ended both a constitutional crisis and a tumultuous chapter in the history of the Fifth Circuit. But that court's preeminent role in the enforcement of civil rights, particularly in the areas of voting and educational opportunity, had only just begun.

108. 346 F.2d at 107, 109.

9

The First Step in
Desegregating the South

Enforcing *Brown*'s Mandate in Louisiana

On a warm, late spring evening, John and Bonnie Wisdom celebrated his forty-ninth birthday with a dinner party at their Garden
District home. Along with their guests, the Wisdoms could not have
imagined the greater significance of this day in reshaping both the legal
and social fabric of their country. Nor could any of the celebrants have
predicted the signal impact that this decision would have on then-lawyer
John Minor Wisdom's future career on the bench or, for that matter, his
impact on the implementation of that nation-changing ruling.

The evening's convivial atmosphere was interrupted by a phone call
informing the Wisdoms that earlier that day, May 17, 1954, the U.S.
Supreme Court had released its anxiously awaited decision in a case
brought by Linda Carol Brown, an African American eight-year-old Kansas schoolgirl, challenging the racially segregated elementary school system operated by the Topeka school board. Brown's father, Ollie, a part-
time minister and railroad welder, along with the parents of a dozen
other African American students, had sued the Topeka school board
seeking a judicial declaration that the maintenance of a racially segregated school system deprived their children of their right to equal pro-

tection under the laws guaranteed by the Fourteenth Amendment to the U.S. Constitution.

At the same time that the Kansas litigation was proceeding, NAACP lawyers instituted similar proceedings to challenge the constitutionality of segregated school systems in South Carolina, Virginia, and Delaware. In all of these cases, the trial court relied on the Supreme Court's nineteenth-century ruling in *Plessy v. Ferguson*[1] that the mandate of the equal protection clause was satisfied by the provision of "separate but equal" facilities.[2] Since these cases raised a common legal question, the Court decided to consider all four appeals together. Oral argument in the consolidated cases was heard on December 9 and 10, 1952, but when a divided Court could not produce a clear majority, re-argument was scheduled on additional issues for December 7 and 8 of the following year.

On Monday, May 17, 1954, perhaps not coincidentally, just one day before the fifty-eighth anniversary of its decision in *Plessy*, the Court convened, as usual, at noon. The session began, as customary, with the ceremonial admission of attorneys to the bar of the Supreme Court. At 12:30, however, Justices Tom Clark and William O. Douglas began reading the opinions in three routine cases. While relative tedium prevailed in the second-floor courtroom, the pace and atmosphere in the press room one floor below suddenly, and dramatically, changed when the Court's press officer, Banning E. Whittington, announced that "reading of the segregation decisions is about to begin in the courtroom."[3]

At 12:52 p.m., with all of his colleagues in attendance (Justice Robert Jackson had suffered a minor heart attack on March 30 and was not expected to return to the bench for the remainder of the term, but he had left his bed to ensure that every member of the Court was present on this historic occasion), Chief Justice Earl Warren intoned, "I have for announcement the judgment and opinion of the Court in

---

1. 163 U.S. 537, 16 S.Ct. 1138, 41 L.Ed. 256 (1896).

2. The plaintiffs were denied relief in the South Carolina and Virginia cases. The Delaware Supreme Court did require the school board to admit black students to white schools, but only because of its determination that the two systems were separate and unequal. *Brown v. Board of Education of Topeka*, 347 U.S. 483, 488, 74 S.Ct. 686, 688, 98 L.Ed. 873 (1954).

3. Luther A. Huston, "High Court Bans School Segregation; 9-to-0 Decision Grants Time to Comply," *New York Times*, May 18, 1954, 1, col. 8; 14, col. 6; Edgar Poe, "Segregation Void In Public Schools: High Court Decides Case but Delays Decree," *New Orleans Times-Picayune*, May 18, 1954, 1, col. 8.

No. 1—Oliver Brown et al v. Board of Education of Topeka."[4] The chief justice then began to read from the Court's unanimous twelve-page decision, which he had authored. The judgment reversed the lower court's ruling and, more significant, expressly renounced the foundation of the "separate but equal" doctrine articulated in *Plessy*. In *Plessy*, the Court had declared that mandated separation of the races did not necessarily imply the inferiority of either race. But in *Brown*, the Court expressly rejected this fundamental premise, proclaiming that racially segregated schools were *inherently* unequal, regardless of whether they were provided in equal facilities and under otherwise equal conditions and ruling that racially segregated schooling deprived black students of their constitutional right to equal protection of the law.

Having made this far-reaching declaration of constitutional principle, the Court then had to tackle the mechanics of its enforcement. Since the four cases arose under different local conditions that could warrant different remedial responses, the Court deferred the implementation question until all of the relevant parties had been afforded an opportunity to prepare for and tender further argument on this crucial remedial issue. On May 31, 1955, the final day of its 1954–1955 term, the Court issued a seven-paragraph decree designed to implement the constitutional edict announced in *Brown I*.[5]

In what became known as *Brown II*, the Court, again both unanimously and in an opinion written by Chief Justice Warren, acknowledged that full implementation of its constitutional mandate might require overcoming a variety of local problems and, therefore, announced that the primary responsibility for examining, assessing, and solving these problems had to be borne by local school authorities.[6] It quickly added, however, that the federal district and appellate courts had to vigilantly monitor whether these local authorities engaged in good faith

4. Kluger, *Simple Justice* (New York: 1975) 664, 665, 693, 702; Huston, "High Court Bans School Segregation; 9-to-0 Decision Grants Time to Comply," *New York Times*, May 18, 1954, 1, col. 8; 14, col. 7.

5. The Court originally had scheduled arguments for this second phase of the *Brown* litigation for December 1954. But Justice Jackson finally had succumbed to heart disease on October 9, 1954, and the Senate did not confirm his nominated successor, John Marshall Harlan, grandson of the first Justice John Marshall Harlan who had dissented from the Court's ruling in *Plessy*, until March 1955. In order to have the case heard by the Court's full complement, arguments in *Brown II* were postponed until April 11–14, 1955.

6. 349 U.S. 294, 75 S.Ct. 753, 99 L.Ed. 1083 (1955).

efforts to comply with this constitutional directive at the earliest practicable date in light of the logistical and other obstacles school boards
would encounter as they migrated to a unitary school system. And so
the Court sent the Kansas, South Carolina, and Virginia cases back to
the trial courts with instructions to issue whatever orders and decrees
were necessary and proper to admit black students in those states to
schools on a nondiscriminatory basis "with all deliberate speed."[7]

Once the Supreme Court announced in *Brown II* that the task of enforcing and implementing the desegregation mandate of *Brown* fell to
the lower federal courts, the judges of the U.S. Fifth Circuit Court of
Appeals suddenly found themselves thrust onto the front lines of the
civil rights battlefield of the 1960s. The Fifth Circuit exercised appellate jurisdiction over the trial courts in six states of the Deep South—
Texas, Louisiana, Mississippi, Alabama, Florida, and Georgia—each
of whose laws mandated racial segregation in public education. Over
the course of the succeeding several decades, the Fifth Circuit assumed
the preeminent role in a decades-long struggle to desegregate not only
public schools, but many other segments of American society, issuing
more opinions in civil rights cases than any federal circuit court.[8] And
no single member of that court played a more pivotal part in formulating and implementing this fundamental reshaping of American society
than its undisputed scholar-in-residence, Judge John Minor Wisdom.
Once the Supreme Court in *Brown* had declared that public school segregation was unconstitutional, Wisdom resolved that it was his obligation as a lower court federal judge to implement the Court's instructions
and aggressively to counteract the efforts by political and other government officials (including federal district judges) to thwart that effort. To
do otherwise, in his judgment, would not only be unfaithful to his oath
to uphold the Constitution, but would deprive blacks of their inalien-
able right to the franchise, an essential component of the democratic

7. 349 U.S. at 3011 75 S.Ct. at 757. The U.S. Supreme Court upheld the Delaware Supreme
Court's order requiring immediate admission of black students to previously all-white schools. But
it did so on the basis of its repudiation in *Brown I* of the separate but equal doctrine, rather than,
as the Delaware court had concluded, because the black school facilities in that state were demonstrably unequal.

8. The task of relegating Jim Crow to the dustbin of history, however, was a role that none of
the members of that court relished or anticipated. For example, shortly after being nominated to
the court in mid-1954, Elbert Tuttle explained that he was leaving his post as chief counsel for the
U.S. Department of the Treasury "to retire on the Fifth Circuit Court of Appeals." Bass, *Unlikely
Heroes*, 15.

form of government that he strove so diligently to promote as leader of his state's Republican Party. And his innate sense of fairness, rather than any desire to promote social change in pursuit of a larger political agenda, demanded nothing less.

The reverberations emanating from the Supreme Court's ruling in *Brown* across the southern portion of the United States ran the spectrum from defiant denunciation through reluctant acquiescence to grudging approval.[9] U.S. senator James Eastland of Mississippi declared that "the South will not abide by nor obey this legislative decision by a political court"; Virginia's senator Harry F. Byrd called *Brown* "the most serious blow that has yet been struck against the rights of the states in a matter vitally affecting their authority and welfare"; and Georgia governor Herman Talmadge vowed that his state would not abide by any desegregation order.[10] On the other end of the spectrum, President Eisenhower urged all Americans, but particularly those located in the South, to exert calm and reason in the wake of the Court's action, stating only that "the Supreme Court has spoken and I am sworn to uphold . . . the constitutional processes in this country, and . . . I will obey."[11]

The response to *Brown I* in Louisiana was mixed. U.S. senator Russell B. Long, while admitting his personal revulsion toward the Court's decision, advised that "my oath of office requires me to accept it as the law. Every citizen is likewise bound by his oath of office of allegiance to his country."[12] Governor Robert F. Kennon, on the other hand, was less accommodating. He predicted that the Louisiana legislature would do whatever it took to ensure the maintenance of "a double-barreled school system" in a post-*Brown* world.[13] The Oracle at Delphi could not have di-

9. See John N. Popham, "Reaction of South: 'Breathing Spell' for Adjustment Tempers Region's Feelings," *New York Times*, May 18, 1954, 1, col. 5; 20, col. 1; Editorial Excerpts on School Bias Ruling, *New York Times*, May 19, 1954, 20, col. 31; "Civil Groups Hail Anti-Bias Ruling," *New York Times*, May 19, 1954, 21, col. 3.

10. William S. White, "Russell Demands Curbs on Use of Court as 'Tool,'" *Atlanta Constitution*, May 18, 1954, 1, col. 2; William S. White, "Ruling to Figure in '54 Campaign," *New York Times*, May 18, 1954, 1, col. 7; 20, col. 2; M. L. St. John, "Court Kills Segregation in Schools; Cheap Politics, Talmadge Retorts: Calls Panel to Set Up Lasting Ban," *Atlanta Constitution*, May 18, 1954, 1, col. 4; "Talmadge's Plan Meets Coolness," *New York Times*, May 20, 1954, 22, col. 3; "Georgia Officials Hint Open Defiance," *New Orleans States*, May 18, 1954, 8, col. 1.

11. "Eisenhower Asks South to Be Calm," *New York Times*, May 20, 1954, 1, col. 7.

12. William S. White, "Ruling to Figure in '54 Campaign," *New York Times*, May 18, 1954, 1, col. 7; 20, col. 2.

13. "Legislators Move to Bypass Ruling on Segregation," *New Orleans States*, May 20, 1954, 3,

vined more accurately the legislature's intent. In Wisdom's hometown of New Orleans, public officials were comparatively muted in their response to the Court's decision. Dr. Clarence Scheps, president of the Orleans Parish school board, prophesied that the ruling in *Brown* would have no immediate effect on New Orleans public schools and that any response by the board and the state legislature to the Supreme Court's forthcoming remedial decree would not occur until after the lapse of "several years at least."[14]

Kennon's speculation turned out to be much more prescient than Scheps's guarded comments. The Louisiana legislature, hell-bent on defying the Supreme Court and maintaining the state's segregationist traditions, enacted statute after statute to frustrate any and every effort to desegregate its public schools. And just as the Supreme Court envisioned in *Brown II*, the obstinate refusal of school boards throughout the state to execute their primary responsibility to end segregated schooling created an enforcement vacuum that had to be filled by the federal courts. But this incessant barrage of subtle and not-so-subtle machinations by state legislators and education officials to frustrate, impede, and delay judicial action did not ultimately succeed in deterring a small number of federal judges, led by Wisdom, from using every mechanism at their disposal to implement the Supreme Court's constitutional directive.

Nowhere in the United States was the battle to desegregate a local public school system more prolonged and contentious than the bitter struggle that erupted between state and federal authorities in Wisdom's native city of New Orleans. For the better part of a decade, Louisiana authorities, particularly its legislators, but also its governor and state judges, employed an unceasing series of contrivances designed to forestall, if not to prevent, compliance with the Supreme Court's declaration in *Brown* that the Constitution forbad the continued maintenance of racially segregated public schools. And as was the case in so many of the crucial civil rights cases decided by the Fifth Circuit, Wisdom played a pivotal role in this legal odyssey, one that actually had begun

---

col. 1; "Kennon Still Sees Segregation in La.," *New Orleans Item*, May 20, 1954, 8, col. 7; Charles D. Pierce, "Dual Schools to Stay—Kennon," *New Orleans Times-Picayune*, May 20, 1954, 1, col. 6.

14. "Segregation Void in Public Schools: Kennon Is Calm on School Edict," *New Orleans Times-Picayune*, May 18, 1954, 1, col. 6; "'No Immediate Effect' Seen Here by Ruling," *New Orleans States*, May 17, 1954, 2, col. 4.

before the Supreme Court outlawed desegregation in *Brown*. For two years prior to this landmark decision, Oliver Bush, an African American insurance salesman and father of thirteen, had taken the first step on the journey for educational equality in New Orleans by allowing his sixteen-year-old son, Earl, to be the public face of the effort to dismantle the Crescent City's segregated schools.

Ollie Bush was the president of the Parent-Teacher's Association of the Macarty Elementary School, one of New Orleans' most overcrowded, neglected, and run-down black schools.[15] After an unsuccessful two-year campaign to convince local and state educational authorities to permit his and other black children to attend all-white schools, Bush and the parents of nearly a hundred other African American students retained Alexander Pierre (A. P.) Tureaud, the legendary black Creole attorney who handled cases for the New Orleans branch office of the NAACP, to file suit in federal court to desegregate the city's public school system. On September 4, 1952, the case was filed and was assigned to the one federal district judge sitting in New Orleans at that time— J. Skelly Wright.[16] But Judge Wright postponed any further proceedings in this case pending the Supreme Court ruling in the desegregation suit brought by Linda Brown.[17]

Since this lawsuit challenged the constitutionality of state law, specifically, a provision of the Louisiana Constitution and two state statutes that mandated the continuation of racially separate public elementary and secondary schools, federal law required that it be tried before a panel of three judges rather than in front of a single district judge. On the afternoon of Wednesday, February 15, 1956, the day after the city's raucous Mardi Gras festivities, New Orleanians received startling news. The three-judge panel (composed of Louisiana native sons Fifth Circuit judge Wayne Borah and District Judges Herbert Christenberry and J. Skelly Wright) in *Bush* unanimously had struck down the state segregation laws as "invalid under the ruling of the Supreme Court in Brown."[18] The trio also concluded that since the Supreme Court in *Brown* had so unambiguously declared the unconstitutionality of public school segregation, this lawsuit did not present a sufficiently serious con-

15. Carl L. Bankston III and Stephen J. Caldas, *A Troubled Dream: The Promise and Failure of School Desegregation in Louisiana* (Nashville: 2002), 58.

16. Baker, *The Second Battle of New Orleans*, 187.

17. *Orleans Parish School Board v. Bush*, 242 F.2d 156, 158 (5th Cir.1957).

18. *Bush v. Orleans Parish School Board*, 138 F.Supp. 336, 337 (E.D.La.1956).

stitutional question to warrant the use of a three-judge district court. Accordingly, the court disbanded itself and turned the case back over to the reserved, but tough-minded James Skelly Wright.

Skelly Wright, as he was known, like Wisdom, was born and raised in New Orleans. But though these two jurists' names have become inextricably linked in any discussion of southern legal history, the pair actually shared little in common beyond their New Orleans upbringing and the heroic and central role each played in overcoming the powerful forces dedicated to preserving the segregationist status quo.

In contrast to the patrician Wisdom, Wright came from a working-class family and grew up in one of the city's many blue-collar neighborhoods, far removed from the tony uptown environs and elite social circles in which the Wisdom clan lived and traveled. Wright, a nominal Democrat, shared neither Wisdom's party affiliation nor his passion for or involvement in political affairs. In 1948, having served as an assistant U.S. attorney for several years, Wright was given the top job when the incumbent U.S. attorney, Herbert Christenberry, was nominated by President Truman to a vacant position on the U.S. District Court in New Orleans.[19] Within a year, however, U.S. district judge Wayne Borah of New Orleans was elevated to the Fifth Circuit and President Truman nominated Skelly Wright to fill Borah's district court seat, making Wright the country's youngest sitting federal judge. When Judge Borah retired from the Fifth Circuit, he was replaced by Wisdom.

On the same Ash Wednesday that the three-judge panel had transferred *Bush* back to his individual docket, Judge Wright issued a decree that required the defendants to desegregate the New Orleans public schools "with all deliberate speed."[20] State officials responded to Wright's decision with predictable outrage and vowed to persevere in their crusade against this unwarranted invasion of states' rights by a Supreme Court gone awry. The state immediately, but unsuccessfully, appealed Wright's order to the Fifth Circuit, which upheld his ruling.[21] Over the next several years, the Louisiana legislature enacted a series of laws designed solely and expressly to prevent school authorities from

19. *J. Skelly Wright*, 24 AMERICAN NATIONAL BIOGRAPHY 39 (John A. Garraty and Mark C. Carnes, eds. 1999).

20. *Bush v. Orleans Parish School Board*, 138 F.Supp. 337 (E.D.La.1956).

21. *Orleans Parish School Board v. Bush*, 242 F.2d 156 (5th Cir.1957), cert. denied, 354 U.S. 921, 77 S.Ct. 1380, 1 L.Ed.2d 1436 (1957).

complying with Wright's desegregation decree.[22] And on each such occasion, Skelly Wright dutifully struck down these patently unconstitutional artifices contrived to circumvent his prior rulings.[23] Yet even though the Fifth Circuit affirmed his decisions, the schools remained segregated.[24] In a bold move designed to overcome the state's pattern of evasion, Wright issued the first federal court decree requiring a local school system to desegregate as of a certain date. On May 16, 1960, one day before the sixth anniversary of *Brown*, he ordered all public schools in New Orleans to desegregate at the rate of one grade per year, with the first grade to be integrated no later than November 14 of that year. But once again, Wright's antagonists remained undeterred. Governor Jimmie Davis called the Louisiana legislature into extraordinary session to draw a final and irrevocable line in the sand in its guerrilla war against the federal government. And the legislature responded to Wright's decree with its boldest and most flagrant attack on the Supreme Court's ruling in *Brown*.

On November 8, 1960, Governor Davis signed a twenty-nine-bill package, the cornerstone of which was an "interposition" statute declaring that the state would not recognize the authority of the Supreme Court's decision in *Brown* or that of any federal court order issued pursuant to *Brown*'s mandate. It also established criminal penalties for any federal judge or marshal who attempted to render or carry out any such order or decision. As one legislature proudly acknowledged, "what we are doing is calling for a showdown between the federal government and the State of Louisiana to find out where we stand."[25] The three-judge court convened to assess the constitutionality of these statutes, composed of Dick Rives, Herbert Christenberry, and Skelly Wright, unanimously rejected this final, dramatic attempt to flout the authority of the federal courts, including a ringing denunciation of the interposition doctrine.[26] Within weeks, the Supreme Court, in a one-paragraph

---

22. See Act 319 of 1956, LSA-R.S. 17:341 et seq; Act 256 of 1958, LSA-R.S. 17:336; Act 496 of 1960, §IV, LSA-R.S. 17:347 et seq.

23. See *Bush v. Orleans Parish School Board*, 163 F.Supp. 701 (E.D.La.1958).

24. See *Orleans Parish School Board v. Bush*, 268 F.2d 78 (5th Cir.1959).

25. James H. Gillis and Robert Wagner, "Interposition Bill Approved by House," *New Orleans Times-Picayune*, November 7, 1960, 22, col. 5.

26. *Bush v. Orleans Parish School Board*, 188 F.Supp. 916 (E.D.La.1960), aff'd, 365 U.S. 569 (Mem.), 81 S.Ct. 754, 5 L.Ed.2d 806 (1961).

per curiam opinion, unanimously affirmed this ruling, declaring the interposition doctrine to be "without substance."[27]

Even a Supreme Court ruling, however, was not enough to deter the Louisiana legislature from pursuing its path of unabashed defiance. It simply enacted and then reenacted anti-integration laws. And notwithstanding that all of these laws were struck down by the federal court, the state's strategy of unyielding confrontation and noncompliance did have the intended effect of frustrating the school board's ability to comply with Wright's desegregation order.[28] Wright had ordered the board to desegregate the first grade of all New Orleans public schools by November 14, 1960. But by the end of that school year, only twelve of more than 13,000 African American children entering the first grade were attending previously all-white schools. So on April 9, 1962, an exasperated Judge Wright issued his most ambitious, and what would turn out to be his final, decree in this tense and extended constitutional impasse between the federal government and the State of Louisiana.[29] Wright ordered the school board to integrate grades 1 through 6 of all public elementary schools in New Orleans by the beginning of the upcoming school year in September 1962.[30] Six weeks later, this effort would be undone by the man chosen by President Kennedy to replace Wright on the federal district court in New Orleans.

Skelly Wright's refusal to back down from his quest to defend the rule of law and to uphold the supremacy of the U.S. Constitution in New Orleans had made him a national figure. Demonized and transformed into a virtual pariah in his home state, Wright was compelled to rely upon armed federal marshals to escort him to and from his office and to guard his home.[31] At the same time, however, scores of news-

27. *U.S. v. State of Louisiana*, 364 U.S. 500, 501, 81 S.Ct. 260, 5 L.Ed. 2d 245 (1960).

28. Acts 3 and 5 of the Second Extraordinary Session of the Louisiana Legislature for 1961, LSA-R.S. §119.1; 122.1; *Bush v. Orleans Parish School Board*, 190 F.Supp. 861, 863n.1 (E.D.La.1960), aff'd, 365 U.S. 569 (Mem.), 81 S.Ct. 754, 5 L.Ed.2d 806 (1961); *Bush v. Orleans Parish School Board*, 191 F.Supp. 871, 872 (E.D.La.1961), aff'd, *Denny v. Bush*, 367 U.S. 908 (Mem.), 81 S.Ct. 1917, 6 L.Ed.2d 1249 (1961); *Bush v. Orleans Parish School Board*, 194 F.Supp. 182 (E.D.La.1961), aff'd, *Gremillion v. U.S.*, 368 U.S. 11 (Mem.), 82 S.Ct. 119, 7 L.Ed.2d 75 (1961).

29. Temporary Injunction, Bush v. Orleans Parish School Board, Civ. Action No. 3630-B (April 9, 1962).

30. *Bush v. Orleans Parish School Board*, 204 F.Supp. 568 (E.D.La.1962).

31. Arthur Selwyn Miller, *A "Capacity for Outrage": The Judicial Odyssey of J. Skelly Wright* (Westport, Conn.: 1984) 14; *J. Skelly Wright*, 24 AMERICAN NATIONAL BIOGRAPHY 40 (John A. Garraty and Mark C. Carnes, eds. 1999).

paper and magazine articles and television reports from outside the Bayou State expressed respect and admiration for his refusal to buckle under the pressure of standing, frequently alone, against the combination of potent forces aligned against him. So when a retirement created a vacancy on the U.S. Circuit Court of Appeals for the District of Columbia, a grateful President Kennedy nominated Wright on December 15, 1961, to fill the open slot. Wright's promotion to the appellate court, however, left a vacuum of authority on the district court bench in New Orleans. And the man President Kennedy chose to succeed Skelly Wright succeeded only in grinding Wright's hard-fought progress in the New Orleans school desegregation case to a slow crawl.

The appointment of Frank B. Ellis, the Democratic Party state chairman in Louisiana, to assume Wright's seat on the district court turned out to be a bitter disappointment to the Kennedy administration. Members of the Justice Department called it "the worst" judicial appointment made during their tenure.[32] Ellis's penchant for falling asleep while on the bench, as well as his less than stellar judicial acumen, were reflected in his colleagues' frequent references to him as "Rip Van Winkle" and to his courtroom as "Sleepy Hollow."[33]

Ellis assumed the bench on April 16, 1962, one week after Wright had issued his final order in *Bush* requiring integration of grades 1 through 6. The Orleans Parish school board immediately requested reconsideration of this decree and Judge Ellis did not disappoint. He issued an opinion on May 23, 1962, that drastically reversed the momentum that had been generated by Wright's bold decree.[34] Under the guise of "modifying" Wright's April 9 order to provide an overwhelmed board of education with more time to meet the enormity of the challenge of integrating its schools, Ellis withdrew the requirement to desegregate grades 1 though 6 by September of 1962 and reinstituted Wright's original annual grade-by-grade stepladder plan. But whereas Wright's stepladder order had required integration of the first grade by November 14, 1960, with one grade per year desegregated thereafter, Ellis's modification meant that desegregation of all grades would be delayed for an addi-

32. Read and McGough, *Let Them Be Judged: The Judicial Integration of the Deep South,* 159.

33. The judges subsequently learned that Ellis's frequent dozing on the bench was the result of a reaction to strong medication that he was taking for a chronically painful back ailment rather than a lack of interest in the proceedings before him. But that realization did not affect Wisdom's overall assessment of Ellis's judicial abilities or performance.

34. *Bush v. Orleans Parish School Board,* 205 F.Supp. 893 (E.D.La.1962).

tional two years.[35] Ollie Bush and the other parents appealed Judge El-lis's modification of Skelly Wright's order and the case was assigned to an appellate panel composed of Dick Rives, John Brown, and John Wisdom. Now, eleven years after Ollie Bush had first sued to enable his child to attend a racially integrated school, and six and one half years after Skelly Wright had ordered the New Orleans schools to be desegregated with all deliberate speed, the final chapter in this saga was about to be written by the Fifth Circuit.

At its conference after hearing oral argument, the members of the Fifth Circuit panel were of one mind that Skelly Wright's final desegregation plan imposed too great an administrative burden on the school board.[36] But they could not agree on the scope of their authority, as an appellate court, to do anything about it. In *Brown*, the Supreme Court clearly had assigned the initial role of formulating desegregation plans to the school boards and the federal district courts were authorized to intervene only when and if a local board defaulted in its responsibility. But there was no specific mention in *Brown I* or *Brown II* of the role of the federal appellate courts in the implementation of the desegregation command. Nevertheless, since the Supreme Court already had upheld several circuit court rulings that had reviewed trial court–ordered desegregation plans, Rives, Brown, and Wisdom agreed that the Supreme Court did not intend to circumscribe the appellate court's traditional power of review on appeal.

Rives argued that Ellis correctly had required desegregation only of the first grade for the impending school year. Brown, however, urged that this was too little too late and proposed that they require desegregation of the first three grades. Wisdom concurred with Brown's view that Ellis's order did not adequately meet the constitutional requirement of achieving total desegregation with all deliberate speed. Consequently, the conference ended with Brown and Wisdom in favor of requiring desegregation of three grades by the beginning of the approaching school term. And Wisdom, once again, was assigned the job of writing what they all expected would be, by its very nature, a controversial, precedent-setting opinion.[37]

Upon further reflection, however, and a more careful study of the

35. 205 F.Supp. at 900.

36. Letter to Elbert P. Tuttle, Richard T. Rives, and John R. Brown from John M. Wisdom July 9, 1962, at 2.

37. Ibid., 2.

mountain of exhibits and other documents generated by the case, Wisdom concluded that it was just too late in the year for the board to do a competent job of desegregating even three grades. He therefore proposed that his colleagues adopt a four-stage compromise plan. Under the first phase of this plan, the dual school system would be retained for the upcoming school year, but all interested African American students in the first three grades would be permitted to transfer to "white" schools. This would trigger the steady eradication of the dual system over the next three stages. The second phase would require the school board to disestablish the dual school system for grades 1 and 2 by the beginning of the following (1963–1964) school year. In its third phase, the board would desegregate grades 3 through 5 by the commencement of the 1964–1965 school year. The fourth and final phase would involve the desegregation of one additional grade per year until the segregated system was completely abolished.[38]

Wisdom realized that this proposal did not fulfill the constitutional mandate to desegregate as cleanly and quickly as Judge Brown would have preferred. But, he suggested to his colleagues, the Supreme Court's articulation of a "deliberate speed" timetable implied that "the Supreme Court seems to have said that, unlike a pregnancy, with a desegregation plan there is such a thing as a little unconstitutionality."[39] Ultimately, the force of Wisdom's argument won over both Rives and Brown, resulting in a united panel and a unanimous decision to adopt his compromise plan.[40]

Wisdom did not join the Fifth Circuit with either the expectation or intent of acting as an agent of social or political reform. He never saw the role of judge as that of reformer. His job was to enforce the law as confected by the Congress and the constitutional framers, and as construed by the Supreme Court. So once the Supreme Court, in *Brown*, declared public school segregation to be unconstitutional, he was intent on doing everything within the legitimate exercise of his judicial authority to implement the desegregation command. And as a federal appellate court judge, Wisdom concluded that he bore a particular responsibility to enforce the Court's constitutional edict in *Brown*.

In light of the pro-segregation public sentiment that pervaded the South, it was, he believed, disingenuous to expect politically sensitive

38. Ibid., 2–3.
39. Ibid., 2.
40. *Bush v. Orleans Parish School Board*, 308 F.2d 491 (5th Cir.1962).

school boards to have the inclination to develop and implement plans that would expeditiously and effectively achieve desegregation. At best, one could only expect them to acquiesce to judicial decree. And even though federal trial court judges were insulated from public pressure by their constitutionally assured life tenure, by virtue of their role as trial judges who dealt with the litigants on a face-to-face, daily basis, they remained in closer contact with the members of their local community and, consequently, typically were loath to change local customs without firm mandates from the appellate court. The circuit courts of appeals, on the other hand, possessed jurisdiction over appeals from district courts in several states and so their members frequently were called upon to decide disputes involving parties from cities and states in which they did not reside.

Consequently, Wisdom believed, it fell to the federal appeals court to step in and provide specific and complete directions to the trial judge. He never claimed that he and his appellate court colleagues enjoyed any claim to moral superiority or intellectual enlightenment. He simply noted that they "are just not on the firing line, not as exposed to built-in pressures and allegiances, not as tied by birth, education, residence, professional experience and other ties to one state and to one section of a state. And they rarely have to condemn and enjoin their golfing, fishing or gin rummy companions."[41]

Wisdom's opinion in *Bush* did more than effectively end Louisiana's eight-year crusade to stalemate all federal efforts at implementing the ruling in *Brown*. Its impact extended beyond New Orleans and the boundaries of Louisiana to the five other states encompassed by the Fifth Circuit. The decision vindicated the supremacy of federal constitutional law, sending a decisive and unequivocal message to public officials throughout the South that continued efforts at thwarting the national policy to end the unconstitutional plague of segregation would not be countenanced. It also created an initial blueprint for implementing that constitutional command in a manner that was sensitive to the administrative and other logistical difficulties associated with this monumental change in the prevailing social order.

But change, as Wisdom anticipated, would be slow in coming. School districts and other local officials attempted to take advantage of Wis-

---

41. John Minor Wisdom, *The Frictionmaking, Exacerbating Political Role of Federal Courts*, 21 Sw. L. J. 411, 420 (1967).

dom's admitted reluctance to have the federal courts replace local authorities as the primary engine of desegregation. After paying respect, in *Bush*, to the school board's members' reputation for "integrity and strength of character," Wisdom had cautioned that "when a case involves the administration of a state's schools, as federal judges we try to sit on our hands."[42] But when, post-*Bush*, local educators consistently failed to uphold their constitutional obligations, Wisdom unhesitatingly unfettered his hands.

For example, although the Louisiana legislature repealed all of its laws mandating public school segregation within five years after *Bush* was decided, some local school boards sought to continue their pattern of obstruction and delay by dredging up other, more novel rationalizations for hanging on to their dual school systems. When the parents of African American children brought suit to desegregate the Bossier Parish public school system in northwest Louisiana, the school board asserted what Judge Wisdom termed a "new and bizarre excuse."[43] These parents were all uniformed members of the armed forces stationed at Barksdale Air Force Base, a military facility located within Bossier Parish. In response to their suit on behalf of all African American school children living in Bossier Parish, the school board shot off a double-barreled defense. The board argued that since the children of the service personnel were living on a federal facility, they were not residents of Bossier Parish and, therefore, were neither entitled to the Fourteenth Amendment guarantee of equal protection nor eligible to bring a class action lawsuit on behalf of parish residents.

District Judge Ben C. Dawkins, Jr. (whose appointment to the federal bench by President Eisenhower had been based on Wisdom's recommendation) rejected both of these arguments and ordered the parish to desegregate. When the case was appealed, Wisdom wrote the opinion for the Fifth Circuit affirming Dawkins's judgment.[44] He agreed with Dawkins that by virtue of accepting federal funding the school district had a statutory and contractual duty to afford "federal children" the same type of schooling it provided to Bossier residents, and that these children therefore could sue on behalf of all black children eligible to

42. 308 F.2d at 501.

43. *Bossier Parish School Board v. Lemon*, 370 F.2d 847, 849 (5th Cir.1967), cert. denied, 388 U.S. 911, 87 S.Ct. 2116, 18 L.Ed.2d 1350 (1967).

44. *Bossier Parish School Board v. Lemon*, 370 F.2d 847 (5th Cir.1967), cert. denied, 388 U.S. 911, 87 S.Ct. 2116, 18 L.Ed.2d 1350 (1967).

attend Bossier Parish schools. Moreover, "for good measure," he also offered a few choice responses of his own to the school board's "opera bouffe" defense.[45] Wisdom reasoned that even if the school district had not accepted any federal funding, once it permitted any student to attend its schools, it was constitutionally prohibited from providing education to that student on a racially segregated basis and that any student attending a district school had standing to enforce his or her constitutional right to a desegregated education.

True to form, the Louisiana legislature did not permit this controversy to end quickly or quietly. The legislators would not abandon their crusade to maintain a racially segregated public school system. And though Wisdom's opinion in *Bush* prevented them from continuing to enact statutes that overtly mandated segregation, they strove mightily and incessantly to confect a series of new subterfuges to accomplish that same end in a more circuitous and deft manner. These artifices, they hoped, would escape, or at least survive, judicial scrutiny.

Perhaps the most insidious of these contrivances was the series of laws enacted between 1958 and 1967 that, in one form or another—each hatching a scheme more subtle in its conception and more sophisticated in its terminology than its predecessor—provided publicly funded tuition grants to white students attending nonsectarian private schools. As Wisdom observed, "as fast as the courts knocked out one school law, the legislature enacted another. Each of these laws, whether its objective was obvious or nonobvious, was designed to provide a state-supported sanctuary for white children in flight from desegregated public schools."[46]

Louisiana took its initial legislative plunge into the tuition grant waters in 1958.[47] Act 258 provided grants to families of students enrolled in private schools "where no racially segregated public school" was available. In 1960, this blatantly discriminatory statute was repealed and reenacted, minus its express racial restriction.[48] That, however, did not signal any legislative retreat. In an effort to evade the constitutional requirements that apply only to public institutions, the legislature created

45. 370 F.2d at 851, 852.

46. *Poindexter v. Louisiana Financial Assistance Commission*, 275 F.Supp. 833, 835 (E.D.La.1967).

47. Acts 257 and 258 of 1958, LSA-R.S. 17:391.1 et seq.

48. Act 3 of the Second Extraordinary Session of the Louisiana Legislature for 1960, LSA-R.S. 17:2901–2917.

a mechanism by which public schools could be metamorphosed into private schools. This so-called local option law provided each parish with the option of closing its schools if a majority of qualified voters in that parish voted to do so.[49] Under this school closing law, the school board was authorized to dispose of the closed school building under any terms and conditions of its choosing. So the board would "sell" the facility to a private educational cooperative that would operate the school. Then, the state funds that previously had been allocated to the administration of the public school would be disbursed, entirely or virtually entirely, to these "private" schools and/or to the families of their students. The clear objective of the scheme was to have these "private" schools operate in the same manner, in identical buildings, under the same supervision, and with the same public financing as the theretofore segregated public schools.

A three-judge court composed of Wisdom and District Judges Herbert Christenberry and Skelly Wright of New Orleans heard the suit brought to challenge the constitutionality of this state law. In a *per curiam* decision prepared by Wisdom, the court struck down what Wisdom called a "transparent artifice designed to deny the plaintiffs their declared constitutional right to attend desegregated public schools."[50] Wisdom's opinion left no doubt about his and his colleagues' disdain for the legislature's pattern of defiance. "This is not the moment in history," Wisdom chided, "to experiment with ignorance."[51] Although the solons deviously eliminated all reference to race "so that, to the uninitiated, the statute appears completely innocuous," Wisdom and his colleagues refused to be blinded to its true purpose, mechanics, and effect.[52] Citing the abundantly available local newspaper reports of public statements made by legislative leaders boldly boasting that the bill represented the keystone to a reformulated plan to perpetuate intact the state's segregated system, Wisdom was able to provide persuasive authority for

49. On April 22, 1961, approximately 80 percent of the registered voters in St. Helena Parish went to the polls and voted 1,147 to 56 in favor of the school closing proposition placed on the ballot pursuant to this local option law. Robert Wagner, "St. Helena Vote Favors Closing," *New Orleans Times-Picayune*, April 12, 1961, 1, col. 2.

50. See initial drafts of opinion bearing holographic revisions by Judge Wisdom; *Hall v. St. Helena Parish School Board*, 197 F.Supp. 649, 651 (E.D.La.1961), aff'd *per curiam*, 368 U.S. 515, 82 S.Ct. 529, 7 L.Ed.2d 521 (1962).

51. 197 F.Supp. at 659.

52. 197 F.Supp. at 652.

his court's finding that although "the state might not be doing business at the old stand; [it] would be participating in the same sort of business."[53]

Undaunted by this temporary setback, the Louisiana legislature concocted a third plan predicated on the use of tuition grants to support "private" schools for white children fleeing from desegregated public schools. Act 147 of 1962 re-enforced the illusory school closing gambit with a state agency chartered to distribute a tuition grant directly to the family of any student accepted by a private nonsectarian elementary or secondary school in Louisiana.[54] By sending the money directly to the parents, instead of to the school, the legislators hoped to circumvent the constitutional reach of *Brown* on the theory that state aid to a student was not the equivalent of state aid to a school.

The suit challenging the constitutionality of this statute was assigned to a three-judge court composed of Wisdom and fellow New Orleanian circuit judge Robert A. Ainsworth, Jr.,[55] and chief district judge Herbert Christenberry.[56] Wisdom's twenty-five-page opinion for the unanimous panel in *Poindexter v. Louisiana Financial Assistance Commission* is another devastating indictment of the legislature's unrelenting refusal to bow to the by-then decade-old ruling in *Brown*.[57]

Wisdom unmasked the purpose and effect of this statute by placing it in the context of a detailed history of public education in Louisiana, featuring its nearly century-old commitment to the perpetuation of a racially segregated school system. Wisdom also forcefully demonstrated that the inevitable (and intended) effect of the tuition grant system was the creation and maintenance of a state-supported system of segregated schools that was constitutionally indistinguishable from its overtly public predecessor. Relying on charts and other quantitative evidence, Wisdom offered a statistical analysis that revealed that the overwhelming bulk of private schools for white children were formed after the formal desegregation of the public system and that all of these schools owed their formation and continued existence to the state's grants-in-aid.

53. 197 F.Supp. at 655. The U.S. Supreme Court affirmed the three-judge court's decision in a one sentence *per curiam* opinion. 368 U.S. 515, 82 S.Ct. 529, 7 L.Ed.2d 521 (1962).

54. LSA-R.S. 17:2951–2959.

55. President Lyndon B. Johnson elevated Ainsworth to the Fifth Circuit in 1966 after five years of service as a federal district judge in New Orleans.

56. Letter to Herbert M. Christenberry from Elbert P. Tuttle, July 7, 1964 (with attached order designating the members of the court).

57. 275 F.Supp. 833 (E.D.La.1967).

This undeniable stamp of official state endorsement of white private schools, Wisdom observed, "perpetuates the open humiliation of the Negro implicit in segregated education."[58] Moreover, the fact that the state subsequently modified this plan after June 1967 so as to limit grants to students attending schools that were not "predominantly maintained" by state funding did not take the state off the constitutional hook and cure the statute's constitutional defect. Wisdom was not about to be drawn down that slippery slope. "The payment of public funds in *any* amount through a state commission under authority of a state law," Wisdom announced, "is undeniably state action."[59] Whether or not the equal protection clause applied to the state's policy of providing financial assistance to private agents of discrimination, he resolved, could not turn "on whether the state aid adds up to 51 per cent or adds up only to 49 per cent of the support of the segregated institution. The criterion is whether the state is so *significantly* involved in the private discrimination as to render the state action and the private action violative of the equal protection clause."[60]

Then, applying his "significant involvement" test to Louisiana's funding scheme, Wisdom concluded that *any* aid resulting from the state's purposeful policy of fostering segregation and encouraging such discrimination reached that constitutional threshold. Finally, as a concluding, stirring rebuke to the state legislature, Wisdom proclaimed that "unless this system is destroyed, it will shatter to bits the public school system of Louisiana and kill the hope that now exists for equal educational opportunities for all our citizens, white and black."[61]

Within six months, this same three-judge court struck down Act 99 of 1967, which the Louisiana legislature had passed as a "standby bill" in the event that Act 147 was invalidated by the federal court.[62] This final incarnation of the tuition grant plan contained a self-serving statement of purpose consisting of a list of statutory objectives unrelated to school segregation. It also tied the amount of the statutory grants-in-aid

58. 275 F.Supp. at 851.

59. 275 F.Supp. at 854 (emphasis added).

60. 275 F.Supp. at 854.

61. 275 F.Supp. at 857. The court's decision was affirmed by the Supreme Court in another of its one sentence *per curiam* opinions. *Louisiana Financial Assistance Commission v. Poindexter*, 389 U.S. 571, 88 S.Ct. 693, 19 L.Ed.2d 780 (1968).

62. *Poindexter v. Louisiana Financial Assistance Commission*, 296 F.Supp. 686 (E.D.La.1968), aff'd *per curiam*, *Louisiana Education Commission for Needy Children v. Poindexter*, 393 U.S. 17, 89 S.Ct. 48, 21 L.Ed.2d 16 89 S.Ct. 48 (1968).

to the individual recipient's level of financial need. But no one, least of all Wisdom, was fooled by this contrivance. Notwithstanding the fact that this most recent ploy "was carefully tailored in its journey through the legislature to avoid *too much* state involvement in the maintenance of private schools (so that the bill would not come under the Fourteenth Amendment)," Wisdom easily and quickly concluded, "Act 99 must go the way of its predecessors."[63]

The significance of Wisdom's opinions in these Louisiana school desegregation cases is not limited to the preeminent role they played in making a reality of the Supreme Court's constitutional dictate in *Brown*. They also had a significant impact on the enforcement of federal civil rights laws.

For example, in striking down the segregated school system in Bossier Parish, Wisdom had referred to Title VI of the Civil Rights Act of 1964 as an alternate basis for his conclusions. This provision prohibits recipients of federal financial assistance, including school districts, from denying participation in their programming to individuals on the basis of their race. But it does not expressly provide individuals with the right to file suit to enforce their right to nondiscriminatory access to such programs. In *Bossier Parish*, Wisdom announced that the absence of an express provision of such a private right of action did not prevent the courts from recognizing such a claim.

In 1972, Congress decided to expand the ban on discrimination by recipients of federal funding to include discrimination on the basis of sex. Title IX of the Education Amendments of 1972 mirrored the language of Title VI except that it prevented recipients of federal funding from discriminating on the basis of sex, rather than race.[64] And like Title VI, Title IX did not expressly provide beneficiaries of, or participants in, federally funded programs from bringing their own suit to enforce its nondiscrimination guarantee. In *Cannon v. University of Chicago*, however, the Supreme Court expressly relied on Wisdom's opinion in *Bossier Parish* as the basis for its ruling that Title IX, like Title VI, should be construed as providing individuals with an implied private right of action for injunctive relief.[65] The Court noted that "a distin-

63. 296 F.Supp. at 688, 691.
64. Pub.L. No. 92-318, 86 Stat. 235 (codified in 20 U.S.C. §§1680-1686 (1976)). See generally, Joel Wm. Friedman, *Congress, the Courts, and Sex-Based Employment Discrimination in High Education: A Tale of Two Titles,* 34 VAND. L. REV. 37 (1981).
65. 441 U.S. 677, 99 S.Ct. 1946, 60 L.Ed.2d 560 (1979).

guished panel of the Court of Appeals for the Fifth Circuit squarely decided this issue in an opinion that was repeatedly cited with approval
and never questioned during the ensuing five years."[66] Thus, by opening the courthouse doors to private litigants, Wisdom dramatically enhanced the enforceability of, and thus the level of compliance with, the
nondiscrimination mandates contained in these two important civil
rights statutes.

Nevertheless, the preeminent historic significance of Wisdom's opinion in *Bush* and the other Louisiana school desegregation cases lies in
their role as the analytic foundation upon which he predicated subsequent rulings that set the pattern for the desegregation of public education throughout the South and the nation. These opinions, grounded
in Wisdom's vigilant and principled concern for fairness as well as his
uncompromising insistence upon enforcing the rule of law, cemented
his reputation as a courageous and scholarly jurist whose brilliantly con-
ceived and artfully delivered opinions led his court to its well-deserved
reputation as a guarantor of civil rights and the driving force behind the
integration of American society.

66. 441 U.S. at 696, 99 S.Ct. at 1957.

10

IMPLEMENTING *BROWN* THROUGHOUT THE NATION

If John Minor Wisdom's opinion in *Bush* constituted the initial blueprint for the demolition of racially segregated public education in Louisiana, his pair of opinions in *Singleton v. Jackson Municipal Separate School District*, issued shortly before his ruling in *Bossier Parish*, represented the next step in his development of a comprehensive and assertive judicial response to segregation throughout all sectors of American society.[1] And these two rulings, in turn, paved the way for the ambitious program he subsequently announced in *U.S. v. Jefferson County*, the monumental opus that nearly all observers, including Wisdom himself, regard as his single most masterful and influential decision.[2]

In March 1963, the Jackson, Mississippi, school board was the target of a school desegregation action. Although the ferocity and duration of the Jackson school board's refusal to embrace *Brown*'s desegregation command did not begin to rival that of its New Orleans counterpart, neither was it setting any land speed records for compliance. Moreover, by 1965, Wisdom's patience was rapidly evaporating as he became increasingly intolerant of the manifest recalcitrance displayed by most

---

1. 348 F.2d 729 (5th Cir.1965); 355 F.2d 865 (5th Cir.1966).
2. 372 F.2d 836 (5th Cir.1966), modified, 380 F.2d 385 (5th Cir.1967) (*en banc*), cert. denied, 389 U.S. 840, 88 S.Ct. 67, 19 L.Ed.2d 103 (1967).

southern communities in response to *Brown*. Near the tail end of his career, Wisdom voiced the frustration and disappointment associated with the battle to enforce the ruling in *Brown*. "At first we thought . . . that the Supreme Court's mandate to desegregate schools with 'all deliberate speed' was a statesmanlike decision. It allowed time for the states to make the transition from segregation to integration. After a while . . . [we] realized that nothing of great importance was happening. 'All deliberate speed' was an excuse for delay by legislatures, school boards, and certain foot-dragging district judges."[3]

The trial judge in the Jackson case, District Judge Sidney C. Mize, approved the school board's grade-a-year segregation plan that offered freedom-of-choice assignment to students entering the first grade. Freedom-of-choice plans were the favored response of school boards to judicial desegregation decrees because they put the onus of desegregation on students and their parents. Under these plans, integration occurred only when and if African American families took the initiative of seeking transfer or admission of their children to previously all-white schools. It imposed no affirmative obligation on the school authorities to take any direct action to produce integrated classes.

The plaintiffs were dissatisfied with the board's decidedly unambitious plan and so they appealed Mize's ruling to the Fifth Circuit. On June 22, 1965, while the appeal was pending, Wisdom authored an interim ruling on behalf of a panel that included Judges Hutcheson and Brown. In what became known as *Singleton I*, Wisdom used the opening line of the opinion to send a resolute and unequivocal message to all of the parties to the case. "The time has come," he announced, "for footdragging public school boards to move with celerity toward desegregation."[4] And although he had acknowledged in *Bush* that the desire to comply with *Brown*'s desegregation decree had to be tempered with an appreciation of the administrative difficulties associated with the transition to an integrated system, Wisdom now insisted that *Brown*'s leavening principle of "deliberate speed" never had been intended to accommodate community hostility to that transformation.

He also declared, in no uncertain terms, that his court rejected the school board's argument that *Brown* merely forbad mandatory segregation, and did not require school boards to take affirmative steps of their own to achieve integration. Only fourteen months after the release of

3. John Minor Wisdom, *In Memorium: One of a Kind*, 71 Tex.L.Rev. 913, 918 (1993).
4. 348 F.2d 729 (5th Cir.1965).

Brown, a three-judge federal district court in *South Carolina v. Elliott* had legitimized that cramped interpretation of the Supreme Court's decision.[5] One particular portion of the South Carolina court's decision in *Briggs* became the rallying cry for devotees of the segregationist status quo and created a safe harbor for those judges who were ready and willing to look the other way at, if not quietly encourage, efforts designed to impede the pace of integration. In a *per curiam* opinion written by aging U.S. Fourth Circuit judge John J. Parker, the court had declared that "the Constitution . . . does not require integration. It merely forbids discrimination."[6] As long as the government did not enforce or compel segregation, this court had concluded, the Constitution was not offended by segregation that was the product of voluntary choice. As far as the court was concerned, if integration was to occur, it would be up to the black students and their parents to make it happen.

Completely aside from the correctness of this statement of the law, the court in *Briggs* had chosen to answer a question that had not been placed before it by the parties. The plaintiffs in *Briggs* never asked the court to require the local school boards to take action to integrate the schools. Their challenge was more fundamental. Because the Constitution and laws of South Carolina mandated racial segregation in public schools, the parents sought merely a declaration that these provisions were unconstitutional and an injunction forbidding state authorities from enforcing them. And since the federal district court was bound by the Supreme Court's ruling in *Brown*, it had no choice but to grant this limited relief. It ruled that such a *de jure* system of racial segregation, that is, one mandated by state law, violated the Fourteenth Amendment of the U.S. Constitution and it ordered state officials to arrange for all students to be admitted to any school on a race-blind basis with all deliberate speed. Nevertheless, the panel went out of its way to rule that the school board was not constitutionally required to take action (affirmative steps toward integration) that no one had asked them to take.

Since, therefore, this question of the scope of the duty to desegregate was not properly before the court in *Briggs*, its discussion of this issue

5. 132 F.Supp. 776 (E.D.So.Car.1955).

6. 132 F.Supp. at 777. President Herbert Hoover had nominated John Parker in 1930 to a vacancy on the U.S. Supreme Court. However, the Senate refused to confirm him, in part, because of racist sentiments expressed during Parker's campaign for governor of North Carolina. Judge Parker served on the Fourth Circuit until 1958. Donald E. Lively, *The Supreme Court Appointment Process: In Search of Constitutional Roles and Responsibilities*, 59 S. CAL. L. REV. 551, 567–568 (1986).

was mere *dictum*, that is, a pronouncement on an issue that is not essential to the resolution of the controversy before the court. And as such, it did not possess the binding effect that attaches to the actual holding in a case. Nonetheless, this *dictum* gained both notoriety and currency in jurisdictions throughout the South, including the Fifth Circuit.

Wisdom was determined in *Singleton I* to discredit the *Briggs* "doctrine." This erroneous interpretation of the Supreme Court's clear message in *Brown* was fashioned, he believed, solely to delay, if not to prevent, the effectuation of the Supreme Court's integration mandate. Once the Court had created the constitutional blueprint for action, Wisdom's commitment to the rule of law compelled him to discredit and eliminate any obstacle placed in the path of that plan's implementation. But though his repudiation of Judge Parker's statement of the law was precise and unambiguous, the power of Wisdom's language was muted by the fact that he chose to place this discussion in a footnote rather than in the main text of the opinion. In that footnote, Wisdom insisted that since the Supreme Court's intervening ruling in *Brown II* unmistakably required school boards to provide integrated school systems, "Judge Parker's well-known dictum in *Briggs* should be laid to rest."[7] In its place, Wisdom promulgated a desegregation game plan containing a specific timetable that could be adopted by school boards throughout the region.

The interim decree in *Singleton I* also threw out the grade-a-year plan that had been approved by Judge Mize. In its place, the court issued an order incorporating the minimum desegregation standards that had been promulgated by the Office of Education of the U.S. Department of Health, Education, and Welfare (HEW) for another purpose—to determine a school's eligibility for federal funding. Pursuant to these guidelines, all grades would have to be desegregated by the fall of 1967. But since the 1965–1966 school year was scheduled to begin in less than three months, Wisdom concluded that a more immediate objective was essential to ensure some measure of progress by the beginning of the upcoming 1965 term. So the interim judgment ordered the Jackson school district to draft a plan that would desegregate at least four grades for the approaching academic year and that would comply with the HEW standards for the remaining grades by 1967.

Two weeks later, the school board submitted a desegregation plan

7. 348 F.2d at 730n.5.

that complied with these directions and that was accepted by the trial judge. Although this satisfied the plaintiffs, the federal government (which had been permitted by Judge Mize to participate in the case because of its public importance) believed that only full and immediate desegregation of *all* twelve grades satisfied the *Brown* requirement that desegregation proceed with deliberate speed nevertheless. Consequently, the government chose to continue the appeal and ask the Fifth Circuit panel to issue a final order.

The panel assembled to rule finally on the merits of the appeal was composed of Wisdom, his Fifth Circuit colleague Homer Thornberry of Texas, and U.S. Court of Claims judge Samuel E. Whitaker. On January 26, 1966, the court issued a unanimous ruling, penned by Wisdom, which rejected the government's aggressive desegregation schedule and adhered to the more protracted HEW timetable.[8] More significant, Wisdom made sure, on this occasion, that his court's rejection of the *Briggs* dictum was both a forceful and integral part of its ruling by shifting the situs of his denunciation of the *Briggs* dictum to the main text of the opinion. In *Singleton II,* Wisdom expressly renounced the "over-simplified dictum" in *Briggs* and proclaimed, "there should be no misunderstanding" that the Constitution, as construed in *Brown,* compelled school authorities to take steps to create a single, integrated school system.[9] He also stated that until the school board had taken affirmative steps to integrate the schools in accordance with the HEW timetable, every individual African American student enjoyed the constitutional right to transfer immediately to a formerly all-white class.

On the same day that this opinion in *Singleton II* was issued, another Wisdom-authored opinion in a related case involving the Jackson school board was released. In *Jackson Municipal Separate School District v. Evers,* an incensed Wisdom disclosed that despite the presence of "decisions too numerous to mention in this Court and in the Supreme Court [that] show unyielding judicial approval of the legal principle that segregated schooling is inherently unequal," the school boards in Jackson and Biloxi, Mississippi, had persisted in justifying their maintenance of racially segregated public schools.[10] "Bewitched and bewildered by the popular myth that *Brown* was decided for sociological reasons untested in a trial," he added, the school boards in these two consolidated cases

8. *Singleton v. Jackson Municipal Separate School District,* 355 F.2d 865 (5th Cir.1966).

9. 355 F.2d at 869.

10. 357 F.2d 653 (5th Cir.1966), cert. denied, 384 U.S. 961, 86 S.Ct. 1586, 16 L.Ed.2d 673 (1966).

had sought to circumvent if not undermine *Brown* by proffering evidence that innate racial differences in educability demonstrated that racially segregated schools operated to the advantage of both races and, accordingly, justified their continued existence. Directing the trial judge, Sidney Mize, to issue a desegregation order that mirrored the terms of the order issued in *Singleton II,* an infuriated Wisdom left no doubt as to his intolerance of the Mississippi school boards' unremitting intransigence. "These cases," he growled, "tax the patience of the Court."[11]

Wisdom's adoption, in all three of these cases, of the HEW timetable as the benchmark for achieving system-wide desegregation was more than just an innovative strategy. It was a cornerstone in the development of an effective, national plan to fulfill the constitutional command of a racially integrated educational system, a tactic adopted soon after by other federal courts.[12] It also served as the intellectual springboard for the final member of the trio of groundbreaking school desegregation decisions produced by this jurist and the one that he, and most observers, proudly and rightfully point to as his most brilliant and momentous opinion. Ironically, as fate would have it, but for the vagaries of one of his colleague's personal schedule, Wisdom would not even have sat on this case, let alone author an opinion that undeniably and irreversibly placed the federal judiciary in the driver's seat in the challenge to accelerate the pace of school desegregation.

Oral arguments before federal appeals court panels are scheduled on a weekly basis in the various venues in which each federal circuit sits. The next to the last sitting of the Fifth Circuit's 1965–1966 term was scheduled for the week of May 23, 1966, in New Orleans before a panel composed of Circuit Judges John Brown and Homer Thornberry of Texas and, sitting by designation, District Judge Harold Cox of Mississippi. Six weeks earlier, however, Brown had informed Wisdom that a scheduling conflict made it difficult for him to be in New Orleans on those dates and had asked Wisdom to substitute for him as the senior member (and therefore presiding judge) of that panel.[13] In exchange, Brown agreed to replace Wisdom on the following week's panel.[14]

11. 357 F.2d at 654.

12. See *Kemp v. Beasley,* 352 F.2d 14, 18–19 (8th Cir.1965); *Wright v. County School Bd. of Greens-ville County, Va.,* 252 F.Supp. 378 (E.D.Va.1966).

13. Memorandum to John M. Wisdom from John R. Brown, April 12, 1966; Letter to Homer Thornberry and William H. Cox from John M. Wisdom, April 16, 1966.

14. Memorandum to Harold Cox and Ben Dawkins from John R. Brown, April 12, 1966; Letter to All Fifth Circuit Judges from John R. Brown, April 12, 1966.

On Tuesday and Wednesday, May 24 and 25, 1966, in the Louisiana Wildlife and Fisheries Building that housed the U.S. Fifth Circuit Court of Appeals on Royal Street in the heart of New Orleans' French Quarter (the court had moved there from the old New Orleans post office in 1963), the Wisdom-Thornberry-Cox panel heard arguments in twelve school desegregation cases that had been brought against school boards in Mississippi, Louisiana, Georgia, and Alabama. Since seven of these actions involved public schools in Alabama and Louisiana that raised common legal issues, these cases were consolidated for purposes of appeal. As the senior member of the majority (Cox filed a dissenting opinion), Wisdom assigned himself the task of writing the opinion on behalf of the court in *U.S. v. Jefferson County Board of Education*.[15] Wisdom's mammoth, seminal opus, which was more than half a year in the making and occupies nearly seventy-five pages in the official case reports, is widely regarded as the single most influential non–Supreme Court decision in the area of school desegregation. It signaled the end of the judiciary's preoccupation with the "deliberate" component of *Brown*'s "all deliberate speed" mantra and kick-started the engine of public school desegregation.

Wisdom's prior experience with the dilatory and obstructionist tactics employed by state and local government officials in *Bush* and *Singleton* already had persuaded him that the federal courts could most effectively fulfill their role of preserving the constitutional rights of all school children, while acting within the bounds of their judicial function, by strictly enforcing the desegregation guidelines issued by the federal Department of Health, Education, and Welfare. And though, in *Singleton*, he purposefully and carefully had insisted that this deference to administrative guidelines was not intended to signal the court's abandonment of its judicial function, Wisdom also had come to the conclusion that continuing judicial micromanagement of school desegregation was "perilously close to the perimeter of the judicial function."[16] Nevertheless, in the absence of any meaningful action by state and local officials to fulfill their obligation to enforce the law of the land, Wisdom was con-

15. 372 F.2d 836 (5th Cir.1966), modified, 380 F.2d 385 (5th Cir.1967) (*en banc*), cert. denied, 389 U.S. 840, 88 S.Ct. 67, 19 L.Ed.2d 103 (1967). Jefferson County encompasses the City of Birmingham. The other six appellees were the school boards of Fairfield and Bessemer Counties in Alabama and the school boards of Caddo, Bossier, Jackson, and Claiborne Parishes in northwest Louisiana.

16. Letter to Homer Thornberry and William H. Cox from John M. Wisdom, April 16, 1966.

vinced that the federal courts had to take affirmative steps to ensure that the Constitution, as interpreted by the Supreme Court, was not ignored. As he subsequently acknowledged, "we had a void. . . . It was a case of having to act."[17]

But Wisdom also had become comfortable with looking to federal administrative agencies for help in enforcing the Supreme Court's instructions. Not only did he believe that federal agencies were better equipped to perform this supervisory function than he and his judicial colleagues, he was anxious to relieve the courts of the time-consuming burden of monitoring desegregation efforts. Moreover, he had been persuaded that a "rigid, uniform mandate to district courts and to school boards is in the interest of everyone."[18] The job of reviewing the more than ninety court-approved desegregation plans pending within the Fifth Circuit was weighing on his mind and Wisdom was prepared to grasp the opportunity presented by this case to impose a uniform solution throughout the six states that comprised the Fifth Circuit.[19] Moreover, the potential for influencing the pace of integrating public schools throughout the rest of the country also did not escape his attention.

To those ends, and with the concurrence of his colleagues Thornberry and Cox, Wisdom instructed the court clerk to send a letter to counsel for all of the parties in the consolidated appeal directing them to file supplemental briefs focusing on (1) the extent to which it was permissible and desirable for federal trial and appellate courts to give weight to or to rely on HEW guidelines in all pending public school desegregation cases; and (2) suggestions as to practical means and methods by which the courts could make these guidelines judicially effective.[20] While purposefully couching the instructions in sufficiently broad language to eschew any claim that the court had prejudged the case, Wisdom nevertheless sent a clear signal to the parties of the direction the court was likely to take, an intimation that ultimately became fact.

Sending out this request to counsel, however, was not actually Wisdom's idea. The day after Wisdom agreed to substitute for Brown at the court's May 23 sitting in New Orleans, Brown sent Wisdom a brief

17. Bass, *John Minor Wisdom and the Impact of Law,* 69 Miss. L. J. 25, 31 (1999).

18. Letter to Homer Thornberry and William H. Cox from John M. Wisdom, April 16, 1966, 2.

19. U.S. Department of Justice Memorandum in Support of Motion to Consolidate and Expedite Appeals in *U.S. v. Jefferson County* et al., April 1966, 8.

20. Letter to All Counsel in *U.S. v. Jefferson County* et al. from Edward W. Wadsworth, April 21, 1966.

note suggesting that he send instructions of this type to counsel. Brown told Wisdom that he regretted the fact that the federal courts had become "the haven for the reluctant or recalcitrant" and that he had come to believe that "at this very, very late date some way ought to be found, I would think, to make the demands of the Federal Government—speaking through the Judiciary and the Executive—uniform."[21]

After hearing arguments in the seven consolidated cases from Alabama and Louisiana, Wisdom began the process of drafting his opinion. By now, with nearly a decade of judicial service under his belt, Wisdom had developed a modus operandi with which he felt comfortable. This process, which relied principally upon his personal involvement, yielded a product reflecting exhaustive legal, historical, and statistical research, rigorous analysis of both the issues before him as well as the legal and extralegal consequences of his intended ruling, and detailed attention to expressing his conclusions in compelling, eloquent, and unambiguous language.

As was his custom, Wisdom prepared thoroughly for the oral arguments. He carefully read and annotated a summary of the briefs filed by all of the parties to the case that had been prepared by one of his law clerks. This, in turn, was supplemented with some of his own preliminary research into relevant case law and scholarly publications. During the course of each attorney's presentation, Wisdom took dozens of pages of handwritten notes on the long, yellow tablets favored by most attorneys, summarizing the points made by counsel, jotting down questions and notes to himself regarding additional potential research topics or ideas for the opinion that had been inspired by the argument, and sketching the occasional doodle.

Unlike many of his colleagues, Wisdom did not rely exclusively, or even extensively, on his law clerks for the research that frequently was necessary to supplement what had been provided in the parties' briefs. Moreover, because of the unique importance of this case, Wisdom explained, *Jefferson* was "a case I wrote almost entirely by myself, without much help from the law clerks. It was an extremely sensitive case that had to be exactly right and I spent months on it."[22] He also noted, with undisguised pride, that "virtually all of the history came from my li-

21. Memorandum to John M. Wisdom from John R. Brown, April 12, 1966, 2.
22. According to one of Wisdom's law clerks during this period, the judge did all of the research and composition of the first draft of *Jefferson County* without any assistance. Alan Black, *John Minor Wisdom: A Tribute and Memoir by One of His Law Clerks*, 69 Miss. L. J. 43, 48 (1999).

brary."[23] As was his wont in all important civil rights cases, Wisdom limited his law clerks' participation to the preparation of lists of relevant or otherwise helpful cases, law review articles, and other materials for his consideration, most, if not all, of which Wisdom read. Whenever he found any particularly useful concept, suggestion, or quotation, Wisdom would write down information he had gleaned from each separate case or article onto a single, short piece of memo paper and stick it into his case research file.

At a time decades removed from the presence, let alone ubiquity, of computers, the task of producing and editing large amounts of text was an infinitely more time-consuming and labor-intensive process than it would later become. And Wisdom habitually devoted long hours to crafting and re-crafting his opinions until they met his exacting standards for accuracy, precision, and fluency. This laborious enterprise began with Wisdom's preparation of a handwritten outline of the various divisions of the opinion. This was followed by a handwritten initial draft of the opinion penned on scores of pages torn from yellow legal pads. This document, in turn, would be transformed by his secretary into a typed manuscript that underwent endless revisions, with Wisdom either inscribing annotations directly on the typed page or, more typically, attaching a separate page or pages of handwritten insertions. This methodical effort, which occupied much of Wisdom's attention for more than six months, eventually yielded a final draft that was ready for evaluation by the other two members of the panel in early December 1966.[24]

Ordinarily, the members of each appellate panel hold a conference relatively quickly after the oral argument to exchange their preliminary views about the case and to determine who should be assigned the task of writing the opinion. But Wisdom, Thornberry, and Cox did not follow this custom after hearing argument in the seven consolidated desegregation cases in New Orleans. Instead, as presiding judge, Wisdom decided to take the first crack at drafting a judgment, expecting that

23. Robert G. Pugh, Jr., *An Interview with the Honorable John Minor Wisdom*, 39 La. B. J. 254, 255 (1991).

24. Wisdom sent Judge Thornberry a "dirty" copy of the opinion on December 6. Letter to John M. Wisdom from Homer Thornberry, December 12, 1966; Letter to John M. Wisdom from William H. Cox, December 12, 1966. Wisdom also sent a copy to Chief Judge Tuttle, who "approve[d] it with enthusiasm." Letter to John M. Wisdom from Elbert P. Tuttle, December 13, 1966.

Thornberry would join with him to constitute a majority. This did not sit well with Cox. After receiving his copy of Wisdom's proposed opinion, Cox dashed off a letter to Wisdom, urging him to schedule a conference, regardless of the logistical difficulty occasioned by the fact that Thornberry lived in Austin, Texas, and Cox in Jackson, Mississippi. Cox insisted that because of the "far reaching effect and the great importance of the issues involved" a conference was essential "to satisfy a proper discharge of our duty to provide a three judge hearing and determination after discussion of these cases."[25] Wisdom eventually acquiesced to Cox's request, and the trio conferred most of one day, going over the opinion page by page and often paragraph by paragraph.[26] But at the end of the day, the discussion did nothing to dissuade Cox from predictably disagreeing with his colleagues and issuing a dissenting opinion.

The court released its decision on December 29, 1966. From its opening passages, Wisdom's exhaustive opinion left no doubt about his heightened level of frustration with the exceedingly languid pace of desegregation efforts in these seven jurisdictions and his consequent determination to take all steps necessary to bring *Brown*'s declaration of the right to equal educational opportunity, finally, to fruition. In classic Wisdom style, the opinion's lead paragraph was crafted precisely to highlight the disappointing current state of affairs and to underscore the legitimacy of the court's proposed solution.

"Once again," the opening sentence laments, "this Court is called upon to review school desegregation plans to determine whether the plans meet constitutional standards."[27] Wisdom then put a human face on the truly devastating consequences of the seemingly mundane observation that a dozen years had passed since the issuance of the Supreme Court's ruling in *Brown*. He pointed out that the members of the graduating class of the high schools targeted by this lawsuit had not even entered the first grade when the Court decided *Brown*. Yet the African American members of the class of 1966 had been forced to live, and suffer, through the same racially segregated experience that had plagued the twelve preceding classes. Then turning, as he often did, to Shakespeare for inspiration, Wisdom ruefully opined that these facts

25. Letter to John M. Wisdom from William H. Cox, December 12, 1966.

26. Letter to All Judges of the Fifth Circuit Court of Appeals from John M. Wisdom, February 1, 1967, at 5 (document on file with author).

27. 372 F.2d at 845.

had rendered the hopeful promise of *Brown* "of such stuff as dreams are made of."[28]

For more than a decade since the ruling in *Brown*, Wisdom reported, the seven school districts targeted by this lawsuit had made no effort of any kind to begin desegregating their schools. In fact, by the middle of the 1965–1966 school year, less than one percent of all African American students in Louisiana and Alabama were enrolled in racially mixed schools.[29] Wisdom's response to this sad history was clear and unequivocal. "Now after twelve years of snail's pace progress toward school desegregation, courts are entering a new era. . . . The clock has ticked the last tick for tokenism and delay in the name of 'deliberate speed.'"[30]

What particularly irked Wisdom was the fact that the school boards had used the federal courts, including those district courts under his court's appellate supervision, as a safe haven from the rigors of the Office of Education's integration schedule. The HEW guidelines contained an unfortunate loophole; school boards that failed to comply with the Department of Education's desegregation standards were not subject to forfeiture of their federal funding as long as they were operating under a federal court's desegregation order.[31] Consequently, Wisdom explained, school boards that could convince sympathetic federal district judges to impose less stringent and/or more leisurely desegregation timetables than those imposed by HEW readily cashed in on this incentive to "seek refuge in the federal courts."[32]

After reiterating his view that the Supreme Court's decisions in *Brown* I and II laid waste to any doubt as to whether the Constitution imposed an affirmative duty upon states to fully integrate their public schools, Wisdom provided an answer to the fundamental legal issue presented by this case in language that was both pragmatic and elegant in its simplicity and straightforwardness. "The only school desegregation plan that meets constitutional standards," he averred, "is one that works."[33] It was another example, as Supreme Court justice William J. Brennan, Jr.,

---

28. 372 F.2d at 845, quoting from Shakespeare's *The Tempest*, Act IV.

29. 372 F.2d at 845n3.

30. 372 F.2d at 896.

31. Nondiscrimination under Programs Receiving Federal Assistance through the Department of Health and Human Services Effectuation of Title VI of The Civil Rights Act of 1964, 45 CFR §80.4(c).

32. 372 F.2d at 859.

33. 372 F.2d at 847.

once noted, of Wisdom's uncanny ability to "forthrightly ground the opinion in practical realties, rather than platitudinous theory."[34]

Moreover, Wisdom continued, since "the courts acting alone have failed," the country's best hope for providing African American students with some true measure of their long denied constitutional rights was a uniform, coordinated effort between all three branches of government predicated on a comprehensive, nationwide program of compliance with HEW desegregation guidelines.[35] These administratively generated guidelines—which set forth benchmarks to mark the pace and success of efforts to integrate schools operating under a freedom-of-choice plan—offered, in Wisdom's judgment, the best chance for producing an effective, prompt, and orderly transition from a racially segregated dual system to a single, integrated one. Thus, without abdicating their judicial responsibilities, every federal district court in the entire Fifth Circuit, Wisdom announced, could and thereafter should employ these administratively created guidelines as the yardstick by which they measured the constitutionality of freedom-of-choice desegregation plans.[36]

Having now tied the courts to terms of the HEW guidelines, Wisdom also had to deal with the fact that these guidelines expressly relied on race as a basis for assigning students and faculty to particular schools in order to attain the specified level of integration. This government-mandated reliance on race raised a thorny constitutional problem for Wisdom and his colleagues, and particularly for Wisdom. For in 1958, during only his second year on the bench, he had renounced any and all reliance on race in governmental decision-making. Writing for a unanimous court in *Dorsey v. State Athletic Commission*, he had struck down those portions of Louisiana's Anti-Mixing Law and its State Athletic Commission's Rule that prohibited white and black fighters from competing against one another or appearing on the same fight card.[37] Relying on the Supreme Court's ruling in *Brown*, Wisdom had concluded in *Dorsey* that any such state-imposed racial classification was "inherently discriminatory and violative of the Equal Protection Clause of the Four-

34. William J. Brennan, Jr., *"Dispositions That Are Lovely": In Tribute to Judge John Minor Wisdom,* 60 Tul. L. Rev. 237, 238 (1985).

35. 372 F.2d at 847.

36. 372 F.2d at 894.

37. *Dorsey v. State Athletic Commission,* 168 F.Supp. 149 (E.D.La.1958).

teenth Amendment."[38] And he had done so in the clear and unequivocally stated belief that the Fourteenth Amendment's equal protection
clause mandated total colorblindness by the government in the conduct
of its various activities.

Moreover, *Dorsey* wasn't the only case in which Wisdom previously
had adopted the position that a colorblind Constitution precluded any
governmental reliance on racial classifications. In 1960, just two years
after *Dorsey*, as part of a package of segregation laws, the Louisiana legislature had enacted a statute that required, for the first time, that the
race of every candidate for elective office be designated on the ballots
for all primary, general, and special elections. By that act, Louisiana assumed the dubious distinction of being the only state in the nation with
a racial labeling requirement for election ballots.[39]

Dupuy Anderson and Acie J. Belton, two unsuccessful African American candidates in a Democratic Party primary election for the East
Baton Rouge Parish School Board, challenged the constitutionality of
this ballot labeling law. The case was assigned to a three-judge federal district court on which Wisdom was joined by U.S. district judges
E. Gordon West of Baton Rouge and Frank B. Ellis of New Orleans.
Like Ellis, West had been appointed to the federal bench by President
Kennedy. And he was nearly as great a disappointment to the Kennedy
administration as his colleague from New Orleans. In a case in which
he reluctantly ordered the school board of East Baton Rouge to prepare
a desegregation plan, Judge West had referred to the Supreme Court's
opinion in *Brown* as "one of the truly regrettable decisions of all time."[40]
Not surprisingly, then, he was a particularly frequent target of blistering
reversals from Wisdom's caustic pen.

After hearing argument in the ballot labeling case, Judges Ellis and
West agreed with the defendants that the state law did not discriminate
against anyone on the basis of race since it required all candidates for
elective office, regardless of their race, to list their racial classification
on the election ballot. Writing for the majority in *Anderson v. Martin*,[41]

38. *Dorsey v. State Athletic Commission*, 168 F.Supp. 149, 151 (E.D.La.1958).

39. "Racial Labeling on Ballet Upset in Supreme Court," *New York Times*, January 14, 1964, 1,
col. 3; 17, col. 1.

40. *Davis v. East Baton Rouge School Board*, 214 F.Supp. 624, 625 (E.D.La.1963).

41. *Anderson v. Martin*, 206 F.Supp. 700 (E.D.La. 1962), rev'd, 375 U.S. 399, 84 S.Ct. 454, 11
L.Ed.2d 430 (1964).

Judge West rejected the plaintiffs' claim that providing this information to the electorate would cause electors to vote against them on the basis of their race and, therefore, result in racial discrimination. Just as he had done in *Labat* in rejecting the constitutional challenge to the practice of granting exemptions from jury duty to all laborers, West chose to ignore the obvious racially disparate results that were produced by this superficially race-neutral policy.

Wisdom's unusually brief dissenting opinion in *Anderson* rested on one simple but unshakeable belief: that the evil of desegregation lay not so much in the forced physical separation of the races as in the "stamp of classification by race" manifested in the "Colored Only" signs that proclaimed the fact of separation.[42] In his view, a determination of the statute's constitutional infirmity was not dependent on any demonstration of actual injury to African American candidates. Rather, as in *Dorsey*, Wisdom concluded in *Anderson* that "the vice in the law is the State's placing its power and prestige behind a policy of racial classification inconsistent with the elective processes." It was simply "no part of the business of the state to put a racial stamp on the ballot."[43] Wisdom, after all, had spent years prior to joining the court fighting even more blatant attempts by the Louisiana legislature to frustrate any and every attempt by African Americans to exercise this most treasured civil right. So he was unwilling to tolerate this more sophisticated and cynical effort to stimulate private racial prejudice by facilitating the ability of individuals to vote their prejudice and directly and insidiously impede the ability of black candidates to prevail.

The Supreme Court reversed the majority's ruling and unanimously agreed with Wisdom that the statute was unconstitutional, although it did not incorporate his reasoning in every respect.[44] Like Wisdom, the Court ruled that the Constitution prohibited any state from requiring or encouraging its voters to discriminate on racial grounds and that this ballot labeling scheme aroused racial prejudice that operated to disfavor one group and favor another because of race. The fact that the candidate's racial classification was the only piece of identifying information on the ballot other than his name, the Court reasoned, sent a message to voters that the state viewed race as an important consideration in the exercise of their franchise when it should be irrelevant to a candi-

42. *Anderson v. Martin*, 206 F.Supp. 705 (Wisdom, J., dissenting).
43. *Anderson v. Martin*, 206 F.Supp. 705 (Wisdom, J., dissenting).
44. *Anderson v. Martin*, 375 U.S. 399, 84 S.Ct. 454, 11 L.Ed.2d 430 (1964).

date's qualifications for office. Echoing Wisdom, the Court concluded that "the vice lies in the placing of the power of the State behind a racial classification that induces racial prejudice at the polls."[45]

Unlike Wisdom, however, the members of the High Court did not believe that the mere presence of a state-mandated racial classification rendered the state's electoral system constitutionally defective. They did not endorse Wisdom's reliance on Justice Harlan's famous admonition in his dissenting opinion in *Plessy v. Ferguson*[46] that "our Constitution is colorblind."[47] In his dissenting opinion in *Anderson*, Wisdom had stated that "if there is one area above all others where the Constitution is colorblind, it is the area of state action with respect to the ballot and the voting booth. In the eyes of the Constitution, a man is a man. He is not a white man. He is not an Indian. He is not a Negro."[48] But although the Supreme Court did not share Wisdom's view that any use of race was absolutely forbidden, the Court struck down this particular racial classification because it did not serve the government's legitimate interest in providing relevant information about the candidates to the electorate.

Despite his impassioned defense of a colorblind Constitution in *Dorsey* and *Anderson*, and his having been the first federal judge to interpret *Brown* (in *Dorsey*) to require a constitutional rule of colorblindness,[49] Wisdom summarily dispatched the school district's claim in *Jefferson County* that a district court's desegregation plan could not incorporate HEW guidelines since the HEW rules took race into account in creating their desegregation standards. He relied upon a difference in the fact patterns in *Dorsey* and *Jefferson County* that, he said, justified a different approach to the facially parallel legal issue. And although he did not cite or otherwise refer expressly to his earlier ruling in *Dorsey*, Wisdom sashayed his way around that ruling. And he did so by creating an analytic dichotomy that eventually was embraced by the Supreme Court as the guiding principle for deciding school desegregation and affirmative action cases over the succeeding four decades.

With his customary flair for phrasing the boldest statements in the most simple, yet emphatic terms, Wisdom declared that "the Constitu-

---

45. 375 U.S. at 402, 84 S.Ct. at 456.

46. 163 U.S. 537, 16 S.Ct. 1138, 41 L.Ed. 256 (1896).

47. 163 U.S. 1144, 1146; 85 S.Ct. 552, 559 (Harlan, J., dissenting).

48. *Anderson v. Martin*, 206 F.Supp. 705 (Wisdom, J., dissenting).

49. Andres Kull, *The Color-Blind Constitution* (Cambridge, Mass.: 1992), 179.

tion is both color blind and color conscious."[50] When, as in *Dorsey*, the government utilized race to deprive someone of a benefit or otherwise impose a burden, he declared, the Constitution had to be construed to require colorblind decision-making. But, as in *Jefferson County* and other school desegregation cases, when race was used to prevent the continuation of prior discrimination and to undo its continuing effects, the Constitution should be interpreted to countenance reliance on a color-conscious remedy. Thus, he was able to conclude that "here race is relevant because the governmental purpose is to offer Negroes equal educational opportunities. The means to that end, such as disestablishing segregation among students, distributing the better teachers equitably, equalizing facilities, and selecting appropriate locations for schools, and avoiding resegregation must necessarily be based on race."[51] This ruling, one commentator observed, "identifies . . . the moment at which the color-blind ideal was jettisoned by its former proponents [and] banished . . . from contemporary constitutional law."[52]

To justify this bifurcated view of the constitutionality of race-based state action, Wisdom emphasized that the HEW guidelines did not require the placement of white or black children in particular schools merely for the purpose of striking a racial balance in a school or school district proportionate to the racial population of the local community. Rather, he maintained, the racial percentages were used merely as a "general rule of thumb" or an "objective administrative guide" to measure the success of integration efforts.[53] He also underscored the fact that this case involved only the review of desegregation plans for formerly *de jure* segregated school systems and not school systems that, while racially desegregated *de facto*, were not separated by force of law.[54]

In deciding to countenance a limited use of race, Wisdom was also guided, as he frequently was, by purely pragmatic factors. "The Courts and HEW cannot measure good faith or progress," he explained, "without taking race into account." Once racial imbalance "infects a private

50. 372 F.2d at 876.

51. 372 F.2d at 877.

52. Kull, *The Color-Blind Constitution*, 181.

53. 372 F.2d at 886, 887.

54. 372 F.2d at 868, 869, 873–876, 886. In its *en banc* opinion in *Jefferson County* adopting Wisdom's panel opinion, the Fifth Circuit also "express[ed] no opinion as the applicability of HEW Guidelines" to the integration of school districts outside of the Fifth Circuit where racial imbalance was the result of *de facto* segregation and not state-compelled apartheid. *U.S. v. Jefferson County*, 380 F.2d 385, 390 (5th Cir.1976) (*en banc*).

school system, there is simply no way to alleviate it without consideration of race. . . . Common sense suggests that a gross discrepancy between the ratio of Negroes to white children in a school and the HEW percentage guides raises an inference that the school plan is not working as it should in providing a unitary, integrated system."[55]

The persuasive power of this reasoning soon extended beyond the confines of school integration law. Wisdom's reference to the use of racial percentages as a yardstick to measure progress, rather than as an end in themselves, subsequently was incorporated by the Supreme Court and served as the underpinning of its acceptance of the use of race-based remedies designed to respond to the legacy of racial discrimination in education, employment, and public contracting.[56]

Yet even within the limited context of school desegregation law, Wisdom's opinion had the enormously powerful effect of requiring all of the six states that made up the Fifth Circuit (Texas, Louisiana, Mississippi, Alabama, Georgia, and Florida) to adhere to a single, uniform, comprehensive plan for desegregating all grades by the impending 1967–1968 school term and for achieving substantial faculty desegregation by the following year. The opinion also is noteworthy for its reliance on statistical and historical evidence and its display of Wisdom's unique writing style. He buttressed his conclusions concerning the need for more rapid integration of the defendant school districts with detailed statistical analyses of both the racial composition of every school's student body and faculty and the impact on the district and circuit court dockets of the multitude of lawsuits and appeals occasioned by the school boards' consistent refusal to voluntarily engage in meaningful integration. Wisdom also crafted a comprehensive historical analysis of Congress's evolving appreciation of the importance of keeping effective integration of the nation's public school system a matter of national priority, a process that culminated in its enactment of Title VI of the Civil Rights Act of 1964, which banned racial discrimination by schools and other programs receiving federal financial assistance.[57]

---

55. 372 F.2d at 877, 888.

56. Wisdom's use of this same analysis to sanction the use of race-based affirmative action in employment, and its influence on Supreme Court jurisprudence concerning affirmative action is described in chapter 14, *infra*.

57. In 1965, Congress passed the Elementary and Secondary Education Act, 20 U.S.C.A. § 6301 et seq (1965), the first federal statute authorizing the grant of general federal financial aid to elementary and secondary education in the nation's history. As a consequence of that enact-

Style as well as substance, however, was another hallmark of Wisdom's opinion. Throughout the decision, he was able to emphasize a particularly important point with a graceful turn of phrase. For example, to underscore the role that clear and uniform standards would play in discouraging local school boards from continuing their pattern of delaying actions, Wisdom artfully paraphrased Cicero, declaring that "in Georgia, for example, there should not be one law for Athens and another law for Rome."[58] And in some of his most stirring prose, Wisdom summarized the impact and message of *Brown* in words that reflected his own deeply felt sense of the moral imperative that justified, and, in fact compelled, the implementation of an expeditious and effective integration plan. "Brown erased Dred Scott, used the Fourteenth Amendment to breathe life into the Thirteenth, and wrote the Declaration of Independence into the Constitution. Freedmen are free men. They are created as equal as are all other American citizens and with the same unalienable rights to life, liberty, and the pursuit of happiness. No longer 'beings of an inferior race'—the Dred Scott article of faith— Negroes too are part of 'the people of the United States.'"[59]

The seemingly perpetual pattern of official obstructionism that Wisdom and his colleagues had confronted in every case was, as Wisdom previously had decried in both *Singleton I* and II, the legacy in large part of language found in the South Carolina federal court's ruling in *Briggs*. The *Briggs* dictum had legitimized the use of "freedom-of-choice" desegregation plans that placed the onus of desegregation on the parents of African American students by providing them with the opportunity to choose to send their children to previously all-white schools. But as his statistical analysis in *Jefferson County* persuasively demonstrated, where school boards were not required to take affirmative steps to integrate the schools, parent-initiated "free choice" was largely ineffective in removing the racial identification of historically segregated schools.

Nevertheless, Wisdom's concern over freedom-of-choice plans was tempered by his cognizance of certain political realities. He was astute enough to recognize that while he might convince Homer Thornberry

---

ment, Title VI of the 1964 Civil Rights Act, which prohibits any recipient of federal funding from engaging in racial discrimination (upon penalty of losing some or all of that funding), became applicable to public schools that received federal funds.

58. 372 F.2d at 861.

59. 372 F.2d at 873.

to join him in an opinion that struck down all further use of freedom-of-choice plans, the regional importance and national profile of this case made the panel's opinion a likely target for *en banc* reconsideration by the whole court. And the last thing that Wisdom wanted was a lukewarm affirmance by a highly divided court, or, even worse, a reversal. He needed to make sure that the entire court would ratify whatever decision his panel rendered. So to garner that needed support, Wisdom limited the scope of the opinion by permitting the continued use of freedom-of-choice plans, subject, however, to severe constitutional restraint in the form of adherence, at a minimum, to HEW's stringent desegregation guidelines.

Wisdom previously had attempted to lay the *Briggs* dictum (that school boards have no affirmative duty to integrate but merely to stop promoting segregation) to rest in a footnote in *Singleton I.* And he had reiterated the court's rejection of that ill-conceived notion in the main body of *Singleton II.* In *Jefferson County,* he drove the final nail into *Briggs*'s jurisprudential coffin. Wisdom devoted a significant portion of the main body of his opinion to a thorough dismantling of the "pure dictum" that had produced such a "frustrating effect" on efforts to implement the Supreme Court's ruling in *Brown.*

The fundamental error in *Briggs,* beyond the fact that its entire discussion was pure dictum, Wisdom explained, lay in the notion that rights codified in the Fourteenth Amendment inured exclusively to the benefit of individuals, rather than to the groups of which they were members. First of all, this statement ignored the critical fact that *Brown* was a class action in which the Supreme Court sought to secure, for all African Americans, the benefits of the constitutional right to equal educational opportunity. This oversight, in turn, drained *Brown* of the significance of its core finding that the maintenance of a segregated school system injured black students, as a collectivity, by causing psychological damage, denying them access to the dominant culture, diminishing their opportunity to participate meaningfully in political and other aspects of the life of the community and affairs of state, and imposing upon them, as a group, the stigma of apartheid that flew in the face of the constitutional mandate to abolish all the badges and incidents of slavery.[60]

Additionally, Wisdom wrote, *Briggs*'s focus on the individual nature

60. See Civil Rights Cases, 109 U.S. 3, 20, 3 S.Ct. 18, 28, 27 L.Ed. 835 (1883).

of Fourteenth Amendment rights was inconsistent with *Brown II*'s explicit recognition of the right of blacks as a class to a unitary, nonracial system of public education. By requiring states only to provide relief to discrete individuals, the opinion in *Briggs* permitted, and even encouraged, the perpetuation of a dual, segregated system because it failed to address, let alone cure, the systemic constitutional wrong of legally mandated educational apartheid. This state-coerced separation of the races was, in and of itself and without regard to the harm it imposed on any individual, a denial of the constitutional guarantee of equal protection under the law.

This was a boldly innovative statement, unique in its conception and far-reaching in its implications. For the first time, a federal appellate judge had concluded that when a state sought to remedy its own history of discrimination in education, the Constitution required more than a plan providing relief solely to *individual* African American students. Since the evil perpetrated by *de jure* segregation was an injury to an entire race, any meaningful, constitutionally appropriate remedy had to address that class-wide wrong. Writing in italics for emphasis, Wisdom proclaimed that "*the only adequate redress for a previously overt system-wide policy of segregation directed against Negroes as a collective entity is a system-wide policy of integration.*" Equally important, this concept—that the Constitution could require group-based relief for victims of racial discrimination—would later serve as the analytical lynchpin for the Supreme Court's evolving jurisprudence in the area of affirmative action in employment and government contracting as well as in education.

Moving from the theoretical to the practical, Wisdom explained that the collective damage inflicted by the unconstitutional, state-coerced segregation in *Jefferson County* demanded a plan for comprehensive and complete integration not only of the student body but of the entire educational system. "Faculties, facilities, and activities as well as student bodies," Wisdom boldly announced, "must be integrated."[61] Faculty integration was an indispensable component of an effective desegregation plan, Wisdom explained, because as long as a school retained an all- or nearly all-black faculty, it never would attract a white student body. Thus, irrespective of its impact on the constitutional rights of individual black teachers, the discouraging effect that teacher segregation would have on student body integration was sufficient to render it unconstitutional in its own right.

61. 372 F.2d at 867.

Wisdom's thorough dissection of the erroneous theoretical under-pinnings of *Briggs*, particularly his acknowledgment of a group-based theory of constitutional entitlements and his related declaration of the constitutionality of race-conscious remedies, went far beyond relegat-ing *Briggs* forever to the dustbin of history. Like a smooth-faced stone cast into a placid pond, it produced ripple effects that would have far-reaching implications extending way beyond the contours of this and other school desegregation cases.

This opinion also contained a detailed decree giving school boards and district courts specific directions on how to achieve integration of students, faculties, facilities, and programs. Every public school stu-dent was required to make an annual choice of school. Any student who failed to do so within a week after the opening of the school year would be assigned to the school closest to his or her home where space was available. Furthermore, no student's choice could be denied for any reason other than overcrowding, in which case preference would be given on the basis of the proximity of the school to the student's home. The decree also required all school districts to bring the quality of the physical facilities, equipment, and instruction in formerly all-black schools to the level provided in theretofore all-white schools. Thus, not-withstanding his cautionary proposal to the contrary in *Bush*, Wisdom, his colleagues on the Fifth Circuit, and district judges throughout the circuit would no longer be sitting on their collective hands.

Within a week of the release of the opinion in *Jefferson County*, the Of-fice of Education of HEW, with President Lyndon Johnson's approval, published its 1967 desegregation guidelines. Prior to the release of *Jeffer-son County* there had been concern among HEW officials that President Johnson might not endorse the tough, aggressive standards contained in these regulations.[62] And, in fact, these proposed guidelines had lin-gered on the president's desk for several weeks prior to the release of *Jefferson County* while the administration pondered the political ramifi-cations that might be created by the court's ruling. But the persuasive power of Wisdom's opinion convinced President Johnson to authorize the promulgation of these guidelines.[63]

The decision in *Jefferson County* did not, however, meet with univer-sal acclaim. In addition to the predictable and widely reported denun-

62. Title VI of the 1964 Civil Rights Act authorizes the U.S. Office of Education of HEW to issue implementing guidelines but also expressly provides that these guidelines cannot become ef-fective until the president approves them. 42 U.S.C. §2000d-1 (1964).

63. Editorial, "Tokenism's Last Tick," *Atlanta Constitution*, January 9, 1967, 4, col. 1.

ciations of Wisdom's opinion by several southern governors, Wisdom received scores of private communiqués once the court's decision was made available to the public. The range of reactions is reflected in two letters he received within one day of each other.

One Florida citizen informed Wisdom that "you will go down in history as one of the people that wrecked the public school systems in the southern states. Either your knowledge of the law is quite vague, or you are just a stooge for the federal government. I hope you can sleep nights. Yours truly, Frank Hill."[64] At the other end of the spectrum was a letter from Louis Berry, a self-described "Negro lawyer" from Alexandria, Louisiana. "I read your December, 1966, opinion with pride and deep emotion. I shall never forget the profound analysis which you made of the disabilities under which Negroes have had to toil and labor since slavery. I am convinced that your opinion and your reasoning will go down in the history of this country as a legal masterpiece." And lauding Wisdom's record in civil rights cases, Berry added that "your role as a Federal Judge in the area of Civil Rights has been monumental. May the good Lord keep you well, because the masses of downtrodden people need you more and more in their struggle toward the American Dream of equality and brotherhood under our constitutional democracy."[65]

Harold Cox, the third member of the *Jefferson County* panel, did not join with Wisdom and Thornberry and wrote a stinging dissenting opinion.[66] An adherent to the *Briggs* principle that desegregation did not mandate integration, Cox was incensed by Wisdom's repudiation of that doctrine in the face of the Fifth Circuit's previous endorsement of it in several of its earlier decisions. "Surely," Cox grumbled, "only two of the judges of this Court may not now single-handedly reverse those decisions and change such law of this Circuit."[67] And though he acknowledged the legitimacy of *Brown* and that the time for "deliberate speed" in desegregating the public schools had expired, Cox rejected Wisdom's "extreme view and harsh and mailed fist decision" that *Brown* required schools to take specific steps to achieve integration.[68] Most significant, however, although Cox did not overtly suggest or request the granting of *en banc* review of the panel ruling, his additional statement that the majority's decision "does not reflect the well considered and

64. Letter to John M. Wisdom from Frank Hill, April 4, 1967.
65. Letter to John M. Wisdom from Louis Berry, April 3, 1967.
66. *U.S. v. Jefferson County,* 372 F.2d 905 (5th Cir.1966) (Cox, J., dissenting).
67. 372 F.2d at 906.
68. 372 F.2d at 906.

firmly stated composite decision of this Circuit"[69] left no doubt about his intentions in that regard.

Surprisingly, however, the official request to poll the members on a rehearing came not from Cox but from John Brown. Even though Judge Brown believed that the majority decision was correct and that no good would be served by hearing school desegregation cases *en banc,* he perceived that several of his colleagues harbored genuine doubts about the opinion and he wanted them to have "a legitimate way of giving a judge-like public utterance to these views."[70] But Brown assumed that the motion to reconsider would fail, and that these "utterances" would take the form only of opinions concurring or dissenting from a decision to *deny* reconsideration.[71]

The first ten announced votes from the twelve active (that is, non-senior status) members of the court split 6–4 against granting reconsideration.[72] Under the court's rules, *en banc* consideration is denied whenever a majority of the active circuit judges vote against it. And although Wisdom had good reason to believe that he could obtain that seventh "no" vote from one of the two undecided judges, he chose not to force the issue in a case that he knew would have broad, if not nationwide, impact. To the contrary, he ultimately urged his colleagues to vote in favor of reconsideration.

Wisdom's esteemed colleague Dick Rives, now a senior judge and therefore ineligible to participate as a member of the court *en banc,* was deeply distressed by Wisdom's rejection of the *Briggs* "dictum" and believed that if previous rulings by the Fifth Circuit were replaced by *Jefferson County*'s holding "that integration lock, stock and barrel is required," future orders issued by the Fifth Circuit "may or may not be enforced, [but] I do not believe that they will be respected."[73] So Rives chose to send a nine-page letter to all the active circuit judges on January 30 setting forth the reasons why he did not agree with the rulings of the majority in *Jefferson County*.[74] Rives's letter convinced Wisdom that the case

69. 372 F.2d at 909.

70. Letter to Elbert P. Tuttle from John M. Brown, January 10, 1967.

71. Ibid. Memo with attached draft order to Elbert P. Tuttle from John R. Brown, January 11, 1967.

72. Judges Tuttle, Goldberg, Simpson, Thornberry, Brown, and Wisdom voted against and Judges Gewin, Godbold, Coleman, and Bell voted in favor of *en banc* rehearing. Judges Ainsworth and Dyer had not voted by this date.

73. Letter to The Circuit Judges of the Fifth Circuit from Richard T. Rives, January 30, 1967, 9.

74. Ibid.

was too important to the court and the country to be resolved by only a three-member panel. On February 2, Wisdom sent a letter to his colleagues urging them to vote with him to grant rehearing en banc of the case whose majority opinion he had authored.[75] All of the other judges immediately jumped on the bandwagon, and on February 9 the court announced its unanimous decision to reconsider the case en banc.[76]

In 1964, three years before the court released the panel opinion in *Jefferson County*, Congress had authorized three new positions for the Fifth Circuit to deal with its expanding caseload. The addition of these new slots made the Fifth Circuit the nation's largest federal court of appeals with twelve active members. President Lyndon Johnson filled these posts in 1966 with Texan Irving L. Goldberg, New Orleanian Robert A. Ainsworth, Jr., and Floridian Bryan Simpson. In addition, two other roster changes occurred during that same year. President Johnson promoted District Judges John C. Godbold and David W. Dyer to replace retired judges Rives and Warren Jones, respectively. Consequently, by the time oral argument in *Jefferson County* was held before the en banc court in Jacksonville, Florida, on March 10, 1967, the Fifth Circuit had its full complement of twelve active judges in place.[77] The hearing on that day was not only the first time the Fifth Circuit had sat en banc in Jacksonville,[78] it was the first time in American history that a case had been argued in front of a panel of a dozen judges.[79] In fact, the government had to construct special plywood platforms in District

75. Letter to All Active Judges of the Fifth Circuit Court of Appeals from John M. Wisdom, February 2, 1967.

76. See Letter to All Active Circuit Judges of the Fifth Circuit from Elbert P. Tuttle, February 3, 1967; Letter to The Circuit Judges from James P. Coleman, February 4, 1967.

77. Since he expected the en banc court's judgment to be reviewed by the Supreme Court, Chief Judge Tuttle sought to minimize the delay in obtaining an en banc decision by drafting an order that permitted additional briefing but did not allow further oral argument by the parties. Letter from Chief Judge Elbert P. Tuttle to All Active Circuit Judges of the Fifth Circuit, February 8, 1956 (with attached draft order granting reconsideration en banc without oral argument). But when several of his colleagues urged him to allow argument, he relented and sent out an amended order setting oral argument in the consolidated cases for March 10, 1967, in Jacksonville, Florida. Order of the Fifth Circuit in *U.S. v. Jefferson County* et al., filed February 21, 1967. See also "Mixing Orders to Be Reviewed," *New Orleans Times-Picayune*, February 10, 1967, 1, col. 3; "U.S. Court to Reopen Guides Case," *New Orleans States-Item*, February 22, 1967, 1, col. 3; "Ban on School Bias in South Is Upheld," *New York Times*, March 30, 1967, 1, col. 7; 37, col. 3.

78. "Old Integration Arguments Renewed," *Jacksonville Journal*, March 10, 1967, 1, col. 1.

79. "Race Pressure Is Blasted in School Decree," *New Orleans States-Item*, March 10, 1967, 1, col. 1.

Judge William A. McRae's courtroom in the Federal Building to accommodate those judges who could not be seated either behind the bench or in the area normally used by the courtroom clerks.[80]

Making good on its promise to render a decision as quickly as possible, the court released its ruling on March 29, 1967.[81] Wisdom's decision to subject his opinion to *en banc* review, whether the product of a selfless desire to avoid rancor among his colleagues or a shrewd political calculation of the most effective way to achieve meaningful school integration (or some combination thereof), achieved both of these objectives. By a vote of 8-4, the full court voted to adopt Wisdom's original opinion subject to a few minor clarifying statements and some technical changes to the decree.[82] Most important, the court's *per curiam* opinion, which Wisdom prepared, endorsed his panel opinion's rejection of the *Briggs* dictum and his affirmation of the school boards' constitutional duty to engage in affirmative steps to achieve integration.[83] The *en banc* opinion also expressly overruled all prior Fifth Circuit decisions that had adopted *Briggs*'s distinction between desegregation and integration, and embraced the adoption of HEW guidelines as the minimum standards for measuring progress toward attaining an integrated, unitary school system.

Less than three weeks later, the Supreme Court turned back a last-ditch effort by Louisiana and Alabama officials to prevent the Fifth Circuit's ruling from taking effect before the opening of the fall school term. It denied the school boards' motion to stay enforcement of the Fifth Circuit's decision pending review of that ruling by the High Court.[84] Then, on October 9, 1967, the Supreme Court issued the final word in this historic case when, consistent with its treatment of other

80. George Harmon, "History-Making Court to Sit Here," *Jacksonville Journal*, March 9, 1967, 1, col. 1.

81. *U.S. v. Jefferson County Board of Education*, 380 F.2d 385 (5th Cir.1967) (*en banc*). See "U.S. Court Ruling on Bias Is Fought," *New York Times*, March 11, 1967, 14, col. 3.

82. Judges Gewin, Bell, and Godbold wrote dissenting opinions while Judge James P. Coleman of Mississippi wrote a "separate" opinion agreeing with the decision to reverse the lower courts' rulings but disagreeing with the majority's rulings on the two key issues in the case—the repudiation of the *Briggs* dictum and the mandate to adhere to the HEW guidelines. They were the same four judges who had voted in favor of *en banc* reconsideration prior to Wisdom's decision to call for *en banc* review. See note 72, *supra*.

83. Letter to Judges Tuttle, Brown, Thornberry, Goldberg, Ainsworth, Dyer, and Simpson from Judge John M. Wisdom, March 13, 1967.

84. *Caddo Parish School Board v. U.S.*, 386 U.S. 1001, 87 S.Ct. 1342, 18 L.Ed.2d 430 (1967).

Fifth Circuit desegregation rulings, it denied the school boards' request for review.[85]

The impact and significance of Wisdom's opinions in *Jefferson County* on both the pace of integration and the development of constitutional equal protection doctrine cannot be overestimated. For over a dozen years, the Supreme Court's breathtaking pronouncement in *Brown* of a constitutional mandate to end racial discrimination in public education had been stymied at every turn by an unspoken but willing collaboration between determined state and local public officials and accommodating federal district judges. But, as one judicial chronicler accurately remarked, "it was John Minor Wisdom's pen, fueled by his intellect and his will, that transfigured [*Brown's*] promise into reality."[86] Wisdom's opinions in *Bush*, *Singleton I* and *II*, and *Jefferson County*, this scholar adjudged, "changed the course of desegregation law, moving the lower federal district courts from token desegregation to immediate, massive integration."[87] As a result, he concluded, "no judge in America contributed more to the evolution of school desegregation law than John Minor Wisdom."[88] A respected member of the U.S. Fourth Circuit Court of Appeals, Judge J. Harvie Wilkinson seconded that assessment, stating that Wisdom's opinions in these cases "transformed the face of school desegregation law."[89] And reflecting back on the legacy of Wisdom's *Jefferson*

85. *Caddo Parish School Board v. U.S.*, 389 U.S. 840, 88 S.Ct. 67, 19 L.Ed.2d 103 (1967); *Board of Education of City of Bessemer v. U.S.*, 389 U.S. 840, 88 S.Ct. 77, 19 L.Ed.2d 104 (1967). The Supreme Court's action, however, did not signify the end of this litigation. Within two years, the Jefferson and Bessemer County school boards were back before the Fifth Circuit. After two years of experience with the freedom of choice plan prescribed in the Fifth Circuit's model decree, not one white student in either of these two school districts had attended an all-black school and less than 4 percent of black students attended previously all-white schools in each of these districts. These facts impelled the Justice Department to request a modification of the decree with respect to student assignment. After the district judge denied this request for additional relief, the case came to a Fifth Circuit panel composed of Circuit Judges Griffin Bell of Atlanta and Irving L. Goldberg of Dallas and District Judge C. Clyde Atkins of Miami. The unanimous panel reversed the trial judge on the ground that the freedom of choice plan had failed to accomplish any meaningful level of desegregation. It sent the case back to the trial judge with instructions to come up with a revised desegregation plan. *U.S. v. Jefferson County Board of Education*, 417 F.2d 834 (5th Cir.1969).

86. Frank T. Read, *The Penman of the Court: A Tribute to John Minor Wisdom*, TUL. L. REV. 264, 265 (1985).

87. Frank T. Read, *The Penman of the Court: A Tribute to John Minor Wisdom*, TUL. L. REV. 264, 272 (1985).

88. Frank T. Read, *The Penman of the Court: A Tribute to John Minor Wisdom*, TUL. L. REV. 264, 271 (1985).

89. J. Harvie Wilkinson, *From Brown to Bakke* (New York: 1979), 111.

County opinions more than two decades later, Jack Greenberg, the man who, along with Thurgood Marshall, oversaw all of the NAACP's litigation efforts in scores of desegregation cases throughout the South during this period, observed that Wisdom's opinion "was an extraordinary leap in judicial supervision of the schools. After *Jefferson County*, the federal courts boldly took on the unenviable job of supervising school desegregation. The case was the progenitor of the broad equitable discretion federal courts later would exercise as school litigation moved away from segregation to the problems of integration. It brought judicial involvement in the schools to a plane undreamed of in the Brown era and gave plaintiffs real reason to hope that they could force the dismantling of segregated school systems."[90]

Yet even as the rulings in *Jefferson County* impelled the U.S. Justice Department to reopen nearly two hundred desegregation cases throughout the South to compel school boards to adhere to the *Jefferson County* standard, it was essential that the Supreme Court place the prestige of its endorsement on the path blazed by the Fifth Circuit. It was one thing for the Fifth Circuit, even sitting *en banc*, to declare that the Constitution demanded not only the dissolution of legally mandated segregated schools, but also affirmative governmental action to integrate those schools. It was another thing to have that bold interpretation of *Brown* ratified by the High Court through an official opinion, as opposed to a decision not to review the Fifth Circuit's ruling. For even though Wisdom and his colleagues hoped that their *en banc* ruling in *Jefferson County* would set the blueprint for the desegregation of *de jure* segregated school systems located outside of their jurisdiction, other courts, particularly the Fourth Circuit comprising the Carolinas, Virginia, and West Virginia, were free to chart their own course. The only words that would bind the entire nation would have to come from the nine justices in Washington, D.C.

Those words were not long in coming. On May 27, 1968, in *Green v. County School Board of New Kent County*, the Supreme Court struck down an eastern Virginia school district's freedom-of-choice desegregation plan.[91] In arriving at this conclusion, the Court drew heavily from the concepts, terminology, and analysis contained in Wisdom's *Jefferson County* opinions. Confronted with a dual system that had operated

90. Jack Greenberg, *Foreword: A Civil Rights Symposium Honoring Judge John Minor Wisdom*, 64 TUL. L. REV. 1351, 1353–1354 (1990).

91. 391 U.S. 430, 88 S.Ct. 1689, 20 L.Ed.2d 716 (1968).

under compulsion of state law and school board fiat, the Court unanimously followed Wisdom's lead by declaring the official demise of both "deliberate speed" and *Briggs*'s purported distinction between the duty to desegregate and the obligation to integrate, and by relying on statistical measures of integration to assess the constitutional adequacy of desegregation efforts.

Echoing the strains of *Jefferson County*, the Supreme Court acknowledged that the ultimate objective of its rulings in *Brown I* and II was "the abolition of dual systems"[92] in favor of "a unitary, nonracial system of public education."[93] Precisely as Wisdom had explained in *Jefferson County*, the High Court declared that the command of *Brown II* was to charge school boards in such situations with "the affirmative duty to take whatever steps might be necessary to convert to a unitary system."[94] Furthermore, such affirmative action, the Court pronounced, embellishing upon Wisdom's succinct refrain, must consist of a plan "that promises realistically to work, and promises realistically to work now."[95] Actual success in attaining classroom integration was now the measure of constitutional muster.

The High Court also incorporated Wisdom's strategic compromise in *Jefferson County* by refraining from outlawing the use of all freedom-of-choice plans. The Court, expressly citing *Jefferson County* for the first and only time in the opinion, announced that freedom of choice, while not a legitimate end in itself, would be an acceptable means to the constitutionally dictated end where no reasonably available alternative mechanism could more speedily and effectively effectuate conversion to a unitary school system. But since Virginia board's freedom-of-choice plan had not, after three years of operation, resulted in a single white child choosing to attend the district's all-black school and as 85 percent of all African American students continued to attend a "black" school, the Court struck down the county's freedom-of-choice plan.

The Court did not, however, require adherence to the HEW guidelines among its suggested methods for achieving acceptable levels of integration. Nevertheless, in ordering the school board to formulate a new plan, the Supreme Court again parroted some of Wisdom's phraseology in *Jefferson County*. Wisdom had concluded in *Jefferson County* that

92. 391 U.S. at 437.
93. 391 U.S. at 436.
94. 391 U.S. at 437–438.
95. 391 U.S. at 439.

"freedom of choice means the maximum amount of freedom and clearly understood choice in a bona fide unitary system where schools are not white schools or Negro schools—just schools."[96] In *Green*, the Supreme Court declared that the Constitution demanded conversion to a system "without a 'white' school and a 'Negro' school, but just schools."[97]

But even the Supreme Court's decisive endorsement of the Fifth Circuit's ruling in *Jefferson County* that school boards had an affirmative duty to take steps to demonstrably expedite the pace of integration did not prevent Wisdom and his Fifth Circuit colleagues from continuing to be confronted by a pattern of recalcitrance that required their vigilant review and supervision. Two cases in particular reflect Wisdom's unceasing post-*Jefferson County* efforts to hold school boards', the federal district judges', and even some of his colleagues' feet to the fire.

In May 1965, nearly two years prior to the release of the Fifth Circuit's *en banc* opinion in *Jefferson County*, the Houston school district had authorized, per voter referendum, a $59 million bond issue dedicated to public school construction. In deciding how and where to allocate those funds to build new and renovate existing schools, the school board had considered a host of non-race related factors. It ultimately had adopted, post-*Brown*, a freedom-of-choice plan in which each student had the right to choose to attend any school in the district. But since most neighborhoods were racially segregated, and most students continued to choose to attend the school in closest proximity to their residence, the composition of the student body of each public school reflected the racial composition of the neighborhood in which it was located.

A group of black students in the Houston area filed suit to enjoin the local school board from following through on its construction and improvement program until a new site location program that would not promote *de facto* segregation could be designed and implemented. The plaintiffs claimed that the decision to build new schools in predominantly African American neighborhoods was designed to perpetuate *de facto* segregation by depriving the black students in these neighborhoods of the right to go to a truly integrated school. The trial judge in *Broussard v. Houston Independent School District* denied this request for relief on the ground that the school board system had not acted with the intention or purpose of maintaining or perpetuating segregation but, in good faith, had acted upon a collection of relevant, nondiscriminatory

96. 372 F.2d at 890.
97. 391 U.S. at 442.

factors such as accessibility of facility, safety, and due regard for prevailing traffic patterns.[98]

On appeal, a majority of the Fifth Circuit panel (composed of Wisdom, Dick Rives, and District Judge Ben C. Connally of Houston) voted to affirm the trial court's ruling on the ground that the board was under no affirmative obligation to compel integration by preventing individuals from choosing to attend a neighborhood school.[99] Rives's decision to side with Judge Connally rather than with Wisdom was consistent with the position he had communicated to his colleagues when he urged them to vote to reconsider the panel opinion in *Jefferson County*.

In a sharply worded dissenting opinion, Wisdom remarked that it seemed "scarcely possible that in the Fifth Circuit a school board in a great city could look a judge in the eye and say that in spending sixty million dollars for school buildings the board need not consider residential racial patterns as a relevant factor in the selection of a school site."[100] After all, Wisdom reminded, "everyone knows that the location of schools is highly relevant to school segregation."[101] More important, he emphasized, the majority's continued reliance on the "*Briggs* word-magic" distinction between desegregation and integration was "flatly contrary" to the Fifth Circuit's repudiation of this concept in its *en banc* opinion in *Jefferson County* more than a year before.[102] The defendants' failure to affirmatively consider race in selecting school sites, Wisdom declared, flouted that part of the *en banc* decree in *Jefferson County* that required local authorities to locate new schools and substantially expand existing facilities with the objective of eradicating the vestiges of dual system of segregated schools. And even though his was a dissenting opinion, Wisdom chose to offer some words of caution and advice to school districts throughout the Deep South. "With deference, I suggest that such school boards bear in mind that the majority's decision is irreconcilable with Jefferson and that recent decisions fully support Jefferson, in general and specifically as to school construction. It is not

98. 262 F.Supp. 266 (S.D.Tex.1966).

99. *Broussard v. Houston Independent School District*, 395 F.2d 817 (5th Cir.1968).

100. 395 F.2d 822 (Wisdom, J., dissenting).

101. 395 F.2d at 822.

102. Although the majority and dissenting opinions in *Broussard* were officially released three days *after* the Supreme Court issued its opinion in *Green*, the members of the panel did not have the benefit of the Supreme Court's ruling before deciding *Broussard* because their opinions were completed and sent to the printer *before* the release of *Green*. *Broussard v. Houston Independent School District*, 403 F.2d 35 (Wisdom, J., dissenting).

too late to heed these decisions." And with respect to the lingering devotion to *Briggs,* Wisdom emphasized that "Briggs has fallen. There is a bridge under construction, resting on the Constitution, connecting whites and Negroes and designed to lead the two races, starting with young children, to a harmonious, peaceful, civilized existence. That bridge is a plan for equal educational opportunities for all in an integrated, unitary public school system based on school administrators affirmatively finding ways to make the plan work."[103]

Although arguments in this case had been held before the Fifth Circuit panel in January 1967, the opinion did not see the light of day until May 30, 1968, nearly seventeen months later. On December 11, 1967, Judge Rives had gently reminded his colleagues that although nearly a year already had passed since the arguments, and though he and Connally had distributed their opinions six months ago, they were still awaiting receipt of Wisdom's dissent. Rives also predicted that, at this pace, construction on the schools whose site selection was the subject of the lawsuit would likely be completed before the court was ready to rule.[104] And that is precisely what happened. As a result, on October 2, 1968, a little more than four months after releasing their opinion, Rives and Connally voted to dismiss the case as moot.[105] Wisdom wrote a short opinion dissenting from the dismissal in which he emphasized that although these schools had been constructed, it was not too late to enjoin future construction of buildings pursuant to the existing selection plan.[106]

Wisdom's insistence upon full compliance with the rule of law and his concomitant willingness to acknowledge and condemn the overt and subtle stratagems by which state officials sought to perpetuate the now constitutionally outlawed culture of legally mandated segregation also was front and center in a dissenting opinion he wrote in a much heralded case that challenged the City of Jackson, Mississippi's decision to close all five of its municipal swimming pools. In 1962, a trio of African American residents of Jackson brought an action to enjoin the enforcement of state laws that mandated the racially segregated use of public parks, swimming pools, golf links, and other public recreational

103. 395 F.2d at 828 (Wisdom, J., dissenting).

104. Letter to John M. Wisdom and Ben C. Connally from Richard T. Rives, December 11, 1967.

105. *Broussard v. Houston Independent School District,* 403 F.2d 34 (5th Cir.1968).

106. 403 F.2d 35 (Wisdom, J., dissenting).

facilities. District Judge Sidney Mize found, as the plaintiffs had admitted, that the city had not taken any affirmative steps to enforce these statutes, but, rather, had acquiesced to the custom of segregated use of these public facilities located in the city's totally segregated residential neighborhoods.[107] These voluntary acts of self-segregation by private individuals, he reasoned, did not directly implicate the city and therefore the plaintiffs could not assert any constitutional claim, which required some form of governmental action. The Fifth Circuit summarily affirmed Mize's ruling in a one-paragraph *per curiam* opinion and the Supreme Court refused to hear the case on appeal.[108]

The City of Jackson subsequently officially desegregated all of its public recreational facilities, but also decided to shut down its five public pools rather than operate them on an integrated basis. A suit was filed to compel the reopening of the pools on a desegregated basis. In *Palmer v. Thompson*, the trial judge rejected the plaintiffs' claim that the closure decision was motivated by a desire to avoid desegregation and accepted the city's explanation that its decision was based on its good faith determination that it could not operate the pools safely or efficiently on an integrated basis.[109]

A Fifth Circuit panel composed of Judges Rives, Coleman, and Godbold unanimously affirmed the trial court's ruling.[110] On the very day that this opinion was released, Wisdom had completed a "semifinal" draft of his opinion for the majority in a case involving the closure of public pools in Tallahassee, Florida. Wisdom and Irving Goldberg had agreed in that case, *Steele v. Taft*, to declare the city's decision unconstitutional under the Fourteenth Amendment. The third member of the panel, Judge Warren Jones, had announced his intention to dissent from such a ruling.[111] Wisdom was adamant that the pool closures in both the Tallahassee and Jackson cases had been racially motivated and, therefore, disagreed strongly with the result reached by the panel in the Jackson case (*Palmer*). In a letter to Judge Goldberg, Wisdom

107. *Clark v. Thompson*, 206 F.Supp. 539, 543 (S.D.Miss.1962).

108. *Clark v. Thompson*, 313 F.2d 637 (5th Cir.1963), cert. denied, 375 U.S. 951, 84 S.Ct. 440, 11 L.Ed.2d 312 (1963).

109. 391 F.2d 324 (5th Cir.1967), aff'd *en banc*, 419 F.2d 1222 (5th Cir.1969), aff'd, 403 U.S. 217, 91 S.Ct. 1940, 29 L.Ed.2d 438 (1971).

110. *Palmer v. Thompson*, 391 F.2d 324 (5th Cir.1967).

111. Letter to All Judges of the Fifth Circuit Court of Appeals from John M. Wisdom, September 21, 1967; Letter to All Judges of the Fifth Circuit Court of Appeals from Warren L. Jones, September 26, 1967.

discussed whether the pair should simply stick to their guns in *Steele* and attempt to distinguish it from *Palmer* or instead of adopting that "weaselly" approach, simply "throw either *Palmer* or *Steele en banc* if the parties failed to request rehearing." Wisdom ultimately concluded that the best course would be to "throw" one or both of the cases *en banc*.[112] When Goldberg agreed with Wisdom's recommendation, the pair requested *en banc* rehearing in *Palmer* and re-argument before the original panel in *Steele*.[113]

A majority of the entire court voted to grant *en banc* rehearing in both cases.[114] But before a judgment could be issued in *Steele*, the City of Tallahassee reopened its municipal swimming pools on an integrated basis, which led to the dismissal of the appeal in *Steele* on mootness grounds.[115] *Palmer*, on the other hand, was resolved on the merits. By a one-vote margin, the thirteen-member court upheld the original panel decision in the city's favor.[116] Judge Rives, the author of the majority opinion, explained that the city's decision to shut down the pools did not implicate any constitutional rights since it had chosen to close the pools to all citizens, regardless of race, and was not funding or otherwise involved with privately owned, segregated swimming facilities. The majority also accepted the city's contention that it had acted in the interests of preventing violence and preserving fiscal integrity. Finally, the court rejected the plaintiff's argument that the closure had a particularly deleterious impact on black citizens since, as a group, they did not have the same degree of access to private swimming pools that was available to their generally more affluent white neighbors.

Wisdom wrote a dissenting opinion on behalf of all six members of the *en banc* minority.[117] Just as he had done in *Broussard*, Wisdom made no effort to hide his frustration at his colleagues' refusal to acknowl-

112. Letter to Irving L. Goldberg from John M. Wisdom, September 5, 1967.

113. Letter to All Judges of the Fifth Circuit Court of Appeals from John M. Wisdom, September 21, 1967.

114. Orders granting rehearing *en banc* in *Palmer v. Thompson* and *Steele v. Taft*, October 25, 1967.

115. *Steele v. Taft*, 415 F.2d 1005 (5th Cir.1969); Letter to Carl Rachlin, John D. Due, Jr., Roy T. Rhodes, and Rivers Buford, Jr., from Edward W. Wadsworth, July 28, 1969 (with attached note from Wadsworth to all Fifth Circuit Judges) (documents on file with author).

116. *Palmer v. Thomson*, 419 F.2d 1222 (5th Cir.1969) (*en banc*). Fifth Circuit judge Claude F. Clayton of Mississippi had attended the oral argument before the *en banc* court, but he passed away before the court reached its final decision, thereby reducing the number of participating judges from fourteen to thirteen. *Palmer v. Thomson*, 419 F.2d 1222, 1223n* (5th Cir.1970).

117. *Palmer v. Thompson*, 419 F.2d 1229 (5th Cir.1969) (Wisdom, J., dissenting).

edge that which, to him, was manifest. "Long exposure to obvious and non-obvious racial discrimination," his opinion commenced, "has seasoned this Court. It is astonishing, therefore, to find that half of the members of this Court accept at face value the two excuses the City of Jackson offered for closing its swimming pools and wading pools."[118] He refused to turn a blind eye to what every southerner knew, and what most white southerners felt to the core of their being. It was one thing to comply with the constitutional mandate to permit white and black citizens to share use of large, open air spaces. But it was totally another matter to expect most white residents of Jackson, Mississippi, to share the same enclosed space and splash around in the same water with African Americans. The decision to close the pools rather than open them to members of both races, Wisdom uniquely observed, amounted to a "forced display of a racial badge of inferiority. . . . Just as certainly as did the Jim Crow law considered in *Plessy v. Ferguson*, the swimming pool closing proceeds on the ground that Negroes are so inferior and degraded that they cannot be allowed to use public swimming pools with white people."[119] Wisdom entreated his colleagues to "recognize the actual traumatic impact of the action on Negroes for what it was. This is the badge of servitude, the sign of second-class citizenship, the stigma that the Thirteenth, Fourteenth, and Fifteenth Amendments were designed to eradicate."[120] Upholding the city's decision, he charged, "was a reaffirmation of the *Dred Scott* article of faith that Negroes are indeed 'a subordinate or inferior class of beings, who had been subjugated by the dominant race' and are not members of the 'people of the United States.'"[121] That this proud southerner and member of the privileged class was willing and able, unlike nearly any of his peers, to lay bare the racist face of his regional community, and to do so in powerful, compelling prose, was a testament not only to his courage and talent, but also to his unflagging devotion to the rule of law and regard for human dignity.

One by one, Wisdom gutted every argument raised in support of the City of Jackson's decision. Its insistence that the municipal pools could not be operated profitably was summarily dismissed as "frivolous." He

---

118. 419 F.2d at 1229.

119. 419 F.2d at 1233 (Wisdom, J., dissenting).

120. 419 F.2d at 1237 (Wisdom, J., dissenting).

121. 419 F.2d at 1237 (Wisdom, J., dissenting) (citing *Dred Scott v. Sanford*, 60 U.S. [19 How.] 393, 15 L.Ed.691 [1857]).

turned the city's assertion that its integrated operation of other public recreational facilities belied any intent to circumvent its constitutional duty on its head. To Wisdom, this fact served only to undercut the city's claim that it could not integrate public facilities without endangering public safety. And the facile claim that closing the pools to all was race-neutral, Wisdom countered, either disingenuously or cruelly ignored the decision's conspicuously more harmful impact on black children for whom pools in private country clubs or summer camps were virtually inaccessible. Moreover, and perhaps more important, the closure decision also produced a more enduring and insidious result. "The closing of the City's pools has done more than deprive a few thousand Negroes of the pleasure of swimming. It has taught Jackson's Negroes a lesson: In Jackson the price of protest is high. Negroes there now know that they risk losing even segregated public facilities if they dare to protest segregation. Negroes will now think twice before protesting . . . segregated facilities."[122]

Wisdom's dissent generated a caustic concurring opinion by Griffin Bell that was joined in by all other six members of the majority. Bell, a confident, outspoken, former lawyer from Atlanta, was not at all reluctant to cross swords with his more senior colleagues, a trait he previously had demonstrated. Only three months before Wisdom issued his dissenting opinion from the *en banc* ruling in *Palmer*, Bell openly and stridently had criticized Wisdom for relying on a law review article that had been submitted to him by one of the parties after oral argument in the *Local 189* case.[123] A proud man who zealously guarded his reputation, Wisdom rarely, if ever, ignored or left uncontested any perceived challenge to his integrity. And he had a memory like an elephant when it came to personal attacks. Not surprisingly, therefore, as a result of these and other actions by Bell over the years, Wisdom held his colleague in increasingly low personal regard.

Bell's one-page concurrence in *Palmer*, directed entirely at Wisdom's dissent, did not focus solely on the merits of the case. He began the opinion with a not very subtle jab at Wisdom. After noting that the pools had been closed in 1963, that the lawsuit had been filed in 1965,

122. 419 F.2d at 1236 (Wisdom, J., dissenting). The Supreme Court turned out to be as divided on this difficult case as the Fifth Circuit. By its own one-vote margin, a majority of the Court voted to uphold the circuit court's *en banc* ruling. *Palmer v. Thompson*, 403 U.S. 217, 91 S.Ct. 1940, 29 L.Ed. 438 (1971).

123. This squabble is discussed in detail in chapter 7, *supra*.

that a "prompt" hearing had been held and judgment rendered by the trial judge in 1965, that the original circuit panel decision had been rendered in 1967, and that all members of the majority had signed on to Rives's opinion in February 1968, "now almost two years later, the dissenting opinion has been filed." This led him to conclude, and to openly charge that "this is not to attribute the long delay to the parties; it is court produced."[124] Additionally, in support of his claim that Wisdom's dissent had departed from the record in concluding that the City of Jackson had acted in bad faith in deciding to close the pools, Bell chose to drop a cutting footnote. "Judge Rives wishes it noted that the City of Montgomery parks, contrary to footnote 14 of [Wisdom's] dissenting opinion, are open and have been since 1965. This fact was called to the attention of the court by Judge Rives prior to the filing of the dissenting opinion."[125]

Wisdom, however, had the last word. He responded to Bell's footnote with an addendum to his dissenting opinion acknowledging his error but wryly pointing out that "visitors to Montgomery's park will find no animals in the City Zoo and no water in the public swimming pools."[126]

Although Wisdom was piqued by this public criticism of his delay in producing his dissent in Palmer, Bell was by no means the only colleague to voice frustration over his frequent lack of dispatch in completing his opinions. In fact, substantial pressure from other colleagues had been applied to encourage Wisdom to bring forth his Palmer dissent. In a April 14, 1969, letter to the other members of the court concerning the progress of the en banc reconsiderations in both Steele and Palmer, Judge Rives noted that his proposed majority opinion for the en banc court in Palmer had been distributed "considerably more than a year ago," and asked whether it was "possible that we can get this case decided sometime in the near future?" Rives also remarked that "the only time I can remember a dissent being held for more than a year was when Judge Cameron's heart trouble delayed him, and then he graciously agreed for the majority opinion to be filed with a notation that his dissent would be filed later, and that was done."[127] And on July 29, in a letter to then-

124. Palmer v. Thompson, 419 F.2d 1228 (Bell, J., concurring).

125. 419 F.2d at 1228n.2 (Bell, J., concurring).

126. Palmer v. Thompson, 419 F.2d 1237 (January 22, 1970) (Wisdom, J., Addendum to dissenting opinion).

127. Letter to All Fifth Circuit Judges in Regular Active Service, Elbert P. Tuttle, and Warren L. Jones from Richard T. Rives, April 14, 1969.

Chief Judge John Brown, Warren Jones tweaked, "we have not had the opportunity of seeing the magnum opus (not to be confused with sub judice) Judge Wisdom has refrained from filing."[128]

Eventually, John Brown felt compelled to call his ally to task. In a letter to all of the judges, Brown acknowledge that *en banc* disposition of *Palmer* had been "held up now for many, many months for the preparation of Judge Wisdom's dissent." He ended the note by urging Wisdom "to give this the top priority."[129] When, six weeks later, Brown's gentle nudge had not produced the desired result, the chief dashed off a brief note to Wisdom expressing his agreement with the rest of the judges "that we can no longer justify holding up a dissent" and imploring him to "move heaven and earth to get it in the hands of the Judges."[130] In the end, Rives's majority opinion was released on October 9, 1969, with a notation that six dissenters had reserved the right to file a dissenting opinion at a later date. Wisdom's dissent was published six weeks later, on November 25.

Although some of his colleagues may have wondered privately whether this delay was attributable to Wisdom's penchant for taking afternoon breaks to play cards with his cronies at the Boston Club that also included, on more than the rare occasion, the consumption of alcohol, no one ever publicly raised such a complaint. Wisdom consistently maintained that the time that it took him to produce his opinions was a function of his extensive personal involvement in the research and drafting of his work product and the care he lavished on choosing the clearest, most precise, and most artful way to express his thoughts. His colleagues also knew that even though he did indulge in frequent afternoon respites, Wisdom invariably took several large briefcases of files and draft opinions home to work on at night. Indeed, it was the welcomed task of one of his law clerks to drive the judge home and to carry at least one large black briefcase filled with briefs and other documents. In fact, it was well known by his clerks that the chief reason that Wisdom did not hire a single female law clerk during his first seventeen years on the bench was his belief that it was inappropriate to ask a woman to carry such a heavy object. Though he ultimately relented, this is but one example of the traditional component of his personality. Like his steadfast refusal to resign from several racially and religiously

128. Letter to John R. Brown from Warren L. Jones, July 29, 1969.

129. Letter to The Judges Comprising the En Banc Courts from John R. Brown, August 12, 1969.

130. Memo to John M. Wisdom from John R. Brown, September 23, 1969.

restrictive private clubs, it also demonstrates that his civil rights opinions were not the result of a reflexive liberal orientation.

Although the Supreme Court's ringing denunciation of segregation in *Brown* occurred in the context of public education, its broadly phrased articulation of the meaning of the constitutional guarantee of equal protection under the laws subsequently was seized upon as the basis for upending racial segregation in other public arenas as well. And here too, the Fifth Circuit, and especially its intellectual leader, John Wisdom, were in the vanguard of judicial efforts to enforce the Supreme Court's constitutional edict.

In June 1953, Louisiana's capital city of Baton Rouge had adopted an ordinance that mandated racially segregated seating on local buses. A suit challenging the constitutionality of this statute, the likes of which pervaded the South during the height of the Jim Crow era, was brought in a Louisiana state court. The state court dismissed the action without addressing the merits of the plaintiffs' constitutional claim because, the court ruled, the plaintiffs' constitutional objection had not been pleaded with sufficient specificity. When the plaintiffs failed to appeal this ruling, it became final.

Several years later, after the Supreme Court had issued several post-*Brown* rulings expressly outlawing racial segregation of interstate or intrastate transportation facilities, a group of African American residents of Baton Rouge brought a second action challenging the constitutionality of that ordinance. This time, however, they filed their complaint in federal court and the trial judge issued an injunction forbidding the continued enforcement of that law. Despite the existence of a collection of express rulings by the Supreme Court striking down other such enactments as unconstitutional, state officials nevertheless appealed the case to the Fifth Circuit on the back of a cynical interpretation of a venerable rule of procedure.

Nearly four months before issuing his opinion in *Bush*, Judge Wisdom, writing for a unanimous panel that also included Judges Richard Rives and John Brown, affirmed the lower court's decision. In a terse but authoritative opinion, Wisdom characteristically cut right to the chase, making quick work of each of the defendants' arguments. With respect to the state's halfhearted defense of the statute's constitutionality, only two sentences were required. "The central issue in this case," Wisdom responded, "is cut and dried. The Supreme Court has settled beyond question that no State may require racial segregation of interstate or intrastate transportation facilities."[131]

The defendants' more insidious argument was that the plaintiffs' lawsuit was precluded by the doctrine of *res judicata*, a doctrine of preclusion that denies parties the opportunity to re-litigate a previously adjudicated claim. The defense maintained that since a state court already had upheld this law, the plaintiffs were not entitled to a second bite at the apple before a federal judge.

Wisdom would have none of this. He carefully detailed how the Supreme Court consistently had recognized an exception to the general rule of preclusion when a significant change in the law had intervened between the time of the first judgment and the filing of the second lawsuit. The state court ruling, he noted, "was issued before the sands ran out on the 'separate but equal' doctrine."[132] But three months after the state court decision, the Supreme Court had released its opinion in *Brown* and that decision to overturn the "separate but equal" dogma subsequently was extended to cases involving segregated local transportation facilities. Consequently, Wisdom concluded, if ever there had been a change in the law that justified, if not mandated, exemption from the operation of *res judicata*, "this is it."[133] And to underscore his disdain for both the ordinance and the official intransigence reflected in the defense of its continued enforcement, he declared that "it would be a senseless absurdity to sanction in Baton Rouge segregated seating under a law patently unconstitutional while everywhere else in the country segregated seating is prohibited. The Constitution is not geared to patchwork geography. It tolerates no independent enclaves."[134]

Wisdom manifested this same intolerance for cruelly distorted interpretations of the law in a public accommodations case involving the City of Jackson, Mississippi. Pursuant to the policy codified in several federal statutes that prohibited interstate carriers from engaging in discriminatory practices, the federal Interstate Commerce Commission (ICC) had issued an order barring interstate carriers from operating racially segregated railway and bus terminal facilities. That 1961 order also prohibited the posting of any signs indicating that the facilities inside

---

131. *Christian v. Jemison*, 303 F.2d 52 (5th Cir.1962), cert. denied, 371 U.S. 920, 83 S.Ct. 287, 9 L.Ed.2d 229 (1962).

132. 303 F.2d at 55.

133. 303 F.2d at 55.

134. 303 F.2d at 55.

the terminal were racially segregated. Nonetheless, in utter disregard of these regulations, the City of Jackson had continued to maintain signs on the public sidewalks directly outside all of its rail and bus terminals that designated one waiting room "For Whites Only" and the other "For Colored Only." Each of these signs also stated that this designation was "By Order Police Department." And the Jackson police routinely arrested African Americans who refused to leave a "white only" waiting room.

The Justice Department brought suit in federal court against three carriers, the City of Jackson, and several city officials to desegregate the terminal facilities. The case was assigned to District Judge Sidney C. Mize of Meridian, Mississippi, the trial judge whose incredulous finding that the University of Mississippi had not discriminated against James Meredith on the basis of his race had been reversed by the Fifth Circuit in a scathing opinion penned by John Wisdom.

True to form, Judge Mize upheld the city's continued posting of these racist signs.[135] The carriers that operated the terminals had fully complied with the ICC orders, Mize held, because the signs were not located on terminal premises. The city had not violated any statutory or constitutional prohibition on racial discrimination, he reasoned, because the racially segregated nature of the terminal waiting rooms was a matter of voluntary individual choice and not city mandate. (Mize had relied on this same "voluntary self-segregation" argument in refusing to sanction the City of Jackson for its refusal to integrate its segregated public recreational facilities in *Palmer.*) Neither was the city in violation of the ICC rule, since that regulation only applied to carriers. Finally, Mize concluded that placing and retaining signs on public property to encourage voluntary segregation was a valid exercise of the city's police powers since all the city had done was provide passengers with useful information to guide their choice of waiting room. He did rule, however, that the word "Only" and the phrase "By Order Police Department" should be removed from the signs because they were unsuited to their intended purpose of providing guidance to the patrons.

Judge Mize's decision was reversed unanimously by the Fifth Circuit panel comprised of Wisdom and District Judges Robert A. Ainsworth, Jr., of New Orleans and William A. Bootle of Macon.[136] In his

---

135. U.S. v. *City of Jackson, Mississippi,* 206 F.Supp. 45 (S.D.Miss.1962).
136. U.S. v. *City of Jackson, Mississippi,* 318 F.2d 1 (5th Cir.1963).

opinion for the court, Wisdom ridiculed Mize's finding that the passengers' choice of waiting rooms was exclusively the product of individual choice and that the signs were nothing more than a helpful and welcomed suggestion. Citing his own ruling thirteen months earlier in *Meredith*, Wisdom once again took judicial notice of the fact that "Mississippi has a steel-hard, inflexible, undeviating official policy of segregation. The policy is stated in its laws. It is rooted in custom."[137] And the signs, he added, "were commands. A sign reading 'By Order Police Department' carries no inference that travelers may exercise their volition in choosing waiting rooms. We find it impossible to believe that a single Negro misunderstood the plain peremptory meaning and all the implications of the signs."[138]

It also was immaterial to Wisdom that the signs were located on the public sidewalk rather than inside the terminal. With a nod to John Donne, he observed that "a terminal is not an island, entire of itself: the adjacent sidewalks are necessary to passenger use of the terminal."[139] Consequently, he concluded, when the City of Jackson posted signs on the sidewalks commanding or even encouraging segregation that resulted in the harassment and arrest of individuals unless they submitted to the humiliation of using segregated facilities, the city violated federal statutory and constitutional law.

At the same time that Wisdom was crafting his opinion in *City of Jackson*, he also was busily preparing an opinion in another case that involved a challenge to segregated public accommodations. In this case, however, the issue was a great deal starker, and to some extent, therefore, easier to resolve than the question posed in *City of Jackson*. As Wisdom bluntly acknowledged, "it was in the cards that sooner or later the question would someday be put to the Court. It was in the cards too that the Court would give the answer we give here."[140]

A statute originally enacted by the Louisiana legislature in 1921 made it a crime for the owner of any apartment house or other dwelling place to rent to a black person when any part of that building already was occupied by a white person.[141] Two separate lawsuits, consolidated for

---

137. 318 F.2d at 5.

138. 318 F.2d at 7.

139. 318 F.2d at 7.

140. *McCain v. Davis*, 217 F.Supp. 661, 663 (E.D.La.1963).

141. The statute similarly prohibited renting to a white person when a black individual or family occupied any part of that building. It did, however, permit mixed housing of employees of

trial before a three-judge district court, were brought by African Americans who alleged that three New Orleans hotels—the Royal Orleans, Sheraton-Charles, and Hilton Inn—had refused them accommodations on the basis of their race.[142] The hotels admitted the fact of the discrimination, but insisted that they had acted under compulsion of state law. The plaintiffs asked for a declaration that the state law was unconstitutional and an injunction against its future enforcement by government officials and local hotels.

Wisdom's opinion for the panel (which also included District Judges Herbert Christenberry and E. Gordon West of New Orleans) in *McCain v. Davis* was released only two days after the issuance of his ruling in *City of Jackson*.[143] The statute, he pronounced, was "one part of an elaborate, developed, overall legislative plan for dealing with the racial problem in Louisiana. Louisiana laws forbid the mixing of races in every activity in almost every phase of life from birth to death."[144] In his typically direct and to-the-point manner, Wisdom declared that this state-mandated separation of the races, just like the state law prohibiting mixed-race athletic contests that he had voted to strike down in *Dorsey*, clearly ran afoul of the Fourteenth Amendment.[145]

Wisdom also took the occasion in *McCain* to voice his deep-seated revulsion toward this racist policy and to assure the public that his court would not shut its eyes to the manifestly unjust legacy of the region's segregationist history. Although the Supreme Court in *Brown* already had discredited the separate but equal doctrine, Wisdom pointed out that the result of this criminal statute was to subject black travelers not only to separate, but to unequal hotel accommodations. "We take judicial notice that in Louisiana, as a general rule, 'white' hotels are far superior to 'Negro' hotels, and the 'white' traveling public has a relatively wide choice of hotels as to price range; 'Negro' hotels are few, inferior, and offer rooms within a limited price range. What all Louisianians know, this Court knows."[146] Accordingly, Wisdom predicted with a full mea-

---

different races in hotels, boarding houses, or private homes when housing under the same roof was shown to be a necessary part of the job. LSA-R.S. 14:317.

142. "Hotel Segregation Law Held Invalid," *New Orleans Times-Picayune*, May 19, 1963, 1, col. 1; 11, col. 1.

143. 217 F.Supp. 661 (E.D.La.1963).

144. 217 F.Supp. at 665.

145. The statute formally was repealed in 1972.

146. 217 F.Supp. at 666.

sure of delight, "doors closed to Negroes in Louisiana since Reconstruction will be opened."[147]

The unshakeable dedication to ensuring the full implementation of the Supreme Court's broad desegregation mandate in *Brown* that Wisdom demonstrated in all of these opinions never diminished over the entirety of his more than forty years on the federal bench. Tragically, more than forty-five years after *Brown*, the Fifth Circuit continued to hear appeals in school desegregation cases. And it was in such a case that Wisdom wrote the last of his more than 1,100 judicial opinions.

In 1965, a group of African American children had sued the school board of Rapides Parish, Louisiana, to compel desegregation of that northern Louisiana public school system. Over the succeeding thirty-three years, the trial court in Alexandria had issued an increasingly aggressive series of decrees designed to dismantle the dual-school system and to replace it with an integrated, unitary system. Thirty years later, with full knowledge of these efforts to attain, and then maintain, racial balance, the voters in Louisiana nevertheless approved a legislatively generated ballot initiative to amend the Louisiana Constitution to divide the Rapides Parish School District into two separate districts. The newly formed district split out the northern part of Rapides Parish consisting of the predominantly white suburbs outside the racially mixed city of Alexandria. The state legislature also passed a statute that authorized the creation of election districts for the members of the board of this new suburban school district. In response, the original Rapides Parish school board filed suit seeking a ruling that this state law was unconstitutional because it interfered with the board's ability to fully comply with extant federal court desegregation orders.

Federal district judge Nauman Scott, a lifelong resident of Alexandria who had been appointed to the bench in 1970 by President Richard M. Nixon, found that by extracting the suburban areas from the original school district, the statute so altered the racial balance in the two resulting districts that it unconstitutionally infringed upon the school district's ability to comply with the federal court's desegregation orders.[148] The appeal from Judge Scott's ruling was heard by a Fifth Circuit panel composed of Wisdom and Houstonians Jerry E. Smith and Harold R. DeMoss, Jr., who had been appointed to the Fifth Circuit by Presidents Ronald Reagan and George H. W. Bush, respectively.

147. 217 F.Supp. at 664.
148. *Valley v. Rapides Parish School Board*, 960 F.Supp. 96 (W.D.La.1997).

Judge Smith wrote a majority opinion vacating the trial court's ruling on the ground that the case was not ripe for review because it failed to satisfy the constitutional requirement of a justiciable case or controversy.[149] In his view, unless and until the suburban school board declared its intention to take action that would interfere with the desegregation orders, there was no imminent threat to the original school board's ability to comply with the desegregation decrees. Thus, he concluded, all judicial action should be postponed until the new school board was in place and had developed its plan for running the newly created district.

After beginning his dissenting opinion with the customarily polite "I respectfully dissent," Wisdom unleashed an extremely caustic condemnation of Smith's majority opinion, belittling its conclusion that the case was not ripe for review. "This case is so bursting with over-ripeness," Wisdom proclaimed, "that it emits an unpleasant odor."[150] By ignoring the facts "well known to Louisiana and to this Court," that the newly created district "is clearly defined as the predominantly white section of Alexandria," the majority, Wisdom charged, knowingly had countenanced "a blatant attempt to establish a special public school district for whites in a limited area known as the white section of Alexandria."[151]

Wisdom's dismay at the fact that he, his court, and the country should still be combating efforts at retaining segregated public schools is evocatively reflected in the lament with which he closed the opinion. "It is incredible," Wisdom complained, "that half a century after *Brown*, one should have to ask for an *en banc* judgment to prevent the establishment of a school for whites in a public school system. That is necessary in this case where ripeness 'is a cape for unauthorized appellate rule making.' Here, however, the cape has rubbed hard against the rock of controlling fact. The cape is in tatters."[152]

A majority of his Fifth Circuit colleagues, however, ultimately agreed with Wisdom and voted to grant *en banc* reconsideration.[153] The opinion for the unanimous *en banc* court was written by Wisdom; it would be

149. *Valley v. Rapides Parish School Board*, 145 F.3d 329 (5th Cir.1998).

150. *Valley v. Rapides Parish School Board*, 145 F.3d 334 (Wisdom, J., dissenting).

151. 145 F.3d at 334.

152. 145 F.3d at 335, quoting *Marathon Oil Corp. v. Ruhrgas*, 145 F.3d 211, 225 (5th Cir.1998) (Higginbotham, J., dissenting).

153. *Valley v. Rapides Parish School Board*, 169 F.3d 216 (5th Cir.1999) (*en banc*).

his last, issued less than a month before his death.[154] Amazingly, every member of the court, even Judges Smith and DeMoss, the members of the original panel majority, signed onto Wisdom's carefully drafted ruling. The judgment ordered the trial judge to "grant promptly" the state's request to defend its creation of the new school board and to take other steps that would ensure an expeditious resolution of the legal issue that the original panel had found unready for adjudication.[155] After forty-two years on the bench and more than thirty years after writing *Jefferson County*, Wisdom finally had been able to convince all his colleagues of the correctness of his vision of their crucial role in integrating American society.

But Wisdom's incessant pressure on state and local officials, federal district judges, and, on occasion, his own colleagues, to fully adhere to the dictates of *Brown* had its own institutional costs. From the early 1960s, dissension on the Fifth Circuit over the handling of civil rights cases began to build until it reached a level that placed the court's ability to continue to operate effectively in serious peril.

154. *Valley v. Rapides Parish School Board*, 173 F.3d 944 (5th Cir.1999).

155. See generally Barry Sullivan, *John Wisdom, Watchman of the Republic, Forester of the Soul*, 69 Miss. L. J. 1, 15 (1999).

11

INTERNAL DISCORD
THREATENS THE COURT

Not every member of the Fifth Circuit shared the zeal with which John Minor Wisdom and some of his colleagues strove to combat and overcome the unwavering obstructionist tactics employed by state officials and federal trial judges hell-bent on thwarting the Supreme Court's will and preserving the segregationist status quo. To the contrary, the legal reasoning and procedural tactics employed by a majority of the court's members in the early 1960s to compel adherence to the Supreme Court's 1954 constitutional decree in *Brown* became an increasing source of internal discord, irritation, and conflict that soon escalated to a point that threatened the court's continued ability to function and to retain any semblance of public confidence.

The most celebrated, though not the first, instance of the Fifth Circuit's use of a controversial procedural device designed expressly to accelerate the theretofore-languid pace of public school integration occurred in *Armstrong v. Board of Education of the City of Birmingham.*[1] It, along with other stratagems, was designed to thwart the techniques that many district court judges in the circuit's six-state jurisdiction had devised and utilized solely to frustrate and delay compliance with the Su-

1. 323 F.2d 333 (5th Cir.1963).

preme Court's edict in *Brown* that school boards begin the process of dismantling racially segregated public schools "with all deliberate speed."

The traditional appellate process is, by its very nature, protracted. Moreover, it is fraught with multiple opportunities for additional delay. Absent extraordinary circumstances, the losing party must first wait until the trial court has delivered a final judgment. Papers requesting an appeal must then be filed, docketed with the court, and delivered to the opposing party or parties, as must a copy of the trial court proceedings. Each side then is entitled to a reasonable opportunity to prepare and file written briefs supporting their respective positions and, typically, additional time to submit briefs responding to the arguments offered by the other side. The members of the panel that will decide the case must be designated and given time to consider the briefs before the parties are permitted to argue their case.[2] After oral argument, the panel deliberates and eventually prepares and distributes a written opinion or opinions. Consequently, it is the rare case where the parties can expect to receive the appellate court's ruling within less than a year, if not longer.

Authority for invoking the procedural tool that the Fifth Circuit used in *Armstrong* to expedite the standard appellate timeframe was predicated on the All Writs Act.[3] This federal statute, dating back to the Judiciary Act of 1789, was designed, among other things, to provide federal appellate courts with authority to deviate from the general rule that review is only available from either "final" judgments or a finite category of interlocutory (mid-case) orders. The Fifth Circuit, under Chief Judge Tuttle's leadership, construed the language of the All Writs Act (which authorized federal appellate courts to issue "all writs necessary or appropriate in aid of their respective jurisdictions and agreeable to the usages and principles of law") to permit it to issue a "temporary" order compelling certain action by the district court pending the circuit court's final disposition of the appeal. The use of this "injunction pending appeal" enabled Tuttle and some of his colleagues quickly and efficiently to circumvent the attempts by recalcitrant district judges to adhere to the spirit of the Supreme Court's ruling in *Brown*.

On June 17, 1960, Dwight Armstrong and other African American

2. In the 1960s, requests for oral argument were routinely granted; the movement toward deciding appeals on the briefs in the absence of oral argument did not begin to appear until the beginning of the twenty-first century.

3. 28 U.S.C. §1651.

students sued the Birmingham, Alabama, board of education to enjoin it from continuing to operate its public school system on an admittedly racially segregated basis. Although the school board conceded that it never had formulated any specific desegregation plan, it maintained that it would assign and transfer all students to schools on a race-blind basis in accordance with the terms of Alabama law. And this state law, like the freedom-of-choice desegregation plan Wisdom had criticized in *Jefferson County*, shunted the burden of requesting assignment or transfer onto the parents or guardians of the students. So the fact that no parent or guardian of a black student in Birmingham ever had applied for assignment or transfer to a previously "white" designated school, the school board argued, was simply a matter beyond its control.[4]

These arguments persuaded District Judge Seybourne H. Lynne. But his opinion was not released until May 23, 1963, barely three months before the opening of the fall school term, which meant that any meaningful desegregation of the Birmingham schools prior to the beginning of the new academic year would require the nearly immediate intercession of the court of appeals. The appeal was assigned to a panel composed of Chief Judge Tuttle and Judges Rives and Gewin. Loathe to countenance Judge Lynne's more-than-willing acquiescence to a student placement regime, Tuttle and Rives wanted to ensure, at a minimum, that the board would make a good faith start toward desegregating its schools. In an opinion authored by Rives, the majority issued an injunction pending the panel's ruling on the merits of the appeal from Judge Lynne's decision. The injunction required the school board to submit a desegregation plan directly to their court, rather than to Judge Lynne, by August 19.[5]

Judge Gewin, the third member of the panel, wrote a withering dissent in which he not only set forth his disagreement with the majority's ruling, but also accused Tuttle and Rives of intentionally perverting the normal appellate process. Gewin, a born-and-bred Alabamian who had come to the court after twenty-five years at the bar and four years as a state legislator, was not inclined to judicial activism. Under the guise of

---

4. *Armstrong v. Board of Education of the City of Birmingham*, 220 F.Supp. 217 (N.D.Ala.1963).

5. Judge Tuttle would have preferred to go even further and require the complete desegregation of at least one grade. But he acquiesced to Rives's proposal in order to constitute a majority to overturn Judge Lynne's total denial of relief. 323 F.2d 339 (Tuttle, C.J., concurring specially). See also Burke Marshall, *Southern Judges in the Desegregation Struggle*, 95 HARV. L. REV. 1509, 1512 (1982).

ruling on a temporary injunction pending full review of the appeal on the merits, Gewin charged, Judges Tuttle and Rives effectively had resolved all of the issues in the case "without any pretense that the court has taken so much as a hurried glance at the record."[6] Because he believed that the panel's precipitous decision left little, if anything, for the court to resolve when it actually addressed the full appeal on the merits, Judge Gewin formally requested an *en banc* reconsideration of the majority's interim order.

By this time, another of Gewin's colleagues, Judge Warren LeRoy Jones, also had become concerned, if not perturbed, by the lengths to which some of his colleagues would go in civil rights cases. A native Nebraskan, Jones had transplanted himself to Jacksonville, Florida, a few years after graduating from the University of Denver's law school. In Jacksonville he joined, and later became senior partner of, a highly successful corporate law firm, and eventually served as president of both the city and state bar associations. When Louie W. Strum, the only Floridian on the Fifth Circuit, died in 1954, President Eisenhower, whom Jones actively had supported in 1952, nominated Jones to fill this vacancy.[7] Known for his dry wit and good-naturedly called "our poet laureate" by his colleagues, Gewin indulged his penchant for doggerel to defuse the brewing controversy over what he and others deemed an overly aggressive approach toward civil rights cases by some of their brethren.[8] In a gentle attempt to voice his concerns to his ideological antagonists, Jones composed the following verse, which he dispatched to Rives, Brown, and Wisdom.

> Quickly my brother
>   Gather you down
> Assemble the panel
>   Of Rives, Wisdom and Brown.
> The troops we will muster
>   And cancel all leaves

---

6. 323 F.2d 339 (Gewin, J., dissenting). Judge Gewin also believed that the trial court's ruling was fully compliant with the Supreme Court's decision in *Brown* and, therefore, should have been affirmed on the merits.

7. Allison Herren Lee, William W. Shakeley, and J. Robert Brown, Jr., *Judge Warren L. Jones and the Supreme Court of Dixie*, 59 LA. L. REV. 209, 215–216 (1998).

8. Letter to All Fifth Circuit Judges from John R. Brown, July 17, 1963 (document on file with author).

Report ye for duty
    Brown, Wisdom and Rives.
There is a rebellion
    In old Chatham Town
We quell it instanter
    By Rives, Wisdom and Brown.
We'll follow the pattern
    That gave us renown
Remember the Meredith
    Rives, Wisdom and Brown.
If this shall be treason
    Upon it please frown
And may I be shriven
    By Rives, Wisdom and Brown.[9]

On July 22, ten days after the release of the panel opinion in *Armstrong,* the Fifth Circuit voted 5–4 to deny Gewin's request for rehearing.[10] Ordinarily, that would have been the end of the matter, at least as far as the Fifth Circuit was concerned. But this was no ordinary situation. Like Gewin, Judge Ben Cameron had been outraged by the deployment of what he viewed as manipulative strategies by a group of his colleagues. Moreover, only four days before the court's denial of the request for rehearing, Cameron had begun to isolate and alienate himself from his benchmates in the James Meredith case by taking the unprecedented, unilateral step of issuing the first of four stays of execution of a Fifth Circuit panel opinion in which he had not participated.

The decision by Tuttle and Rives to issue an injunction pending appeal in *Armstrong* simply pushed Cameron over the edge. But unlike Gewin, who had restricted his objections to internal communications, Cameron chose to air his concerns publicly by taking the exceptional step of issuing a detailed dissenting opinion to the court's decision denying the request for *en banc* rehearing. And though three other judges— Gewin, Jones, and Griffin Bell—had voted with Cameron to grant the request for rehearing, none of them signed on to his dissenting opinion.

9. Letter to John R. Brown, Richard T. Rives, and John M. Wisdom from Warren L. Jones, May 17, 1963.

10. *Armstrong v. Board of Education of City of Birmingham,* 323 F.2d 333 (5th Cir.1963), cert. denied sub nom *Gibson v. Harris,* 376 U.S. 908, 84 S.Ct. 66, 11 L.Ed.2d 606 (1964).

Benjamin Franklin Cameron, born in the 1890s in Meridian, Mississippi, was a teetotaling sports enthusiast who, after completing his college and law school studies in Tennessee, returned to his hometown, where he developed a reputation as a successful litigator. The retirement of Edwin R. Holmes of Yazoo, Mississippi, at the end of 1954 provided President Eisenhower with his second opportunity to place a judge on the Fifth Circuit, Elbert Tuttle being the first. But unlike Tuttle or, subsequently, John Brown and John Wisdom, Cameron was not a mover and shaker in Republican Party circles. Rather, his appointment was due, ironically, in no small part to Wisdom's influence with Attorney General Herbert Brownell. Eisenhower had needed a suitable replacement from Mississippi for the slot previously held by a judge hailing from that state and Wisdom convinced Brownell that Cameron was the best of a small list of moderate Republicans from that heavily Democratic state.[11] As Wisdom explained decades later, "no one was under any illusions about how Cameron or anyone in Mississippi felt about civil rights or desegregation. We just wanted to get an honest man who would have some reputation in the community so his appointment would reflect credit on the administration. There were no Republicans of any reputation in Mississippi at that time, certainly none with Cameron's reputation for being a good, honest lawyer."[12]

Wisdom's recommendation also received a strong endorsement from the NAACP, a decision the organization would come to deeply regret. With his longtime friend James Eastland chairing the Senate Judiciary Committee, Cameron's nomination sailed through Congress and, at the age of sixty-four, he joined the court in March 1955. It was not long, however, before Cameron's bedrock conservative philosophy grounded in a distrust of the federal government and a concomitant conviction that most decisions should be left to state control began to manifest itself in his judicial opinions.

Cameron released his dissent to the denial of *en banc* rehearing in *Armstrong* on July 30, 1963. He charged that the panel's issuance of temporary injunctive relief reflected a disturbing pattern by a majority of his deeply divided court to misuse the judicial process by "invent-

11. Although Wisdom was forever hounded by the charge that he subsequently enlisted Cameron's influence with Senator Eastland to smooth the way for his own Senate confirmation, Wisdom fervently denied this allegation. See chapter 6.

12. Transcript of interview of Judge John M. Wisdom by Jeffrey Young, in New Orleans, La., February 22, 1991.

ing special procedures" in order to achieve preordained results in civil rights cases with which he and much of the public disagreed.[13] In support of this general observation, Cameron inserted a footnote in which he quoted from a recent article in a Birmingham newspaper that had praised the Fifth Circuit for having blazed new trails in civil rights cases over the past decade. The article credited a "hard core" majority of four members—Tuttle, Rives, Wisdom, and Brown—with having "stood together consistently in decision on civil rights cases."[14] Cameron took a significantly less appreciative view of the quartet, ending this footnote with what was destined to become his most famous judicial utterance. "These four Judges," Cameron cynically added, "will hereafter sometimes be referred to as The Four."[15]

Based on his survey of what he termed "racial" cases decided by the Fifth Circuit over the past few years, Cameron charged Chief Judge Tuttle with stacking the composition of the panels assigned to civil rights cases with members of the court's liberal bloc in order to promote Tuttle's desegregation agenda. Specifically, Cameron alleged, a majority of the panel in twenty-two of these twenty-five cases "was composed of some combination of The Four," while in only two cases did two of the circuit's other five members sit together. Cameron further stated that a member of "The Four" wrote the opinion in twenty-three of these twenty-five cases.

Judge Cameron also accused Tuttle of "gerrymandering" the composition of three-judge district courts in cases filed in Mississippi. The federal statute providing for the empanelling of three-judge district courts authorizes the chief judge of each circuit to designate the two other judges who will sit on the panel with the district judge that initially was assigned to hear the case. Beyond stating that at least one of those two other judges will be a circuit judge, the statute does not expressly limit the chief judge's discretion in assembling the panel. But until Tuttle became its chief judge, Cameron insisted, the practice in the Fifth (and every other) Circuit had been to appoint one circuit judge and one district judge who resided in the state in which the suit had been filed. Yet though Mississippi had one resident circuit judge (Cameron) and three active district judges, in each of the three Mississippi-filed cases involv-

13. 323 F.2d 352, 354 (Cameron, J., dissenting).

14. Jack Steele, "5th Circuit Has Major Part In Civil Rights Conflicts," *Birmingham Post-Herald*, July 20, 1963, 10, cols. 3, 4.

15. 323 F.2d 352, 353n.1 (Cameron, J., dissenting).

ing three-judge district courts, Cameron reported, "a member of The Four was substituted for the resident Circuit Judge . . . and another member of The Four was substituted for the additional District Judge."[16]

Judge Cameron's angst over the assignment of Fifth Circuit judges to panels hearing appeals in civil rights cases, however, had not originated in *Armstrong*. His suspicions had been building over the course of the past several months. Nearly five months before issuing his dissent in *Armstrong*, Cameron had circulated a letter to all of his colleagues in which he noted that Judges Brown and Wisdom had been assigned, along with District Judge Harold Cox of Mississippi, to sit on a case involving a constitutional challenge to Mississippi's election laws. In stark contrast to the custom his colleagues routinely followed of placing a high priority on the polite, even solicitous expression of divergent points of view, Cameron expressed his dissatisfaction with the composition of this panel in unusually scathing and personal terms. "I cannot refrain from voicing my personal protest against this action," he announced, "and my astonishment that Judges Brown and Wisdom will be participants in such a crass betrayal of honorable dealings between gentlemen charged with responsibility of public office." As far as he was concerned, the appointment of Brown and Wisdom to the panel on a Mississippi case demonstrated that the four federal judges residing in

16. 323 F.2d 352, 359 (Cameron, J., dissenting). Ben Cameron's growing disenchantment with his colleagues also manifested itself in another dissenting opinion that he wrote on the same day that he issued his dissenting opinion in *Armstrong*. In *Davis v. Board of School Commissioners of Mobile County, Alabama*, 322 F.2d 356 (5th Cir.1963), cert. denied, 375 U.S. 894, 84 S.Ct. 170, 11 L.Ed.2d 123 (1963), a panel composed of Judges Brown, Wisdom, and Bell issued a *per curiam* opinion, written by Wisdom, granting an injunction pending appeal in a case where the trial judge had decided not to require the immediate integration of the Mobile public school system. Since a majority of the appellate court (with Judge Bell dissenting) believed that the school boards of Mobile and Birmingham faced the same difficulties in desegregating their schools, it conformed its order in the Mobile case to mirror the one it had issued in *Armstrong* to govern desegregation of the Birmingham schools. Wisdom's initial draft of the opinion for the court, however, had contained a desegregation order more aggressive than the one issued in *Armstrong*. But because he anticipated that Cameron would request *en banc* reconsideration of the court's decision, he toned down the order to conform to the decree in *Armstrong* in order to assure that Judge Rives would join with him, Hutcheson, Brown, and Tuttle in voting against granting a rehearing. The strategy worked to perfection as the court voted 5–4 to deny *en banc* review. Letter to All Judges of the Fifth Circuit from Richard T. Rives, July 13, 1963; Letter to All Judges of the Fifth Circuit from Elbert P. Tuttle, July 15, 1963; Letter to All Judges of the Fifth Circuit from Griffin B. Bell, July 15, 1963; Letter to John Minor Wisdom from Griffin B. Bell, July 17, 1963. True to form, Cameron filed a dissenting opinion from the denial of rehearing in which he incorporated the contents of his simultaneously issued dissent in *Armstrong*. 322 F.2d 362, 363 (Cameron, J., dissenting).

Mississippi "have been divested of our rightful place on such courts and outsiders substituted solely because the Chief Judge does not trust our integrity and wishes to displace us with Judges whose minds are slanted as his own."[17]

And Cameron's consistently hostile attitude toward civil rights claims had not begun in 1963. In a 1960 case challenging the racially segregated operation of buses in Birmingham, for example, Cameron had dissented from the Fifth Circuit's decision to strike down the policy on the ground that the private company's monopolistic franchise to operate on Birmingham's public streets made it an agent of the city government and therefore subjected its policy to constitutional inquiry.[18] In his dissenting opinion, Cameron insisted that the most lamentable event in the period following the Civil War was the repudiation of the "separate but equal" doctrine that occurred when "*Brown* sprang Pallas-like full-fledged from the Jovian forehead of the Supreme Court."[19] That regrettable and unsupportable decision, Cameron charged, "based upon assumed psychological knowledge alone, changed the 'law of the land' and repudiated principles which had formed the basis of action upon which the citizenship of a considerable portion of this nation had built up a happy and productive civilization."[20] To Cameron, "decisions . . . in cases brought by or on behalf of Negroes and involving the equal protection clause of the Fourteenth Amendment, have not been in harmony with the spirit, thought and desires of the people, the vast majority of whom, in both races, know that their common problems can best be worked out if they are left alone to continue the unbroken improvement in relationships which has taken place in the last eight decades."[21]

After learning of Cameron's charges, Dick Rives felt compelled to come to the aid of Tuttle, whom he had preceded as chief judge. In a letter sent to all members of the court, Rives declared that Cameron's charges were not only unfounded but also "inexcusable, impertinent, and reprehensible."[22] Chastened by the passage of a fortnight, however, Rives subsequently withdrew his uncharacteristically harsh criticism of

17. Letter to Judges Tuttle, Hutcheson, Rives, Jones, Brown, Wisdom, Gewin, and Bell from Ben F. Cameron, March 7, 1963.

18. *Boman v. Birmingham Transit Company*, 280 F.2d 531 (5th Cir.1960).

19. 292 F.2d at 17 (Cameron, J., dissenting).

20. 292 F.2d at 20 (Cameron, J., dissenting).

21. 292 F.2d at 28.

22. Letter to Judges Tuttle, Hucheson, Jones, Brown, Wisdom, Gewin, and Bell from Richard T. Rives, March 8, 1964.

his brother Cameron and apologized for his intemperate language.[23] Cameron, on the other hand, chose never to respond to Rives's initial retort. Nevertheless, to placate Cameron's ruffled feelings, Tuttle, at Wisdom's request, replaced Wisdom with Cameron on the three-judge court in the Mississippi election law case.[24] This decision, as anticipated, directly affected the court's resolution of the case. Cameron teamed with Harold Cox to constitute a majority upholding the state laws, with Judge Brown dissenting.[25] But Cameron's victory was short-lived; the Supreme Court unanimously reversed this ruling.[26]

Predictably, Cameron's frontal and public assault on Chief Judge Tuttle's integrity contained in his *Armstrong* dissent, as well as his allegations of acts of complicity by Rives, Brown, and Wisdom, sent shock waves through the court and mobilized the members of each of its two factions. Judges Griffin Bell and Warren Jones, along with Walter Gewin, emboldened by Cameron's documentation, demanded an explanation if not some remedial response from Tuttle.

A few weeks later, in early August 1963, Jones, the court's third most consistently conservative jurist after Cameron and Gewin, demanded that the clerk of the Fifth Circuit, Edward W. Wadsworth, provide him with an answer to one simple question: "Did Judge Brown or any other Judge direct or suggest that any segregation cases be assigned to or kept from any particular panel or Judges?"[27] Wadsworth, naturally, was reluctant to respond to such a request without appropriate authorization.

23. Letter to Judges Tuttle, Hutcheson, Cameron, Jones, Brown, Wisdom, Gewin, and Bell from Richard T. Rives, March 22, 1963.

24. According to Judge Warren Jones, the replacement of Wisdom by Cameron was part of a deal to ensure that Cameron would convince Senator Eastland to terminate his investigation of the Fifth Circuit. Moreover, Jones recounted, once Cameron was appointed as Wisdom's replacement, Cameron convinced Senator Eastland to indefinitely postpone his investigation. Jones also reported, however, that as "Eastland's forbearance was on the basis of . . . Cameron's expressed view that the Court was being run on a proper basis, it may be assumed that if there is any further stacking of the Court, or handling Mississippi differently than elsewhere in three judge district court cases, then the investigation can be resumed." Diary Memorandum prepared by Judge Warren Jones, September 13, 1963, at 1; September 17, 1963, at 1, 2. There is no corroborating evidence of such a deal, however. This may be explained by the fact that though Cameron and Jones agreed that while they would "pass the word" on Cameron's "agreement with Senator Eastland" to Tuttle, Rives, Bell, and Gewin, they also promised not to inform either Judges Hutcheson, Brown, or Wisdom. Diary Memorandum prepared by Judge Warren Jones, September 17, 1963, at 3.

25. *U.S. v. Mississippi*, 229 F.Supp. 925 (S.D.Miss.1964).

26. 380 U.S. 128, 85 S.Ct. 808, 13 L.Ed.2d 717 (1965).

27. Letter to Edward W. Wadsworth from Warren L. Jones, August 11, 1963.

At the same time, however, he was fearful of alienating the third most senior member of the court. So Wadsworth, who had served as Dick Rives's law clerk for four years before being appointed as clerk of court during Rives's brief stint as chief judge, came up with a brief stalling maneuver. He informed Jones that because Chief Judge Tuttle was vacationing in the Rocky Mountains and unreachable by phone, his office would release the report if given the go ahead by the court's senior member and his former boss, acting Chief Judge Rives.[28]

A "shocked" but undeterred Jones reasserted his demand, this time directly to Rives.[29] Rives acknowledged that his colleague had a right to know all of the facts, particularly in light of the public assurances he and Wisdom had given that no panel-packing had occurred. Rives promised Jones that he would receive all the requested information and instructed Wadsworth to accumulate the requested information from his docket and files.[30] Later that afternoon, Wadsworth telephoned Jones to reassure him that he was giving his full and immediate attention to compiling the requested report. In his personal diary, Jones reported that he informed Wadsworth that he would be delighted to receive such a detailed report, but that "in the meantime I thought he [Wadsworth] could give me a direct answer to the question, which I read to him, and which he copied: 'Did Judge Brown direct or suggest that any segregation or other civil rights cases be assigned to or kept from any particular panels or judges? And, if so, had he followed the direction or suggestion?'" Jones's diary entry concluded with a blockbuster response to that question. "He [Wadsworth] said he could answer that question and the answer was 'yes.'"[31]

Four days later, on August 11, Wadsworth dashed off a letter to all of the judges informing them that Judge Rives had told him to "fully and truthfully" respond to Judge Jones's query. He also reported that, "to my best recollection," Tuttle had ordered him not to calendar any "racial cases" for hearing during the weeks that Judges Gewin and Bell were assigned to sit prior to the Senate's confirmation of their presi-

28. Diary Memorandum prepared by Judge Warren L. Jones, August 7, 1963, at 5. Although Judge Rives was the senior active member of the Fifth Circuit, Tuttle was the chief judge because Rives had resigned from that post on December 5, 1960, after only a year on the job, because of his distaste for the position's administrative obligations. As the next most senior member of the court, Tuttle succeeded Rives and remained chief judge until July 17, 1967.

29. Diary Memorandum prepared by Judge Warren L. Jones, August 7, 1963, 3.

30. Letter to Elbert P. Tuttle from Edward W. Wadsworth, August 11, 1963.

31. Diary Memorandum prepared by Judge Warren Jones, August 7, 1963, 5.

dential appointment. Wadsworth also conveyed his recollection that although Judge Tuttle initially had instructed him, in consideration of Cameron's failing health, not to calendar racial cases for panels to which Cameron was assigned; this order subsequently had been rescinded and that Tuttle "instructed me with respect to regularly calendaring of such cases to 'let them fall.'"[32] Wadsworth's letter also addressed Jones's concern over John Brown's part in the alleged court-packing scheme. He acknowledged that on several occasions Brown had given him "advice and suggestions about the advisability of not setting racial cases while Judge Cameron or District Judges were sitting at Montgomery." He also recalled that although Brown had told him that "such cases ought not to be assigned during weeks when Judges Gewin and Bell were sitting," the records revealed that "I have not followed his suggestions and advice in these respects as to the racial cases being regularly calendared without special order, as Chief Judge Tuttle has never given me any such instructions. No Judge has ever directed or suggested that racial cases not be assigned while you [Jones] are sitting."[33]

In a follow-up letter to Jones the next day, Wadsworth expanded a bit on Judge Brown's role in panel assignments and calendaring. Wadsworth admitted to Jones that on more than one occasion, Brown had reminded Wadsworth that Brown would likely become the chief within the next three or four years, if he lived, and had intimated that Wadsworth should accustom himself to operating "his" way. "I am devoted to him personally," Wadsworth concluded, "even though I have many times not agreed with or followed his ideas and suggestions. I shall always believe, however, that he was in good faith in thinking that he had the right to make them."[34]

Once Wadsworth completed his survey of the assignment of judges to racial cases from 1959 through June 30, 1963, he relayed his findings to Judge Rives. Composed of a series of reports detailing and analyzing statistical records for each of the past four fiscal years, the contents were explosive. Wadsworth's report officially confirmed that Water Gewin and Griffin Bell had been excluded from sitting on racial cases pending their Senate confirmation. The documents also reported that some combination of "The Four" constituted a majority in twelve of the sixteen racial cases submitted to panels from February through the end of

32. Letter to Warren L. Jones from Edward W. Wadsworth, August 11, 1963.
33. Ibid.
34. Letter to Warren L. Jones from Edward W. Wadsworth, August 12, 1963.

June 1962, with seven of those assignments made by special order or direction, while only five were the result of the clerk's regular assignment protocol.[35] Similarly, members of "The Four" constituted a majority in twenty of the twenty-three racial cases heard over the succeeding twelve months. The composition of these panels was the result on six occasions of the clerk's regular assignment protocol and, in the remaining fourteen instances, of a special order or direction.[36]

This information was so potentially divisive that Rives hesitated in distributing it to his colleagues. Instead, he called Jones at 10:00 p.m. on August 10, 1963, and asked him to agree to a postponement of the release of the report until the court's next Judicial Council meeting. When pressed for an explanation for this delay, Rives admitted that "the report showed a worse condition than he had expected, and he hoped, that as a personal favor to him, [Judge Jones] would not insist on seeing the report."[37] This acknowledgment served only to further infuriate Jones, who immediately and forcefully reminded Rives that he had an absolute right to a report that he had requested from the clerk's office. Unable to withstand the pressure, Rives asked Jones to hold his fire on the promise that Jones would receive the report as soon as Rives spoke with Tuttle. Jones reluctantly agreed to wait for a few days, but threatened that "if I do not get the information requested, I will consider whether to ask a member of Senator Eastland's staff to meet me in New Orleans."[38] Two days later, after finally contacting Tuttle in Colorado and urging him to return to Atlanta as quickly as possible to deal with this impending crisis, Rives fulfilled his promise.[39] On August 17, at Rives's direction, Wadsworth sent a copy of his report on panel assignments to every member of the court.[40]

By the time Tuttle returned to Atlanta, the unrest generated by Cameron's denunciation of "The Four" and his indictment of Tuttle's alleged panel-rigging maneuvers had pushed an already disgruntled

---

35. Clerk's Report and Analysis of Statistical Facts of Record Concerning Attached List of Racial Cases for Fiscal Year 1962 (July 1, 1961, through June 30, 1962).

36. Ibid.

37. Diary Memorandum prepared by Judge Warren Jones, August 10, 1963, at 2.

38. Ibid., 5.

39. Frank T. Read and Lucy S. McGough, *Let Them Be Judged: The Judicial Integration of the Deep South* (Metuchen, N.J.: 1978), 269.

40. Letter to Judges Elbert P. Tuttle, Joseph C. Hutcheson, Jr., Richard T. Rives, Ben F. Cameron, Warren L. Jones, John R. Brown, John M. Wisdom, Walter P. Gewin, and Griffin B. Bell from Edward W. Wadsworth, August 17, 1963.

quartet of the court's nine active members into a state of total exasperation, if not near rebellion. *Armstrong,* after all, was but the latest in a series of cases in which, under Tuttle's direction and with Wisdom's active participation, a variety of procedural techniques had been employed to ensure that the Supreme Court's desegregation order in *Brown* was fully implemented by the district and appellate judges in the Fifth Circuit.[41] In fact, his objecting colleagues previously had called Tuttle to task on this score.

Nearly three months earlier, on May 29, 1963, the Fifth Circuit's Judicial Council had held its spring meeting in New Orleans. Although the chief judge is the administrative head of each circuit court, he or she does not have unlimited authority over all administrative matters. In each circuit, a Judicial Council composed of the active members of the court oversees the court's administrative workload. It was the practice in the Fifth Circuit for the judges to convene as the Judicial Council on at least a semiannual basis, although the extent of the council's direct involvement in administrative matters varied according to the proclivities of each incumbent chief judge.

The council's spring 1963 meeting started promptly at 9:30 in the morning. Within minutes, Cameron voiced his strenuous objection to the unilateral action that Tuttle had undertaken just one week earlier in a case arising out of a series of mass protests against segregated schools, employment, and lunch counters in Birmingham. On May 20, the Birmingham school board had decided to suspend or expel more than a thousand African American students who had been arrested for taking part in these local demonstrations and had declared that it would not hear any appeals from its decision until after the conclusion of the school year. This meant that hundreds of high schoolers would not graduate with the rest of their class.[42]

Within two days of the school board's announcement, suit was filed in federal district court seeking a temporary order restraining the board from following through with the announced expulsions and suspen-

---

41. *Armstrong* was far from the first instance of the Fifth Circuit's use of the injunction pending appeal mechanism in a civil rights case. That distinction belonged to a voting rights case decided by a panel that, unlike *Armstrong,* did include John Wisdom. In *U.S. v. Lynd,* 301 F.2d 818 (5th Cir.1962), the court, consisting of Judges Tuttle, Wisdom, and Hutcheson, relied, as did the *Armstrong* court, on the All Writs Act as authority for issuing, pending a full determination of the case on appeal, a temporary order that enjoined the authorities in Forrest County, Mississippi, from denying individuals the right to register to vote on the basis of race.

42. "Pupils Take Case to Federal Court," *New York Times,* May 22, 1963, 27, col. 3.

sions. District Judge Clarence W. Allgood, an enthusiastic and unflinching segregationist who, like Frank Ellis and Gordon West, had been
appointed to the bench by President Kennedy, denied the plaintiffs' request for relief. Six hours later, Tuttle, on his own authority, heard argument in a courtroom in the Old Post Office Building in Atlanta from
attorneys for the school board and the students.[43] With his "expression
and tone of voice reflect[ing] anger and distress over the treatment of the
students," Tuttle announced from the bench that the board's retaliation
against students for participating in constitutionally protected protests
was patently unlawful and ordered the school board to reinstate all of
them by the following day.[44]

After heated discussion at the Judicial Council meeting concerning Cameron's denunciation of Tuttle's action in the Birmingham case,
the group of eight attendees (Judge Hutcheson, now eighty-four years
old and in failing health, was unable to attend any meetings outside
his home base in Houston) found themselves split right down on the
middle on whether a single judge held the power to grant injunctive relief.[45] The official, though confidential, minutes of the meeting that
were taken by Judge Griffin Bell in his role as Judicial Council secretary
are intentionally sketchy. They report only that "it was not possible to
resolve the question of power by rule or otherwise due to an even division among the members of the Council as to the presence or absence
of such power, and because some felt that it was not the appropriate subject matter of a rule."[46]

The council's response to his concerns at its May 29 meeting did
little, if anything, to mollify Cameron. Despite the long tradition of
maintaining the confidentiality of all Judicial Council sessions, Cameron chose to break the seal on the proceedings by revealing the council's split vote in his *Armstrong* dissent, which was released on July 30,
just two months after the conclusion of the council meeting. With the
lid now blown off the controversy, public interest mounted as other
members of the court chose to support their chief judge via well-placed
leaks to the press. This unprecedented public revelation of tradition-

43. Sitton, "U.S. Appeals Judge Orders Birmingham to Reinstate Pupils," *New York Times*,
May 23, 1963, 1, col. 7; 19, col. 2.

44. Ibid.

45. Minutes of Meeting of Judicial Council of the Fifth Circuit Held in New Orleans on
May 29 and 31, 1963, at 1.

46. Ibid., 3.

ally confidential court matters led in quick fashion to an announcement on August 2 by Mississippi senator James O. Eastland, chairman of the Senate Judiciary Committee, that he was ordering an investigation of his friend and fellow Mississippian Ben Cameron's court-packing charges.[47] Two days after Eastland's pronouncement, the editors of the *Houston Chronicle* opined that "it's unfortunate that Judge Ben Cameron believed it necessary to question publicly the operation of the US Ct of Appeals for the 5th Circuit. Such matters are better resolved among the judges themselves."[48]

That same August 4 issue of the *Houston Chronicle* also contained a jaw-dropping front-page article that revealed the reactions of some of his colleagues to Cameron's court-packing accusations. Judge Rives was quoted as telling the reporter that "no such thing as Judge Cameron has charged has occurred on the appeal cases heard by panels." Rives also offered his own thinly veiled critique of Cameron and the Mississippi district judges when he added that "Chief Judge Tuttle has the responsibility to appoint judges who will follow the law honestly and fairly and without prejudice. There has been no effort to pattern the cases, they are set and assigned as they come to the court."[49]

Other quotes contained in the *Houston Chronicle* article, however, were not attributed to identified members of the court, a fact that subsequently generated more than a little heat among the brethren. A "source close to the court," echoing Rives's sentiments, intimated that "Cameron would not complain about Judge Tuttle's procedures if the decisions were not contrary to his views. Cameron's views are well known, and so are the views of the district judges of Mississippi. Cameron is a mass of predilections. The Chief Judge wants honest judges to decide according to law." And another "angry" source fervidly rejected Cameron's suggestion that Tuttle's use of "special procedures" diminished the stature the court previously enjoyed during Hutcheson's lengthy tenure as chief judge. "It has always been the practice of the Chief Judge," this source explained, "to appoint the panels and the three-judge courts

47. Ted Lippman, "U.S. Probes Panel Picks by Tuttle," *Atlanta Constitution*, August 2, 1963, 1, col. 7; Saul Friedman, "U.S. Circuit Court Packing Charge Sets Off Probe," *Houston Chronicle*, August 2, 1963, 1, col. 8; "Eastland Calls for Probe of Federal Court," *New Orleans States-Item*, August 2, 1963, 1, col. 6.

48. Editorial, *Houston Chronicle*, August 4, 1963, Section 2, 4.

49. Saul Friedman, "Appeals Court Facing Revolt," *Houston Chronicle*, August 4, 1963, 1, col. 4; 6, col. 1.

as he saw fit. And that's the way it's done on every circuit court in the United States."[50] Finally, a judge characterized as "eager to talk but not to have his name used" supported Tuttle's unilateral action in the Birmingham case because the situation demanded a quick response. According to one report, "Judge Eager," as some members of the court dubbed this confidential informant, was John Brown.[51]

Within a few days, every member of the court had been mailed a copy of the *Houston Chronicle* article.[52] Griffin Bell opened the floodgates by sending an impassioned six-page letter to each of his colleagues in which he lambasted Rives, Brown, and Wisdom for their "disgraceful" public airing of the court's dirty linen.[53] He was particularly stinging in his rebuke of the colleague who had chosen to hide behind the veil of anonymity while challenging the integrity and professionalism of a group of colleagues that Bell took to include him as well. "I wear no man's collar," Bell insisted. "I am a free agent, accountable only to my own oath and conscience. No one of you has the right to speak for me or to judge me. Therefore for the writer to imply, as is clear from the full context, that I am in league with any group on this court is insulting. I take it as an insult from any member of this court who may have in any way furnished any basis for such an implication."[54] Bell also recommended that all future methods of assigning judges be subject to approval by the entire court. To that end, he urged the calling of a Judicial Council meeting in Houston for the purpose of providing all of the active judges with a forum in which to discuss the issues of panel assignment and the power of a single judge to issue temporary injunctive relief.[55]

50. Ibid.

51. J. Robert Brown, Jr., and Allison Herren Lee, *Neutral Assignment of Judges at the Court of Appeals,* 78 TEX. L. REV. 1037, 1051n.78 (2000). .See Letter to All Fifth Circuit Judges from Warren L. Jones, August 15, 1963, at 3, 5, 6.

52. J. Robert Brown, Jr., and Allison Herren Lee, *Neutral Assignment of Judges at the Court of Appeals,* 78 TEX. L. REV. 1037, 1051n.79 (2000).

53. Letter to All Fifth Circuit Judges from Griffin B. Bell, August 9, 1963, at 1.

54. Ibid., 3.

55. Letter to All Fifth Circuit Judges from Griffin B. Bell, August 9, 1963, at 5. According to Judge Warren Jones's diary, Bell had intended to distribute this letter immediately after reading the *Chronicle* article, but delayed doing so because he believed that a resolution calling for an investigation of the Fifth Circuit was going to be introduced at an upcoming American Bar Association meeting. Diary Memorandum prepared by Judge Warren Jones, August 8, 1963, 2. This hypothesis is supported by a postscript to Bell's letter stating that "since dictating the above, I have been advised that the American Bar Association may be asked to look into this matter. This shows how out of hand it is getting." Letter to All Fifth Circuit Judges from Griffin B. Bell, August 9, 1963, 6. Moreover, according to Warren Jones, an earlier draft of Bell's letter also had contained,

The combination of the public discourse generated by Cameron's al-legations, the Bell letter, and the distribution of Wadsworth's report on the assignment of judges in race cases compelled Tuttle to convene a meeting of the Judicial Council to respond to the discord that threat-ened to tear his court apart.[56] The historic meeting was set for August 22 and 23 in Houston to enable the sickly Judge Hutcheson to partici-pate. As it turned out, Cameron, the person singularly responsible for igniting the controversy, was unable to attend because of his own poor health. In a prior conversation with Jones, Cameron had confessed that the strain of the May 29 Judicial Council meeting in New Orleans had forced him to seek medical assistance and that he feared "that any greater strain might be the cause of sending him home 'feet first.'"[57] Nevertheless, he wrote to all of his colleagues in advance of the Hous-ton meeting, urging them to come out of the conference with a collec-tively fashioned, regularized procedure for the assignment of judges to both regular and three-judge court panels.[58]

Although members of the news media uncovered the fact of the meet-ing, its precise location was a carefully guarded secret. The *Houston Press* reported that "the judges were huddled somewhere in the new Federal Building. But officials would not say exactly where the judicial council was being held. Said one obviously nervous official of the court: 'I don't even want to be quoted as saying no comment.'"[59] And when queried as to the reason for the meeting, Circuit Clerk Ed Wadsworth responded: "I have no comment and that's off the record."[60]

---

as Jones characterized it, a recommendation that "the Chief Judge resume the functions of Chief Judge; meaning, of course, that Judge Brown's services as 'bat boy' be dispensed within making appointments." Diary Memorandum prepared by Judge Warren Jones, August 8, 1963, at 2. This suggestion did not appear in the final version that was sent to all the other judges.

56. Since Tuttle was still in Colorado at the time, he authorized acting Chief Judge Rives to send out the call for the meeting in a letter to all judges under Rives's signature but on Tuttle's sta-tionery. J. Robert Brown, Jr., and Allison Herren Lee, *Neutral Assignment of Judges at the Court of Ap-peals*, 78 TEX. L. REV. 1037, 1056n.109 (2000). The letter tersely announced that the Judicial Coun-cil would meet on August 22 at the Federal Courthouse in Houston "to consider rules of Court and any other appropriate matters." Letter to All Active Fifth Circuit Judges from Richard T. Rives, August 13, 1963.

57. Diary Memorandum prepared by Judge Warren Jones, August 12, 1963, 3. Judge Rives con-firmed these concerns, informing his colleagues that Cameron had suffered from acute fibrilla-tion, kidney infection, and high fever as a result of their last council session.

58. Letter to All Active Judges of the Fifth Circuit from Ben C. Cameron, August 19, 1963.

59. John Russell, "Eight U.S. Judges Huddle Secretly," *Houston Press*, August 22, 1963, 1, col. 1.

60. Bob Tutt, "Appeals Justices Weigh Pro-Integration Charges," *Houston Chronicle*, August 22, 1963, 1, col. 3.

In keeping with tradition, Griffin Bell, the court's junior member, served as secretary of the Judicial Council and kept the official minutes. But Bell's minutes are not the only source of information about what transpired during the secret conclave. Just as he had done during the *en banc* conferences in the Meredith and Barnett cases, Wisdom kept a record of the meeting with his own extensive set of holographic notes. For the entirety of the two-day session, he produced a nearly verbatim account of the proceedings on one standard yellow legal pad. For the better part of the next four decades, he kept the original and only copy of this unique record of the historic occasion in a plain, unmarked manila folder locked in the top drawer of a wooden credenza located to the side of his desk in his judicial chambers. These detailed notes, however, provide a bird's-eye view of what turned out to be an extremely confrontational and contentious gathering.[61]

The council met on Thursday, August 22, in chambers assigned to Judge Tuttle in Houston's federal courthouse.[62] The proceedings began innocently enough at 9:30 a.m. with a prayer offered, at Judge Tuttle's request, by Rives.[63] Tuttle then opened the discussion with an impassioned declaration that he "did not consciously do anything improper."[64] Tuttle explained that he had delegated all panel and three-judge court assignments to Judge Brown. Brown had been appointed assignment judge during the latter part of Hutcheson's tenure as chief judge and both Tuttle and his immediate predecessor, Rives, had chosen to retain Brown in that position when they assumed the post of chief judge. Jones then turned to Brown and insisted that the Fifth Circuit's clerk of court, Wadsworth, had informed Jones that Brown had directed Wadsworth to exclude certain judges from sitting on certain cases. Brown coldly replied, "He is in error." Bell shot back, "He says you did."[65]

Tuttle did admit, however, that *he* had instructed Wadsworth not to assign Judges Gewin and Bell to civil rights cases, but only until their recess appointments by President Kennedy became permanent upon being

61. Warren Jones also took contemporaneous notes of the conference. These notes, which are included in his diary, are significantly less detailed than those produced by Judge Wisdom and, on occasion, refer to matters not contained in Wisdom's contemporaneous account. See, for example, note 73, *infra*.

62. Wisdom Minutes of the Meeting of En Banc Court, U.S. Court of Appeals for the Fifth Circuit, August 22 and 23, 1963, Houston, Texas, 1 (hereinafter Wisdom Minutes).

63. Diary Memorandum prepared by Judge Warren Jones, August 22, 1963, 1.

64. Wisdom Minutes, 1.

65. Wisdom Minutes, 7.

confirmed by the Senate. Tuttle insisted that he had decided upon that course solely as a well-intentioned attempt to protect the pair from being involved in decisions that might cause them to fall out of favor with ardent segregationist and Senate Judiciary Chairman James Eastland of Mississippi. But, he also emphasized, he reversed these instructions once the Senate confirmed the pair's permanent appointment. Tuttle's admission, however, enraged Bell. "You mean you could not trust us until we made a record?" he shouted at Tuttle. After a few moments of awkward silence, Tuttle replied, "What actuated [this] was consideration."[66] Bell, however, wasn't placated by that reply. "Tuttle and Brown set themselves up as judges of the judges' honesty," Bell complained.[67] "I object to a guardianship. Brown has seized the Clerk's office like a Central American country; we can't have an Assistant Chief Judge."[68]

With tempers flaring, former chief judge Hutcheson sought to defuse the escalating conflagration. "I won't say John Brown has sinned," Hutcheson suggested, "but I say go in peace and sin no more." However, the usually unflappable and stern Texan could not resist launching a couple of grenades of his own. "There is not a man on this court I do not have the highest respect for, except Ben Cameron." And in response to Gewin's reference to Cameron's participation in the cases involving James Meredith, Hutcheson blurted, "I can't help it if a man's a damn fool!"[69] Finally, turning to Bell, an exasperated Hutcheson asked, "Would you piss on the whole court because you are mad with one judge? Ben disappointed me. Bad bird to befoul his own nest."[70]

Tuttle then offered a series of responses to Judge Cameron's charge that Tuttle intentionally had shut Cameron out from sitting on three-judge court cases filed in Mississippi. First, Tuttle stated, "Cameron was trapped by what he has written." The unambiguous text of Cameron's dissenting opinion in the Birmingham bus and other comparable cases, while honestly reflecting his convictions, demonstrated, in Tuttle's view, a manifest unwillingness to impartially consider and evaluate Fourteenth Amendment civil rights claims.[71] Such an unbending predispo-

66. Wisdom Minutes, 8.
67. Wisdom Minutes, 9.
68. Wisdom Minutes, 13.
69. Wisdom Minutes, 12.
70. Wisdom Minutes, 13.
71. See *United States v. Wood*, 295 F.2d 772, 785 (5th Cir.1961) (Cameron, J., dissenting), where Cameron refused to join Judges Rives and Brown in a ruling that ordered District Judge Harold Cox of Mississippi to issue a temporary restraining order against a disturbing the peace prosecu-

sition, Tuttle maintained, disqualified Cameron from sitting on other race discrimination cases. But anticipating that Tuttle would offer this explanation at the council meeting, Cameron had sent a letter to his colleagues one week prior to the Houston conclave in which he tendered a very different perspective on his voting record. Cameron denied that "I have disavowed neither the Fourteenth Amendment nor the decisions of the Supreme Court," insisting that none of his dissents were "justly susceptible of such a conclusion." These opinions, he maintained, "only pleaded for understanding of the enormity of the undertaking with which Mississippi and other portions of the South are confronted; that patience and understanding are needed, and that gradualism is absolutely required in some instances. I have not sought to offend, and I have not taken any offense."[72]

Tuttle, however, did not limit his remarks to his concern over Cameron's close-mindedness. He further explained to his colleagues that in staffing three-judge courts in Mississippi-filed cases, his hands also had been tied by a variety of other factors. First among them was Cameron's own request not to sit on the same panel with Tuttle. Plus, Jones had asked Tuttle not to pair him with Cameron on any cases because of the delays caused by Cameron's demand for a lengthy siesta between morning arguments and afternoon conferences. And on top of all that, aging Judge Hutcheson's frail condition prevented him from sitting anywhere outside of Houston, thereby severely restricting his availability for assignment. With Bell and Gewin admittedly kept off of all civil rights cases pending Senate confirmation of their recess appointments, this left Tuttle with only four of the nine members—himself, Rives, Brown, and Wisdom—available for unrestricted duty.

At 5:30 p.m., after hours of vigorous discussion on these and other matters, the meeting was adjourned. But the evening's respite didn't dampen either the emotions or the rhetoric that flowed freely at the following day's meeting. Tuttle opened the Friday session at 9:30 a.m. with a blistering attack on his colleague from Mississippi. "It is a caricature of justice," Tuttle professed, "to have Cameron sit on the civil rights cases. Judge Cameron is the thing that caused this turmoil. I have studied the facts and conclude that there has been no case assigned to a judge for

---

tion that the Walthall County authorities had brought against an African American male for helping other African Americans to register to vote.

72. Letter to All Active Judges of the Fifth Circuit from Ben F. Cameron, August 19, 1963, 4.

a prejudiced decision." Tuttle was deeply hurt and offended by Cameron and Senator Eastland's challenge to his honor and integrity. According to notes taken during the meeting by Jones, Tuttle offered, for the good of the court, to resign as chief judge in favor of the next most senior member, Judge Jones. His colleagues quickly and uniformly rejected that gesture.[73]

Gewin admitted that Cameron's thinking was "difficult," but asked his colleagues to remember that Cameron was ill and characterized his decisions as the product of "a lonesome and disappointed man."[74] Jones then predicted that if Tuttle would agree to put Cameron back on the regular rotation for assignment to three-judge cases, Cameron would consent to "realign" with the Fourteenth Amendment. In that same vein, Judge Hutcheson proposed that "if I were Tuttle, I would go to Cameron and say, 'You've been a s.o.b.; now if you're sincere about changing [your refusal to adhere to and enforce the Supreme Court's Fourteenth Amendment decisions], I'll appoint you.'" Tuttle, however, refused to budge. "I read Cameron's dissents," he replied, "as meaning that he intends to make Mississippi an island of resistance."[75]

After prolonged discussion, Rives recommended that the group issue a short press release, the first public statement concerning internal court matters in Fifth Circuit history. Wisdom, who had been noticeably silent throughout the two-day session save for a few comments in support of Judges Tuttle and Brown, and Gewin joined forces to confect language that the group eventually and unanimously approved just before adjourning.[76] The sparsely worded statement announced that "the problems alleged to exist in this Court have been considered by the Court. The Court believes that in no given case has there been a conscious assignment for the purpose of accomplishing a desired result. Action has been taken to avoid any appearance of inconsistency in the assignment of judges or the arrangement of the docket."[77]

This tepid pronouncement (Jones called it "a conglomerate of mean-

73. Diary Memorandum prepared by Judge Warren Jones, August 23, 1963, at 1; Allison Herren Lee, William W. Shakeley, and J. Robert Brown, Jr., *Judge Warren L. Jones and the Supreme Court of Dixie*, 59 LA. L. REV. 209, 249 (1998). Judge Wisdom's handwritten notes of the meeting, unlike those taken by Judge Jones, make no mention of Tuttle's offer to resign.

74. Wisdom Minutes, 15.

75. Wisdom Minutes, 16.

76. Diary Memorandum prepared by Judge Warren Jones, August 23, 1963, 4; Wisdom Minutes, 3.

77. Wisdom Minutes, 3.

ingless phrasing") intentionally omitted any reference to the details of the new assignment policy approved at the Houston meeting.[78] Judges Gewin, Bell, and Jones, despite their outrage at what they repeatedly and emphatically characterized as Brown's abuse of authority as assignments judge, ultimately agreed to acquiesce to their colleagues' readiness to retain Brown in that position. During a lunch break, Jones had convinced Bell and Gewin that for the good of the order it would be best to let bygones be bygones.[79]

As a result of this conversation, the group voted to authorize Judge Tuttle to continue to allow Brown to fashion the panel assignments, but subject to a distinct set of conditions. Assignments could not be made until after Brown and Tuttle had determined the site of each sitting. In addition, Brown's panel assignments could not be released to the clerk's office until after the clerk had scheduled all the cases to be heard at each sitting. Finally, requests to be relieved from sitting with another member no longer would be honored.[80] At 2:30 p.m., the Judicial Counsel meeting ended. The court had survived this threat to its ability to function in a reasonably civil, if not harmonious, fashion.

But the passage of more than forty years after this rancorous, tumultuous thirty-hour session has not yielded a definitive resolution to the controversy over whether Tuttle, with or without Brown, had stacked the panel assignments to ensure pro-integration results. Tuttle and Brown remained forever steadfast in their position that although Judges Gewin and Bell were sheltered from these controversial cases for the short period preceding their Senate confirmation, no member of the court was banished from sitting on race cases on ideological grounds. Wisdom consistently supported the actions of his chief judge, publicly declaring that panels generally had been assigned by "pure chance," with the temporally limited exception carved out for Gewin and Bell, which he characterized as "benign distortions."[81] And although he acknowledged privately his concurrence in Tuttle's judgment that Cameron was irrevocably opposed to integration and therefore should be banished from

78. Diary Memorandum prepared by Judge Warren Jones, August 23, 1963, 4.

79. J. Robert Brown, Jr., and Allison Herren Lee, *Neutral Assignment of Judges at the Court of Appeals*, 78 TEX. L. REV. 1037, 1063 (2000); Allison Herren Lee, William W. Shakeley, and J. Robert Brown, Jr., *Judge Warren L. Jones and the Supreme Court of Dixie*, 59 LA. L. REV. 209, 250 (1998).

80. Wisdom Minutes, 3–8.

81. "Feud over Racial Cases Flares in U.S. Appeals Court in South," *New York Times*, July 31, 1963, 12, col. 6; J. M. Wisdom [Graham], March 7, 1981, 43.

cases involving this issue, he insisted that such a stratagem did not rise
to the level of panel-rigging. He explained that "it would have been a
mockery of justice to have a three judge court composed of Cameron,
Mize, and Cox. That is just like deciding the case in advance against the
plaintiffs in a civil rights case."[82] Wisdom believed that Tuttle had decided that replacing such a panel with a trio that included Wisdom and
Brown "would be in the interest of upholding the law." Consequently,
Wisdom "oppose[d] the use of the word 'stacked' to characterize what
Tuttle did. I mean, when you say stacking or loading, you are implying
that he wanted a particular result. I don't think he wanted a particular result, but he thought that we would be much more objective than
Cameron."[83]

On April 3, 1964, less than eight months after the Houston Council meeting, Cameron passed away. The aged and fragile Mississippian
had become an alienated, embittered, and ineffectual voice on the
court; continually disposed to writing increasingly vituperative dissenting opinions. His degree of detachment was such that only two of his
colleagues attended the funeral in Meridian. The presence of Gewin,
Cameron's most ideologically compatible colleague, was to be expected.
And though the identity of the other member of the court might have
astonished some of the attendees, it came as no surprise to those who

82. The undeniable fact that Wisdom held Cox in professional disdain because of Cox's uniformly hostile views toward all civil rights claims did not, however, prevent Wisdom from writing an opinion that upheld Cox's decision not to recuse himself from presiding over a series of
civil rights cases. After two cases alleging racial discrimination in employment by various Mississippi state agencies had been assigned for trial to Judge Cox, the plaintiffs filed a motion requesting that Cox recuse himself on the ground of racial prejudice. They claimed that Cox's opinions
and remarks from the bench demonstrated his bias against all black people and his hostility to
civil rights actions. Cox denied the motion and the case was appealed to the Fifth Circuit. Wisdom wrote the opinion for the unanimous panel upholding Cox's refusal to disqualify himself.
In it, Wisdom stated that the federal statute governing recusal of federal district judges required
a demonstration of either personal bias that would produce a result based on matters outside of
what the judge learned from participating in the case, or of a clearly evinced policy of disregarding the merits in a particular class of cases. But, Wisdom insisted, disqualification could not be
justified solely on the basis of a judge's ruling in related cases or upon a demonstration of a tendency to rule in any particular way. Thus, he concluded, although many of Cox's racial comments
were "not only outmoded, but improper," and were in no way condoned by the Fifth Circuit, they
did not constitute a sufficient basis for disqualification. *Phillips v. Joint Legislative Committee on Performance and Expenditure Review of the State of Mississippi*, 637 F.2d 1014, 1020 (5th Cir.1981), cert.
denied, 456 U.S. 960, 102 S.Ct. 2035, 72 L.Ed.2d 483 (1982).

83. Transcript of interview of Judge John M. Wisdom by Fred Graham, New Orleans, La.,
March 7, 1981, at 38.

knew him. Wisdom attended his colleague's funeral because, simply, it was the right thing to do. Wisdom, unlike the rest of "The Four," eventually was able to come to terms with the man who had so vociferously challenged the integrity of two of his most esteemed colleagues. As Wisdom later explained, "I respect anybody who on constitutional grounds takes even as a conservative or reactionary position as he takes." Unlike demagogues like Governors George Wallace or Ross Barnett, Cameron had no political axe to grind. In Wisdom's eyes, "Ben was doing what he thought was right. I think he was misguided. I went to his funeral because I wanted to show my respect for him and we had, notwithstanding our very great disagreements, managed to be friends and respect each other."[84]

Albeit badly splintered by the ill feelings generated on both sides of the allegations of court-packing and procedural overreaching, the Fifth Circuit emerged from this difficult period in its history structurally intact, if not ideologically balkanized. But the mere fact of its structural integrity would soon face a determined challenge from agents within and without the court, an effort that Wisdom and his supporters initially succeeded in forestalling, but ultimately failed to avert.

84. Ibid., 34–35.

12

HONORING THE PROMISE OF THE FIFTEENTH AMENDMENT
THE VOTING RIGHTS CASES

On March 30, 1870, nearly five years after the conclusion of the Civil War, the Fifteenth Amendment to the U.S. Constitution was declared to be ratified by the legislatures of twenty-nine of the thirty-seven states.[1] For the first time in American history, the federal government had officially embraced and codified the principle that the most fundamental and cherished of civil liberties—the right to vote—no longer could be systematically denied to individuals solely because of their race. In stirring language, this antebellum amendment guarantees that every citizen's right to vote "shall not be denied or abridged by the United States or by any State on account of race, color, or previous condition of servitude."

Nevertheless, for more than a century after the end of the Civil War, the promise embodied in this compact remained an unfulfilled dream. Through the implementation of a collection of initially overt and subsequently more sophisticated, covert devices and artifices, state legislative

---

1. Ratification technically was completed on February 3, 1870, when Iowa became the twenty-ninth state to vote in favor of ratification, unless the withdrawal of ratification by New York State was effective; in which event the process of ratification was formally completed on February 17, 1870, when Nebraska ratified.

and administrative officials, particularly in the South, pursued a shamefully relentless policy of denying African American citizens the opportunity to exercise the franchise.

Discriminatorily administered literacy tests, poll taxes, amorphous "good character" requirements, racial gerrymandering of election districts, and promulgation of grandfather clauses that exempted descendants of individuals who were registered voters as of 1867 (that is, before the ratification of the Fifteenth Amendment) from having to satisfy even the most elementary literacy requirement were among most commonly and effectively employed stratagems devised to block African Americans from enjoying their right of suffrage. And when these invidiously motivated tools no longer operated to exclude black citizens from voting, other devices that served to dilute the effectiveness of these votes, such as at-large voting for legislative representatives from multi-district voting units, were either put or kept in place.

Over the succeeding century, Congress enacted a series of measures to implement this constitutional mandate. Just two months after the Fifteenth Amendment's ratification, Congress passed the country's first federal voting rights act, providing all otherwise qualified citizens with a statutory right to vote without regard to their race, color, or previous condition of servitude, irrespective of any contrary directive of state constitution, law, regulation, or custom.[2] But this 1870 enactment proved to be largely ineffectual because of its lax enforcement by the federal courts. And for nearly ninety years thereafter, Congress took no further action, despite the widespread adoption and enforcement by southern states of Jim Crow laws that eviscerated the pledge memorialized in the Fifteenth Amendment.

Congress eventually reentered the arena with its passage of the Civil Rights Act of 1957, which prohibited private and public acts of interference with the right to vote in federal elections and authorized the U.S. attorney general to bring actions in federal court to enjoin any such interference.[3] But as these provisions proved to be unsuited to combating the subtle discriminatory voter qualification and registration techniques that already had been implemented in some states, Congress beefed up the litigative authority of the attorney general through its passage of Title VI of the Civil Rights Act of 1960.[4] Under this law, the attorney general could obtain a judicial determination of the existence of

2. Enforcement Act of May 31, 1870, ch. 114, §1, 16 Stat. 140.
3. Civil Rights Act of 1957, Pub. L. 85-315, §§ 131(c), 71 Stat. 634.
4. Civil Rights Act of 1960, Pub. L. 86-449, §601, 74 Stat. 86.

a pattern or practice of race- or color-based discrimination in voter registration, the exercise of the franchise, and the counting of ballots. Additionally, any individual member of a racial group who had been victimized by such a discriminatory practice could obtain a court order declaring him or her qualified to vote.

John Minor Wisdom's initial foray into the voting rights area, as he would be the first to admit, was an abject failure. Alabama, like many southern states, had engaged in racial gerrymandering by passing a variety of reapportionment statutes. One of these enactments reconfigured the shape of the City of Tuskegee's boundaries from a square to a twenty-eight-sided boundary line for municipal elections. In 1959, Wisdom voted to reject the claim of African American residents of Tuskegee that by eliminating nearly all black voters from the city limits while retaining all existing white residents, the statute—by design as well as by operation—disenfranchised black citizens in violation of their constitutional rights under the Fourteenth and Fifteenth Amendments. In the firm belief that the absence of any explicit reference to race in the statutory text precluded him from considering either the legislature's motivation or the statute's impact on members of the affected racial group in adjudicating its constitutionality, Wisdom, to his everlasting regret, wrote a concurring opinion in *Gomillion v. Lightfoot* upholding the law.[5] Within a year, the Supreme Court reversed both the majority's ruling and Wisdom's analysis.[6]

Four years passed before Wisdom's next voting rights case. In an action brought under the 1960 Civil Rights Act, District Judge Edwin F. "Chug" Hunter, Jr., of Lake Charles, Louisiana, had found that the registrar of voters for East Carroll Parish had engaged in a pattern and practice of racial discrimination against black applicants for registration and had directed the registrar to qualify twenty-eight voters.[7] This decision motivated the State of Louisiana to file a separate lawsuit challenging the constitutionality of the 1960 law, which was assigned to a three-judge district court composed of Wisdom, District Judges Herbert W. Christenberry of New Orleans, and Hunter.[8] The state maintained that by authorizing federal judges to make decisions on voting qualifications,

5. 270 F.2d 594, 599 (5th Cir.1959) (Wisdom, J., concurring).

6. *Gomillion v. Lightfoot*, 364 U.S. 339, 81 S.Ct. 125, 5 L.Ed.2d 110 (1960).

7. *U.S. v. Manning*, Civ. Action #8257 (W.D.La.), Order by Judge Edwin F. Hunter, Jr., July 25, 1962.

8. *U.S. v. Manning*, 206 F.Supp. 623 (W.D.La.1962); Letter to Alton L. Curtis from Elbert P. Tuttle, July 24, 1962.

Congress had invaded the powers reserved to the state governments by the Tenth Amendment to the Constitution.

All three judges voted to uphold the constitutionality of the 1960 statute in *U.S. v. Manning*. As senior member of the panel, Wisdom assigned himself the task of writing the opinion, in which he rejected both of the state's arguments.[9] His opinion stands as a powerful refutation of the state's interposition-premised Tenth Amendment argument, a claim that, if embraced, would have allowed state governments free rein over voting qualifications unchecked by the federal judicial guardians of the Constitution.

The Civil War, Wisdom declaimed, had forever settled "the misguided doctrine of interposition" by affirming that "the reality of national sovereignty prevailed over metaphysical state sovereignty."[10] Although the State of Louisiana enjoyed an unquestioned right to confect and administer voting qualifications, Wisdom explained, nothing in the Tenth Amendment provided the state with *exclusive* sovereignty over the election process. To the contrary, he insisted, the federal government had an equally manifest right and obligation to ensure that the state's exercise of its authority was faithful to the commands of the federal Constitution. "If a State shirks this responsibility," he added, "it must expect the Nation to honor the obligation the State has evaded."[11]

Wisdom grounded his explication of the constitutionally fashioned balance of federal and state sovereignty on a mini-dissertation detailing the history of the Tenth Amendment. His comprehensive and thoroughly documented study compared the Tenth Amendment with the corresponding provision in the Articles of Incorporation, reviewed the debates on ratification of the Constitution contained in the *Federalist Papers*, and analyzed Supreme Court cases that had construed this constitutional provision. This thoroughgoing examination impelled him to conclude that the Tenth Amendment never had been intended to preclude the federal government from operating in areas, such as the regulation of elections, in which the states also were authorized to act. Rather, he concluded, the real question in this case was whether Congress was constitutionally authorized to enact the Civil Rights Act.

Wisdom's answer to this question would prove to be the most momentous aspect of the opinion. He explained that the language of Article I,

9. 215 F.Supp. 272, 290 (W.D.La.1963).
10. 215 F.Supp. at 295.
11. 215 F.Supp. at 296.

Section 4, of the Constitution that authorized Congress to regulate the time, places, and manner of holding federal elections carried with it the implied power, under the Necessary and Proper Clause of Article I, Section 8 (which authorizes Congress "to make all Laws which shall be necessary and proper for carrying into Execution the Powers vested by this Constitution in the Government of the United States") to take all appropriate action plainly adapted to accomplishing that objective.

The next step in Wisdom's chain of reasoning was the masterstroke. He boldly announced that the entire electoral process was a single, indivisible event. "The act of casting a ballot in a voting booth," he reckoned, "cannot be cut away from the rest of the process. It is the last step in a process that starts with registration." By creating this nexus, Wisdom was able to conclude that since Congress had the power to regulate the scheduling and conducting of an election, it legitimately could legislate to protect the integrity of "the entire electoral process, from the first step of registering to the last step, the State's promulgation of honest returns."[12]

Wisdom did not, however, rest there. He reasoned that since Section 2 of the Fifteenth Amendment expressly authorized Congress to enforce the amendment's substantive provisions, the Fifteenth Amendment constituted an independent, broad source of authority for Congress to attack and remedy racial discrimination in voting. Moreover, unlike Article I, Section 4, of the Constitution, the Fifteenth Amendment was not limited to elections for federal office. And employing the same link-in-the-chain metaphor initiated in his examination of Article I, Section 4, Wisdom concluded that Congress enjoyed a correlative power to assure that states did not engage in racial discrimination in any part of the electoral process, including, of course, registration.

Wisdom's opinion was hailed as "magnificent" by Chief Judge Elbert Tuttle and as "a monument" by John Brown.[13] In his congratulatory note to Wisdom, Brown went on to state that "to keep this from being too drippy, I can only repeat again what I said once before after reading one of your masterpieces: I feel like the Indian over the horizon at Los Alamos after the initial atomic explosion and the mushroom cloud: I wish I had said that."[14] Wisdom's ruling was the first federal court decision addressing the constitutionality of the 1960 Civil Rights Act. As

12. 215 F.Supp. at 283–284.
13. Letter to John M. Wisdom from Elbert P. Tuttle, February 28, 1963.
14. Letter to John M. Wisdom from John R. Brown, March 6, 1963.

such, and particularly because of the deference accorded to Wisdom-authored judgments, the opinion placed an authoritative stamp of constitutional legitimacy on this important law. But perhaps more significant, it served as the analytical springboard for yet another Wisdom voting rights opinion, an acknowledged judicial masterpiece released later that same year.

Louisiana's Constitution had been amended in 1960 to provide that every voter "shall be able to understand and give a reasonable interpretation of any section of either [the Louisiana or U.S.] Constitution."[15] Additionally, a Louisiana statute required that all applicants for voting registration "be able to read any clause in the Constitution of Louisiana or of the United States and give a reasonable interpretation thereof."[16] The Justice Department brought suit in the federal district court in New Orleans claiming that these understanding and interpretation requirements violated the 1960 Civil Rights Act as well as the Fourteenth and Fifteenth Amendments to the U.S. Constitution.

A trio of Louisiana judges—Wisdom and District Judges Herbert Christenberry and E. Gordon West—made up the three-judge court constituted to rule on this constitutional challenge to state law. Wisdom's forty-three-page opinion in *U.S. v. State of Louisiana*, released only four days after President Kennedy's assassination in Dallas, opened in classic Wisdom style—with a characteristically vivid depiction of both the legal and pragmatic issues before the court.[17] The state Constitution's interpretation test, he proclaimed, had created "a wall" between registered voters and unregistered, eligible African American voters, a wall that operated as "the highest, best-guarded, most effective barrier to Negro voting in Louisiana."[18] In both design and operation, the interpretation test was nothing more than "a sophisticated scheme to disenfranchise Negroes."[19] Having tangled for years with state election officials when he sought to register black voters in Louisiana as part of his overall strategy to revive his state's Republican Party, Wisdom was intimately familiar with the intricacies and connivances of his state's voting eligibility requirements. And he penned an unambiguous, blunt, and

15. Article VIII, Section 1(d), La. Constitution of 1921, as amended in 1960.
16. LSA—R.S. 18:35.
17. 225 F.Supp. 353 (E.D.La.1963).
18. 225 F.Supp. at 355.
19. 225 F.Supp. at 356.

forceful reply to the issue in the same metaphoric terms he had used to frame it. "We hold: this wall, built to bar Negroes from access to the franchise, must come down."[20]

Under Louisiana law, parish voting registrars were accorded the discretion to select any constitutional provision for any individual applicant to interpret. They also possessed the sole, unreviewable authority for evaluating the sufficiency of the prospective elector's answer. And, as Wisdom noted in measured understatement, "in many parishes the registrar is not easily satisfied with constitutional interpretations from Negro applicants."[21]

In response to the state's predictable assertion of the states' rights doctrine, that is, that the Tenth Amendment precluded the federal government from interfering with any state's exercise of its exclusive and plenary power to establish voting qualifications, Wisdom simply reaffirmed the positions he had taken nine months earlier in *Manning*. This left him only with the task of countering the state's claim that because the text of Louisiana's constitutional and statutory interpretation test contained no reference to the race of voting applicants, there could be no finding that its enactment had been motivated by a discriminatory motivation.

In language that would echo for decades thereafter as the doctrinal baseline for Supreme Court opinions in civil rights cases ranging from voting to employment rights, Wisdom declared that unconstitutional racial bias could be found in the administration as well as the declaration of governmental policies. Both "the legislative purpose and inevitable effect of a law non-discriminatory on its face," he boldly declared, "may be decisive in determining the unconstitutionality of the law."[22] Ironically, Wisdom based this conclusion on the Supreme Court's decision in *Gomillion*, the voting reapportionment case in which the High Court had reversed the contrary position taken by Wisdom in his first voting rights opinion.

Having concluded that inquiry into both the purpose and impact of the interpretation test was essential, let alone appropriate, to the constitutional inquiry, Wisdom employed the same technique he had used so masterfully and effectively in his school desegregation opinion in

20. 225 F.Supp. at 356.
21. 225 F.Supp. at 356.
22. 225 F.Supp. at 362.

Jefferson County. He launched into an exhaustive and compelling recitation and indictment of the over two hundred-year history of Louisiana's campaign, dating from colonial times, to perpetuate white supremacy by denying black citizens the right to vote. Wisdom fastidiously
documented the devastatingly discriminatory legacy of that sorry tradition. Beginning with the overtly exclusionary Louisiana *Codes Noir* of
colonial times through the Black Codes, property ownership requirements, educational tests, and grandfather clauses of the late nineteenth
century, as well as periodic purging of those few blacks who had overcome these obstacles to registration, Wisdom recounted precisely how
the State of Louisiana had consistently and systematically engaged in a
conscious plan to exclude black citizens from the franchise. And this
historical survey propelled him to the inescapable conclusion that the
present-day interpretation test, its purpose rooted in that same regrettable history, was designed to perpetuate that longstanding disenfranchisement of African American citizens.

The process of unearthing and revealing the fruits of this painstaking research, which one former Wisdom clerk referred to as "the life
force of the opinion," was, as Wisdom subsequently confided to several
of his correspondents, "pure fun."[23] He also reveled in telling any interested listener that this massive research effort had been conducted entirely within the confines of the extensive library housed in his judicial
chambers.[24]

23. Letter to George Simpson from John M. Wisdom, December 3, 1963; Letter to Edmond
N. Cahn from John M. Wisdom, December 3, 1963.

24. Joel Wm. Friedman, *John Minor Wisdom: The Noblest Tulanian of Them All*, 74 TUL. L. REV.
1, 31 (1999); Jack Bass, *John Minor Wisdom and the Impact of Law*, 69 MISS. L. J. 25, 33 (1999). Another glorious example of Wisdom's enthusiasm for historical research appears in his opinion in
Block v. Compagnie National Air France, 386 F.2d 323 (5th Cir.1967), cert. denied, 392 U.S. 905, 88
S.Ct. 2053, 20 L.Ed.2d. 1363 (1968). After the downing of an Air France jet that had been chartered by the Atlanta Art Association for an excursion by its members to visit the Louvre, the families of the passengers, all of whom had perished in the crash, brought an action in federal court
against Air France. The sole issue before the Fifth Circuit was whether or not the terms of the
Warsaw Convention, which limit recovery in such cases to $8,291.87 per deceased passenger, ap-
plied to a charter flight. Wisdom's thirty-page opinion for the majority examined the history of
the Warsaw Convention and the legislative history of the limitation on liability provision in exhaustive detail, with extensive reference to, and analysis of, contemporary and successive scholarly
commentary as well as relevant opinions by other American and European courts. As one of his
former law clerks reported, "after various law clerks had struggled with the case for two years, the
Judge took the research into his own hands. He consulted not only the original text of the Con-

Wisdom's reliance on the history of Louisiana's voting requirements had strategic as well as scholarly objectives. As he later acknowledged, he was hopeful that "by tying the future with the past we may be able to reduce the invention of a new series of schemes."[25] By revealing and formally repudiating the state's historical pattern of voting discrimination, he wished to lay the foundation for the invalidation of any future statutory or constitutional "gimmick" that the state might one day employ to achieve that same end.[26] Wisdom also hoped that this narrative would persuade the public at large, and particularly those unfamiliar with Louisiana's history of racial disenfranchisement, of the unlawfulness of the state's registration regime and the absolute necessity for taking aggressive measures to remove every vestige of this discriminatory tradition.[27]

Wisdom's assessment of the purpose behind the challenged interpretation test, however, did not rest solely on his historical analysis. He meticulously detailed the massive evidence of an organized, pervasive pattern of unequal administration of the inherently subjective and standardless interpretation test by voting registrars throughout Louisiana. Wisdom revealed that registrars had been clothed with unlimited, unreviewable discretion to use or not to use the interpretation test, to choose which applicants would be subjected to the test, to select

---

vention (in French), but also the Convention's legislative history (also in French), the Code Civile of France, and numerous scholarly works on the Convention and on international air law in general." The result, this former clerk continued, was "a tour de force of legal scholarship, in which he weaves together underlying concepts from the common law and civilian systems, compares French and English texts of the Convention, discusses the pertinent scholarly writings, and, finally, analyzes the few prior decisions that are helpful by analogy." Alan Black, *John Minor Wisdom: A Tribute and Memoir by One of His Law Clerks*, 69 Miss. L. J. 43, 47 (1999). But though he thoroughly enjoyed the journey, Wisdom took no pleasure in the destination. As he acknowledged to his panel colleagues, Wisdom spent an inordinate amount of time "trying to find a way to decide in favor of the passengers." Unfortunately, his research did not permit him to indulge his desire to circumvent the Convention's stark limitation on liability. To the contrary, it left him no alternative but to conclude that the Convention applied. Letter to Warren L. Jones and Leo Brewster from John M. Wisdom, August 31, 1967.

25. Letter to Arthur J. Freund from John M. Wisdom, December 3, 1963.

26. Letter from Judge John M. Wisdom to Dean Erwin Griswold, December 3, 1963; Letter from Judge John M. Wisdom to Professor John Kaplan, December 3, 1963; Letter from Judge John M. Wisdom to Professor Edmond N. Cahn, December 3, 1963.

27. Barry Sullivan, *The Honest Muse: Judge Wisdom and the Uses of History*, 60 Tul. L. Rev. 314, 341 (1985).

which of the 443 sections of the 600-page Louisiana Constitution to require the applicant to interpret, and to determine on an ad hoc basis
whether or not a particular interpretation was acceptable. As Wisdom
ruefully concluded, "pity the applicant asked to interpret the interpretation test."[28]

Finally, Wisdom pointed out that since the interpretation test did not
measure literacy, intelligence, or citizenship, it did not gauge any skill
or ability reasonably relevant to the state's legitimate interest in an informed electorate. This inevitably meant that the right to vote turned
"more upon the caprice of the registrar than upon the possession of
measurable qualifications."[29] Consequently, he deduced, "the ugly intractable truth"[30] was that the unrestricted raw power vested in the registrars was linked solely to the state's intention to promote unlawful
racial discrimination. Thus, he resolved, not only did the racially disenfranchising purpose and effect of the interpretation test render it invalid under the Fifteenth Amendment, the constitutional and statutory
delegation to government officials of unrestrained discretion to apply a
capricious test without guidance or standards rendered that test so in-
curably subjective, unreasonable, and incapable of equal enforcement as
to be invalid under the Fourteenth Amendment. Accordingly, the court
enjoined its further use.

But merely prohibiting the use of the challenged voting test would
not accomplish Wisdom's objectives. The State of Louisiana, in antici-
pation of just such a judicial ruling, previously had enacted a fallback
voting qualification policy. In the event any court struck down the interpretation test, the state would require registrants to demonstrate their
understanding of the federal Constitution as a whole. Under this alternate standard, a registrant was required to select one out of ten cards,
each of which contained six multiple-choice questions. To pass, the applicant was required to answer four of the six questions correctly, each
of which required a comprehension of the theory of the American system of government as well as knowledge of specific constitutional provisions. But although previously enacted changes to Louisiana's voting
qualifications had been accompanied by a general re-registration of all
voters, that did not happen on this occasion. After all, as Wisdom wryly
observed, "general re-registration would in large measure destroy the

28. 225 F.Supp. at 382.
29. 225 F.Supp. at 390.
30. 225 F.Supp. at 386.

continuing usefulness of the past discriminations designed to keep Negroes off of the registration rolls."[31]

Instead, this new procedure was applied only to previously unregistered voters. Moreover, since African Americans represented the vast bulk of this group, they were disproportionately disadvantaged by the new system that undoubtedly would have resulted in the disqualification of many white voters who had successfully registered under the prior, less demanding regime. Clearly, Wisdom noted, the necessary effect of the newly adopted system was "to perpetuate the differences created by the discriminatory practices of the past."[32]

The remedy that Wisdom fashioned, born of equal parts pragmatism and imagination, is perhaps the single most enduring portion of his opinion. He explained that the court needed to do more than merely order the cessation of these intrinsically discriminatory practices. "An appropriate remedy," he declared, "should undo the results of past discrimination as well as prevent future inequality of treatment. A court of equity is not powerless to eradicate the effects of former discrimination. If it were, the State could seal into permanent existence the injustices of the past."[33] And the state's alternative scheme, Wisdom determined, operated to "freeze the result of the past illegal practices."[34]

Accordingly, Wisdom declared that the federal courts possessed inherent authority to grant relief that would both rectify past inequities and prevent future inequalities. Certain remedies, such as mandating re-registration of all voters in the state, purging those white voters who could not have passed a nondiscriminatory qualification test, or qualifying those African Americans who either would have passed such a test or who were deterred from even seeking registration by the state's deserved reputation for unfairness, were dismissed as impracticable or unworkable because they would generate excessive federal interference with state and local procedures. Instead, Wisdom offered the state two options. In those parishes that previously had used the interpretation test, the state could choose either to re-register all voters who could pass a uniform voting test, or totally "freeze" further use of the examination and subject all candidates to the requirements (such as voting age and residency) previously imposed only on nonwhite applicants until the

31. 225 F.Supp. at 393.
32. 225 F.Supp. at 393.
33. 225 F.Supp. at 393.
34. 225 F.Supp. at 394.

court was satisfied that the now-discarded interpretation test had lost its discriminatory effect.[35]

Wisdom was well satisfied with the fruits of his extended labors on this opinion. As he typically did in cases that he deemed unusually significant or interesting, he sent letters to many of his friends and acquaintances informing them of the content and likely impact of the ruling.[36] Fourteen months later, Wisdom was delighted to learn that the U.S. Supreme Court had affirmed, unanimously, his judgment and adopted all of his findings, rationale, and conclusions.[37] It marked the first occasion on which the High Court approved the use of a reparative injunction, that is, one designed not only to preclude future acts of discrimination but also to undo the continuing effects of past unlawfully biased conduct. Moreover, it laid the theoretical groundwork for subsequent Fifth Circuit and, eventually, Supreme Court, decisions validating and implementing this form of broad-based affirmative action in response to other forms of public- and private-sector discrimination in areas such as employment, jury selection, and education.[38]

In terms of its direct and immediate impact, Wisdom's ruling effectively eliminated the use of the understanding test throughout the nation, thereby withdrawing one of the most potent weapons from the arsenal available to local officials bent on depriving blacks of the franchise. But despite its clear and powerful language, this ruling was not instantly successful in convincing the voting registrars in all of the Louisiana parishes subject to its remedial decree to put an end to their race-based disenfranchisement tactics. In East and West Feliciana Parishes, for example, the registrars closed their offices to all voting applicants on the precise day that the ruling in *U.S. v. Louisiana* was rendered. Four months later, when the Justice Department initiated separate law-

35. Judge West did not join Wisdom and Christenberry in the majority, choosing instead to file a dissenting opinion primarily on the Tenth Amendment–based theory that regulation of voting fell within the exclusive control of the States. *U.S. v. State of Louisiana*, 225 F.Supp. 353, 398 (West, J., dissenting).

36. See notes 23, 25, and 26.

37. *Louisiana v. U.S.*, 380 U.S. 145, 85 S.Ct. 817, 13 L.Ed.2d 709 (1965). Justice Harlan agreed with the ruling that the interpretation test was unconstitutional, but limited that ruling to Fifteenth Amendment grounds. He fully subscribed to the Court's opinion in all other respects. 380 U.S. at 156, 85 S.Ct. at 823.

38. See *Taylor v. McKeithen*, 499 F.2d 893, 910 (5th Cir.1974); Philip P. Frickey, *Judge Wisdom and Voting Rights: The Judicial Artist as Scholar and Pragmatist*, 60 Tul. L. Rev. 276, 280–81 (1985); Bass, *Unlikely Heroes*, 272n.15.

suits against each of registrars to obtain orders compelling the reopening of their offices, District Judge Gordon West, the lone dissenter in *U.S. v. Louisiana*, denied the federal government's request for that injunctive relief. The ruling in *U.S. v. Louisiana*, in his view, had placed the voting registrars in an untenable position. The effect of the court's order to cease using both the original interpretation test and its subsequent replacement was to leave the registrars without any usable criteria for voter qualification. Consequently, West reasoned, it was completely understandable and nondiscriminatory for the registrars to close their offices to all applicants, white and black, until legally enforceable standards were put into place.

Wisdom wrote a vigorous opinion for the Fifth Circuit panel that unanimously reversed Judge West's ruling and imposed a "freezing" remedy.[39] "The registrars' excuses," he began, "are a patent sham."[40] In parishes where nearly all whites, though few African Americans, of voting age were registered, Wisdom caustically reported, "we cannot take seriously a registrar's wry defense that since the office was closed to applicants of both races, there was no discrimination."[41] Judge West also had erroneously concluded that the decision in *U.S. v. Louisiana* had left the registrars with no usable voting qualifications. Since Louisiana law prescribed several lawfully enforceable standards, including minimum age and residency requirements, by closing their offices rather than applying these qualifications, the registrars had failed to abide by the Fifth Circuit's freezing principle. Accordingly, the registrars were directed to reopen their office and apply the standards previously imposed upon white applicants.

Notwithstanding such temporary bumps in the road, the impact of Wisdom's opinion in *U.S. v. Louisiana*, particularly its application of the freezing principle to invalidate practices that were racially neutral on their face when they operated to perpetuate the effects of prior discrimination, extended far beyond the development of civil rights jurisprudence by the federal courts.[42] It also was part of a chain of events that resulted in the enactment of new voting rights legislation by Congress.

39. *U.S. v. Palmer*, 356 F.2d 951 (5th Cir.1966).

40. 356 F.2d at 953.

41. 356 F.2d at 952.

42. Although the initial adoption of a remedy for voting discrimination based on the "freezing" principle is found in District Judge Frank Johnson's opinion in *U.S. v. Penton*, 212 F.Supp. 193 (N.D.Alab.1962), Judge Wisdom's more fulsome development and refined articulation of that

Notwithstanding the ruling in *U.S. v. Louisiana* and subsequent cases, communities throughout the South that fell within the jurisdiction of the Fifth Circuit nevertheless continued to erect barriers to the registration of black voters. One of the most vigorous and notorious examples of this strategy was Dallas County, Alabama. And perhaps the most vicious enforcer of this invidious policy was Dallas County sheriff "Big Jim" Clark. In January 1965, Clark had responded to a series of public demonstrations over Alabama's voter registration testing requirements in the county seat of Selma by arresting more than three thousand protestors. In response, in part to Clark's actions, black leaders planned a march from Selma to the state capital in Montgomery. On March 7, in front of a stunned nation watching the events transpire on live television, as the marchers traversed the Edmund Pettus Bridge, they were confronted by a phalanx of Alabama state police officers. The state troopers, abetted by Clark's forces, brutally beat and tear-gassed the marchers into submission, forcing them to cross back over the bridge and injuring nearly eighty demonstrators.

The public reaction to this horrific event finally convinced President Johnson that the extant voting provisions of the Civil Rights Acts of 1957, 1960, and 1964 were not adequate to combat the seemingly endless variety of stratagems and ploys concocted by state legislature to continue to block African Americans from the voting rolls. Before the Selma marchers eventually reached Montgomery, President Johnson presented a tougher and more comprehensive voting rights act to Congress, which Congress thereafter enacted as the Voting Rights Act of 1965.[43] Chief among its innovations, this enactment codified Wisdom's freezing principle by expressly prohibiting the implementation of any "test or device" as a prerequisite to voter registration that was discriminatorily motivated or that generated a discriminatory effect. As further evidence of the impact of Wisdom's ruling on this legislative development, John Doar, by then the chief of the Civil Rights Division in the Justice Department, recalled frequently hearing other Justice Department lawyers refer to "that wall that must come down" as they de-

---

concept in *U.S. v. Louisiana* is generally recognized as the opinion that gave life and credibility to the doctrine and served as the springboard for its adoption by the Supreme Court in voting and other civil rights cases.

43. James B. Zouras, *Shaw v. Reno: A Color-Blind Court in a Race-Conscious Society*, 44 DePaul L. Rev. 917, 924 (1995).

veloped drafts of the bill that became the Voting Rights Act of 1965.[44] Additionally, in its report to the House concerning this proposed legislation, the Judiciary Committee Report referred approvingly to Wisdom's freezing principle and expressly affirmed that "that is what Congress will be doing in the present bill."[45]

Wisdom's mammoth opinion in *U.S. v. Louisiana*, however, demonstrated more than his resolute dedication to eradicating the lingering effects of the coldly calculated and faithfully observed stratagems designed to disenfranchise generations of otherwise qualified black voters. It, like so many other of his opinions, also reflected his ability and habit of tempering his doctrinal analysis with his innate pragmatism and common sense. Supreme Court justice Stephen Breyer, in a letter read at the memorial service following Wisdom's death, wrote that in response to Breyer's asking Wisdom whether it was better for a judge to be theoretical or practical, Wisdom had replied "practical."[46]

In fact, it was in large part due to Wisdom's unfailingly pragmatic outlook and his overarching devotion to fairness that he invariably bridled at being called a reformer. Far from being a dogmatic, knee-jerk ideologue, Wisdom possessed a temperament and a judicial philosophy marked by a clear recognition of the practical and an understanding that change, when necessary to ensure fairness, was only a means to an end and not an objective worthy of pursuit in its own name. Moreover, his voting rights decision reflected his abiding dedication to the constitutional separation of powers and its allocation of responsibility between the judicial and legislative branches of the federal government.

A 1966 voting case is a notable example of Wisdom's evenhanded, non-reflexive approach to voting rights claims. A little more than a month before the scheduled date of a primary election, a group of African American citizens of Mississippi sued to obtain a court order re-

44. See Bass, *John Minor Wisdom and the Impact of Law*, 69 MISS. L. J. 25, 31 (1999); Bass, *Unlikely Heroes*, 276-277 .

45. H.R. Rep. No. 439, 89th Cong., 1st Sess. 10-12, *reprinted at* 2 U.S. Cong. & Admin. News 2446-7, 89th Cong., 1st Sess. (1965). Coincidentally, in a Senate Committee report drafted in opposition to the voting rights bill, the authors relied on the Supreme Court's ruling in *Minor v. Happersett*, 88 U.S. (21 Wallace) 162 (1874) in which the Court unanimously rejected the argument of one of Wisdom's ancestors, Virginia Minor, that she enjoyed a Fourteenth Amendment right to vote. S. Rep. No. 162 3, *reprinted at* 2 U.S. Cong. & Admin. News 2510-2511, 89th Cong., 1st Sess. (1965).

46. See Philip P. Frickey, *Wisdom on Weber*, 74 TUL. L. REV. 1169, 1171 (2000).

quiring the state's Democratic Party to postpone the election for about two months. They alleged that since black citizens had been victimized by the state's hundred-year policy of racially based disenfranchisement in violation of the Fifteenth Amendment, the court should exercise its equitable power to provide African American citizens with additional time to register so that more of them could participate in that election.

After the district court denied the request for relief, the plaintiffs appealed to the Fifth Circuit. Wisdom, sitting with Circuit Judge Homer Thornberry of Texas and District Judge William Harold Cox of Mississippi, wrote the opinion for the unanimous panel affirming the lower court's refusal to postpone the election.[47] Citing his own opinion in *U.S. v. Louisiana*, Wisdom noted that his court had "not been backward in exercising its equity power to fashion remedies appropriate in analogous situations; for example, the 'freezing principle.'"[48] Nevertheless, he recounted, the State of Mississippi had abolished all of its registration requirements other than age, residency, and literacy standards. Consequently, he continued, the record demonstrated that for a year there had been no serious impediment to the registration of black citizens in Mississippi. And though he sympathized with the plaintiffs' claim that the legacy of the state's century-old tradition of racial disenfranchisement warranted extraordinary relief, the fact was that the election in this case was just around the corner. Postponing this election at the last moment, Wisdom reasoned, would be enormously disruptive to the state and public by, among other things, subjecting the candidates and the public "to an unbargained for, expensive, and exacerbating extension of the current campaign." Consequently, he reluctantly concluded, "weighing competing values and balancing the inconveniences, we feel compelled to affirm the district court."[49] And although it undoubtedly was of small comfort to the plaintiffs, Wisdom offered these final, nearly poetic words of consolation. "The tight grip of a long dead hand is hard to break. More than one summer may pass before that grip is broken and the effect of its clasp on the present completely undone."[50]

47. *The Mississippi Freedom Democratic Party v. The Democratic Party of the State of Mississippi*, 362 F.2d 60 (5th Cir.1966).

48. 362 F.2d at 62.

49. 362 F.2d at 63.

50. 362 F.2d at 63.

Nevertheless, when doing so would not offend the rule of law, Wisdom never retreated from using the full force of the federal courts to counteract some very imaginative efforts at interfering with the exercise of the franchise. In May 1963, in response to the commencement of a voter registration drive, the sheriff of Selma, Alabama, had ordered the arrest and prosecution of several visible campaign leaders for vagrancy, breach of the peace, and other minor offenses. He also had ordered the incarceration of twenty-nine African American attendees at a voter registration meeting and prosecuted them for operating a motor vehicle with improper license-plate lights. The Justice Department filed suit under the Civil Rights Act of 1957, alleging that these actions had the effect and purpose of intimidating African Americans with respect to their right to vote. The trial court denied the request for injunctive relief, finding that each of the allegedly coercive acts was justified to maintain law and order.

Writing for a unanimous Fifth Circuit panel in *U.S. v. McLeod*, Wisdom emphasized that the challenged acts could not be assessed in a vacuum, but, rather, had to be considered in the context of specific contemporaneous events as well as in light of the general climate that prevailed in Selma.[51] From that perspective, he concluded, it was "difficult to imagine anything short of physical violence which would have a more chilling effect on a voter registration drive than the pattern of baseless arrests and prosecutions revealed in this record."[52] Moreover, when it came to unearthing the motivation behind the conduct of the Selma officials, Wisdom did not shrink from calling it exactly as he saw it. In the context of Selma's history of systematic racial discrimination, he could draw but one reasonable inference from the fact that several registration drive leaders had been arrested on trumped-up charges. Since "the police often overlook violations of relatively trivial traffic laws," Wisdom rejected the disingenuous notion that the Selma police had mounted a "massive law enforcement drive to eradicate the sinful practice of driving with burned out license-plate lights."[53] Rather, the undeniable purpose of this coordinated campaign was to obstruct the voter drive and to deter others from taking part in it. Accordingly, the appellate panel ordered the local authorities to cease any future such coercive activity

51. 385 F.2d 734 (5th Cir.1967).
52. 385 F.2d at 734.
53. 385 F.2d at 744.

and to return all fines, expunge all arrests and convictions, and re-imburse those prosecuted for the costs and attorney fees incurred in their defense.

The formulation and implementation of a deliberate strategy to frus-trate the ability of African Americans to exercise their constitutional right to vote was not, of course, the sole province of public officials. Pri-vate individuals and groups were not reluctant to get into the act as well. The most notorious, malevolent, and violent of these groups was the Ku Klux Klan. And when the U.S. Justice Department finally decided to go after the Klan, John Wisdom played the central role in the federal government's assault on this lawless organization through his authorita-tive and compelling invocation and articulation of the rule of law.

One of the most sinister repercussions, if not the direst response, to the nascent civil rights movement in the early 1960s was the migration of many extreme opponents of integration to the burgeoning ranks of the Ku Klux Klan. This cancerous movement's public rallies, covert conclaves, lynchings, cross-burnings, and associated terrorist atrocities quickly spread throughout Wisdom's home state of Louisiana. By 1965, membership in the local klavern in Bogalusa, a sawmill-dominated town of twenty-five thousand residents (40 percent of whom were black) lo-cated just seventy miles north of New Orleans had swelled to more than eight hundred. So fertile was the Bogalusa environment for this infes-tation of hatred and bigotry that the city quickly became home to not only the largest Klan group in the entire state,[54] but, as one journalist reported, "possibly the largest Ku Klux Klan concentration per capita of any community in the South."[55]

In February 1965, the Deacons for Defense and Justice set up a chap-ter in Bogalusa. This armed self-defense group had been founded by a group of African American men in Jonesboro, a small mill town in Jackson Parish, for the express purpose of protecting Congress of Ra-cial Equality (CORE) volunteers from the Klan. The primary goal of the Bogalusa office was to combat the Klan's increasingly militant cam-paign of terror directed against the residents of that city. Klan intimida-tion had led to the cancellation of a speech by a congressman who had traveled to Bogalusa to discuss the experiences of other southern towns

54. Adam Fairclough, *Race and Democracy: The Civil Rights Struggle in Louisiana, 1915–1972* (Athens: 1995), 340–345.

55. Paul Good, "Klantown, USA," *The Nation*, February 1, 1965, 110, col. 1.

in dealing with racial problems. A local Episcopal minister and former combat bombardier in Korea had a cross burned in his front yard for daring to offer to host the speech at the parish meeting hall.[56] Finally, a series of violent confrontations, including the murder of a black deputy sheriff and the beating of several civil rights workers, forced the federal government's hand.[57] Led by John Doar, who had been promoted to replace Burke Marshall as chief of the Civil Rights Division by Attorney General Katzenbach in 1965, the Justice Department filed suit on July 19, 1965, against the Bogalusa Klan in the federal district court in New Orleans.[58]

The Justice Department alleged that as part of its campaign to preserve total racial segregation and white supremacy in the City of Bogalusa and throughout Washington Parish, Klan members had conspired to deprive black citizens of their constitutional and statutory civil rights. The complaint requested an injunction ordering the Klan to cease engaging in that course of conduct. The case was assigned to a three-judge district court consisting of Wisdom and District Judges Herbert W. Christenberry and Robert A. Ainsworth, Jr., of New Orleans.[59]

The practical and symbolic significance of the Justice Department's decision to go after the Klan was not lost on Wisdom, as evidenced by the opening sentence of his opinion for the unanimous court. "This," he declared, "is an action by the Nation against a klan."[60] Fully aware that the government was ready to call over a hundred witnesses who would testify to the Klan's unlawful activities, the defendants did not even attempt to deny participating in the various acts of lawlessness detailed in the Justice Department's complaint.[61] Instead, they hung their hat on the implausible contention that the Klan did not exist and the legal argument that the U.S. attorney general lacked the authority to

56. Ibid., 110–112.

57. "U.S. Court Bars Klan Anti-Rights Activities: Bogalusa Chieftains Enjoined," *New Orleans States-Item*, December 1, 1965, 1, col. 4; "U.S. Court Orders Klan to Halt Intimidation of Louisiana Negroes," *Houston Chronicle*, December 1, 1965, 1, col. 7.

58. Fairclough, *Race and Democracy: The Civil Rights Struggle in Louisiana, 1915–1972*, 357–371.

59. Letter to Dallam O'Brien, Jr., from Elbert Parr Tuttle, July 28, 1965 with attached Order by Chief Judge Tuttle, *U.S. v. Original Knights of the Ku Klux Klan*, Civ. Action #15793 (E.D.La.), July 28, 1965.

60. *U.S. v. Original Knights of the Ku Klux Klan*, 250 F.Supp. 330 (E.D.La.1965).

61. Roy Reed, "Bogalusa Klan, at Trial, Admits Harassing Negroes," *New York Times*, September 9, 1965, 27, col. 2; Gordon Gsell, "Three Jurists Ban La. Klan Violence: Issue Injunction in Washington Parish Case," *New Orleans Times-Picayune*, December 2, 1965, 1, col. 1; 20, col. 2.

seek an injunction against private groups or individuals under the civil rights acts.

Wisdom summarily dispatched the nonexistence defense, noting, simply, "the proof shows that the Klan continues to exist."[62] Exposing, in detail, many specific incidents of violence and terror perpetrated by the Klan in Washington Parish and other areas of the South, Wisdom observed that the "ineradicable evil" of the Klan and its members was its obsessive adherence to a policy of coercion, intimidation, and violence designed to deprive black citizens of their civil rights, "whether cloaked and hooded . . . or skulking in anonymity."[63] Barely containing his outrage, Wisdom branded the members of this "anti-Roman Catholic, anti-Semitic, hate-breeding organization" as nothing more than a hate-filled collection of "ignorant bullies, callous of the harm they know they are doing and lacking in sufficient understanding to comprehend the chasm between their own twisted Konstitution and the noble charter of liberties under law that is the American Constitution."[64]

The remainder of his thirty-nine-page opinion is devoted to a methodical dismemberment of the Klan's claim that the federal government lacked authority to prevent private acts of interference with civil rights. Citing both the text and legislative history of the relevant statutes, as well as the long and sad history of private acts of interference with black voter registration in the South, Wisdom concluded that there was "no doubt" that these laws applied to private individuals, and that interpreting the statutes in this broad manner did not do violence to any provision of the U.S. Constitution. He also relied on his own prior rulings in *Manning* and *U.S. v. Louisiana* to reiterate the point that since registration was an integral, indispensable part of the voting process, Congress had intended for these statutes to outlaw interference with registration as well as with voting.

Finally, noting that until the adoption of the federal Civil Rights Act of 1964, Washington Parish had been "segregated from cradle to coffin," Wisdom agreed with the Justice Department that the Bogalusa Klan's admitted pursuit of a policy of terror and intimidation could be halted only by a broadly worded order enjoining it and its members from any further interference with the exercise by African Americans of their civil rights.[65] Granting the government's request, the court's de-

62. 250 F.Supp. at 334n.1.
63. 250 F.Supp. at 334.
64. 250 F.Supp. at 335.
65. 250 F.Supp. at 337.

cree not only prohibited the defendants from assaulting, intimidating, threatening, or otherwise harassing African Americans in the exercise of their various civil rights, it forbad similar acts of retaliation against any public or private individual who did anything to support the exercise by any African Americans of these civil rights. It further required the Bogalusa Klan and its leaders to maintain membership records, to file monthly reports documenting its membership and meetings, and to post copies of this decree at all of its meeting places at all times.[66] Leaving no doubt that the Klan now would be under the watchful eye of federal judges across the region, Wisdom declared that judicial "tolerance of secret societies must cease at the point where their members assume supra-governmental powers and take the law in their own hands. We shall not allow the misguided defendants to interfere with the rights of Negro citizens."[67]

According to one noted historian, by using the pages of the official court reports to lay bare the ugly truth of the Klan's calculated, systematic campaign of violence, economic coercion, and intimidation against black citizens and those who spoke out on their behalf, Wisdom "punctured the Klan's mystique and eroded its power to intimidate."[68] In a similar vein, an editorial in a Los Angeles daily newspaper cheered, "the tremendous mass of Americans, applauding Judge Wisdom for living up to his name, will shout, 'So say we all.'"[69] And John Brown handwrote a short note to Wisdom offering his unique brand of encouragement and support:

> The
> Klan
> Klaque Does Not
> Kotten to
> Klan
> Klobberers And
> Konfidently
> Kalculates voters will
> Kontemptuously
> Kick out such
> Kindred thinkers and would not

66. Preliminary Injunction in U.S. v. Original Knights of the Ku Klux Klan.
67. 250 F.Supp. at 335.
68. Fairclough, Race and Democracy: The Civil Rights Struggle in Louisiana, 1915–1972, 373.
69. Editorial, "Naming the Klan, Los Angeles Herald-Examiner," December 9, 1965, G-2, col. 1.

> Konfirm even to
> Kanine
> Katchers some appointive
> Kontemporaries.[70]

Although most of Wisdom's opinions in voting rights cases addressed claims of racial discrimination, his contribution to the development of voting rights jurisprudence is not limited to these cases. Rulings that he authored also resulted in the overturning of voting requirements that operated to disenfranchise other, nonracial groups. His lifelong struggle to make the southern political process more than just a democracy for the few was grounded in an unwavering conviction that any limitation or encumbrance of this most fundamental of civil rights must be subject to the most withering scrutiny. His unflinching fidelity to this tenet impelled Wisdom to strike down residency and property taxpaying prerequisites to voter eligibility that operated to impede access to and participation in the electoral process. This deeply held principle even caused him to part company with one of his most esteemed colleagues in a voting rights case.

Alvin Rubin, a native of northern Louisiana and graduate of Louisiana State University, was universally regarded as a brilliant, scholarly judge. Appointed to the federal district court in New Orleans by President Lyndon Johnson in 1966, the erudite Rubin was promoted to the Fifth Circuit in 1977 when Wisdom chose to retire from active service on the court and assume senior status. Wisdom counted Rubin among the finest jurists with whom he had ever served. And that level of esteem is nowhere better reflected than in the manual of style Wisdom prepared for and distributed to all of his law clerks. Among "Wisdom's Idiosyncrasies," a list of stylistic, organizational, and grammatical commandments that each successive cohort of law clerks honored only in the observance, was the following: "Do not use the trial judge's name in the opinion unless the judge was Ed Weinfeld, Ed Gignoux, Frank Johnson, or Alvin Rubin."[71]

When a resident of the city of Houma, Louisiana, filed suit challenging the constitutionality of various provisions in Louisiana law that allowed only property owners to vote in municipal utility bond elections, a three-judge district court composed of Wisdom and District Judges

---

70. Note to John M. Wisdom from John R. Brown, January 3, 1966.
71. John Minor Wisdom, *Wisdom's Idiosyncrasies*, 109 YALE L. J. 1273, 1277 (2000).

Rubin and James A. Comiskey of New Orleans was assigned to hear the case. The panel split 2-1, with Rubin writing the majority opinion and Wisdom dissenting. In his majority opinion, Judge Rubin reasoned the Supreme Court's ruling that a poll tax was constitutionally impermissible in the context of elections for political representatives or for general governmental purposes, did not necessarily apply to referendums on limited subjects.[72] Since the election in this instance was for the limited purpose of authorizing the issuance of government bonds, the court only had to determine whether the Louisiana legislature's decision to limit the franchise to property holders was so unreasonable as to be considered irrational, arbitrary, or invidious. And without agreeing with the sagacity of the legislature's choice, Rubin concluded that its determination that property owners had a special pecuniary interest in utility bond elections was neither arbitrary nor irrational.

Wisdom rejected Judge Rubin's reliance on the contextual difference between an election for political office and an election for the issuance of municipal bonds. As far as he was concerned, there was only one important and undisputed fact in each situation—the right to vote was tied to the payment of a property tax. All otherwise eligible voters, regardless of whether or not they owned property, had a stake in all governmental decision-making and, therefore, enjoyed the right to participate in *all* elections without regard to whether or not they paid property taxes.[73] The Supreme Court sided, unanimously and in every respect, with Wisdom, declaring that the constitutional infirmity of poll taxes was not limited to strictly political elections.[74]

Although Louisiana was one of only a minority of states that limited voting in bond elections to property owners, it was solidly in the mainstream in also maintaining residency requirements for voting in state elections.[75] In addition to age and citizenship requirements, Louisiana law did not permit anyone to register unless he or she had been a resident of the state for one year, of the parish for six months, of the municipality for four months, and of the chosen precinct for three months preceding the election in which he or she sought to vote. Louisiana law also discouraged voters from changing their political party affiliation by

---

72. *Cipriano v. City of Houma*, 286 F.Supp. 823 (E.D.La.1968).

73. 286 F.Supp. 828 (Wisdom, J., dissenting).

74. *Cipriano v. City of Houma*, 395 U.S. 701, 89 S.Ct. 1897, 23 L.Ed.2d 647 (1969).

75. *Stewart v. Parish School Board of Parish of St. Charles*, 310 F.Supp. 1172,1173 and n.1 (E.D.La.1970).

providing that any registered voter who changed party affiliation could not vote for six months in a primary held by the party to whom he or she had shifted allegiance.

When four plaintiffs filed a lawsuit in federal court in New Orleans challenging the constitutionality of these state and parish laws, a majority of the three-judge district court voted to deny relief. In *Fontham v. McKeithen*, District Judge R. Blake West, writing for himself and fellow district judge Jack M. Gordon of New Orleans, ruled that the residency requirements fell solidly within the state's authority to create rational, nondiscriminatory voting standards and therefore did not violate the constitutional rights of equal protection or due process.[76] The court also held that the state's decision to suspend voting rights for those who chose to shift their party allegiance promoted its legitimate interest in protecting the integrity of political parties within its territory.

In dissent, Wisdom reiterated the position that he had espoused, and that the Supreme Court had endorsed, in the Houma bond election case. To pass constitutional muster, any state-imposed restriction on the fundamental right of voting had to be justified by a compelling governmental objective; it was insufficient to establish only a rational connection to any conceivably reasonable public interest.[77] "I am unable to discern even a flickering gleam of a twinkle," Wisdom decried, "which might help to explain the majority's decision to apply the rational relation test to both the Louisiana voter eligibility standards under attack today."[78]

Wisdom conceded that a durational residency requirement could be justified as a method of promoting an informed electorate (by ensuring that voters have been exposed to the relevant issues for some period of time) and by minimizing the opportunity for multiple voting. Yet he also believed that a residency requirement was a far too imprecise tool for accomplishing the former objective since it excluded many knowledgeable transplants and posed no obstacle to voting by uninformed long-term residents. And though he also was willing to admit that Louisiana's residency requirement did minimize the opportunity for a "would-be fraudulent voter" to register in a locale in which he or she did not reside and vote both there and in his or her home district, Wisdom was

76. 336 F.Supp. 153 (E.D.La.1971), appeal dismissed, 409 U.S. 1120, 93 S.Ct. 932, 34 L.Ed.2d 704 (1973).

77. *Fontham v. McKeithen*, 336 F.Supp. 163 (E.D.La.1971) (Wisdom, J., dissenting).

78. 366 F.Supp. at 164 (Wisdom, J., dissenting).

convinced that the residency requirement did not completely prevent such abuse. Since the statute authorized voting registrars to require potential registrants to tender documentary proof of length of residency, anyone intent on fraud had to do more than merely avow falsely as to the length of her or his residency. This led Wisdom to conclude that a uniform durational residency requirement was a constitutionally permissible method of deterring fraudulent registration and that each state should be granted significant discretion in determining the length of that residency requirement.

But instead of enacting a single, uniform residency requirement, the Louisiana legislature had concocted a patchwork of differential standards of state, parish, municipality, and district residence. To uphold the constitutionality of this scheme, Wisdom explained, would require a determination that though six months was sufficient to deter fraudulent migration from parish to parish, a year was needed to deter fraudulently bent wayfarers from outside the Bayou State from crossing its borders. This struck Wisdom as both counterintuitive and unsupported by the factual record. Consequently, he announced that he would strike down all but the shortest statutory residency requirement and apply that standard across the board. He also declared that anyone who had resided in the state for more than one year should be permitted to vote for statewide offices regardless of how long they had lived in their current place of residence.

The Louisiana statutory provision suspending voting privileges for six months for individuals choosing to switch their political party affiliation was something with which Wisdom had extensive firsthand experience. As leader of the campaign to rebuild the Louisiana Republican Party in the early 1950s, he was painfully aware of the impact this legislation had on efforts to convince disgruntled Democrats to shift their party alliance. But having severed all political ties and affiliations upon assuming the bench back in 1959, Wisdom was not about to allow his personal political views or experiences to cloud his judicial judgment. Nevertheless, he also refused to ignore what personal experience had taught him about the pragmatic effect of this statutory scheme.

Voters who chose to abandon their independent status and affiliate with any political party, Wisdom observed, were not subject to this statutory provision; they could vote in that party's primary without delay. This led Wisdom to forecast that if the case ever went to trial, the evidence would demonstrate that "the practical effect was to benefit the dominant party by imposing a high barrier to change of registration."[79] In his judgment, the state had offered no evidence to establish that the six-month period was anything other than "a rough, easily circumvented device which may reduce badly motivated crossovers, but only at the expense of the right to vote of countless other well-meaning citizens."[80]

Although this case did not reach the Supreme Court, Wisdom's views on the residency requirement ultimately prevailed.[81] In *Dunn v. Blumstein,* the Court declared unconstitutional a set of non-uniform durational residency requirements codified in Tennessee law.[82] It held, just as Wisdom had maintained in *Fontham,* that adherence to both a one-year in-state and three-month in-county residency requirements could not be necessary to achieving its compelling interest in preventing migratory voter fraud. The Court also rebuffed, for precisely the same reasons offered by Wisdom in *Fontham,* the claim that the durational residency requirement promoted the interest of ensuring an informed electorate. Within less than four months after the Court's ruling, the Louisiana legislature amended its laws to replace the durational residency requirements with a prerequisite of bona fide residence in the state, parish, municipality, and precinct in which the applicant sought to register.[83]

Although Wisdom's most enduring legacy in the voting rights area lies in his opinions striking down policies that encumbered the right of black citizens to vote, he also produced several significant decisions that set forth the conditions under which race could and could not be used as a factor in the fashioning of reapportionment plans designed to remedy the effects of that history of race-based discrimination. In *Tay-*

79. 366 F.Supp. at 174 (Wisdom, J., dissenting).

80. 366 F.Supp. at 174 (Wisdom, J., dissenting).

81. The losing plaintiff initially sought review by the Supreme Court, but subsequently decided to dismiss his appeal before the Court ruled on the merits. *Fontham v. Edwards,* 409 U.S. 1120, 93 S.Ct. 932, 34 L.Ed.2d 704 (1973). After the Supreme Court struck down Tennessee's durational residence requirement in *Dunn v. Blumstein,* 405 U.S. 330, 92 S.Ct. 995, 31 L.Ed.2d 274 (1971), Louisiana's attorney general, Jack P. F. Gremillion, issued an opinion that the Louisiana residency requirement was no longer unenforceable. He also assured plaintiff Fontham that the state would not enforce the six-month suspension provision for party switchovers. Based on those assurances, Fontham, a young attorney representing himself and the other three plaintiffs, agreed to dismiss the appeal. Transcript of Telephonic Interview of Michael R. Fontham by Joel Wm. Friedman, May 11, 2004.

82. 405 U.S. 330, 92 S.Ct. 995, 31 L.Ed.2d 274 (1971).

83. 1972 La. Acts, No. 379, §1. The state voter eligibility requirements were recodified in 1976 at LSA-R.S. 18:101.

lor v. McKeithen, for example, he wrote an opinion overturning a "well intentioned" but misguided district judge's adoption of a reapportionment plan that created both majority black and majority white election districts for the purpose of promoting the electability of African American candidates to the state legislature in some of these districts.[84]

In 1970, the Louisiana legislature had enacted self-reapportionment legislation for all of its legislative districts. This legislative package was challenged in a series of lawsuits filed in federal court in Baton Rouge, the state capital. After a series of interim decisions, the parties agreed that the controversy had been reduced to a fight over the reapportionment of four state senatorial districts in Orleans Parish.[85] Historically, these districts had been configured according to the geographical boundaries of the wards that they encompassed. But District Judge E. Gordon West redrew these four districts so that two were transformed into predominantly black districts and two became nearly entirely white in their composition. West determined that the composition of Orleans Parish's historical ward boundaries was the primary cause of the fact that only two African Americans had been elected to the Louisiana legislature during the twentieth century.[86] Thus, he concluded, it was appropriate to radically redraw the contours of four of the parish's seven senatorial districts to ensure the election of black candidates from at least two of these districts, even though he acknowledged that the shape of the other two reapportioned senatorial districts would ensure that they would remain traditionally "safe" districts for white candidates.

Wisdom wrote the opinion for the unanimous Fifth Circuit panel. And in his standard fashion, he crystallized the issue and grabbed the attention of the public by opening his decision with a bold and dramatic statement of the question before his court. "This case," he began, "involves a racial gerrymander not by a state legislature but by a federal district court."[87] And if framing the question with that loaded language did not sufficiently adumbrate his views on the merits of the case, Wisdom later pulled no punches in voicing his rejection of the factual predicate underlying Judge West's decision. "There is absolutely nothing in the record," Wisdom declared, to support the trial judge's finding that reliance on ward boundaries was the culprit for the near total exclusion

---

84. 499 F.2d 893, 894 (5th Cir.1974).

85. *Taylor v. McKeithen,* 499 F.2d 893, 899n.15 (5th Cir.1974).

86. *Bussie v. McKeithen,* 333 F.Supp. 452, 462 (E.D.La.1971).

87. *Taylor v. McKeithen,* 499 F.2d 893,894 (5th Cir.1974).

of African Americans from the halls of the state Senate over the past seventy-five years. "As a statement of Louisiana history," he proclaimed, "it is an error of monumental magnitude."[88] Wisdom decried the "spectacularly false premise on which the district court based its approval of gerrymandering" and insisted that "any student of history and certainly anyone familiar with Louisiana politics . . . knows that the district court's 'finding' was not just clearly erroneous; it was dead wrong."[89]

Thus, notwithstanding the fact that Wisdom already had demonstrated his willingness to employ race-conscious means to ensure the constitutional right of every American to exercise the franchise and to ensure that black Americans, in particular, were not denied full and equal access to the political system, his resolution of this case reflects his clear recognition of the limitations of the judicial process. Where a case could be decided on its specific facts, he felt no urgency to address far-reaching constitutional questions. And so, relying on his own wealth of knowledge about Louisiana's electoral politics, Wisdom concluded that this dispute did not require a drastic race-based remedy to ensure that African American citizens of his state enjoyed the full measure of their constitutionally protected franchise.

Modifying the shape of the election unit was not the only reapportionment tool relied upon by state legislators to dilute the impact of the votes cast by members of racial minority groups. Adjusting the size of the voting constituency for elected positions was another frequently utilized method of accomplishing this objective. The combination of racial bloc voting and de facto segregated residential patterns meant that black voters often could elect African American candidates where the electoral unit was small, that is, ward- or district-based. But where the electoral structure was expanded to a city- or municipality-wide unit, where white voters represented the majority of electors, the opportunity for black voters to constitute a majority was frustrated, if not lost.

By the mid-1970s, the federal courts had developed a body of case law dealing with such attempts to dilute the voting strength of African American citizens. Suits had sprung up in a variety of locations in which the plaintiffs challenged the constitutionality of geographically large voting districts that tended to submerge the ability of minority racial groups to elect candidates sympathetic to their interests. The common thread in all of these cases, however, was the notion that to establish a

88. 499 F.2d at 896.
89. 499 F.Supp. at 906.

constitutional violation, the plaintiffs had to establish that the legislature had been motivated by a racially discriminatory purpose.

Plaintiffs faced a difficult hurdle in attempting to establish the existence of discriminatory intent in voting dilution cases. The geographical
size of most voting constituencies typically had been set at a time when
African Americans had been denied the right to vote. Consequently, it
hardly could be demonstrated that the legislature had chosen to *adopt* a
system of at-large voting in citywide election units in order to dilute the
impact of nonexistent black votes. Nevertheless, the *retention* of these
large electoral units after the elimination of overt obstacles to registration and voting by African Americans had the undeniable effect of frustrating the opportunity for black voters to constitute majorities in most
election districts.

The Fifth Circuit was confronted by just this problem in four cases
that challenged at-large municipal election schemes in four southern
jurisdictions—Mobile and Fairfield (a Birmingham suburb), Alabama;
Shreveport, Louisiana; and Thomas County, Georgia. All four cases
were heard by the same Fifth Circuit panel and decided on the same day.
In all of these cases, Judges Bryan Simpson and Gerald Bard Tjoflat,
both of whom hailed from Florida, adhered to the view that both Fourteenth and Fifteenth Amendment challenges to legislative apportionment schemes required proof of a racially discriminatory purpose. In
concurring opinions in three of the cases (dissenting only in the Shreveport case), Wisdom maintained that proof of discriminatory intention
was not necessary to establish a violation of the Fifteenth Amendment.

In the Fairfield, Alabama, case, Wisdom took the position that dilution of voting rights was enough by itself, without evidence of a racially
discriminatory objective, to constitute the type of abridgment of the
"fundamental political right" of voting that the Fifteenth Amendment
forbad.[90] He noted that overtly discriminatory voting requirements had
been replaced with more sophisticated, facially neutral schemes that
nevertheless continued to produce racially discriminatory results. The
fact that the at-large voting scheme in all four consolidated cases operated to demonstrably reduce the value of each African American elector's vote was sufficient, in his judgment, to render them unlawful under the terms of the Fifteenth Amendment. To demand an additional
demonstration of discriminatory motivation on the legislature's part, he

90. *Nevett v. Sides,* 571 F.2d 209 (5th Cir.1978), cert. denied, 446 U.S. 951, 100 S.Ct. 2916, 64
L.Ed.2d 807 (1980).

cynically observed, would burden the plaintiffs "with the necessity of finding the authoritative meaning of an oracle that is Delphic only to the Court."[91]

Although the Supreme Court did not endorse Wisdom's effects-based analysis, Congress subsequently did. The Supreme Court agreed to review the Fifth Circuit's ruling in one of these four consolidated voter dilution cases. In *City of Mobile v. Bolden*, a four-member plurality of the Court held that Mobile's system of citywide election of city commissioners was not unconstitutional.[92] Citing several of the Court's prior rulings, including *Gomillion*, the plurality declared that maintenance of an at-large system violated the Fourteenth and Fifteenth Amendments only if it had been motivated by a racially discriminatory purpose. The plurality similarly ruled that legislative apportionment would be struck down under the equal protection clause of the Fourteenth Amendment only if its purpose was invidiously to minimize or cancel out the voting potential of racial or ethnic minorities. Only Justices Marshall and Brennan agreed with Wisdom that proof of discriminatory impact was sufficient to establish a Fifteenth Amendment violation.[93]

Nevertheless, in response to the Court's ruling in *City of Mobile*, Congress amended the 1965 Voting Rights Act in 1982.[94] As originally en-

91. *Nevett v. Sides*, 571 F.2d 209, 238 (5th Cir.1978) (Wisdom, J., concurring).

92. 446 U.S. 55, 100 S.Ct. 1490, 64 L.Ed.2d 47 (1980).

93. *City of Mobile v. Bolden*, 446 U.S. 55, 94 100 S.Ct. 1519, 64 L.Ed.2d 47 (1980) (Brennan, J., dissenting) and 446 U.S. at 103, 100 S.Ct. 1519, 64 L.Ed.2d 47 (1980) (Marshall, J., dissenting). Justice White, who also dissented, took a slightly different approach. He did not expressly repudiate the requirement of proof of discriminatory intent. But he disagreed with the plurality's conclusion that there was insufficient evidence of a racially discriminatory purpose in this case. As far as he was concerned, the totality of circumstances, including the undeniable fact that racial bloc voting at the polls makes it impossible to elect a black commissioner under the at-large system, amply supported an inference of purposeful discrimination in violation of the Fourteenth and Fifteenth Amendments. *City of Mobile v. Bolden*, 446 U.S. 94, 94 100 S.Ct. 1514 (1980) (White, J., dissenting).

94. Wisdom opinions also led to legislative reform on the community and state levels. In *Brown v. Vance*, 637 F.2d 272 (5th Cir.1981), Wisdom authored the opinion for a unanimous court striking down as unconstitutional a Mississippi statutory scheme for compensating state justices of the peace. Under that system, justices of the peace (who had jurisdiction over small civil claims and petty criminal charges) were paid a specific fee for each criminal and each civil case filed in their courts. Since most civil suits were filed by collection agencies and business with a heavy volume of litigation, these plaintiffs were more likely to file their complaints in the court of the judge they believed was most likely to rule in their favor. The same was true of arresting officers: they were more likely to make arrests in the counties where there was a judge with a high conviction rate. Wisdom pragmatically recognized that this created a temptation for judges to take a biased

acted, §2 of that statute prohibited the use of any voting standard or practice that operated "to deny or abridge the right of any citizen of the United States to vote on account of race or color." In *City of Mobile,* the plurality had concluded that §2 did no more than elaborate the command of the Fifteenth Amendment, that is, prevent purposeful racial discrimination in voting. To overturn that bit of statutory construction, and to circumvent the necessity of proving discriminatory intent to establish a constitutional violation, Congress amended §2 to prohibit the use of any election procedure or standard that "results in a denial or abridgement of the right of any citizen of the United States to vote on account of race or color."[95] This provision expressly codified Wisdom's view that demonstrably discriminatory effects of racially neutral election practices should be struck down, albeit as a matter of statutory, rather than constitutional, law. In fact, as one constitutional law scholar and former Wisdom law clerk has reported, "the committee report concerning the Senate bill that Congress subsequently enacted into law as the 1982 amendment expressly concluded that Judge Wisdom, and not the plurality of the Supreme Court in *Mobile,* had correctly interpreted" the Court's prior voting rights cases and that this amendment to §2 was both necessary and appropriate to fully protect the Fourteenth and Fifteenth Amendment rights of African American voters.[96]

Over the course of a quarter-century, with but one lamentable exception at the outset of his judicial career, Wisdom's voting rights decisions reflected his bedrock view that democracy was best served by ensuring that the franchise was impervious to arbitrary or capricious restrictions, including those that incorporated some form of racial or economic categorization. That same former Wisdom clerk and consti-

---

view that would favor the positions of litigating creditors and arresting officers. "The vice," he explained, "inheres in the feed system. It is a fatal constitutional flaw." 637 F.2d at 276. And the mere fact that it created a potential temptation for judges to be biased against civil and criminal defendants, Wisdom ruled, rendered the compensation system constitutionally defective by depriving defendants of their right to due process of law. Accordingly, the court struck down the compensation system. This, needless to say, created a crisis for the state. For although Wisdom had not abolished the justice of the peace courts, he had invalidated the method of funding its operation. Consequently, in 1981, the Mississippi legislature passed a law providing salaries for these members of the state judiciary. See Mary Libby Payne, *The Mississippi Judiciary Commission Revisited: Judicial Administration: An Idea Whose Time Has Come?* 14 Miss. C. L. Rev. 413, 492–493 (1994).

95. 42 U.S.C. §1973(a).

96. Philip P. Frickey, *Judge Wisdom and Voting Rights: The Judicial Artist as Scholar and Pragmatist,* 60 Tul.L.Rev. 276, 286 (1985).

tutional scholar also offered this informed assessment of Wisdom's impact on voting rights law. "In evaluating a judge, then, one must look not only for genius, but also for pragmatism and humanitarianism, not only for ideas, but also for results. On all these fronts, as his voting opinions suggest, Judge Wisdom is unsurpassed by any judge of his generation."[97]

97. Philip P. Frickey, *Judge Wisdom and Voting Rights: The Judicial Artist as Scholar and Pragmatist*, 60 TUL. L. REV. 276, 313 (1985).

13

A Vigilant Steward of Fairness

John Minor Wisdom's reputation as a resolute defender and protector of civil rights is most commonly, and justifiably, linked to his decisions in school desegregation and voting rights cases. But his civil rights legacy manifestly is not limited to those high-profile, and unquestionably seminal, rulings. Wisdom opinions blazed new trails in a wide range of areas. Notable among these are his rulings recognizing a civilly and criminally detained individual's right to psychiatric treatment, a prison inmate's right to recover damages for a sexual assault by a prison guard, and government workers' and students' rights to freedom of speech, religion, and association. And the common strand that ties all of these and hundreds of other opinions together is the manifest influence of Wisdom's innate humanity and sense of decency and fairness. Not only was he devoted to preserving and enforcing the rule of law, he was motivated by a passionate desire to ensure that operation of the law provided everyone with a fair and square shake with respect to both result and process. The lessons taught by his mother about the importance of treating everyone with fairness and dignity were never lost on her son.

In 1974, Wisdom wrote the first federal appellate court opinion holding that persons who were involuntary committed, through civil proceedings, to state mental hospitals possessed a federal constitutional right to treatment.[1] This ruling came out of an extraordinary case involving a thirty-five-year-old man who had been confined by a Florida state court to a state mental institution for fifteen years without receiving any occupational therapy or psychiatric treatment. Toward the end of his confinement, the man had filed suit seeking damages against several hospital and state mental health officials, alleging that they had deprived him of his constitutional right to receive treatment. A jury found that the boy had never posed a physical danger to himself or to others and returned a verdict in his favor. The defendants' appeal to the Fifth Circuit was heard by a panel composed of Wisdom, Richard Rives, and Lewis R. Morgan, a former federal district judge from Georgia who had been nominated by President Lyndon Johnson to fill the circuit court vacancy created by Elbert Tuttle's retirement in June 1968.

On behalf of a unanimous panel, Wisdom boldly and unambiguously announced that "a person involuntarily civilly committed to a state mental hospital has a constitutional right to receive such individual treatment as will give him a reasonable opportunity to be cured or to improve his mental condition."[2] His formal explanation was that where the involuntary confinement, as in this case, was predicated on the subject's need for treatment, rather than on his posing a threat to himself or others, the due process clause of the Fourteenth Amendment compelled the government to provide adequate treatment. But the true impetus for the ruling was Wisdom's outrage at the harrowing facts of this case. By the time he filed his damage claim, the plaintiff had been confined involuntarily in a locked ward with sixty other patients for nearly fifteen years without a shred of commonly accepted psychiatric treatment. It was these shocking circumstances that convinced Wisdom that his case was a compelling vehicle for proclaiming the existence of this important constitutional entitlement.[3]

1. Three years earlier, noted district judge Frank M. Johnson, Jr., of Montgomery, Alabama, had recognized the existence of this constitutional right to treatment for civilly committed mentally ill patients in *Wyatt v. Stickney*, 325 F.Supp. 781 (M.D.Ala.1971). Wisdom not only credited Johnson with being the first to formulate such a right, but incorporated Johnson's formulation of the scope of the constitutional right to treatment, that is, one that provided individuals with a realistic opportunity to be cured to improve his or her mental condition. In addition, back in 1966, Chief Judge David Bazelon of the D.C. Circuit Court of Appeals had written an opinion in *Rouse v. Cameron*, 373 F.2d 451 (D.C.Cir.1966), holding that the federal Mentally Ill Act of 1964 created a *statutory* right to treatment on behalf of mental patients in the District of Columbia.

2. *Donaldson v. O'Connor*, 493 F.2d 507 (5th Cir.1974), vacated and remanded, 422 U.S. 804, 95 S.Ct. 2486, 45 L.Ed.2d 396 (1975).

3. Letter to Griffin B. Bell and James P. Coleman from John M. Wisdom, April 2, 1974.

On this occasion, however, the Supreme Court was unwilling to follow Wisdom's lead. All of the justices on the High Court agreed that because this case could be decided on a much more limited ground, there was no reason to address "the difficult issues of constitutional law dealt with by the Court of Appeals."[4] The Court focused only on the lawfulness of the decision to commit the plaintiff to the state hospital, rather than on the conditions of his confinement. And with respect to that limited issue, the Court recognized a "constitutional right to freedom" that precluded involuntary commitment when the individual was not a danger to anyone and was capable of surviving safely in freedom on his own or with the help of willing family members or friends. Thus, the Court held that only the plaintiff's right to freedom from unwarranted confinement that had been infringed. The Court chose not to reach the question of whether the patient also enjoyed the more expansive right to reasonable treatment that Wisdom had formulated. Nonetheless, it went out of its way to declare that the effect of its order vacating the Fifth Circuit's judgment was to deprive Wisdom's opinion of any precedential effect.[5] And to this date, the Supreme Court has yet to rule affirmatively on the existence or nonexistence of a civilly committed mental patient's constitutional right to treatment. Nevertheless, or perhaps because of the absence of a definitive statement by the Supreme Court, Wisdom's opinion is consistently cited in scholarly publications as the original and definitive articulation of a civilly committed person's constitutional right to treatment.

A dozen years later, Wisdom took another stab at the right to medical treatment. On this occasion, the issue arose in the context of a criminal defendant being held in pretrial custody. In 1976, the Supreme Court had ruled that prison administrators were obliged by the Fourteenth Amendment's due process clause not to be deliberately indifferent to the serious medical needs of a pretrial detainee.[6] In 1986, Wisdom wrote the first opinion that extended that Supreme Court ruling to a detainee's psychiatric or psychological, as well as medical, needs. By reading the Court's opinion in this expansive manner, he was able to

---

4. 422 U.S. at 573, 95 S.Ct. at 2492. In a concurring opinion, Chief Justice Burger went even further in distancing himself from Wisdom's analysis than the eight justices who signed on to Justice Stewart's opinion for the Court. Burger expressly rejected Wisdom's conclusion that the due process clause guaranteed the right to treatment for involuntarily civilly confined mental patients. 422 U.S. 578, 95 S.Ct. 2495 (Burger, Ch.J., concurring).

5. 422 U.S. at 578n.12, 95 S.Ct. at 2495n.12.

6. See *Estelle v. Gamble*, 429 U.S. 97, 97 S.Ct. 285, 50 L.Ed.2d 251 (1976).

conclude that the due process clause also required attention to a prisoner's mental health needs.[7]

Wisdom's impact on the development of constitutional jurisprudence also can be felt in a collection of cases implicating the First Amendment freedoms of religion, speech, and association. In these cases, his characteristically even-handed, non-dogmatic, pragmatic approach to constitutional adjudication is reflected in the fact that he was as apt to deny the existence of an alleged constitutional violation as he was to rule in favor of a constitutional claim.

When, for example, a majority of his colleagues concluded that public high school students did not enjoy a constitutionally protected right to wear their hair as they like, Wisdom wrote a lengthy dissent. Chesley Karr, a sixteen-year-old student at Coronado High School in El Paso, Texas, had been prevented from enrolling until he cut his hair to conform to the hair-length provision of the school district's dress code. He sued the school authorities, claiming that enforcement of this policy violated his First Amendment–guaranteed right to freedom of expression. The trial judge ordered the school board officials to enroll Karr and to cease enforcing its hair-length regulation.[8] When the case was appealed, the judges of the Fifth Circuit voted to hear the case *en banc* rather than to submit it to a three-member panel. By a one-vote margin, a majority of the fifteen-member court rejected the schoolboy's constitutional claim, ruling that the right to a certain hairstyle was neither protected speech under the First Amendment nor a fundamental right protected under any other constitutional amendment.[9]

In his dissenting opinion, Wisdom chastised the court for its "belittling characterization of a young person's right to present himself to the world as he pleases so long as he causes no one any harm."[10] His stirring advocacy of the view that personal appearance is a fundamental right deserving of constitutional protection has been called "the classic statement" of this position, and has been embraced by other circuit courts in cases challenging the constitutionality of dress codes.[11] "Hair," he ob-

7. *Partridge v. Two Unknown Police Officers of the City of Houston*, 791 F.2d 1182 (5th Cir.1986).

8. *Karr v. Schmidt*, 320 F.Supp. 728 (W.D.Tx.1970).

9. *Karr v. Schmidt*, 460 F.2d 609 (5th Cir.1972) (en banc).

10. 460 F.2d at 621.

11. Robert Post, *Prejudicial Appearances: The Logic of American Antidiscrimination Law*, 88 CAL. L. REV. 1, 5n.22 (2000). See, for example, *East Hartford Education Association v. Board of Education*

served, "is a purely personal matter—a mater of personal style which for centuries has been one aspect of the manner in which we hold ourselves out to the rest of the world . . . . a symbol: of elegance, of efficiency, of affinity and association, of non-conformity and rejection of traditional values." Unable to resist the temptation to engage in a bit of lighthearted punnery, Wisdom noted that "a person shorn of the freedom to vary the length and style of his hair is forced against his will to hold himself out symbolically as a person holding the contrary, perhaps, to ideas he holds most dear. Forced . . . hair style humiliates the unwilling complier, forces him to submerge his individuality in the 'undistracting' mass, and in general, smacks of the exaltation of organization over member, unit over component, and state over individual." To Wisdom, a free society "does not condone such repression."[12]

Nonetheless, Wisdom also authored a Fifth Circuit opinion that upheld the constitutionality of hair-grooming standards imposed upon prison inmates by the State of Mississippi.[13] A group of inmates at the state penitentiary at Parchman who subscribed to the Rastafari religion had challenged Mississippi prison regulations requiring short, neatly cut hair. They maintained that this policy violated their First Amendment right to freely exercise their religious beliefs, which included never cutting one's hair and growing it in dreadlocks.

Since this case involved a prison regulation, Wisdom explained, the court's greater deference to the decisions made by the governing authorities than would be accorded, for example, a decision by educational authorities. Thus, as long as the prison regulation reasonably related to legitimate penological interests, it would survive constitutional challenge despite its impact on the inmates' constitutional rights. Wisdom agreed with the prison authorities that their short hair requirement served legitimate identification, discipline, health, and security interests. And though the regulation deprived Rastafarians of the opportunity to engage in certain forms of religious expression, it permitted them to engage in other aspects of religious observance, such as the opportunity to adhere to their dietary rituals and to be identified by their Rastafarian name. Consequently, he reasoned, "although we could imagine a

---

of the Town of East Hartford, 562 F.2d 838, 842 (2d Cir.1977) (citing Wisdom's "eloquent" defense of a person's freedom to dress as he pleases).

12. 460 F.2d at 621 (emphasis added).

13. *Scott v. Mississippi Department of Corrections*, 961 F.2d 77 (5th Cir.1992).

prison that feasibly accommodated the religious expression locked into a Rastafarian's hairstyle, it is not for us to impose our own ideas about prison management upon those who attempt the reasonable regulation of that nearly impossible task."[14]

Another of Wisdom's opinions influenced the way most circuit courts resolved a particular knotty aspect of the controversial and seemingly indeterminable constitutional right to privacy. In response to a growing concern over the mounting presence of alcohol and contraband drugs in public schools, a Texas school district had implemented a policy of random and unannounced use of trained dogs to sniff students' lockers, automobiles, and persons in search of alcohol and contraband drugs. When this policy was challenged as an unreasonable search and seizure in violation of the students' Fourth Amendment rights, the trial court ruled in favor of the school district. The appeal was heard by a Fifth Circuit panel consisting of Judges Wisdom and Albert Tate, Jr., of New Orleans and Carolyn Randall of Houston, Texas. Although the panel decided to issue an unsigned *per curiam* opinion, it was written by Wisdom. The unanimous court held that dog-sniffing of lockers and cars did not constitute a search because the students did not enjoy a reasonable expectation of privacy in either cars parked on public parking lots or in their lockers.[15] The aromas emanating from these unattended objects, Wisdom reasoned, were exposed to public detection, and therefore, were not entitled to the protections afforded by Fourth Amendment.

Using dogs to sniff a student's person, however, was an entirely different matter. Distilling the holdings of a host of Supreme Court decisions, Wisdom declared that the Fourth Amendment prohibited unreasonable intrusions on the human body, but not on inanimate objects. And since the dog-sniffing techniques employed in this case put the dogs in direct contact with the students' bodies, these contacts were sufficiently embarrassing and intrusive to be considered a search subject to scrutiny under the Fourth Amendment, thereby requiring the court to balance the intrusiveness of that search against the school district's legitimate need for the information that it had yielded.

To accommodate both the school's obligation to provide its students with a safe environment conducive to education and the students' pri-

14. 961 F.2d at 82.

15. *Horton v. Goose Creek Independent School District*, 690 F.2d 470 (5th Cir.1982), cert. denied, 463 U.S. 1207, 103 S.Ct. 3536, 77 L.Ed.2d 1387 (1983).

vacy interests, Wisdom declared that the Fourth Amendment required the school to demonstrate that it possessed a factually based suspicion of the need to search each specific student. But since the trial court had not made any factual findings on the reliability of the dog alerts, Wisdom's court remanded the case back to the district court for a determination of whether the reaction of the dogs provided the authorities with a reasonable suspicion that the subject of the sniffing was currently in possession of contraband. As the Supreme Court has never ruled on this matter, Wisdom's opinion, which has received widespread endorsement by the other circuits, now represents the prevailing view of the lower federal courts.[16]

The scope of the constitutional right to privacy also was at the heart of another Wisdom dissenting opinion whose analysis subsequently was adopted by the Supreme Court. In *U.S. v. Sanders*, several defendants convicted of transporting obscene materials in interstate commerce had based their appeal, in large part, on the trial judge's refusal to suppress evidence that they claimed had been illegally seized by the government.[17] The defendants had shipped cartons of 8 mm films to Atlanta via Greyhound Bus Lines. The packages contained a nonexistent return address and fictitious names for the shipper and the recipient. When the cartons reached their destination, the local Greyhound office contacted one of its regular local customers whose name was nearly identical to the fictitious consignee and who accepted the cartons. When this customer opened them up and saw that they contained sexually explicit movies, he immediately notified the Federal Bureau of Investigation (FBI). FBI agents thereupon retrieved the cartons, opened the individual boxes, and screened the contents, all of which, however, without benefit of a search warrant. Thereafter, the defendants were indicted, tried, and convicted based, in part, on the films that the trial court had refused to exclude from the jury's viewing, despite the fact that they had been seized without a warrant

The defendants appealed their convictions, urging that the trial judge had erred in refusing to suppress the films that had been seized in violation of the Fourth Amendment rights. A Fifth Circuit panel composed of Wisdom, Robert Ainsworth, and Charles Clark heard the ap-

16. See *Horton v. Goose Creek Independent School District*, 693 F.2d 524, 525 (5th Cir.1982) (a *per curiam* opinion denying the plaintiffs' request for a panel rehearing).

17. 592 F.2d 788 (5th Cir.1979), rev'd sub nom *Walter v. U.S.*, 447 U.S. 649, 100 S.Ct. 2395, 65 L.Ed.2d 410 (1980).

peal. The majority, in an opinion written by Judge Ainsworth, held that since the cartons initially had been opened and their contents recognized as pornography by a private customer, the FBI's subsequent possession and viewing of the contents did not constitute a governmental "seizure" within the meaning of the Fourth Amendment. Thus, the failure to obtain a search warrant prior to taking and viewing these films did not require suppression of this evidence at trial.

Wisdom did not share this view. In his judgment, the fact that the materials had been delivered in error to a third party did not, as far as he was concerned, destroy the shipper's expectation of privacy. To the contrary, he insisted, the careful manner in which each carton had been wrapped, as well as the use of a fictitious name for the addressee, demonstrated the shippers' desire to maintain their privacy interests. Consequently, Wisdom reasoned, the shippers retained their right to privacy even after the films had been viewed by a private individual. The FBI's subsequent projection and viewing of the films was an independent invasion of that right by a government entity and, therefore, was subject to the protection of the Fourth Amendment. And since the FBI had not obtained a search warrant prior to opening the boxes and viewing the films, the agents' conduct constituted an unconstitutional warrantless seizure.

The government appealed the Fifth Circuit's decision and the Supreme Court reversed the Fifth Circuit in favor of Wisdom's position and ordered that the convictions be overturned.[18] A majority of the Court agreed with Wisdom that the defendants had retained an enforceable constitutional right of privacy to the contents of their shipment, that the FBI's warrantless search violated their Fourth Amendment rights, and, therefore, that the trial court had erred in refusing to suppress the introduction of the films into evidence at trial.

In November 1967, a Houston-based company, Zapata Offshore Company, contracted with a German corporation, Unterweser Reederei, GMBH, to tow one of Zapata's drilling rigs from Venice to Ravenna, Italy. But since the Venice in this instance was the small southeastern Louisiana town near the mouth of the Mississippi River, and not the home of the Grand Canal and the Piazza San Marco, the contemplated

---

18. *Walter v. United States*, 447 U.S. 649, 100 S.Ct. 2395, 65 L.Ed.2d 410 (1980).

voyage involved traversing the Gulf of Mexico, crossing the Atlantic Ocean, and navigating up the Adriatic Sea to the rig's final destination.

Unfortunately for both parties, a mighty storm erupted in the Gulf of Mexico barely four days into the journey, causing the rig's legs to break off and tumble piecemeal into the sea. When informed of this emergency, the rig owner instructed the tug owner to haul the rig to the nearest port. Once the convoy arrived in Tampa several days later, the tug was seized by a U.S. marshal in response to a lawsuit filed by Zapata against Unterweser in that city's federal district court seeking $3.5 million in damages. This relatively commonplace maritime event, however, raised a hugely important legal issue, the resolution of which produced a significant change in American procedural law. And though the Supreme Court had the final word in this saga, its milestone opinion was shaped nearly entirely by the analysis developed and articulated in Wisdom's dissenting opinion in the case.

With the expansion of nationwide and, later, international commerce in the twentieth century, parties to consumer and other contracts increasingly included forum selection clauses in their commercial agreements. These clauses provide that any litigation arising under the contract must be conducted exclusively in the designated forum. By agreeing to a particular litigation site in advance of the institution of any particular lawsuit, the parties seek to eliminate, or at least reduce, the expense and uncertainty associated with litigating jurisdictional and other disputes over the appropriate locale for the resolution of their contractual disputes.

The towage agreement between Zapata and Unterweser contained such a clause. It designated the London High Court of Justice as the exclusive forum for all contract-related disputes. Nevertheless, Zapata had brought its damage action against Unterweser in a federal court in Tampa, Florida. In response, Unterweser filed a countersuit against Zapata in the London High Court to recover moneys due it under the towage contract. Unterweser also asked the federal judge in the Tampa case to suspend those proceedings in order to enforce the forum selection clause, at least until the English court had resolved Unterweser's breach of contract claim against Zapata. Alternatively, Unterweser asked the Tampa court to limit the scope of its potential liability in Zapata's damage action.

District Judge Ben Krentzman of Tampa decided not to enforce the forum selection clause and ruled that his court retained jurisdiction over all aspects of the controversy. Consequently, he issued an order prohibiting either party from litigating any part of this dispute in England or any other location until he had ruled on the merits of the dispute. Unterweser appealed this ruling to the Fifth Circuit. A majority of the panel voted to uphold the district judge's decision. In keeping with the prevailing view of nearly all American courts, the Fifth Circuit majority refused to enforce the contractual forum selection clause. It adhered to the standard view that such clauses were contrary to public policy because they represented private attempts to oust courts of their otherwise admitted jurisdiction and because they were frequently instruments of oppression invoked by the more powerful party to an agreement to compel the other side to litigate in a highly inconvenient forum.[19]

The majority's decision was heavily influenced as well by the fact that allowing the dispute to be litigated in England would likely produce a devastating effect Zapata's right to recover. The towage contract contained a provision immunizing Unterweser from any liability for damages suffered by the rig while being towed. This type of exculpatory provision was unenforceable in American courts. But in England it was considered valid and enforceable. Consequently, if Unterweser, a German corporation, was permitted to enforce the forum selection clause, it would strip the American court of its jurisdiction and compel the case to be decided by an English court. This, in turn, would mean that Zapata, an American company, would be barred from recovery on a claim that could lead to recovery in an American court. On the basis of these and other factors, the Fifth Circuit majority upheld the trial judge's decision to retain authority to adjudicate the case and not force the parties to resolve their differences in England.

In contrast to his two colleagues, Wisdom did not feel constrained to follow what he viewed as an outmoded judicial aversion to forum selection clauses.[20] After all, he noted, this contract was the product of a voluntary agreement between two sophisticated corporations and Zapata, the party seeking to be excused from the terms of the forum selection clause, had made no effort to alter or delete this provision during its negotiations over the entire agreement with Unterweser. Wisdom also calculated that since Zapata chose to contract with Unterweser because of Unterweser's relatively low bid price, whatever advantage Unterweser

19. In Re Unterweser Reederei, GMBH, 428 F.2d 888 (5th Cir.1970).
20. In re Unterweser Reederei, GMBH, 428 F.2d 896 (5th Cir.1970) (Wisdom, J., dissenting).

believed it would reap from the forum selection and exculpatory clauses was reflected in the bid price it had tendered to Zapata. Therefore, to allow Zapata to negate an important component of that total deal would unjustly enrich Zapata and, therefore, be unfair to Unterweser. Moreover, from a more global perspective, Wisdom concluded that the failure to enforce such provisions in commercial agreements would cause a level of unpredictability that would wreak havoc in the international mercantile industry.

But Wisdom did more than simply base his dissenting opinion on the notion that changing commercial circumstances demanded a fresh look at the legal system's conventional treatment of forum selection agreements. He challenged and debunked the traditional wisdom upon which that custom was predicated. And he did this via another of his now legendary history lessons—this time, a discourse on British and American judicial attitudes toward forum selection clauses dating from the seventeenth century.

According to Wisdom's research, the supposed judicial antipathy toward forum agreements was not as entrenched as the Fifth Circuit majority had reported. Wisdom revealed that English courts consistently had enforced forum clauses as far back as 1796. And although, he conceded, most American courts habitually disfavored these clauses, the historical record revealed that not all American courts shared this hostility. Some, in fact, already had broken away from the pack and had begun enforcing forum agreements as early as 1951. Thus, rather than any wholesale repudiation of forum clauses, Wisdom revealed, "what does emerge from the history, the cases, and the commentary is a legitimate concern for the bargaining conditions in which the forum agreement was made and the quality of the remedy available to the parties if the agreement is enforced."[21]

Based on his unearthing of the historical record, Wisdom determined that the better rule was to enforce forum selection clauses unless, in a particular case, the party objecting to the contractually designated forum could convince the court that adherence to the parties' voluntary choice of forum would work a significant hardship. And so Wisdom also proffered a list of factors that a court should consider in determining whether or not enforcement in any particular case would be unreasonable.

21. 428 F.2d at 905 (Wisdom, J., dissenting).

Although a majority of his colleagues voted in favor of Wisdom's request for reconsideration *en banc,* Wisdom couldn't convince a majority to adopt his transformative approach to the enforceability of forum clauses. By an 8–6 margin, the entire court voted to affirm the panel's opinion.[22] The court issued only a one-sentence *per curiam* opinion announcing its adoption of the opinion and judgment of the original panel majority. Wisdom, however, wrote a dissenting opinion, joined in by the five other dissenters, in which he reasserted the virtues of enforcing the agreement reached by the contracting parties and the absence of any factors that would justify permitting Zapata to "welch on its bargain." He decried this "backward step by a forward-looking court" as having "no place in a shrinking world where international commercial transactions are becoming increasingly commonplace."[23]

Though it failed to capture the hearts and minds of a majority of his brethren, Wisdom's boldly innovative opinion received a much more hospitable reception when the case arrived at the doorstep of the Supreme Court. By an 8–1 margin, the Court reversed the Fifth Circuit and relegated the country's traditional antipathy toward forum clauses to the annals of American legal history.[24] Chief Justice Burger's opinion for the Court relied heavily on and quoted extensively from Wisdom's dissenting opinion with respect to both its conclusion and underlying rationale. The Court agreed with Wisdom that the American judiciary's "parochial" aversion to forum selection clauses was anachronistic and needed to be discarded in favor of a policy that would be more hospitable toward the expansion of overseas commercial activities by American businesses. The chief justice announced that the view advanced in Wisdom's "well-reasoned dissenting opinion" that forum clauses should be enforced unless shown to be unreasonable under the particular circumstances was "the correct doctrine" to be followed thereafter by federal courts.[25] The Court also endorsed the list of factors Wisdom had outlined as relevant to that reasonableness determination. Inspired and guided by Wisdom's analysis, the Supreme Court effected what one

22. Letter to Walter P. Gewin from John M. Wisdom, July 14, 1970; Order granting rehearing *en banc,* In Re Unterweser Reederei, GMBH, August 18, 1970; In Re Unterweser Reederei, GMBH, 446 F.2d 907 (5th Cir.1971). Judge Griffin Bell recused himself from the *en banc* review.

23. In Re Unterweser Reederei, GMBH, 446 F.2d 908, 911 (5th Cir.1971) (Wisdom, J., dissenting).

24. *M/S Bremen v. Zapata Off-Shore Company,* 407 U.S. 1, 92 S.Ct. 1907, 32 L.Ed.2d 513 (1972). Justice Douglas was the lone dissenter.

25. 407 U.S. at 11.

noted legal scholar characterized as a "fundamental and epoch-making" transformation of American law concerning the enforcement of forum selection clauses.[26]

Perhaps the least known of Wisdom's most influential rulings dealt with a subject near and dear to his heart. Throughout his adult life, he pursued the love of books that he inherited from his father and shared with his older brother, William B., amassing both a richly eclectic and extensive book collection. He also developed a keen interest in American art, stockpiling a significant collection, with an emphasis on works with a Louisiana theme or connection. And though Wisdom did not personally dabble much in primitive art from other countries, his natural curiosity, as well as his appreciation for diverse cultures, was piqued by a 1977 case involving allegedly stolen pre-Columbian artifacts exported from Mexico in violation of that country's export regulations.

In the early 1970s, five Americans had developed an intricate scheme for unearthing large numbers of pre-Columbian artifacts from archaeological sites in Mexico and smuggling them out of the country for sale to eager and usually unwitting buyers in America. Based on a tip, the FBI conducted a sting operation that led to the conspirators' 1974 arrest, prosecution, and conviction for transporting, concealing, and selling knowingly stolen property through interstate commerce in violation of the National Stolen Property Act (NSPA).[27]

The crux of the defendants' appeal turned on whether cultural property shown to have been exported from a foreign county in contravention of that nation's export laws rendered them "stolen," thereby making their possession a crime under the NSPA. And though this case did not receive any notice from the general public, its resolution was of massive importance to art museums, art dealers, private collectors, and other players in the international art world. For if the American statute was construed to criminalize the *receipt* of unlawfully exported property, then museums, art dealers, and private collectors would be subject to criminal prosecution whenever an exporter with whom they did business failed to comply with the typically rigid export restrictions imposed by other countries, regardless of whether that exporter had lawfully owned or stolen the artifacts.

26. Otto Kahn-Freund, *Jurisdiction Agreements: Some Reflections*, 26 INT'L. & COMP. L.Q. 825, 845 (1977).

27. 18 U.S.C. §371, 2314, 2315.

The Fifth Circuit unanimously agreed to reverse the defendants' convictions. Writing for the court in *U.S. v. McClain*, Wisdom declared that it was not a violation of the NSPA merely to import an item that had been illegally exported from another country.[28] However, and most significant, he also declared that cultural property would be deemed "stolen," and its possessor subject to criminal prosecution under the NSPA, if the item had been declared by the country of origin to be its property prior to its unlawful exportation.

As Wisdom acknowledged in the very first sentence of his opinion, "museum directors, art dealers, and innumerable private collectors throughout this country must have been in a state of shock when they read the news—if they did—of the conviction of the five defendants in this case."[29] The American Association of Dealers in Ancient, Oriental and Primitive Art had even gone so far as to file a friend of court brief in *McClain* urging the Fifth Circuit to overturn the defendants' conviction. And these third parties were equally dissatisfied with the basis upon which Wisdom explained his panel's decision to overturn the defendants' convictions. By declaring that a mere assertion of national ownership (which a country can legislate without ever having actually obtained physical possession of the objects) meant that any subsequent importation constituted criminal transporting in stolen property (assuming the exportation was in violation of the host country's export laws), critics charged that Wisdom and his colleagues had unreasonably expanded the reach of the NSPA. Pursuant to this ruling, these naysayers insisted, a good faith acquirer of such imported cultural property would be deemed to have committed a crime, regardless of whether the artifacts had been lawfully acquired decades prior to the unilateral declaration of state ownership or had only recently been looted from an archaeological site.[30]

Nevertheless, the *McClain* doctrine, as it is now known, is the prevailing law governing the criminal prosecution of antiquities dealers. And though bills were introduced in Congress in 1985 and 1986 to narrow the effect of Wisdom's interpretation of the NSPA with respect to cultural property, neither of these legislative proposals was enacted, and no other federal circuit court has questioned the ruling's soundness.

28. 545 F.2d 988 (54th Cir.1977).

29. 545 F.2d at 991.

30. See Jamison K. Shedwill, *Is the "Lost Civilization" of the Maya Lost Forever? The U.S. and Illicit Trade in Pre-Columbian Artifacts*, 23 CAL. W. INT'L. L.J. 227, 248 (1992).

Consequently, Wisdom's broad interpretation of "stolen" property to include any cultural property subjected to nationalization has provided source countries with an effective method of protecting their cultural treasures and enforcing their own stringent exportation regulations. By "waving a magic wand and promulgating this metaphysical declaration of ownership," a foreign state can invoke the threat of criminal prosecution in American courts of anyone who obtains possession of "its" illegally exported artifacts.[31]

A few states within the United States subsequently seized on Wisdom's ruling in *McClain* as justification for enacting their own umbrella ownership statute in order to protect local natural resources from unlawful export. One such state was Wisdom's own Louisiana. In 1986, its legislature enacted a law declaring state ownership of all resident alligators, a declaration that served as the predicate for a subsequent ruling by a federal district court that unlawful transportation of this form of wildlife violated the NSPA.[32] Thirty years after he joined the Fifth Circuit, the list of beneficiaries of Wisdom's body of jurisprudence had extended to members of the animal kingdom.

---

31. Paul M. Bator, *An Essay on the International Trade in Art*, STAN. L. REV. 275, 350 (1982).

32. LA. REV. STAT. ANN. §56-3 (West Supp. 1986). See also Jonathan S. Moore, *Enforcing Foreign Ownership Claims in the Antiquities Market*, 97 YALE L.J. 466, 481 (1988).

14

THE CIVIL RIGHTS STRUGGLES
OF THE 1970S AND 1980S
EQUAL OPPORTUNITY IN EMPLOYMENT

Just as school desegregation and voting rights cases became the focal point for civil rights litigation in the mid-1960s, Congress's passage of the 1964 Civil Rights Act brought employment discrimination claims to the forefront of the litigation universe in the early 1970s. Unquestionably, Congress's primary objective in 1964 was to respond to the long history of racial prejudice perpetrated by employers and unions against African Americans and to promote the assimilation of members of this minority group into the economic mainstream. Nonetheless, the purposefully expansive language contained in this comprehensive civil rights statute opened up the courts to a broad spectrum of claims alleging discrimination on the basis of sex, religion, and ethnicity, as well as race. And just as it had been in the vanguard of the enforcement of statutory and constitutional rights in voting and education, the Fifth Circuit, led by its resident scholar and wordsmith, John Minor Wisdom, assumed a leading role in the implementation and realization of this statute's broad agenda.

The 1964 Civil Rights Act[1] consists of several separate sections, or

1. Pub.L. 88–352; 78 Stat. 241 (1964).

Titles, each of which prohibits discrimination in a different segment of society. Title IV, for example, forbids discrimination in public accommodations such as hotels and restaurants, while Title IX bans discriminatory access to programming on the basis of sex by entities receiving federal financial assistance. Title VII focuses specifically and exclusively on employment and bans discrimination on the bases of race, color, religion, national origin, and sex.[2]

Once individuals began asserting their rights under Title VII, the federal courts were confronted by a myriad of questions concerning the meaning and scope of this important piece of legislation. These included not only substantive matters such as the extent of an employer's duty not to discriminate, but also issues going to the limit of the courts' own remedial authority. For example, how far was a federal court permitted to go in issuing a remedial order that would effectively combat the continuing consequences of decades of job discrimination while remaining true to the statute's core antidiscrimination principle?

Whenever the courts were called upon to examine the scope of their remedial authority under Title VII, they invariably were confronted with two related issues. First, after finding the existence of unlawful discrimination, to what extent, if at all, could a court compel an employer to take action based, in whole or in part, on race? Second, could an employer or union voluntarily implement a plan that included some form of race-based preference as part of its own effort to undo the effects of past discrimination? And, if so, would this depend upon whether that prior discrimination was traceable to its own conduct, or was it simply the result of societally generated inequities?

One of Wisdom's signal contributions to the development of employment discrimination law dealt with the latter of these two immensely controversial questions. By the beginning of the 1970s, and for a host of reasons ranging from the most altruistic to the merely expedient, employers across the country began to formulate and implement a variety of affirmative action programs designed to open up previously segregated jobs to members of racial minority groups, primarily African Americans, by affording them some manner of preferential treatment.

When lawsuits challenging the legality of these policies came before them, the courts had to come to grips with the thorny question of whether such race-based affirmative action contravened the statu-

2. 42 U.S.C. §2000a et seq.

tory ban on racial discrimination. Since this form of affirmative action was designed to work to the advantage of members of the historically victimized class, seemingly at the expense of members of the tradition- ally favored racial class, the resulting legal issue was most commonly phrased in terms of whether affirmative action amounted to unlawful reverse discrimination. But the technical legal issues presented by these cases required more than a mechanical interpretation of the governing statutory language. They raised complex questions of social policy that quickly became the focus of a highly charged national debate over the core objectives and scope of federal antidiscrimination law.

Thirty miles up the Mississippi River from Wisdom's New Orleans home, a twenty-six-year-old chemical worker named Brian Weber worked at the Kaiser Aluminum plant in Gramercy, Louisiana. When he was denied admission to the company's on-the-job training program, Weber filed suit against his employer and union. The case eventually made its way to the Supreme Court and became the vehicle for the Court's au- thoritative pronouncement on the extent to which a private company voluntarily could grant race-based preferences without simultaneously violating Title VII's ban on racial discrimination.

En route to the Supreme Court, the appeal from the trial judge's rul- ing in favor of the defendants was heard by a Fifth Circuit panel. Un- able to join with his two colleagues, Wisdom wrote a dissenting opinion that reflected the culmination of a nearly two-decade-long evolution of his views on the lawfulness of implementing race-conscious solutions to the systemic problem of racial discrimination in voting, education, and employment. And even though Wisdom was unable to convince either of his brethren to join with him, his views ultimately carried the day with the Supreme Court in a ruling that remains the touchstone for as- sessing the statutory (that is, non-constitutional) validity of race-based affirmative action undertaken by private-sector employers.

On February 1, 1974, Kaiser Aluminum and Chemical Corporation entered into a master collective bargaining agreement with the United Steelworkers of America, the union that represented workers at fifteen Kaiser plants across the country, including the one in Gramercy, Loui- siana. In that master contract, Kaiser agreed to create a joint labor- management committee to review the extent to which minority group members were employed in its trade, craft, and maintenance jobs in various locations, including Gramercy. Additionally, the company and union agreed that, where necessary, they would establish goals and timetables to achieve a "desired" minority ratio in those classifications in which minorities presently had been and continued to be under-represented. The agreement further provided that in filling apprentice and craft jobs, assuming the availability of qualified minority candidates, not less than one minority employee would be hired for every non-minority employee. A separate memorandum setting forth the desired goal for each covered Kaiser plant prescribed a goal of 39 percent minority representation for each "craft family" at the company's Gramercy location.

To enhance its ability to recruit qualified minority workers for its skilled craft positions, Kaiser agreed to create an on-the-job training program for those of its unskilled workers who were interested in obtaining the expertise necessary to transfer to the higher-paying craft jobs.[3] Most important, for the purposes of this case, the master agreement prescribed that one African American Kaiser employee would be admitted into the training program for every white Kaiser employee admitted until the percentage of minority craft workers at the plant roughly approximated the percentage of minority individuals in the general population of the surrounding area. This meant that all candidates competed for entry into the program solely against members of their racial group. And within each racial group, applicants were chosen based on their years of seniority with Kaiser.

Since the company based its apprentice program admissions decisions on race-segregated seniority lists, some of the African American employees admitted to the program had less seniority than some unsuccessful white applicants. Weber, a laboratory technician at Kaiser's Gramercy plant since 1968,[4] was one of those unchosen white workers.

Weber, an active member of the Steelworkers local union that represented Kaiser's Gramercy plant employees, decided to bring his claim to the federal court in New Orleans. Far from being a bayou redneck, Weber was regarded by his union cohorts as a strong proponent of civil

3. In 1974, a skilled craftsman at the Gramercy plant made $25,000 per year, whereas Brian Weber earned an annual salary of only $17,000 as a lab technician tasked with completing routine chemical tests. Barry Bearak and David Lauter, "U.S. Anti-Bias Regulations Disrupt Lives, Workplaces," *Los Angeles Times*, November 4, 1991, 14, col. 1; 15, col. 1.

4. Citron, "Blue Collar Bakke Wants Rights for All," *New Orleans Times-Picayune*, December 21, 1978, 14, col. 1.

rights. Few of his co-workers viewed Weber's motives in filing this action as racially suspect.[5] To the contrary, he was mortified when members of the local Ku Klux Klan demonstrated their support of his actions in front of the Gramercy plant.[6] Moreover, and perhaps most ironical, as chairperson of the plant grievance committee, Weber actively had supported Kaiser's implementation of the training program. But when he learned that the company's admissions standards contained a racial preference, Weber simply and sincerely concluded that he had been cheated out of the sort of benefit that traditionally had been doled out on the basis of seniority. He was hoping to be trained to be a pipefitter and welder, a transfer that would raise his annual income by as much as $15,000 per year.[7] And so Weber filed suit against Kaiser on behalf of himself and all the other white workers at the Kaiser-Gramercy plant who were eligible to apply for admission to its on-the-job training program.[8] His complaint alleged that by reserving 50 percent of the spots in its training programs for minority workers, the master agreement had established a racial quota system in violation of Title VII's prohibition against racial discrimination. Weber asked the federal district court in New Orleans to stop Kaiser and the union from implementing the terms of the plan.

Although African Americans represented approximately 40 percent of the population of the geographic area from which Kaiser drew nearly all of its employees, less than 15 percent of Kaiser's Gramercy workers and less than 3 percent of its craftsmen were black. This manifest dearth of black workers at the Gramercy plant was of particular concern to Kaiser and the union. As a government contractor, Kaiser was subject to investigation, and possible termination, of its lucrative federal government contracts by the Office of Federal Contract Compliance Programs

5. Barry Bearak and David Lauter, "U.S. Anti-Bias Regulations Disrupt Lives, Workplaces," *Los Angeles Times,* November 4, 1991, 1, col. 5. But see Citron, "Anti-Weber Forces Fear Rights Setback," *New Orleans Times-Picayune,* December 22, 1978, 12, col. 1 (quoting one organizer of the New Orleans Committee to Overturn the Weber Decision and Defend Affirmative Action as calling Weber "a straight up racist" and a "sort of Klansman without a sheet speaking for the anti-black wing of this country").

6. "Speaking of Race," *New Orleans Times-Picayune,* November 16, 1993, A-7, col. 4.

7. Citron, "Blue Collar Bakke Wants Rights for All," *New Orleans Times-Picayune,* December 21, 1978, 14, col. 1.

8. Weber was represented from the commencement of suit through the appeal to the U.S. Supreme Court by Michael Fontham, a thirty-two-year-old partner in the law firm that had been co-founded by John Wisdom.

(OFCCP). Pursuant to Executive Order No. 11246, all companies entering into contracts with the federal government were obliged to "take affirmative action" to ensure that individuals were hired, and treated during their employment, without regard to their race. Enforcement of this obligation was ceded to the OFCCP. Since termination or even suspension of Kaiser's government contracts would deal a serious blow to both the company and its workers, Kaiser and the union had a strong interest in avoiding such a result.

The trial judge sided with Weber. He did not accept Kaiser's contention that race-based decisions implemented for the salutary or benign purpose of redressing a history of racial subordination fell outside the intended scope of this federal law's antidiscrimination mandate. To the contrary, he characterized the Kaiser–United Steel Workers of America effort as a blatant racial quota that violated the statute's "clear and unequivocal" prohibitions against discrimination against "*any*" individual on the basis of her or his race.[9] He also noted that Kaiser and the union had implemented this race-based affirmative action plan in the absence of any finding that they had engaged in unlawful racial discrimination.

Kaiser and the union's appeal to the Fifth Circuit was assigned to a panel composed of Wisdom and two of his junior colleagues, Thomas G. Gee of Austin, Texas, the court's most ardent and vocal supporter of Wisdom's fifteen-year crusade against the congressional campaign to split up the Fifth Circuit, and Peter T. Fay, a former U.S. district judge from Miami. Judges Gee and Fay voted to affirm the trial court's ruling.[10] They found that the plan's preference could not be sustained because there had been no demonstration that Kaiser had previously engaged in racial discrimination in its hiring or promotion practices. They also reasoned that since all of Kaiser's black workers were eligible for the preference afforded by the one-to-one admissions policy, this advantage was not limited to identifiable victims of prior acts of discrimination. The combination of these two factors convinced the majority that the racial preference amounted to an unlawful racial quota designed to attain racial balance for its own sake.

This was certainly not the first time that Wisdom had been confronted by the question of whether federal law mandated colorblindness or whether it allowed for the consideration of race in decisions affecting

9. *Weber v. Kaiser Aluminum & Chemical Corp.*, 415 F.Supp. 761, 766, 769 (E.D.La.1976).

10. *Weber v. Kaiser Aluminum & Chemical Corp.*, 563 F.2d 216 (5th Cir.1977).

employment or other matters. In only his second year on the bench, he had authored an opinion striking down a Louisiana statute that prohibited black and white prizefighters from competing against one another.[11] His decision in that case had rested squarely and expressly on the determination that the equal protection clause of the Fourteenth Amendment prohibited *all* race-based governmental conduct. Similarly, in his dissent from a 1960 case in which the majority of the Fifth Circuit panel voted to sustain the validity of a Louisiana statute requiring the listing of the racial identity of candidates on all election ballots, Wisdom reaffirmed his view that the Constitution mandated colorblindness on the part of governmental actors.[12]

Both of those earlier cases, however, involved racial classifications that operated to burden African Americans. It was not until 1966, in a series of school desegregation cases, that Wisdom faced head-on the question of whether race could be used by the government to benefit members of a historically disadvantaged racial group. In his twin opinions for the Fifth Circuit in *Singleton,* and in his monumental opus in *Jefferson County,* Wisdom embraced and enforced school desegregation standards that openly incorporated race as a factor in pupil placement. This form of racial affirmative action was permissible, he had concluded, because race was being used solely as a means of eradicating the manifest effects of generations of segregation. As such, race-based relief was not only appropriate, but essential in order to accomplish the desired objective of integrating the public schools.[13]

Wisdom's evolved view of the legitimacy of race-conscious governmental action also had migrated to the private sector's use of race to combat job discrimination. In a 1969 case, a group of minority employees had challenged the use of a seniority-based promotion policy which, although racially neutral on its face, operated to perpetuate the consequences of the employer's decades of previously lawful racial segregation in hiring and initial job assignment. In *Local 189, United Paperworkers v. U.S.,* Wisdom's opinion for a unanimous panel declared that the com-

11. *Dorsey v. State Athletic Commission,* 168 F.Supp. 149,152 (E.D.La.1958).

12. *Anderson v. Martin,* 206 F.Supp. 700, 705 (E.D.La.1962) (Wisdom, J., dissenting).

13. *Singleton v. Jackson Municipal Separate School District,* 348 F.2d 729 (5th Cir.1965); *Singleton v. Jackson Municipal Separate School District,* 355 F.2d 865 (5th Cir.1966); *U.S. v. Jefferson County,* 372 F.2d 836, 876 (5th Cir.1966), modified, 380 F.2d 385 (5th Cir.1967) (*en banc*), cert. denied, 389 U.S. 840, 88 S.Ct. 67, 19 L.Ed.2d 103 (1967). Wisdom's rulings in these cases are explored in chapter 10.

pany's African American workers deserved a remedy that would put them in their "rightful place" even though their competitive disadvantage was the product of then-lawful racially discriminatory practices.[14] He announced that the employer was under a duty to undo the effects of its prior discriminatory, though lawful, conduct, and ordered the company and the union to base all subsequent promotion decisions on a modified calculation of seniority whenever one of the candidates for promotion was an African American worker who had been hired during the preexisting racist hiring and job assignment regime.

Having crossed that ideological Rubicon in *Local 189*, Wisdom was predictably unwilling to abide by his colleagues' insistence in *Weber* that race could be used only to remedy proven acts of discrimination with respect to the identifiable victims of that prior unlawful conduct. Such a limit, Wisdom insisted, effectively precluded employers from taking the initiative to respond to the consequences of decades of subordination of black workers. It forced employers wishing to put an end to the perpetuation of the effects of previously lawful policies of racial discrimination "to walk a high tightrope without a net beneath them."[15] For any company choosing to implement race-conscious affirmative action to combat the impact of its antecedent acts of racial basis would face the threat of reverse discrimination suits (such as Weber's) by its non-preferred white workers. On the other hand, failing to respond to the legacy of prejudice left the company liable to either private suit by black workers or sanctions by the OFCCP under Executive Order 11246.

To avoid placing the employer in this legal no-man's land while simultaneously encouraging voluntary efforts to eliminate what he termed "the blight of racial discrimination," Wisdom devised a novel yet characteristically pragmatic standard by which to evaluate the lawfulness of affirmative action. "If an affirmative action plan, adopted in a collective bargaining agreement, is a *reasonable* remedy for an *arguable* violation of Title VII," he prescribed, "it should be upheld."[16]

By sanctioning affirmative action predicated solely upon a showing of an "arguable" violation (a concept that originated in the brief submitted by counsel for the Steelworkers Union), Wisdom sought to provide em-

14. 416 F.2d 980 (5th Cir.1969), cert. denied, 397 U.S. 919, 90 S.Ct. 926, 25 L.Ed.2d 100 (1970). Wisdom's ruling in this case is examined in chapter 7.

15. 563 F.2d 227, 230 (Wisdom, J., dissenting).

16. 563 F.2d at 230 (Wisdom, J., dissenting) (emphasis added).

ployers with a net under this juridical tightrope.[17] He also hoped to re-lieve the courts of the obligation to determine the existence of a fact—the existence of unlawful discrimination—that none of the parties had any incentive to prove. Employers and unions obviously did not want to subject themselves to the financial exposure that would accompany any admission of complicity in unlawful conduct. Similarly, employees, like Weber, who were attempting to challenge employer-instigated affir-mative action, clearly had no incentive to litigate this issue since a find-ing of prior discrimination on the employer's part would only weaken their case. In fact, the only individuals interested in establishing the ex-istence of past discrimination—minority employees or job applicants—were not parties to these cases. Wisdom's response to this dilemma, once again, was to devise a fundamentally pragmatic and commonsense solution to one of the nation's most sensitive and controversial prob-lems. Affirmative action was acceptable if it took the form of a reason-able remedy for an *arguable* violation of Title VII.

Wisdom then listed two factors relevant to determining whether or not a particular form of affirmative relief was a "reasonable" response to arguable violations. First, a court should determine whether or not the affirmative action was the result of a joint agreement between labor and management. Since unions are under both a legal duty and political mandate to fairly serve the interests of their non-minority members, he reasoned, the union's participation in an affirmative action plan oper-ated as a meaningful check on its fairness. Second, the more limited the impact of the preference on the non-preferred workers, the more likely it would be deemed a reasonable effort at eradicating the lingering effects of past arguable violations. Thus, for example, in Kaiser's case, the vol-untary affirmative action did not result in the displacement of a single white worker. Moreover, it actually provided white workers with access to on-the-job training that had not existed prior to the adoption of the affirmative action plan. Both of these factors, in Wisdom's view, sup-ported the conclusion that this affirmative action plan was a reasonable response on Kaiser and the union's part.

In stark contrast to the reasoning of the majority, Wisdom offered an alternative validation for affirmative action. Race-based policies, he proclaimed, also were justified as a necessary response to societal dis-crimination. His panel colleagues had declared that Title VII's ban on

17. Bench Memorandum to Judge John Minor Wisdom from (Law Clerk) Steven A. Reiss, March 28, 1977, at 11.

racial discrimination forcefully and unequivocally forbad the use of race to correct the evils produced by decades of undeniable societal discrimination.[18] Wisdom, on the other hand, refused to condemn a generation of incumbent black workers to a permanently subordinated status that was directly attributable to the past practices of their employers or others. It was high time, he concluded, to break this insidious cycle of disadvantage.

The incidence of discrimination against women and minorities by craft unions was so pervasive that Wisdom took judicial notice of it. But even though the existence of this discrimination was undeniable, he observed, it often was difficult to establish the identity of all of its victims. For example, the inevitability of a hostile reception certainly operated to deter many women and minority group members from even applying for union membership in the first place. But the mere fact that its victims often were invisible, he believed, neither diminished the impact of that tradition of bias on all members of the disadvantaged class nor eroded their claim to meaningful relief. Therefore, he concluded, where societal discrimination was as egregious and recent as in this case, the implementation of a reasonable race-based preference was warranted.

At the same time, however, Wisdom freely acknowledged that any consideration of race was "troubling" and tended to pull a society committed to equal rights "perilously close to self-contradiction." Nevertheless, he ultimately was persuaded that "the pervasive effects of centuries of societal discrimination still haunt us"[19] and demanded reasonable reliance on racial preferences to remedy their impact.

After reading the majority and dissenting opinions, John Brown, then the chief judge of the Fifth Circuit, became convinced that the case should be reconsidered en banc.[20] So he polled his colleagues to determine if he could muster a majority in support of such review.[21] Surprisingly, Wisdom opposed reconsideration. He desperately wanted to avoid the delay incident to reconsideration by the entire court. In a brief letter to his colleagues informing them of his opposition to Brown's proposal, Wisdom predicted that voting to rehear the case would mean that it "will be delayed nine months to a year . . . before finding its way to the

18. 563 F.2d at 225.

19. 563 F.2d at 239 (Wisdom, J., dissenting).

20. Letter to All Active Fifth Circuit Judges from John R. Brown, February 10, 1978, and attached memorandum.

21. Ballot on Granting En Banc & Oral Argument, February 10, 1978.

Supreme Court. The issue is too important to be subjected to such a delay." Moreover, he correctly predicted, "this case is absolutely certain to go to the Supreme Court, whichever way it is decided."[22] Most of his colleagues agreed with this assessment and strategy. In the memorandum he circulated informing his colleagues that the vote was 11–4 against reconsideration, Brown good-naturedly acknowledged that "Judge Wisdom has persuaded us not to delay the train by an *en banc* sidetrack. He may be right, and I cheerfully submit. I only hope he is as good a prognosticator as he is an advocate."[23]

He was. Not only did the Supreme Court agree to hear the case, it reversed the Fifth Circuit majority's judgment.[24] And although it also declined to endorse Wisdom's proposed "arguable violation" standard, the five-member majority did adopt Wisdom's more far-reaching proposition that Title VII did not prohibit employers and unions from taking voluntary steps to eradicate the effects of societal discrimination.[25]

But the Supreme Court's endorsement of affirmative action was not unlimited. And it is with respect to its demarcation of the boundaries of lawful race-conscious affirmative action that the persuasive power of Wisdom's dissenting opinion was most clearly evidenced. Justice Brennan, author of the majority opinion, agreed with the fundamental principles underlying Wisdom's opinion. By declaring that voluntary race-conscious affirmative action was permitted by Title VII when it was designed "to eliminate conspicuous racial imbalance in traditionally segregated job categories," Brennan acknowledged that an employer could implement racial preferences even when it had not been an active participant in prior incidents of job bias.[26] His opinion for the Court agreed with Wisdom that preferences were justified "when there has been a societal history of purposeful exclusion of blacks from [a] job category."[27]

Freeing the proponents of affirmative action from the evidentiary straitjacket of an underlying statutory violation, arguable or otherwise, represented a wholehearted incorporation of Wisdom's view that remedying societal discrimination was both a laudable and statutorily per-

22. Letter to All Active Judges of the Fifth Circuit Court of Appeals from John M. Wisdom, February 13, 1978.

23. Letter to Thomas G. Gee from John R. Brown, February 23, 1978.

24. *United Steelworkers of America v. Weber*, 443 U.S. 193, 99 S.Ct. 2721, 61 L.Ed.2d 480 (1979).

25. Justices Powell and Stevens recused themselves from ruling on the case. 443 U.S. at 209, 99 S.Ct. at 2730.

26. 443 U.S. at 209, 99 S.Ct. at 2730 (Blackmun, J., concurring).

27. 443 U.S. at 212, 99 S.Ct. at 2731 (Blackmun, J., concurring).

missible objective. Similarly, in determining that the extent of the racial preference in Kaiser's training program was reasonable, the Court referenced the factors set forth in Wisdom's dissent. Like Wisdom, Justice Brennan relied on the facts that the plan did not result in the discharge of any white workers and did not preclude admission of white workers into the training program.[28]

The impact of Wisdom's dissenting opinion in *Weber*, however, did not end there. Only a year earlier, in *Regents of the University of California v. Bakke*,[29] four justices—Brennan, White, Marshall, and Blackmun— had voted to uphold the use of affirmative action in admission to the medical school at the University of California. In *Bakke*, these justices had rejected both the constitutional and statutory challenges to this public school's race-based affirmative action plan. Most Court-watchers anticipated, therefore, that this quartet similarly would line up in support of a private entity's use of affirmative action.

But four other members of the *Bakke* Court (Chief Justice Burger and Justices Stewart, Rehnquist, and Stevens) had eschewed the constitutional issue and voted to invalidate the university's use of race solely because it violated statutory bans on discrimination set forth in Title VI of the 1964 Civil Rights Act. Justice Powell, the crucial ninth and swing vote in *Bakke*, chose not to participate in the decision of *Weber* since he had been unable to attend the oral argument due to illness. So when Justice Stevens also decided to sit *Weber* out (because he had provided legal counsel to Kaiser while in private practice[30]), it appeared, based on their respective positions in *Bakke*, that the seven remaining justices in *Weber* would split 4–3 in support of Kaiser's affirmative action plan.

Justices Brennan, White, Marshall, and Blackmun did indeed stay true to form and voted to ratify Kaiser's affirmative action plan. And Justice Potter Stewart, who had voted to strike down the medical school's affirmative action plan in *Bakke*, switched sides, which produced a five-member majority in support of Kaiser's limited use of race-based affirmative action. (Chief Justice Burger and Justice Rehnquist dissented, consistently with their votes against the use of affirmative action in *Bakke*.)

But Justice Harry Blackmun, who had approved the use of race in

28. 443 U.S. at 208, 99 S.Ct. at 2730.

29. 438 U.S. 265, 98 S.Ct. 2733, 57 L.Ed.2d 750 (1978).

30. Linda Greenhouse, "High Court Backs a Preference Plan for Blacks in Jobs," *New York Times*, June 28, 1979, 1, col. 6.

medical school admissions in *Bakke,* harbored serious reservations about Justice Brennan's assessment in *Weber* of the legislative history underlying Title VII and was uncomfortable with Brennan's less-than-rigorous analysis of the statutory text. Nevertheless, Blackmun ultimately decided to join in Justice Brennan's opinion for the majority in *Weber.* But he also decided to write a concurring opinion, one that reflects the decisive impact that Judge Wisdom's dissenting opinion had on Blackmun's ultimate decision to vote in support of the Kaiser-Steelworkers affirmative action plan.

Referring expressly to Wisdom's dissenting opinion, Blackmun agreed with Wisdom that a wooden construction of the statute placed employers on a "high tightrope without a net" and placed voluntary compliance with Title VII "in profound jeopardy."[31] Moreover, Blackmun explained, because Wisdom's "arguable violation" theory was "the soundest way to approach this case," his preference was to adopt it as the justification for the use of reasonably drawn voluntary, race-conscious affirmative action.[32] Nevertheless, at the end of the day, Blackmun concluded, notwithstanding the fact that Wisdom's formulation was more "conceptually satisfying" than Justice Brennan's prescription, the differences between the two approaches were insignificant enough to make the majority's framework acceptable and to allow Blackmun to join in Justice Brennan's opinion.[33] But without the comfort level Justice Blackmun received from Wisdom's analysis, in terms of both its content and the identity of its author, he might not have been willing to join in the majority's opinion. And although there still would have been a four-member majority of the seven-member Court even without Blackmun, the fact that Justice Brennan's opinion for the Court attracted five of the seven votes significantly contributed to its landmark status and its subsequent wholesale adoption by the Court in a case upholding the use of sex-based affirmative action.[34]

Wisdom's opinion in *Weber* clearly is his most significant and enduring contribution to the development of Title VII jurisprudence. But it was not the only area in which his opinions played a path-breaking role. Along with its antidiscrimination mandate, Title VII contains a num-

31. 443 U.S. at 209–10, 99 S.Ct. at 2730–2731 (Blackmun, J., concurring).

32. 443 U.S. at 210, 99 S.Ct. at 2731 (Blackmun, J., concurring).

33. 443 U.S. at 213, 99 S.Ct. at 2732 (Blackmun, J., concurring).

34. See *Johnson v. Transportation Agency,* 480 U.S. 616, 107 S.Ct. 1442, 94 L.Ed.2d 516 (1987).

ber of procedural provisions designed to guide litigants in the prosecution of employment bias claims. And although the public's attention inevitably and understandably focuses primarily on the statute's substantive terms, a party's failure to abide by these procedural rules can doom her or his lawsuit even before it begins. Consequently, the interpretation and enforcement of these procedural provisions has played and continues to play a crucial role in the effective implementation of the broad congressional directive to stem the tide of discrimination in employment.

Wisdom authored the first appellate court decision holding that a claimant's failure to comply with the statutory requirement to file a discrimination charge with the Equal Employment Opportunity Commission (EEOC) within ninety days of the alleged discriminatory act did not necessarily preclude him or her from pursuing that claim in court. In *Reeb v. Economic Opportunity Atlanta, Inc.*, Wisdom's opinion for the court bears the hallmark of his pragmatic approach toward problem-solving.[35] He calculated that since EEOC charges typically were filed by laymen without the benefit of legal counsel, it was unreasonable and unnecessary to insist on unforgiving enforcement of such a technical filing requirement. Although several other circuit courts initially adopted the contrary position, the Supreme Court ultimately agreed with Wisdom, holding that the ninety-day requirement was not an unshakeable jurisdictional prerequisite to suit but, instead, was more in the nature of a statute of limitations that could be subject to equitable exceptions.[36]

Long hair, and the right to wear it, an issue that Wisdom previously had examined from a constitutional perspective, also was the factual backdrop for another visionary opinion that served as a crucial link in the evolution of federal employment discrimination law. The Macon Telegraph Publishing Company required all applicants for positions requiring contact with the general public to adhere to a grooming code. This code, which required all such workers to be neatly dressed and groomed in accordance with standards customarily accepted in the business community, was construed to exclude the employment of males, but not females, with long hair. When Alan Willingham, a twenty-two-year-old male with shoulder-length hair, applied for a layout artist position in the newspaper's advertising department, the company refused to hire him. He brought an action under Title VII, alleging that since

35. 516 F.2d 924 (5th Cir.1975).
36. *Zipes v. Trans World Airlines, Inc.*, 455 U.S. 385, 102 S.Ct. 1127, 71 L.Ed.2d 234 (1982).

female job applicants were not subject to any hair-length restriction, the application of this portion of the grooming code to him amounted to unlawful sex discrimination.

Even though the company admitted that Willingham had been denied a position solely because of his refusal to comply with its grooming code, it still asked the court to throw out his lawsuit. District Judge William A. Bootle agreed with the newspaper that it had not discriminated against Willingham because of his sex. Because the newspaper had imposed some grooming requirements on both male and female applicants, and since there was no suggestion that the company was using its code as a pretext for refusing to employ men in general, Bootle concluded that it was "not unreasonable for an employer to expect differences in grooming between men and women—and such expectations are not indicative of sexual discrimination."[37]

The appeal from Bootle's ruling was heard by a panel composed of Elbert Tuttle, Wisdom, and Bryan Simpson, a former federal district judge from Jacksonville. Simpson consistently sided with Wisdom in school desegregation cases and had signed onto Wisdom's dissenting opinion in *Karr v. Schmidt*, the case in which Wisdom supported the recognition of the constitutional right of public high school students to wear long hair.[38] Less than a year after that decision, however, the two jurists parted company when it came to deciding whether or not enforcement of the Macon newspaper's grooming code was forbidden by the federal antidiscrimination statute.

Judges Tuttle and Wisdom voted to reverse Judge Bootle's decision. In his opinion for the majority in *Willingham v. Macon Telegraph Publishing Company*, Wisdom repudiated the newspaper's claim that since it required all its employees to groom their hair according to the prevailing community standard, it was not discriminating on the basis of sex.[39] He ignored the superficial appeal of the company's argument and focused instead on the more nuanced issue raised by the case. The fact that both male and female employees were subject to a community standards–based grooming code did not divert Wisdom to the reality that the content of that code reflected sex-stereotyped notions of proper and acceptable behavior. Title VII, he concluded, "was in-

37. *Willingham v. Macon Telegraph Publishing Co.*, 352 F.Supp. 1018 (M.D.Ga.1972).
38. 460 F.2d 609 (5th Cir.1972) (*en banc*). This ruling is discussed in chapter 13.
39. 482 F.2d 535 (5th Cir.1973).

tended to strike at the entire spectrum of disparate treatment of men and women resulting from sex stereotypes."[40]

Within less than a month, a slim majority of Fifth Circuit judges voted in favor of the request by Judge J. P. Coleman of Mississippi, another of the court's most consistently conservative members, to grant rehearing *en banc*.[41] And by a markedly greater margin, 11–4, the court voted to reverse the original panel's ruling and to adopt the reasoning offered by the panel's dissenting member, Simpson. The *en banc* opinion, authored by Simpson, ordered the reinstatement of District Judge Bootle's judgment dismissing Willingham's complaint on the grounds that the newspaper had not discriminated against Willingham on the basis of his sex.[42] Simpson construed the statutory ban on sex discrimination to preclude only those policies that differentiated between men and women on the basis of sex plus a factor that either involved an immutable characteristic or abridged a fundamental, constitutionally protected right. But hair length, Simpson discerned, was most assuredly not immutable and did not enjoy constitutional protection, at least in the employment context. Consequently, the company's decision to regulate hair length for men but not for women did not amount to proscribed sex-based discrimination.

Over the succeeding years, Simpson's analysis was adopted by all the other circuit courts and was applied not only to male-specific grooming codes, but to most other sex-differentiated dress codes as well. Invariably, the courts justified these decisions on the theory that the intrusion into personal autonomy occasioned by rules requiring men to wear short hair or forbidding women from wearing pants was relatively trivial and, in any event, amounted to little more than a refusal to indulge individual fashion proclivities. Moreover, the circuit courts typically opined, catering to these preferences would significantly, and unreasonably, curtail management's ability to best manage its business.

It took nearly fifteen years for the Supreme Court to come around to Wisdom's recognition of and sensitivity to the fact that unspoken, and often deeply rooted, cultural norms can operate to reinforce and to enable sex-based prejudices and stereotypes in ways that are as debilitating

40. 482 F.2d at 538.

41. Letter to John M. Wisdom from James P. Coleman, June 30, 1973; Letter to John R. Brown from John M. Wisdom, July 24, 1973.

42. *Willingham v. Macon Telegraph Publishing Company*, 507 F.2d 1084 (5th Cir.1975) (*en banc*).

to the assimilation of women into the workplace as those generated by more transparent, traditional, and explicit forms of bias. The metamorphosis occurred in a case brought by a woman employed by the Price Waterhouse accounting firm who had been denied partnership on the basis of, among other things, comments in her dossier from some of the firm's male partners that she was "macho" and in need of "a course in charm school." She also was described in that portfolio as "a lady using foul language" and someone who had been "a tough-talking somewhat masculine hard-nosed manager."[43] The Supreme Court ruled that this form of gender stereotyping, if causally linked to the challenged decision, did indeed constitute a form of sex-based discrimination forbidden by Title VII. This ruling, in turn, paved the way for the lower federal courts to begin to recognize that even though Title VII does not prohibit discrimination on the basis of sexual orientation or sexual identity, adverse action taken against male or female employees on the grounds that they behave in an untraditional manner or otherwise do not conform to gender expectations, similarly violates the statutory ban on sex-based bias.[44] And the Supreme Court's appreciation of the impact of sex-stereotyped attitudes traces directly back to Wisdom's visionary dissenting opinion in the Macon newspaper case.

43. *Price Waterhouse v. Hopkins*, 490 U.S. 228,235, 109 S.Ct. 1775, 104 L.Ed.2d 268 (1989).

44. See, for example, *Nichols v. Azteca Restaurant Enterprises, Inc.*, 256 F.2d 864 (9th Cir.2001); *Doe v. City of Belleville, Illinois*, 119 F.3d 563 (7th Cir.1997), vacated and remanded, 523 U.S. 1001, 118 S.Ct. 1183, 140 L.Ed.2d 313 (1998).

15

THE UNSUCCESSFUL CAMPAIGN
TO SAVE THE FIFTH CIRCUIT

In 1869, Congress enacted the first of what would become a series of laws governing the retirement of federal judges. A half-century later, it established the concept of "senior status," which enables a federal district or circuit judge to retire from full-time active service when that judge's combination of age and years of service in the federal judiciary totals at least eighty.[1] Any judge who exercises this option retains his or her judicial position and full salary and is permitted, subject to a few express limitations, to continue to perform as many or as few of the duties of an active judge as he or she is willing and able to undertake.

Three of these limitations are particularly meaningful to the judges. Moreover, they played a crucial role in a struggle for control over the Fifth Circuit that would be more than fifteen years in the resolution. The moment a federal circuit court of appeals judge assumes senior status, he or she is precluded from further participation in *en banc* rehearing of all cases save those on which he or she served as a member of the original panel.[2] Second, no senior judge can serve as chief judge of his or her court.[3] Finally, and most significant with respect to the second

1. 28 U.S.C. 21371(b) (1).
2. 28 U.S.C. §46(c).
3. 28 U.S.C. §45(a) and (d).

of two related conflicts that would engulf the Fifth Circuit in the 1960s and 1970s, a senior judge is disqualified from attending meetings of the circuit's Judicial Council.[4]

On January 15, 1977, nineteen and a half years after being sworn in as a member of the Fifth Circuit, John Minor Wisdom decided to retire from active service and became a senior judge of that court. Although he could have requested a reduced caseload, the prospect of retiring held no interest for him. Instead, he chose to retain his full complement of case assignments. The fact that he declined the opportunity to lighten his caseload is one reflection of the fact that his decision to "go senior" was not based principally on health concerns. The primary motivation was Wisdom's desire to provide the Fifth Circuit with the additional active judgeship that his retirement would produce.[5]

Yet even though he continued to pull his full share of panel assignments, taking senior status did relieve Wisdom of many of the administrative chores associated with being a member of the Judicial Council. Consequently, he now found the time to accept the Supreme Court chief justice's frequent invitation to sit temporarily ("by designation") as a member of another federal circuit court.[6] But as the years progressed and traveling to the site of the appellate arguments became more of a chore than a pleasure, he began to limit his extra–Fifth Circuit assignments to the geographically adjacent circuit. And while sitting as a member of the Eleventh Circuit offered Wisdom the chance to rejoin several colleagues who, prior to October 1, 1981, had been his brethren on the Fifth Circuit, it was, in many ways, a mixed blessing for him. Although he enjoyed the opportunity to influence the development of this new cir-

---

4. 28 U.S.C. §332(a) (3).

5. Robert G. Pugh, *An Interview with the Honorable John Minor Wisdom*, 39 LA. B. J. 254, 257 (1991).

6. See, for example, Wisdom's opinions in *Craig v. M/V Peacock*, 760 F.2d 953, 957 (9th Cir.1985) (Wisdom, J., dissenting) (maritime law case); *Garcia v. Cecos International, Inc.*, 761 F.2d 76 (1st Cir.1985) (jurisdictional issue in environmental law case); *Matter of Providence Journal Co.*, 820 F.2d 1342 (1st Cir.1986); *Smith v. Kelso*, 863 F.2d 1564 (11th Cir.1989) (whether fundamental fairness required severance of one defendant from co-defendants in criminal trial because of alleged conflict of interest); *Brown v. Clarke*, 878 F.2d 627 (2d Cir.1989) (deposit pick-up service constituted branch banking in violation of the restrictions imposed by federal law); *Step-Saver Data Systems, Inc. v. Wyse Technology*, 939 F.2d 91 (3d Cir.1991) (breach of warranties case involving computer software); *Sivard v. Pulaski County*, 959 F.2d 662 (7th Cir.1992) (prisoner's civil rights claim of wrongful detention); *Scott v. Mississippi Department of Corrections*, 961 F.2d 77 (6th Cir.1992) (rejecting Rastafarian inmates' First Amendment claim that prison hair-grooming standard mandating short, neatly cut hair violated their constitutional right to freely exercise their religious beliefs).

cuit's jurisprudence, he never got over the bitter defeat he had suffered as the most vocal opponent of the action that resulted in the creation of the Eleventh Circuit—the partition of the beloved Fifth Circuit on which he had sat for more than two decades.

As far back as 1963, the lethal combination of an expanding population, increased commercial activity in the six states that fell within its jurisdiction, and the burgeoning influx of appeals in school and jury desegregation, voting rights, and other civil rights cases had caused the Fifth Circuit to become the busiest of the nation's federal appellate courts. For the next twenty years, the Fifth Circuit would retain the dubious distinction of having the largest docket of any federal circuit court. This translated to an average caseload per judge more than 40 percent higher than the national average and 11 percent greater than that borne by members of the second most heavily worked federal appellate court, the U.S. Circuit Court for the District of Columbia.[7] Everyone recognized that there were only two ways to change the status quo. Congress could either authorize more judgeships for the Fifth Circuit or divide it into two separate circuits.

In September 1963, Elbert Tuttle, in his role as chief judge of the Fifth Circuit, urged the Judicial Conference of the United States at its semiannual meeting to endorse his proposal for the creation of additional judgeships for his court. The Judicial Conference, the federal judiciary's chief policy-making body and unofficial lobbying representative before Congress, is chaired by the chief justice of the Supreme Court. Its other members are the chief judge of each of the federal circuit courts, a district judge elected from each federal circuit, and the chief judges of two specialized federal courts—the Court of Claims and the Court of Customs and Patent Appeals. Without the support of this group, Tuttle had no chance of persuading Congress to expand the size of the Fifth Circuit.

Although many of his colleagues on the Judicial Conference were sensitive to Tuttle's concern and supportive of his request, others firmly believed that an appellate court could not function effectively and efficiently once it expanded beyond nine members. Proponents of this "Rule of Nine" insisted that exceeding this limit would undermine the court's ability to function as a collegial body, add to the growing burden

7. Deborah J. Barrow and Thomas G. Walker, *A Court Divided: The Fifth Circuit Court of Appeals and the Politics of Judicial Reform* (New Haven: 1988), 4.

of staying current with the opinions issued by the other judges of that court, and produce *en banc* sessions of unwieldy size. And since the Fifth Circuit had expanded from seven to nine members in 1961, subscribers to this tenet believed that the only way to attack the court's caseload problem was to split it into two separate and independent circuits.

The Judicial Conference was not, however, the only or even the most formidable obstacle standing between the Fifth Circuit and congressional authorization of additional judgeships. Any bill authorizing new judgeships would have to pass through the Senate Judiciary Committee before the matter could reach the Senate floor for a vote. And bills did not receive favorable treatment by the committee without the support, or least acquiescence, of its chairman, the senior senator from Mississippi, James O. Eastland. Eastland, who had presided over the Judiciary Committee since 1956, was an unapologetic segregationist who deeply resented the Fifth Circuit's role in spearheading the integration of public and private institutions in his state and region. Consequently, he was hell-bent on doing whatever it took to thwart, or at least retard, that court's exercise of power and influence.

Only months before the issue of additional judgeships surfaced, Senator Eastland had engaged in a separate brief, but highly visible, contretemps with the Fifth Circuit. Right after Fifth Circuit judge Ben Cameron of Mississippi charged that Chief Judge Tuttle and his lieutenant, John Brown, had conspired to pack the composition of Fifth Circuit panels in civil rights cases in order to cook the results in those actions, Eastland very publicly announced his intention to order an investigation into Cameron's allegations.[8] Although Eastland never followed through on this threat, the outburst planted the seeds of discontent with many members of the court. And within a few weeks of his intervention into the alleged court-packing affair, Senator Eastland let Tuttle know in no uncertain terms that the only way a request for additional judges would get past his committee was if it was part of a plan to split the Fifth Circuit along the banks of the Mississippi River.[9]

But though Senator Eastland was certainly the most redoubtable proponent of a court-splitting solution to the Fifth Circuit's emerging caseload crisis, Tuttle quickly learned that the drumbeat for splitting the court already was resonating with more than one member of his own

8. The court-packing controversy and its aftermath are the subject of chapter 9, *supra*.

9. See Letter to Joseph C. Hutcheson, Jr., Richard T. Rives, Jon R. Brown, and John M. Wisdom from Elbert P. Tuttle, March 25, 1964.

court. Only a short time after his appearance before the Judicial Conference, in fact, it became quite apparent that indeed most of Tuttle's Fifth Circuit colleagues were ambivalent about, if not receptive to, the concept of recasting their court into two smaller circuit courts.

Just months after the tempestuous two-day August gathering in Houston that had been called in response to Cameron's charges of panel rigging by Judges Tuttle and Brown, the Fifth Circuit Judicial Council met again in the late fall of 1963. The national Judicial Conference had voted to establish an ad hoc committee to formulate a recommendation on the best way of addressing the Fifth Circuit's growing caseload problem. And the committee wanted the input of the active Fifth Circuit judges. So Tuttle's plan was to forge a consensus at the council meeting that he could then forward to the Judicial Conference's ad hoc committee. But although everyone in attendance at the council meeting agreed that the best way of handling the court's caseload burden was to expand the size of their court, seven of the nine active members, including, ultimately, Tuttle himself, nevertheless were prepared to accept a circuit split if that was the only way of obtaining the much-needed additional manpower.[10]

Only Wisdom and Dick Rives remained unalterably opposed to splitting their court. Their deeply felt and fervently articulated opposition was multileveled. They were desperately concerned that replacing the Fifth Circuit with two independent circuits, each of which would have jurisdiction over a smaller number of states, would significantly impair what Wisdom termed the court's "federalizing" function. Federal appellate judges drawn from a narrow geographical base, he continuously stressed, were less likely to review vigilantly the decisions of local district judges. Moreover, an appellate court that drew its members from a smaller geographical area would likely become increasingly parochial in its perspective since it would be composed of members who were less diverse in their vision, values, and orientation.

But Wisdom and Rives also were motivated by the same political and practical considerations, albeit from the opposite pole of the ideological spectrum, which fueled the movement to split their court. Senator Eastland wanted the court to be split along the Mississippi River, creating thereby a two-state western circuit and a four-state eastern circuit. This gravely troubled Wisdom and Rives because the more progressive

10. Barrow and Walker, A Court Divided: The Fifth Circuit Court of Appeals and the Politics of Judicial Reform, 30.

judges from Texas and Louisiana would be split apart from their typically more conservative colleagues from Florida, Georgia, Mississippi, and Alabama. The pair feared that isolating Wisdom and the few other members of the liberal wing of the court in one western circuit with jurisdiction over a significantly reduced number of states would dramatically curtail the influence of that court. They also were concerned that this sort of split would yield an eastern circuit in which Tuttle and Rives perennially would be outvoted by those judges who were disinclined to continue this half of "The Four's" pattern of aggressive enforcement of civil rights law.[11]

Additionally, John Brown was in line to become the chief judge of the Fifth Circuit in three years, when Tuttle, at age seventy, would be compelled to retire as chief judge. If the circuit were to be split in the manner favored by Senator Eastland, Brown's influence would be dramatically diminished since he would preside over a court whose jurisdiction extended only over Texas and Louisiana. And the new chief judge of the four-state circuit, on the other hand, would be the Fifth Circuit's most conservative member, Walter Gewin of Alabama.

One possible compromise, of course, would have been to place Mississippi in the western unit, thereby creating two equally sized circuits, each with jurisdiction over three states. But this was a nonstarter for both camps. Wisdom and Rives were opposed to any form of split. And retaining Mississippi in the circuit that was under the administrative control of Tuttle and the intellectual leadership of Wisdom was anathema to Eastland. The senator would never forget the pivotal role that Wisdom had played in desegregating the flagship university in Eastland's home state in the case brought by James Meredith. Eastland simply could not countenance the prospect of his state remaining subject to the authority of such a court.

The Judicial Conference met in mid-March 1964, to take up the matter of the Fifth Circuit's caseload. By a narrow three-vote margin, a majority of the nineteen-member Conference voted to support dividing the

---

11. "Dick Rives felt very keenly that it was a ploy by Eastland to break up the influence that he, Tuttle, Brown, and I had on a small court. The ploy was by dividing the circuit and increasing the number of judges for each new circuit and have Tuttle and Rives in one circuit and Brown and Wisdom in the other, and then have additional judges. Thereby our influence would be undermined." Interview of Judge John Minor Wisdom, New Orleans, Louisiana, May 28, 1985, reported in Barrow and Walker, *A Court Divided: The Fifth Circuit Court of Appeals and the Politics of Judicial Reform*, 71.

Fifth Circuit into two circuits located east and west of the Mississippi River. The fact that their position had been rejected by such a narrow margin suggested to Rives and Wisdom that the die had not been irrevocably cast and that they might still convince Congress, the ultimate decision-maker, not to travel down this road. In fact, the conference's decision served only to spur the pair on to a decidedly more aggressive all-out campaign to save the existing configuration of their court.

As the Fifth Circuit was scheduled to hold a Judicial Council meeting in Fort Worth on May 11, Wisdom and Rives decided to jump-start their anti-split campaign with a request that the Fifth Circuit withdraw its prior recommendation concerning the creation of new judgeships.[12] At that Fort Worth meeting, Wisdom drafted and tendered a resolution that no action be taken to divide the Fifth Circuit until the Judicial Conference had given further study to the issue of circuit court caseload on a national, rather than a piecemeal, basis. Seven of the Fifth Circuit's nine active members attended this council meeting; ill health prevented Joe Hutcheson from attending and Ben Cameron had passed away five weeks earlier. But after extended discussion, Wisdom's resolution was not supported by anyone other than its two sponsors.[13]

This momentary setback, however, did not deter Wisdom and Rives. They vowed to go forward with their crusade and to enlist the help of prominent individuals who, they believed, would help convince Congress to support their cause. Over the course of his decade of participation in the political arena at the local, regional, and national levels, and continuing through his seven-year tenure on the federal bench, Wisdom had cultivated an extensive network of relationships with high-profile members of the legal academy, judiciary, legislature, and media. And Rives also was not without friends in high places. So it was both easy and natural for the duo to mobilize an enthusiastic regiment of influential opinion-makers to mount a nationwide public and private educational campaign in response to the Judicial Conference's recommendation to sever the Fifth Circuit.

Leading lights of the law professoriate, such as Paul Freund of Harvard, Walter Gellhorn of Columbia, Charles Alan Wright of the University of Texas, Delmar Karlen of New York University, and Dean

12. Letter to Elbert P. Tuttle and Joseph C. Hutcheson, Jr., John R. Brown, and John M. Wisdom from Richard T. Rives, March 23, 1964.

13. Minutes of Meeting of Judicial Council, U.S. Court of Appeals, May 11, 1964, Fort Worth, Texas, at 1-2, and attached copy of Wisdom resolution.

Joseph O'Meara of Notre Dame, as well as influential members of the bar such as Bernard Segal of Philadelphia, jumped on the bandwagon. They began a well orchestrated letter-writing campaign directed at members of Congress, newspapers, and others urging the preservation of the Fifth Circuit.[14] In addition, former New Orleanian J. Skelly Wright, now a judge on the D.C. Circuit Court of Appeals, two members of the Judicial Conference, Judge Simon Sobeloff of the Fourth Circuit and Charles Fahy of the D.C. Circuit, as well as District Judge Frank Johnson, Jr., vigorously engaged in their own anti-split lobbying efforts.[15]

Wisdom also made sure his own voice was heard among this chorus of opposition. On May 29, 1964, he sent a lengthy letter to Supreme Court chief justice Earl Warren, the chair of the U.S. Judicial Conference. In it, Wisdom beseeched the Judicial Conference "to take a hard second look at the proposal to split the Fifth Circuit before putting in motion irreversible processes." Respectfully suggesting that the conference "had not faced up to the dimensions of the problem," he emphasized that "fractionating" his court would "lead to parochialistic courts inadequate to perform their federalizing function." He reiterated his view that "the best exercise of this federal function would call ideally for a court consisting of judges with widely disparate backgrounds who are familiar with regional and local thinking but completely insulated from the prejudices and influence of the region and the community." He advised the chief justice that "a single court drawn from all six states would come closer than two courts to performing the federal function."[16]

Wisdom also suggested that other large circuits with heavy dockets, such as the Second and Ninth Circuits, eventually would be targeted for division, at which time these same concerns over insularity and the problems it generates would resurface. Finally, he took direct aim at what he called the "taboo" of the Rule of Nine, supplementing his inherently persuasive advocacy with equal doses of comparative analysis

14. See Letters to Harrison A. Williams, Jr., Philip A. Hart, and Clifford P. Case from Walter Gellhorn, May 14, 1964; Charles A. Wright, Split Court Area Opposed, Letter to the Editor, New York Times, July 10, 1964, 28, col. 6; Letter to John M. Wisdom from Charles A. Wright, June 20, 1964; Letter to John M. Wisdom from Delmar Karlen, June 17, 1964; Letter to John M. Wisdom from Paul Freund, July 4, 1964; Letter to Richard T. Rives from Joseph O'Meara, August 14, 1964; Letter to Bernard Segal from John M. Wisdom, September 1, 1964.

15. See Letter to Richard T. Rives from J. Skelly Wright, June 2, 1964; Letter to John M. Wisdom from Simon E. Sobeloff, June 3, 1964; Letter to Robert F. Kennedy from Frank M. Johnson, Jr., May 27, 1964.

16. Letter to Earl Warren from John M. Wisdom, May 29, 1964, at 2.

and statistical data. He reported that the English Court of Appeal consisted of twelve judges, the English Court of Criminal Appeal was composed of thirty-four or more judges, the World Court comprised seventeen judges, the U.S. Tax Court contained sixteen members, and the intermediate appellate courts of Texas, New York, and California, had thirty-three, twenty-four, and twenty-one judges, respectively. Based on all this evidence, Wisdom concluded, "I fail to see what all the argument is about."[17]

Precisely one month later, Wisdom received an extremely favorable reply from the chief justice. Earl Warren acknowledged that he shared Wisdom's concern with the proposal to break up the Fifth Circuit and that he was "distressed when the Judicial Conference gave its approval to the division." In fact, the chief justice continued, "I argued against it and raised some of the precise points you mention in your letter. I believe there is no particular virtue in fixing the limit for courts of appeals at nine judges. Historically, there is no reason for it."[18]

Meanwhile, Wisdom also had dispatched a copy of that May 29 letter to Supreme Court justice Hugo Black, the justice assigned supervisory authority over the Fifth Circuit. Within a week, he had received a reply stating that Justice Black had conferred with the chief justice several times about the proposal to split the Fifth Circuit and expressing Black's hope that "something can be done to frustrate the plan."[19] And a little over three months later, Justice Black sent Wisdom another short note, stating that he had "talked to several judges and have reason to believe that the campaign of you, Judge Rives and Judge Brown is being felt."[20] Then, two weeks later, Wisdom received a note from Supreme Court justice William Brennan informing Wisdom that "from what I hear around this building your enclosures have done the trick at the Conference. My sincere congratulations!"[21]

Buoyed by both these expressions of support and with an eye toward the Judicial Conference's upcoming meeting in late September, Wisdom accelerated his lobbying efforts. Reaching out to key legislators, he relayed copies of his May 29 letter to his longtime friend Senator Hugh Scott of Pennsylvania and to Congressman Emanuel Celler. Celler was

17. Ibid., 3.
18. Letter to John M. Wisdom from Earl Warren, June 29, 1964.
19. Letter to John M. Wisdom from Hugo L. Black, June 5, 1964.
20. Letter to John M. Wisdom from Hugo L. Black, September 9, 1964.
21. Letter to John M. Wisdom from William J. Brennan, Jr., September 24, 1964.

a pivotal player in this unfolding drama. As chairman of the House Judiciary Committee, he wielded incalculable influence over the House committee that would have first crack at the bill court-splitting bill.[22]

Wisdom also determined that it was important to reach out to the top leaders in the Kennedy administration. Hoping that they would come to the aid of what he was now calling the "Rives-Wisdom Project," Wisdom dispatched copies of the May 29 letter to Attorney General Robert F. Kennedy and Assistant Attorney General Burke Marshall.[23] Wisdom already was well acquainted with Marshall and held him in very high esteem. As chief of the Justice Department's Civil Rights Division, Marshall had argued before Wisdom in several civil rights cases, including James Meredith's suit to enroll at the segregated University of Mississippi.[24]

Marshall's prompt reply exceeded even Wisdom's expectations, assuring him that "you have the Department completely persuaded."[25] Wisdom also received a note from Nicholas Katzenbach, who recently had replaced Robert Kennedy as acting attorney general when Kennedy decided to run for the Senate from New York. In the letter, Katzenbach informed Wisdom that he had spoken against the split at the Judicial Conference's September meeting.[26]

So, slowly but surely, Rives and Wisdom began to reap the sweet fruits of their intense labors. As Wisdom reported in a follow-up letter to Chief Justice Warren, he and Rives had succeeded in converting Fifth Circuit colleagues Joe Hutcheson and John Brown to their cause and were still working on convincing Elbert Tuttle, "stout Presbyterian that he is and conscientious chief judge that he is," to abandon his "moral compulsion not to go back on a proposal he initiated."[27]

When Wisdom and Rives received a polite, but noncommittal response from Congressman Celler, Rives decided to forward a copy of the congressman's note to all of his Fifth Circuit colleagues. Rives's cover letter urged his colleagues to forget their past differences and

22. Letters to Emanuel Celler, Hugh Scott, Simon E. Sobeloff, and Frank M. Johnson from John M. Wisdom, June 8, 1964.

23. See Letter to Elbert P. Tuttle and John R. Brown from John M. Wisdom, June 24, 1964.

24. Letters to Robert F. Kennedy and Burke Marshall from John M. Wisdom, June 17, 1964.

25. Letter to John M. Wisdom from Burke Marshall, September 16, 1964.

26. Letter to John M. Wisdom from Nicholas deB. Katzenbach, undated.

27. Letter to Earl Warren from John M. Wisdom, September 8, 1964, at 2.

suggested that Chief Justice Warren and Associate Justice Black's announced opposition to the splitting plan demonstrated that it was "now
obvious that the presently proposed split of our Circuit is in diametric
opposition to our getting additional Judges in the foreseeable future."[28]
If the Rives-Wisdom letter-writing blitz previously had not been common knowledge around the court, the cat now surely was out of the bag.
And the news of these developments was not well received by most of
Wisdom's colleagues.

The following day, Judge Walter Gewin of Alabama dashed off a
harshly worded response to Rives's letter, expressing his regret that "a
campaign has been, or is being conducted to nullify the recommendation of our own Judicial Council." Gewin bitterly complained that Rives
and Wisdom had sought the aid "of people outside of the Circuit, dis-
associated with it, and who have no responsibility for the performance
of our duties, to decide what should be done about the crowded condition of our docket." The issue having been fairly and fully ventilated at
the Judicial Council meeting, Gewin maintained, "we should abide by
the decision of the majority of the members of our Court and should
not make a national issue out of the matter."[29]

Judge Warren Jones, the court's unofficial poet laureate, chimed in
with a briefer and assuredly tarter riposte. With tongue firmly planted
in cheek, he wrote: "Judge Rives says we should forget our past differences which means, I am sure, that the majority should join the
minority."[30]

Suddenly back on the defensive, Wisdom felt compelled to respond
to his two colleagues. While wanting, where possible, to assuage hurt
feelings, he was not one to retreat from a principled position. And opposition to the circuit split was, to him, a matter of profound principle
on several levels. So he opened his letter by invoking "a truism to justify this letter and some of my activities this summer. Nothing is settled
until it is settled right." He insisted that both he and Rives had advised
their brethren in unambiguous terms at the Judicial Council meeting
"that we regarded ourselves as free agents to oppose division of the Fifth
Circuit." Then, after reiterating his reasons for opposing the split, he
solicited their present views on the matter. He added, however, that if

28. Letter to all Judges of the Fifth Circuit from Richard T. Rives, August 20, 1964.
29. Letter to All Fifth Circuit Judges from Walter P. Gewin, August 21, 1964.
30. Letter to all Circuit Judges of the Fifth Circuit from Warren L. Jones, August 21, 1964.

a majority of his brethren continued to support the split, he would not back down. Rather, he promised, "I propose to appeal to the Judicial Conference of the United States."[31]

The responses to Wisdom's inquiry confirmed his suspicion that only Hutcheson and Brown were aligned with him and Rives in absolute opposition to any attempt to subdivide their court. On the other hand, with the late Ben Cameron's seat not yet filled, the eight-member court now was split right down the middle, a significantly less imposing obstacle than what Rives and Wisdom originally had encountered. So true to his word, Wisdom sent a letter on September 10 to Chief Justice Warren formally requesting that the Judicial Conference reconsider its decision to support dividing the Fifth Circuit.[32] But out of respect for their chief, Tuttle, and to avoid any appearance of pitting themselves against him, Wisdom and Rives declined the invitation to attend the meeting. Instead, Wisdom requested that Warren allow Professor Charles Alan Wright, "as a completely impartial authority in the field of federal courts," to offer his analysis of the proposed court reorganization.[33]

Like his more senior colleagues Brown and Wisdom, Griffin Bell of Atlanta, who had been appointed to the Fifth Circuit by President John F. Kennedy at the age of forty-two, was pragmatic and politically astute. He also enjoyed a reputation as a skilled negotiator adept at the art of compromise. But Bell also shared Wisdom's forcefulness of personality, a fact that, because of Bell's generally conservative ideology, tended to place him and Wisdom in adversarial positions on many of the critical issues before the court. In the midst of the circuit-splitting controversy, Bell chose to float an idea designed both to build a consensus among his colleagues and to offer some short-term relief to their docket crisis.

It had become increasingly obvious to many, if not most, members of the Fifth Circuit that the conflict over the proposed splitting of the circuit had escalated to a point where neither side had much room to maneuver. With Senator Eastland insisting upon the split as the price for obtaining new judges and Congressman Celler equally steadfast in his opposition to the split because of its foreseeable impact on civil rights

31. Letter to all Circuit Judges of the Fifth Circuit from John M. Wisdom, August 27, 1964.
32. Letter to Earl Warren from John M. Wisdom, September 10, 1964.
33. Letter to Earl Warren from John M. Wisdom, September 9, 1964, at 4; Letter to J. Skelly Wright from John M. Wisdom, September 10, 1964; Letter to John R. Brown from John M. Wisdom, September 15, 1964.

decisions, the opposing sides were quickly moving toward a stalemate that would threaten, at least in the short run, any prospect of obtaining the judgeships everyone agreed was essential.[34]

To avert that exceedingly undesirable result, Bell suggested that his colleagues rally around a provisional solution. He proposed that the Fifth Circuit Judicial Council recommend to the Judicial Conference that the conference sponsor legislation creating temporary judgeships equal to the number of Fifth Circuit judges who were eligible to retire but who had not yet chosen to take senior status. Under the terms of this plan, each of these temporary positions would be eliminated upon the actual retirement of each senior-eligible judge.[35]

More than anyone, Tuttle was acutely aware of the political forces that had lined up in support of the plan to hold the additional judge-ships hostage to the splitting of his court. As far back as March of that year, he had received reliable confirmation of statements attributed to Senator Eastland that the only way additional judges would be obtained for the Deep South states was to divide the Fifth Circuit along the lines east and west of the Mississippi River.[36] That was precisely why he grudgingly supported a proposal that he otherwise would have bitterly opposed. He also was keenly distressed by the balkanizing effect this controversy was having on his court. So, only too eager to support any reasonable attempt at compromise, Tuttle immediately endorsed Bell's interim proposal.[37] Walter Gewin and Warren Jones also jumped on board, although Judge Jones opined that the issue had become so polar-ized and divisive that even this conciliatory effort "would probably be futile."[38] Even the four opponents of the split—Wisdom, Rives, Brown, and Hutcheson—endorsed the Bell proposal, although they clearly and

34. Celler often publicly couched his opposition in terms of a desire to avoid piecemeal re-sponses to a nationwide problem. For example, Joseph O'Meara, dean of the Notre Dame Law School, informed Judge Rives in August 1964 that O'Meara had received a memo from a friend that stated that Representative Celler "is very much opposed to the division of the Fifth Circuit Court of Appeals before a nationwide study of the status of all Courts of Appeals is completed." Letter to Judge Richard T. Rives from Joseph O'Meara, August 14, 1964.

35. Letter to All Fifth Circuit Judges from Griffin B. Bell, September 14, 1964.

36. Letter to Joseph C. Hutcheson, Jr., Richard T. Rives, Jon R. Brown, and John M. Wisdom from Elbert P. Tuttle, March 25, 1964.

37. Letter to All Circuit Judges of the Fifth Circuit from Elbert P. Tuttle, September 16, 1964.

38. Letter to All Fifth Circuit Judges from Walter P. Gewin, September 17, 1964; Letter to All Fifth Circuit Judges from Warren L. Jones, September 16, 1964.

unambiguously reaffirmed their continuing commitment to campaign against the circuit split.[39] Eventually, the proposal garnered the court's unanimous support, a fact that Wisdom immediately relayed to the Judicial Conference.[40]

To the consternation of Senator Eastland and his supporters, the Rives-Wisdom project yielded its greatest victory to date at the September 24, 1964, meeting of the Judicial Conference. The conference not only tabled action on the original court reorganization plan, but voted to support the Bell proposal for four temporary Fifth Circuit judgeships.[41] Wisdom and Rives, of course, welcomed not only the endorsement of additional judges but, perhaps more important, this extended opportunity to continue their "project" against the split. Their communications blitz, it now appeared, was paying dividends, at least with a majority of the members of the Judicial Conference.

When he learned of the conference's decision from Wright, Professor Paul Freund of Harvard Law School, a legendary figure whom Wisdom had enlisted to aid in the anti-splitting campaign, dropped Wisdom a congratulatory note. "This," Freund observed, "is good news indeed, and it derives in large measure, I am sure, from the persuasiveness and above all the tactfulness shown in your communications on the subject."[42] In a similar vein, a handwritten "Dear John" note to Wisdom from Supreme Court Justice Tom Clark acknowledged that "in your usual effective way you have 'demolished' those favoring the split."[43] Former New Orleanian Skelly Wright also offered his felicitations, agreeing that Wisdom's "persuasive letters to all the members of the Judicial Conference were most effective in bringing about the desired result."[44] And Wright's D.C. Circuit colleague, Judge Charles Fahy, offered perhaps the most authoritative insight. Fahy was a member of

39. Letter to Elbert P. Tuttle from John R. Brown, September 16, 1964; Letter to All the Judges of the Fifth Circuit Court of Appeals from John M. Wisdom, September 17, 1964; Letter to Elbert P. Tuttle from Joseph C. Hutcheson, Jr., September 17, 1964.

40. Letter to Members of the Judicial Conference of the United States from John M. Wisdom, September 17, 1964.

41. Editorial, "U.S. Fifth Circuit Court of Appeals Must Be Enlarged," *Houston Chronicle*, November 19, 1964, 6, col. 1; "The Week In Law: Court Logjam," *New York Times*, November 1, 1964, E5, col. 1; Letter to John R. Brown from Richard H. Chambers, October 29, 1964; Letter to G. W. Foster, Jr., from John M. Wisdom, October 17, 1964.

42. Letter to John M. Wisdom from Paul A. Freund, September 29, 1964.

43. Letter to John M. Wisdom from Tom Clark, October 5, 1964.

44. Letter to John M. Wisdom from J. Skelly Wright, October 21, 1964.

the Judicial Conference and he, along with fellow Conference member Fourth Circuit judge Simon Sobeloff, had been the principal spear carriers for the anti-split effort at the conference meeting. "I am glad to have been of help," Fahy related, "but I must say your own arguments against the division played perhaps a decisive role at the last testing of the matter at the Conference. The Fifth is a great Circuit and should not be mangled, certainly not without a broader study of the whole circuit problem."[45]

The Judicial Conference's decision also did not escape the notice of the popular media. Wisdom gleefully circulated to his already considerable and continuously expanding list of correspondents an editorial in the *Washington Post* that mirrored the essence of his own opposition to the proposed split. "No one questions the need for more judges in what is now the Fifth Circuit," the newspaper observed, "but there is opposition to appellate courts of more than nine members." Nevertheless, the editorial acknowledged, "some of the Circuit Courts are now working with more than nine judges since their retired judges continue to serve." The *Post* further subscribed to the argument tendered by opponents of the reorganization plan that the reduced Fifth Circuit "would have less inclination than the present court to follow the Supreme Court in civil rights cases" and, "even more important, there is a strong demand for maintaining circuit courts as broad regional tribunals." For all of these reasons, the editorial concluded that "Congress should give the Fifth Circuit the six additional judges it needs, without splitting the court . . . as an experiment to determine whether a large tribunal is manageable." Moreover, the paper proposed, "if the larger court should prove unmanageable, it could be divided later, but the great advantage of maintaining circuits that are national in their outlook and loyalties should not be sacrificed for the imaginary advantage of holding to a maximum of nine."[46]

On June 7, 1965, nearly nine months after Bell initially had placed his compromise proposal before his Fifth Circuit colleagues, a bill creating forty-five new federal judgeships, including Bell's proposed four temporary slots on the Fifth Circuit, was approved by Senator Eastland's Senate Judiciary Committee.[47] The full Senate followed suit on June 30.

45. Letter to John M. Wisdom from Charles Fahy, October 31, 1964.
46. Editorial, "Overburdened Courts," *Washington Post*, October 5, 1964, A-14, col. 1.
47. Edgar Poe, "Committee OK's Judgeship Bill," *New Orleans Times-Picayune*, June 8, 1965, 1, col. 2.

Simultaneously, a bill authorizing the same four temporary Fifth Circuit slots slowly made its way through the House chamber, successfully clearing the House Judiciary Committee and finally receiving a positive vote on the floor of the House on March 2, 1966.[48] When President Lyndon Johnson signed the Omnibus Judgeship Bill later that month, the Fifth Circuit had its four new provisional slots while, at least temporarily, dodging the realignment bullet.

A few months earlier, the Wisdom-Rives anti-split campaign had received good news on another front. In early August 1964, a bit more than six weeks before the Judicial Conference's September 24 meeting, the American Bar Association's (ABA) Section of Judicial Administration recommended the undertaking of a study of the challenges facing all of the federal appellate courts across the country. The ABA formally approved the recommendation in May of the next year and commissioned the American Bar Foundation to prepare the report. This was precisely the type of systemic review that Wisdom and Rives had insisted was a necessary precursor to the adoption of any thoughtful and reasoned solution to the caseload problem. Moreover, it meant that any potential division of their court would be postponed at least for the time it would take to carry out such a study and assess its findings and conclusions. And, as it turned out, the Bar Foundation's study was not released for four years.[49]

But in the midst of these positive developments, other events were combining to dramatically recast both the personality and prevailing ideology of the court, which posed a new challenge to Wisdom and Rives. Congress's 1966 authorization of four new positions, in tandem with the death or retirement of four of the court's active judges, created the potential for effecting a fundamental change in the court's perspective on the reorganization controversy.

The late Ben Cameron had been replaced by former governor James P. Coleman. Coleman had preceded Ross Barnett as governor of Mississippi and then had represented Barnett in his criminal contempt proceedings before the Fifth Circuit from 1962 to 1964. Former chief judge Joe Hutcheson, by then the nation's oldest living federal judge, had retired in November 1964 after thirty-three years of service. President Johnson named then–district judge Homer Thornberry of Aus-

48. "House Approves New Judgeships," *New York Times*, March 3, 1966, 24, col. 1.
49. American Bar Foundation, *Accommodating the Workload of the U.S. Courts of Appeals, Report of Recommendations* (1968).

tin, Texas, to replace Hutcheson. Finally, just a month before President Johnson signed the 1966 judgeship bill, both Rives and Jones assumed senior status.

As a consequence of these personnel changes, the five remaining members of the Fifth Circuit—Tuttle, Wisdom, Bell, Brown, and Gewin—were about to be joined by eight new colleagues. Clearly, the future of the Fifth Circuit's view on court division lay in the hands of its newest members. The five veterans were seemingly unalterably divided on this question. Wisdom and Brown remained opposed to division while Bell and Gewin were prepared to accept it in exchange for a permanent commitment of new judgeships. Chief Judge Tuttle, although naturally sympathetic to Wisdom's position, consistently had insisted on adhering to the stance taken by the majority of his colleagues. Moreover, he continued to believe that the possibility of retaining the new judgeships was tied to acquiescing to the split. Nevertheless, the newly reshaped court's consensus position would remain uncertain until the new members had been confirmed and had staked out their positions on this critical issue.

Adding to the dislocations generated by this seismic shift in the court's composition was the announcement in the middle of the summer of 1967 that, having reached age seventy, Tuttle was stepping down as chief judge of the Fifth Circuit. The man who had spearheaded the procedural innovations that played such a decisive role in the expeditious handling of civil rights claims in the 1960s, and whose unquestioned integrity and sense of fairness had kept the deep emotional and ideological divisions generated by those civil rights claims from irreparably cleaving the court, was now about to be replaced by his longtime deputy, John Brown. Wisdom, like nearly all of his colleagues, sincerely regretted Tuttle's forced relinquishment of the administrative leadership of the court. At the same time, however, he certainly hoped that Tuttle might now, finally, feel liberated from the constraints he believed that his position as chief imposed on his freedom to speak out against the splitting of the Fifth Circuit.

Brown, on the other hand, felt no such compunction against urging both the expansion in size and retention of the six-state composition of the Fifth Circuit. In 1968, Congress passed and President Johnson signed another Omnibus Judgeship Bill that made permanent the four temporary Fifth Circuit slots it had authorized in 1966. This statute also created two more judgeships for the Fifth Circuit, thereby swelling its active roster to fifteen. And once again, as in 1966, there was no linkage to court division. Nevertheless, Wisdom was keenly aware that the threat to his court had not completely disappeared. The ABA study of circuit court realignment that had been commissioned in 1964 was finally completed in 1968 and had concluded that increasing the number of judges in the existing circuits was a more acceptable response to the docket overcrowding problem than increasing the number of circuit courts. At the same time, however, the authors were unable to confect a workable strategy to deal with the many complex issues associated with this systemic problem. This meant, effectively, that the ball was now back in the Judicial Conference's court.

In 1971, at its March meeting, the Judicial Conference agreed to recommend that Congress authorize the appointment of another blue ribbon panel to conduct another study of the viability of a circuit court division plan. The conference also decided, however, to remove itself from further involvement in this controversy, announcing that it would thereafter let the circuit courts speak directly for themselves on the matter.[50] Widely divergent bills moved slowly and contentiously through both houses of Congress, culminating, eventually in a 1972 enactment that established a sixteen-member Commission on Revision of the Federal Court Appellate System.[51] This statute directed the commission to conduct a six-month study and to submit its recommendations to Congress, the president, and the chief justice of the Supreme Court by December 1, 1973. It also charged the commission with conducting a second-phase investigation into additional modifications to the structure or internal procedures of the federal appellate courts that would help solve the caseload problem. This secondary report was due by September 21, 1974.

As part of its first-phase deliberative process, the Commission on Revision (chaired by Senator Roman Hruska of Nebraska) held a series of ten hearings at various locations across the country, including four within the Fifth Circuit in Houston, New Orleans, Jackson, and Jacksonville.[52] At the hearing held in the Fifth Circuit building in New Orleans on August 22, 1973, Wisdom was one of several witnesses.

50. Barrow and Walker, A Court Divided: The Fifth Circuit Court of Appeals and the Politics of Judicial Reform, 156.

51. Pub.L. 92–489, 28 U.S.C. §41, 86 Stat. 807 (1972).

52. Commission on Revision of the Federal Court Appellate System, Hearings: First Phase, August-October, 1973, at i.

In his prepared statement, he reiterated his view that the proposed reorganization of his court was a simplistic and ultimately illusory response to a multidimensional problem that deserved and demanded a multifaceted solution. He proposed a thoroughgoing revision of the entire appellate court system, including the possible realignment of the circuits *on a national scale* to correct the present imbalance among the circuits. But, he urged, "carving up the Fifth Circuit to meet a six-months' deadline provides neither a short-range nor middle-range solution of the root problem. Worse, it is a dangerous step toward proliferation of the circuits that is destructive of the Federal circuit courts' role in the national polity."[53]

The following day, the Hruska Commission members met in the federal courthouse in Jackson, Mississippi, and heard from a contingent of Fifth Circuit judges who offered their boldest declaration yet of support for splitting their court. Two days in advance of this hearing, Walter Gewin had circulated a letter to every member of the court announcing that he would testify before the commission in Jackson along with several of his colleagues. The letter also contained a copy of a statement supporting circuit realignment that already had been, or soon would be, endorsed by Judges Bell, Godbold, Dyer, Simpson, Morgan, Coleman, and Clark. Gewin ended his letter with an invitation for the non-signers to add their names to the statement that he intended to present to the members of the commission.[54]

Once again, the battle lines within the court had been drawn. With but one exception, Judge Paul Roney of Florida, every judge from the four "eastern" states had aligned himself with Gewin's pro-split declaration. Not one judge from Louisiana or Texas had either signed or been asked to sign the statement. This formally captioned "Statement With Reference to Circuit Realignment," or as Brown caustically labeled it, "The Manifesto from the East," declared that the court was "geographically too large and that 15 Judges is definitely 6 too many."[55] "Jumboism," it continued, "has no place in the Federal Court Appel-

53. Commission on Revision of the Federal Court Appellate System, *Hearings: First Phase, August-October, 1973,* at 354.

54. Letter to All Fifth Circuit Judges from Walter P. Gewin, August 21, 1973.

55. Hearings Before the Subcommittee on Improvements in Judicial Machinery of the Committee on the Judiciary, U.S. Senate, 93 Cong., 2d Sess. on S. 2988, S. 2989, and S. 2990, Part 1, Statement of Chief Judge John R. Brown, September 24, 1974, at 78; Text of Statement With Reference To Circuit Realignment, at 1.

late System."[56] Then, after explaining why a fifteen-member court was administratively and functionally inefficient, the manifesto landed a broadside directly at the anti-split argument preeminently and consistently associated with Wisdom. "Some have expressed the fear that any remedy is objectionable. This fear seems to be based upon the concept that any remedy which may be adopted will result in parochialism, provincialism and a lack of cross-pollination amongst Judges of different backgrounds which will seriously interfere with the court's traditional role as a national court. The undersigned Judges reject out of hand this expression of fear."[57]

Not only did the manifesto reject Wisdom's rationale "out of hand," it also included a list of each judge's retirement eligibility date. And the unarticulated, but unavoidable message behind the dissemination of this information was that Wisdom, along with Bryan Simpson, was immediately eligible to take senior status. Wisdom took offense at what he deemed a gratuitous personal attack. And, as always, he was quick to respond to this challenge to his judgment and integrity. He drafted and submitted a supplemental statement to the Hruska Commission designed expressly "to rebut the circuit-dividers."[58] He summarily dismissed their reliance on the Rule of Nine, chastising them for being "bound hand and foot to the Pythagorean mystique in the number '9.'"[59] Wisdom also argued that by ignoring the impact of the explosion of federal legislation in the 1960s and early 1970s and its attendant "mushrooming federal question litigation involving new areas of the law," the "circuit-dividers who fancy the notion that splitting the Fifth Circuit will give temporary relief will always be one step behind the litigants—unless the Fifth Circuit is to be shattered into bits."[60] Finally, with reference to the manifesto, Wisdom charged that his brethren to the East "had scaled new heights of unreality" in ignoring the inescapable trend of continuously increased filings in the Fifth and other circuit courts.[61]

56. Text of Statement with Reference to Circuit Realignment, at 3.

57. Ibid.

58. Letter to Robert Barnett, Jack Weiss, and John Buckley, Jr., from Judge John M. Wisdom, September 20, 1973.

59. Supplemental Statement of Judge John Minor Wisdom, September 19, 1973, at 3.

60. Ibid., 4.

61. Ibid.

This public display of the court's bitter internecine discord over re-organization made it abundantly evident to Wisdom that it was time to reenergize his anti-split campaign. He believed that the statement by his colleagues from the four eastern states was "an Eastland-engineered maneuver" and feared that the commission's hearings "were designed as window dressing" for a preordained political decision to split the Fifth Circuit. Moreover, with Rives now on senior status, the burden of leading this effort fell primarily on his shoulders. As he despairingly reported in a letter to three of his former law clerks, "I am about the only judge on our Court who is still actively fighting against splitting the Fifth." Wisdom also confided to them his severe disappointment with John Brown's lack of leadership on the anti-division front. "'Buster' [a nickname Wisdom and his law clerks derived from the popular shoe brand character "Buster Brown"] has been all wind, no fury, and collapsed like a pricked balloon at the Commission's last hearing in Jacksonville."[62] So Wisdom reopened his extensive mailing list and immediately, and widely, circulated copies of his original and supplemental statements to the commission.

On December 18, 1973, the Hruska Commission delivered its report on circuit court reorganization to Congress, the president, and Chief Justice Burger. The report recommended the division of the Fifth Circuit into a new Fifth Circuit composed only of three of the four western states—Alabama, Georgia, and Florida—and the creation of an Eleventh Circuit that would include Texas, Louisiana, and Mississippi.[63] The commission also offered two alternative schemes in the event that Congress declined to accept its primary recommendation. Either of these options represented, in the commission's view, a "significant improvement over the status quo." The first alternative was to divide the Fifth Circuit into Eastern and Western Circuits, with the Eastern Circuit comprising the four Fifth Circuit states located east of the Mississippi River (Mississippi, Alabama, Georgia, and Florida) and the Western Circuit consisting of the remaining two states—Texas and Louisiana—supplemented by the addition of Arkansas from the Eighth Circuit. Alternative number 2 would simply divide the Fifth Circuit along the Mississippi River, creating a four-state Eastern Circuit and a two-state (plus the Canal

62. Letter to Robert Barnett, Jack Weiss, and John Buckley, Jr., from Judge John M. Wisdom, September 20, 1973, at 2.

63. The plan also called for the Eleventh Circuit to include the Canal Zone.

Zone) Western Circuit. The commission's report affirmatively declined to express any preference between these two options.[64]

After a decade-long valiant campaign against the move to split the Fifth Circuit, Wisdom and his allies had suffered an anticipated, but nonetheless serious setback. Yet Wisdom remained steadfast in his opposition to any attempt to reorganize the Fifth Circuit and was far from ready to throw in the towel. Within days of receiving a copy of the commission report, Wisdom wrote a seething letter to Professor Leo Levin, the commission's executive director.

Wisdom began by unleashing his fury at the suggestion that the name of the court on which he had served for seventeen years be changed. "I am proud of the history of the Court of Appeals for the Fifth Circuit," he affirmed, "and the body of law our Court has developed. I am sure that all of my brothers take equal pride in our Court; each of us regards only with repugnance the mere thought of changing the name of the court on which he serves from the 'Fifth Circuit' to the 'Eleventh Circuit.'"[65] Then, in his most preceptorial tone, Wisdom provided the law professor with a history lesson. The commission, he charged, had "overlooked or ignored" the "significant historical fact . . . that from the time when the memory of man runneth not to the contrary New Orleans has been the headquarters of the Fifth Circuit. The present Circuit was constituted by the Act of July 23, 1866. As far as I can ascertain, the office of the Clerk of the Court of Appeals for the Fifth Circuit and the circuit library have always been in New Orleans."[66] Finally, Wisdom underscored that his objections were not limited to the renaming of his court. "Please do not conclude from this letter," he assured Levin, "that I am reconciled in the slightest to division of the Fifth Circuit. I am still hopeful that Congress will not tolerate the Circuit's being ripped in two when it discovers that the bisection will not bring even temporary relief."[67]

But as Wisdom began to gear up for the next phase of his tilt against the pro-reorganization forces, he learned, to his surprise, that his anti-splitting crusade had just attracted a new champion from within the

64. Commission on Revision of the Federal Court Appellate System, *The Geographical Boundaries of the Several Judicial Circuits: Recommendations for Change* (December 1973), also printed at 62 F.R.D. 223.

65. Letter to A. Leo Levin from John M. Wisdom, January 8, 1974.

66. Ibid., 2.

67. Ibid.

court's junior ranks. Judge Thomas Gibbs Gee, a former air force pilot, had been appointed to the Fifth Circuit by President Richard M. Nixon when Texan Joe Ingraham retired in mid-1973. On December 20, 1973, just five months after his swearing-in, Judge Gee sent a letter to Levin declaring himself to be in "strong agreement" with Judge Wisdom's various presentations to the commission. Gee also decried the move to "dismember a proud and effective institution such as the Fifth Circuit as a preliminary measure and in pursuit of benefits which can only be short-haul." Invoking a Texas-flavored metaphor, Gee suggested that "you have a good horse that is getting the wagon up the hill now. I do not think we should exchange him for two ponies, when it is plan that, by the time we have them in harness, we may be dealing with different wagons and different hills."[68]

About six weeks after the release of the Hruska Commission report, legislation was introduced in both Houses of Congress to implement its recommendation. On February 7, 1974, the four Senate members of the Hruska Commission introduced three bills (S. 2988, S. 2989, and S. 2990) in the second session of the 93rd Congress.[69] The three bills, each of which codified one of the commission's alternative recommendations for reorganizing the Fifth Circuit,[70] were referred to the Senate Judiciary Committee. And that committee was controlled by its chair, Senator James Eastland, the most ardent supporter of the 4–2 state split proposal.

The Judiciary Committee, through its Subcommittee on Improvements in Judicial Machinery, held six days of hearings in late September and early December 1974. Five of the fifteen active Fifth Circuit judges—John Brown, Charles Clark, J. P. Coleman, Walter Gewin, and Wisdom—made appearances. Gee had authorized Wisdom to represent his views in opposition to realignment while Clark, Coleman, and Gewin testified in favor of realignment on behalf of themselves and their solidly aligned colleagues from the four eastern states of the circuit.[71] Up to that time, Judge Paul H. Roney of Florida had been the only "eastern state" judge not to sign the "Manifesto from the East" that

68. Letter to A. Leo Levin from Thomas G. Gee, December 20, 1973, 1–2.

69. 120 Cong. Rec. 2609–2612 (February 7, 1974).

70. The legislation also called for the splitting of the Ninth Circuit.

71. Letter to John M. Wisdom from Thomas Gibbs Gee, September 19, 1974; Hearings Before the Subcommittee on Improvements in Judicial Machinery of the Committee on the Judiciary, U.S. Senate, 93 Cong., 2d Sess. on S. 2988, S. 2989, and S. 2990, Part 1, Letters to Quentin N.

Judge Gewin had submitted to the Hruska Commission back in August 1973. But on September 23, 1974, the day before the Fifth Circuit judges testified in front of the subcommittee, Roney informed Senator Quentin Burdick, the subcommittee chairman, that he too now favored splitting the Fifth Circuit.[72]

The six judges from the Texas and Louisiana, on the other hand, were not of one mind on this question. Although Wisdom, Brown, and Gee opposed division in any form, none of their three other western brethren were willing to take that absolutist position. Wisdom's New Orleans-based colleague, Judge Robert A. Ainsworth, who, along with Irving L. Goldberg of Dallas, had been appointed by President Johnson to one of four newly authorized judgeships in the summer of 1966, would only go so far as to say that if realignment were to become a reality, he preferred the Hruska Commission's prime recommendation of a 3–3 split.[73] The two other Texans on the court, Goldberg and Thornberry, informed the Senate subcommittee that if Congress decided to enact the 4–2 split proposal, it was essential also to authorize additional judgeships for the two-state circuit since it accounted for over 49 percent of the present docket but would host only 40 percent (six) of the circuit's fifteen judges.[74]

Still bristling over the not-so-subtle reference to his eligibility for senior status that had been contained in Gewin's "Manifesto," Wisdom wasted no time assuring the members of the Senate subcommittee, as well as those of his eastern state colleagues in attendance, of his intention to remain in active service. His prepared statement, after the customary expression of appreciation for the invitation to appear, began with a brief, though characteristically feisty introduction: "I have served

Burdick from Lewis R. Morgan, Griffin B. Bell, David W. Dyer, Bryan Simpson, and John C. Godbold, 117–119.

72. Letter to Quentin N. Burdick from Paul H. Roney, September 23, 1974, also printed at Hearings Before the Subcommittee on Improvements in Judicial Machinery of the Committee on the Judiciary, U.S. Senate, 93 Cong., 2d Sess. on S. 2988, S. 2989, and S. 2990, Part 1, 119.

73. Letter to Quentin N. Burdick from Robert A. Ainsworth, September 16, 1974, printed at Hearings Before the Subcommittee on Improvements in Judicial Machinery of the Committee on the Judiciary, U.S. Senate, 93 Cong., 2d Sess. on S. 2988, S. 2989, and S. 2990, Part 1, at 115.

74. Letter to Quentin N. Burdick from Homer Thornberry, September 19, 1974; Letter to Quentin N. Burdick from Irving L. Goldberg, September 23, 1974, both of which are also printed at Hearings Before the Subcommittee on Improvements in Judicial Machinery of the Committee on the Judiciary, U.S. Senate, 93 Cong., 2d Sess. on S. 2988, S. 2989, and S. 2990, Part 1, at 115–116, and 1119, respectively.

on the Court of Appeals for the Fifth Circuit since June 1957, seventeen years. I have no intention of taking senior status."[75] Wisdom then trotted out his by-then familiar arguments against the Hruska Commission's "radical" suggestion which, he insisted, represented "a dangerous step toward proliferation of circuits that may not destroy but will certainly weaken the historic role of the federal courts in American Federalism."[76]

At the conclusion of its hearings, the subcommittee reported out a revised circuit reorganization bill. This "clean bill," denominated S. 729, provided for the reorganization of the Fifth and Ninth Circuits. The Fifth Circuit would be separated into two divisions, rather than circuits, with Texas and Louisiana comprising the Western Division and the four other states and the Canal Zone comprising the circuit's Eastern Division.[77] Each division would have its own chief judge, judicial council, and control over the designation and assignment of circuit and district judges within its division. Finally, to further address the caseload crunch, the Fifth Circuit would receive eight additional judgeships to be divided between these two divisions.

The nine members of the eastern Fifth Circuit states quickly agreed to meet in New Orleans, where they unanimously declared their support for early and favorable passage of S. 729.[78] Brown then called a meeting of the western state judges in his hometown of Houston, where he appointed a committee of the three senior members of the "western tier" (himself, Wisdom, and Thornberry) to meet with a committee formed by Gewin, the senior member of the eastern bloc. He wanted these two groups to exchange ideas how to deal with whatever structural problems might be created by the enactment of S. 729.[79] The summit was held in New Orleans, where the two sides agreed to recommend a package of

75. Hearings Before the Subcommittee on Improvements in Judicial Machinery of the Committee on the Judiciary, U.S. Senate, 93 Cong., 2d Sess. on S. 2988, S. 2989, and S. 2990, Part 1, Statement of Judge John Minor Wisdom, September 24, 1974, at 95.

76. Hearings Before the Subcommittee on Improvements in Judicial Machinery of the Committee on the Judiciary, U.S. Senate, 93 Cong., 2d Sess. on S. 2988, S. 2989, and S. 2990, Part 1, Statement of Judge John Minor Wisdom, September 24, 1974, at 96.

77. 121 Cong. Rec. 3257 (February 18, 1975).

78. Letter to John R. Brown from Walter P. Gewin, December, 16, 1974; Letter to Quentin N. Burdick from Walter P. Gewin, December 16, 1974.

79. Letter to John R. Brown, John Minor Wisdom, Homer Thornberry, Irving L. Goldberg, and Robert A. Ainsworth from Thomas Gibbs Gee, January 8, 1975; Letter to John R. Brown from Walter P. Gewin, January 9, 1975.

technical amendments to S. 729, including one designating Montgomery, Alabama, as the situs for court proceedings of the Eastern Division. Wisdom, Brown, and Thornberry also affirmatively reserved the right to continue to state their opposition to the proposed division.[80]

On December 2, 1975, nearly one year to the day after the subcommittee had come forward with its intra-circuit division plan, a majority of the Senate Judiciary Committee voted in favor of S. 729, although only as it related to the Fifth Circuit. The committee deferred action on the proposal to divide the Ninth Circuit, announcing that it had not been able to confect a workable solution to the unique problems faced by that court.[81]

With Senator Eastland chairing the committee hearings, the decision to support the 4–2 split was hardly a surprise. Neither was its passage by the full Senate. But the measure stalled in the House. The Democrats, who controlled the House, were hoping that their candidate would defeat President Gerald Ford in the upcoming election. Hoping that any new judgeships would be filled by a Democrat resident of the White House, they delayed action on the Senate bill.[82]

The strategy worked. Jimmy Carter defeated Gerald Ford in the 1976 election. Shortly after the convening of the 95th Congress in January 1977, a group of senators, some of whom had supported and others who voted against S. 729, joined together to co-sponsor another Omnibus Judgeship Bill, S. 11. This proposal moved expeditiously through the Judiciary Committee, since Senator Eastland had determined that the committee's extended consideration of the predecessor bills rendered unnecessary separate hearings on this version of the reorganization plan.

The bill S. 11, however, was critically different from S. 729. Like its predecessor, S. 11 provided for a 4–2 split along the Mississippi River. But it divided the Fifth Circuit into two separate circuits. Texas and Louisiana would form a new Eleventh Circuit holding court in New Orleans and Houston, while the other four states and the Canal Zone would constitute the "new" Fifth Circuit, headquartered in Atlanta. The bill also authorized six new judgeships for the Eleventh Circuit and

80. Letter to All Active Fifth Circuit Judges from John R. Brown and Walter P. Gewin, January 16, 1975.

81. S. Rep. No. 94-513, at 1, 5 (1975).

82. See Edgar Poe, "Senate OKs Splitting 5th Circuit," *New Orleans Times-Picayune*, May 25, 1977.

five for the reconstituted Fifth Circuit.[83] It did not provide for any reorganization of the Ninth Circuit.

On May 24, 1977, after brief debate, the Senate passed S. 11 by voice vote and referred this Omnibus Judgeship Bill to the House Judiciary Committee. The campaign to preserve the Fifth Circuit had now shifted to its final battlefield—the U.S. House of Representatives. And though he had retired from active service on January 15 of that year, thereby relinquishing his membership on the court's policy-making Judicial Council, Wisdom remained as tenacious as ever in his opposition to the split.

Just a couple of days after the Senate passed S. 11, Wisdom wrote to Representative Peter Rodino, Jr., the new chair of the House Judiciary Committee. Wisdom urged the chairman to conduct hearings on the reorganization bill that had now moved to the House chamber, expressed his vigorous opposition to the proposed legislation, and requested the opportunity to testify against "the proposed dismemberment of the Fifth Circuit."[84] But this would not be Wisdom's last effort at keeping the pressure on this key legislative leader.

Within two weeks, Wisdom had sent off a second letter to Rodino. In support of its decisions not to include Arizona in the new Eleventh Circuit with Texas and Louisiana and, more important, to align Mississippi with the three eastern Fifth Circuit states rather than with Louisiana and Texas, the Senate Judiciary Committee's report had repeated an argument that previously had surfaced in a variety of legislative reports. "Not only would Arkansas be dislocated," the report declared, "but it would be aligned with *two* states which have a civil law background springing from the Napoleonic Code." The report also stated that "Mississippi's legal antecedents stem from the States to the east, and like Arkansas, it is opposed to prolonging its association with civil law *states*."[85]

Naturally, this inaccurate, even heretical interpretation of the impact of the Napoleonic Code upon American law was too much for a dyed-in-the-wool civil law expert and champion like Wisdom to leave unchecked. "The obvious effect of the statement," he suggested to Rodino, "is to make it appear that the law in Texas and Louisiana is of foreign origin and so alien to the laws of Alabama, Florida, Georgia, and Missis-

83. S. Rep. No. 95-117 (1977).

84. Letter to The Hon. Peter W. Rodino, Jr., from Judge John M. Wisdom, May 26, 1977.

85. S. Rep. No. 95-117, at 45, 46 (1977) (emphasis added).

sippi that these four states should not be in the same circuit with Texas and Louisiana." Then, presenting the same historical analysis that he had employed when schooling Professor Leo Levin on New Orleans' standing as the perennial seat of the Fifth Circuit, Wisdom offered Chairman Rodino a brief refresher course on Texas's common law traditions. He reminded Rodino that in 1840, Texas had enacted a statute making the common law of England the rule of decision in Texas. "The law of Texas," Wisdom reported, "is the common law, to the same extent as it is in Alabama, Florida, Georgia, and Mississippi. Texas law has never had any connection whatever with the Code Napoleon, directly or indirectly."[86]

Despite his best efforts, Wisdom recognized that momentum now clearly was building in the direction of definitive congressional action to split his circuit. Like many others, Wisdom believed that President Carter, who had named former Fifth Circuit judge and split supporter Griffin Bell to be his attorney general, would sign S. 11 into law. These facts also did not escape the attention of Wisdom's pro-split colleagues, who determined that the time was ripe for them to reenter the fray.

Over the preceding year, four members of the court—Griffin Bell, David Dyer, Walter Gewin, and Wisdom—had elected to take senior status. But as only two of these vacancies had been filled by the summer of 1977,[87] the court was down to thirteen active members. At the Fifth Circuit's Judicial Council meeting on July 5, 1977, attended, per court rule, only by the active members, a resolution endorsing the decision to split the court was approved by a 10-3 vote. The only dissenters were three of the court's four Texans—Judges Brown, Goldberg, and Gee.[88]

The House version of the Omnibus Judgeship Bill, H.R. 3685, was considered by the Monopolies and Commercial Law Subcommittee of the House Judiciary Committee. On June 16, 1977, the subcommittee,

86. Letter to Peter W. Rodino, Jr., from John M. Wisdom, June 6, 1977, at 2.

87. Griffin Bell's slot was filled on May 21, 1976, with the swearing in of U.S. district judge James C. Hill of Atlanta, who had been named to the Fifth Circuit by President Jimmy Carter. Four months later, District Judge Peter T. Fay of Miami, similarly nominated for promotion by President Carter, was sworn in to replace David Dyer. District Judge Alvin B. Rubin from Baton Rouge, Louisiana, was nominated by President Carter to fill the vacancy caused by Judge Wisdom's January 15, 1977, retirement, but did not assume his seat on the court until September 19, 1977. Robert S. Vance, an attorney from Birmingham, Alabama, was named by President Carter to replace Walter Gewin and he joined the court on December 15, 1977.

88. Letter to All Senior Circuit Judges of the Fifth Circuit from John R. Brown, July 5, 1977, and attached copy of resolution.

also chaired by Rodino, reported out an amended version of the bill, H.R. 7843, which included the authorization of eleven new judgeships for the Fifth Circuit, but also deleted the circuit-split provision.[89]

The subcommittee held hearings that included presentations by several Fifth Circuit members, who spoke on both sides of the proposed legislation, and representatives of several civil rights groups who insisted that splitting the Fifth Circuit would create a gerrymandered Eleventh Circuit that would be sympathetic to civil rights claims and a larger Fifth Circuit where, in the words of one witness, "civil rights interpretation and enforcement will be disastrous for those blacks residing in those states."[90] A representative from the NAACP presented the subcommittee with an analysis of the Fifth Circuit's last fifty *en banc* decisions, of which eighteen involved civil rights claims. He reported that "the pattern is that the decisions by the liberal—if you will excuse that phrase—members of the Fifth Circuit in the area of criminal law and civil rights, are being reheard and reversed by the majority." Moreover, he continued, "if you look at the membership of the panels whose decisions were overturned by the *en banc* court, you see the same names all the time: Tuttle, Brown, Goldberg, Wisdom."[91]

The week after the committee hearing, Gee sent Wisdom a cryptic note. He relayed to his anti-split comrade-in-arms a statement he had heard at the Fifth Circuit's most recent Judicial Council meeting to the effect that the Omnibus Judgeship Bill would not get past Rodino's subcommittee, at least as long as it contained a circuit-splitting provision. Gee also suggested to Wisdom that "this is something that you might want to pass on to those who are working with you on this matter."[92] This rumor soon became fact. On November 30, 1977, the full House Judiciary Committee voted 31-2 in favor of H.R. 7843, the subcommit-

89. Letter to W. Henson Moore from Peter W. Rodino, Jr., June 16, 1977; Letter to John M. Wisdom from Joe D. Waggoner, Jr., June 21, 1977; Letter to John M. Wisdom from Lindy Boggs, June 29, 1977.

90. Hearings before the Subcommittee on Monopolies and Commercial Law of the Committee on the Judiciary, House of Representatives, 95th Cong., 1st Sess., Testimony of U.W. Clemon, President, Alabama Black Lawyers Association, Birmingham, Alabama, at 99–100 (September 21, 27, and October 19, 1977).

91. Hearings before the Subcommittee on Monopolies and Commercial Law of the Committee on the Judiciary, House of Representatives, 95th Cong., 1st Sess., Testimony of Eric Schnapper, Assistant Counsel, Legal defense Fund, National Association For The Advancement Of Colored People, at 115–116.

92. Letter to John M. Wisdom from Thomas Gibbs Gee, September 30, 1977.

tee's amended judgeship bill that authorized eleven new slots on the Fifth Circuit but did not split that court, and this decision was approved by an overwhelming vote on the House floor on February 7, 1978.[93]

Since S. 11, the Senate version of the judgeship bill, unlike H.R. 7843, did contain a provision splitting the Fifth Circuit, the battleground now shifted to the House-Senate Conference Committee charged with reconciling the differences between the two bills. These efforts were complicated by the fact that just as Senator Eastland continued to insist upon the circuit-split provision, Rodino was equally adamant that any resulting compromise bill retain the House version's requirement that the president promulgate guidelines for merit selection of all future federal district judges. This merit selection proposal, of course, would significantly curtail the prerogatives presently enjoyed by the Senate and, in particular, by the chair of the Senate Judiciary Committee—James Eastland.[94]

The House members' interest in curtailing Senate influence over federal judicial nominations and the desire of Senate Republicans to restrict President Carter's ability to distribute federal judgeships as patronage plums led the conferees to quickly agree on the merit selection provision.[95] The conferees also agreed on the authorization of new district and appellate court positions. Thus, by the middle of May 1978, there remained but one simmering controversy—the status of the Fifth Circuit.[96]

There was little hope of an early break in the impasse caused by the seemingly irreconcilable positions held by Senator Eastland and Congressman Rodino. But on March 22, 1978, Senator Eastland shocked most observers by announcing that he would not run for reelection in November and, therefore, that he would retire from the Senate at the end of his term. The departure of the circuit split's most enthusiastic and powerful proponent gave a measure of hope to split opponents. More-

93. "House Panel OKs Bill for 100 New Judgeships," *New Orleans Times-Picayune*, December 1, 1977, 7, col. 1; Letter to all Fifth Circuit Judges from Thomas H. Reese, November 30, 1977.

94. See Warren Weaver, Jr., "Side Issues Delay Bill to Create New U.S. Judgeships," *New York Times*, March 19, 1978, 21, col. 1.

95. "Conferees Would Require Carter to Set Standards on U.S. Judges," *New York Times*, April 14, 1978.

96. Cragg Hines, "Jordan Marshals Opponents of Appeals Court Split," *Houston Chronicle*, July 27, 1978, 12, col. 1; Warren Weaver, Jr., "Disagreement Delaying Division of Federal Judgeships for South," *New York Times*, June 19, 1978, A-15, col. 3; Editorial, "Eastland's Stall: He Blocks New Judgeships," *Charlotte Observer*, June 25, 1978, B-2, col. 1.

over, Senator Eastland's heir apparent as Judiciary Committee Chairman, Senator Edward Kennedy of Massachusetts, was on record as opposing any attempt to split the Fifth Circuit.

But the early promise of a rosy future did not materialize. Eastland's last hurrah in the chairman's seat would extend for six more months, and he was dead set on producing a compromise bill that would split the Fifth Circuit at the Mississippi River. But as lame ducks tend to carry little water on Capitol Hill, Eastland ultimately was unable to carry the day. Nearly six months after the House and Senate bills were sent to the Conference Committee for reconciliation, the Conference Committee reached a consensus on the Fifth Circuit matter. Fifteen years after he began his tireless campaign against the split, it appeared that Wisdom's arguments, effectively advocated by the anti-split House members on the Conference Committee, had triumphed. But this victory, though sweet, would be short-lived.

On September 20, 1978, the Conference Committee members rejected the Senate bill language that would have realigned the Fifth Circuit. Instead, they unanimously approved a compromise provision brokered by former Fifth Circuit judge and now-U.S. attorney general Griffin Bell.[97] This provision simply authorized any federal appellate court with more than fifteen active judges, at its discretion, to constitute itself into administrative units and to prescribe its own rule for the number of members serving on *en banc* courts.[98] But though this language clearly meant that the Fifth Circuit would remain intact, the Conference Committee's report contained two interesting addenda. First, it stated that Congress retained the power to enact any other legislation it deemed appropriate. And it directed the Fifth Circuit and the Judicial Conference of the United States to issue jointly or separately, a status report to Congress within one year after the appointment of the last of the eleven newly authorized judges. This report was to describe the effect of any new procedures implemented by the court and recommendations, if any, for additional legislative action.[99]

97. Barrow and Walker, *A Court Divided: The Fifth Circuit Court of Appeals and the Politics of Judicial Reform*, 215–216.

98. Conference Report, S.Rep. No. 95-1257 (1978); Sam Hanna, "5th Circuit May Stay Indefinitely," *New Orleans States-Item*, September 23, 1978, A-2, col. 1; "5th Circuit Court Won't Be Altered," *New Orleans Times-Picayune*, September 21, 1978, 5, col. 3; "The 5th to Stay in N.O.," *New Orleans States-Item*, September 21, 1978, A-2, col. 1; Letter to All Federal Judges from William James Weller, September 21, 1978.

99. S. Rep. No. 95-1257, at 9 (1978).

Within a month, the conference bill was adopted overwhelmingly by both the Senate and House. President Carter signed the Omnibus Judgeship Act on October 20, 1978. Chief Judge Brown moved quickly to implement Congress's directive to consider the creation of administrative units. A committee was appointed and the judges debated the matter, both through an exchange of correspondence and at several Judicial Council meetings, for the next two years. However, their sharp division on the many procedural and logistic issues posed by the prospect of creating subdivisions precluded the members of the court from reaching agreement on any particular long-term strategy.

On May 5, 1980, the twenty-four active members of the Fifth Circuit assembled in New Orleans for a meeting of the Judicial Council. But for the first time in nearly thirteen years, a new colleague sat at the head of the table. That past December 10, on the occasion of his seventieth birthday, John Brown reluctantly had turned over leadership of the court to Mississippi's J. P. Coleman. Throughout Brown's tenure as chief, and into the reign of his successor, the difficulties generated by the court's dramatic increase in membership and its perpetually exploding caseload (the annual docket now exceeded four thousand cases) had continued to bedevil the Fifth Circuit. Among the court's most challenging and aggravating problems was the logistical nightmare associated with scheduling *en banc* hearings for two dozen judges dispersed in a circuit that stretched more than 1,100 miles from Fort Worth to Miami. These concerns ultimately proved too much even for Brown (although he was required by statute to step down as chief judge at age seventy, Brown exercised his option to remain on active service and thereby retain his seat on the Judicial Council) and Gee, the two remaining active anti-splittists (Goldberg having retired on January 1) to ignore.[100]

The Judicial Council meeting yielded a unanimous resolution calling for Congress to enact legislation to split the court into two autonomous circuits, each of which would be composed of three states. Mississippi would join Texas and Louisiana in a circuit that, in tribute to Wisdom, would retain the name of Fifth Circuit. Alabama, Georgia, and Florida would comprise the Eleventh Circuit. The headquarters for the Fifth Circuit would remain in New Orleans, while the Eleventh Circuit headquarters would be located in Atlanta. The resolution also

100. See Editorial, "Dividing a Great Court," *New York Times*, August 27, 1980, A-22, col. 1.

stated that until Congress enacted that legislation, pursuant to the authority delegated to it under the 1978 Omnibus Judgeship, the Fifth Circuit, as of July 1, voluntarily would divide itself into two administrative units. Unit A, headquartered in New Orleans, would be composed of Texas, Louisiana, and Mississippi, and Unit B, with its headquarters in Atlanta, would encompass Alabama, Georgia, and Florida. Each unit would hear and decide those cases appealed from district courts located with its three constituent states in panels ordinarily composed of circuit judges residing in those constituent states. All circuit judges, however, still could be assigned to panels in either unit. Finally, although the caseload would be divided according to these administrative units, the court would retain one judicial council, one judicial conference, and one common body of law.[101]

With the active judges of the Fifth Circuit now speaking with one voice on reorganization, a legislative response was swift. A bill implementing these recommendations was submitted to the House on June 19 and to the Senate on June 23.[102] These measures received prompt approval from both chambers on October 14 and President Carter signed the Fifth Circuit Court of Appeals Reorganization Act of 1980 the following day, implementing the split as of October 1, 1981.[103]

More than three and a half years removed from active service, and thereby ineligible to participate in Judicial Council deliberations, Wisdom had privately acknowledged the inevitability of the split. And so when the official word came on October 15, he received the news with mixed emotions. In many way, it was, he subsequently recalled, "a day of mourning" when Congress "sliced a great court in two."[104] Nevertheless, Wisdom was able to take some measure of comfort in the knowledge that the court on which he would continue to serve would retain the name that meant so much to him and to whose legacy he had contributed so mightily.

On October 1, 1981, all twenty-six active judges of the Fifth Circuit, along with Tuttle, Brown, and nine other of their retired colleagues,

101. Letter to All Active and Senior Circuit Judges from Thomas H. Reese, May 7, 1980, and accompanying resolution; Ed Anderson, "Appeals Court Moves to Split," *New Orleans Times-Picayune*, May 8, 1980, 18, col. 1.

102. H.R. 7625 and S. 2839, respectively.

103. Pub.L. 96-452, 94 Stat. 1994, 28 U.S.C. §41(1980). Under this statute, the Canal Zone joined Texas, Louisiana, and Mississippi in the new Fifth Circuit.

104. John Minor Wisdom, *Requiem for a Great Court*, 26 LOY. L. REV. 787 (1980).

joined more than five hundred guests gathered in the vaulted marble Great Hall of the Fifth Circuit building in New Orleans for the formal ceremony marking the official division of the Fifth Circuit into the new Fifth and Eleventh Circuits.[105] Wisdom, however, did not attend. The official explanation for his absence was that he had left town the night before to participate in a meeting of the federal Railroad Reorganization Court, on which he continued to sit. The reality was that he could not bear to participate in the ceremony marking the end of the great court on which he had served with pride and honor for nearly a quarter of a century.

105. Frances Frank Marcus, "Court That Shaped Southern History Ends Long and Busy Life," *New York Times*, October 2, 1981, 14, col. 1; Ed Anderson, "Federal Court Is Split," *New Orleans Times-Picayune/States-Item*, October 2, 1981, 19, col. 1.

EPILOGUE
HONORING THE LEGACY

As testament to John Minor Wisdom's remarkable and varied contributions to American society, those accomplished both in the political sphere and in the juridical arena, he received countless awards and honors from a wide array of admiring and grateful associations and organizations. Wisdom was awarded honorary degrees from Oberlin College, the University of San Diego, Haverford College, Middlebury College, Harvard University, and his beloved alma mater, Tulane University. In 1986, Wisdom became the first recipient of the Louisiana Bar Foundation's Distinguished Jurist Award and, three years later, received Tulane University's Distinguished Alumnus Award.

But towering in importance above all of the other honors that Wisdom received during his lifetime were three extraordinarily prestigious awards—each of which was reserved solely for individuals distinguished by an extraordinary body of lifetime service to the nation—and the naming in his honor of the federal courthouse that served throughout much of his tenure as the headquarters of the Fifth Circuit.

The recipient of the Edward J. Devitt Distinguished Service to Justice Award, originally sponsored by the West Publishing Company, the official publisher of federal trial and appellate court opinions, is selected by a committee composed of three federal judges. The committee is charged with bestowing the annual award upon a federal judge whose exemplary career has been marked by unique contributions to the administration of justice, the advancement of the rule of law, and the improvement of society as a whole. It is widely acknowledged to be the premier honor for outstanding lifetime service by members of the federal judiciary.

In 1988, a committee composed of Supreme Court justice Sandra Day O'Connor, U.S. Second Circuit judge Wilfred Feinberg, and U.S. district judge Edward J. Devitt unanimously chose to confer the seventh annual Devitt award jointly upon Wisdom and Elbert Tuttle in recognition of their leadership in guiding "the Fifth Circuit and, therefore, the nation through the storm of civil rights litigation that followed *Brown v. Board of Education.*"[1] Naturally, both of the recipients were extremely gratified and honored by this prestigious honor. In Wisdom's case, however, the pride and satisfaction shared by him, his family, and legions of friends and admirers was tempered by a temporary period of unwanted, unaccustomed, unanticipated, and unfavorable notoriety.

Five months before receiving the Devitt award, and its accompanying $15,000 prize, Wisdom had sat as a member of a Fifth Circuit panel that heard the appeal in a copyright case brought against West Publishing Company, the Devitt Award's sponsor. For more than seventy-five years, through an agreement reached with the State of Texas, West and its predecessor had published a reorganized and annotated version of all statutes enacted by the Texas legislature. West claimed a copyright in its arrangement of the statutory material, although not, of course, in the text of the statutes themselves.

In 1985, the previously harmonious relationship between West Publishing and Texas hit a rocky patch and the state decided to turn over publication rights to its statutes to another company. This competitor, who also intended to market an electronic version of the Texas statutes, sued West in federal court to obtain a declaration of the invalidity of West's alleged copyright. Two years later, while that action was pending, the State of Texas filed its own action in federal court in Austin seeking a declaration of the invalidity of West's claimed copyright.

The trial judge in the suit brought by the State of Texas dismissed the case on the grounds that there was no actual controversy presently existing between the parties.[2] Since West had not actually threatened a lawsuit or any other action against Texas to protect its claimed copyright, and because West never had accused the state of infringing that

1. Presentation of the Edward J. Devitt Distinguished Service to Justice Award, transcript of remarks reproduced at 888 F.2d at CII (1988).

2. *State of Texas v. West Publishing Co.*, 681 F.Supp. 1228 (W.D.Tx.1988).

alleged copyright, the judge ruled, there was no present need to determine whether or not West actually possessed such a copyright.

The case was appealed to the Fifth Circuit and was assigned to a hearing panel composed of Wisdom and two Reagan appointees, Circuit Judges Will Garwood of Texas and E. Grady Jolly of Mississippi. The panel unanimously agreed to affirm the trial judge's ruling in favor of West.[3] The opinion, written by Judge Garwood, was released on September 5, 1989. Although he did not write an opinion in the case, Wisdom attended the oral argument and fully participated in the panel's deliberations. When the Supreme Court denied Texas's request to hear the appeal,[4] the Fifth Circuit's ruling in West's favor became the final word on the dispute.

Although there was never any suggestion that Wisdom did not deserve the honor embodied in the Devitt award, an issue was raised as to whether or not he should have either recused himself from sitting on the appeal or at least disclosed the fact of this relationship with West prior to the issuance of the panel opinion. Wisdom's response to this public challenge to his integrity, a character trait that he held above all others, was typically instantaneous and emphatic. After insisting that "there wasn't any thought in the mind of anybody" that he should remove himself from the case, Wisdom added that "as I think about it now, I think there might have been some question. But nobody would seriously think that was being used to gain favor for West. Not did it make a difference. Any judge worth his salt wouldn't be influenced by the fact that it was West Publishing Company."[5] And Judge Garwood, the author of the opinion, fully supported his colleague. It was "silly," Garwood opined, to think that Wisdom might have been influenced by the award. Accepting that honor, even with the sponsor a litigant in a case before him, Garwood declared, "does not raise a shadow of a question."[6]

Whatever ripples, if any, that were produced by the Devitt/West con-

3. *State of Texas v. West Publishing Co.*, 882 F.2d 171 (5th Cir.1989).

4. *Texas v. West Publishing Co.*, 493 U.S. 1058, 110 S.Ct. 869, 107 L.Ed.2d 953 (1990).

5. Wisdom also revealed that he used the $15,000 to buy a painting for his home. Sharon Schmickle & Tom Hamburger, "Award Recipient Was on Three-Judge Panel," *Star Tribune—Minneapolis & St. Paul*, 1985, found at http://www.startribune.com/stonline/html/westpub/texas_ru.htm.

6. Schmickle & Hamburger, "Award Recipient Was on Three-Judge Panel," *Star Tribune—Minneapolis & St. Paul*, 1985, found at http://www.startribune.com/stonline/html/westpub/texas_ru.htm.

troversy quickly abated and certainly had no long-lasting impact on Wisdom's reputation. And five years later, Wisdom was on the receiving end of the capstone tribute of his illustrious career, one that he described as "the greatest honor I've ever received."[7]

In early November 1993, Wisdom received a telephone call from one of his former law clerks. Robert B. Barnett, an influential partner in the prestigious Washington, D.C., law firm of Williams & Connolly, had close ties to President Bill Clinton, including acting as his personal attorney and playing a leading role on the team that prepared Clinton for the presidential debates during the 1992 and 1996 election campaigns. Over the years after the completion of his clerkship, Barnett and his family had developed and maintained a particularly close personal relationship with John and Bonnie Wisdom. So it was not unusual for Wisdom to receive a call from his former assistant. But this was not the kind of catching-up conversation that Wisdom anticipated.

To Wisdom's utter astonishment, Barnett had called his mentor with the news that Wisdom was to be awarded the Presidential Medal of Freedom. "I don't recall the exact words, but what he said was, 'Something big is about to happen to you.' And then he almost lost control of himself for a few minutes and then recovered and we proceeded with the conversation. We were both quite emotional over the telephone."[8]

Barnett advised Wisdom to prepare a list of only twenty invitees for an event to take place in Washington, the nature of which could not be revealed to this select group. But since the White House wanted to control the timing of the announcement, Barnett also told Wisdom that in relaying the invitation, Wisdom could not inform his guests of the precise nature of the reason they were being invited to accompany him to the nation's capital. And although Wisdom scrupulously followed this instruction, it was not long before word got out.[9]

Within days of the conversation with Barnett, Wisdom was on a plane to Washington for an unrelated matter. Coincidentally, returning to the nation's capital on that same plane from his wedding to Repub-

7. J. M. Wisdom [Friedman], December 10, 1993, 3.

8. J. M. Wisdom [Friedman], December 10, 1993, 1, 5.

9. The author was one of the invitees. During that conversation, Judge Wisdom simply stated that "you need to go to Washington because I'm going to receive something but I can't tell you what, other than that it's in Washington so get a plane reservation." When the author then said, "Well, I won't try to get you to tell me," Wisdom replied, "You can try, but I won't tell you anyway." J. M. Wisdom [Friedman], December 10, 1993, 6.

lican strategist Mary Matalin in New Orleans was Clinton advisor and Louisiana native James Carville. According to Wisdom, "James went up and down in the plane and said in a loud voice so that all the passengers could hear, 'You've got a very distinguished person on the plane today, the Honorable John Minor Wisdom, who will receive the President's Medal of Freedom.' It was all in good fun. We all laughed."[10]

Wisdom's first call upon hanging up with Barnett was to his Bonnie, his wife of sixty-two years. As she later recalled, "I was deeply touched and quite excited." She then added, in her inimitable style, "And having been a lifelong ardent Republican, well, I thought why in the world didn't the Republicans think of this!"[11]

On a clear sky, brisk winter afternoon, Wisdom and his invited guests gathered with government leaders in the East Room of the White House. The occasion was the annual presentation of the Presidential Medal of Freedom. On November 30, 1993, the highest honor given to civilians by the federal government was awarded to a stellar group of five distinguished Americans whom President Clinton accurately described as "among our nation's great champions of the underdog," "legendary defenders of our freedoms," and "great reformers of the 20th century who changed America for the better."[12]

While the invited guests waited in the East Room for the ceremony to begin, John and Bonnie Wisdom, who had arrived a bit earlier than their guests through the White House East Gate, and the other honorees (or, in the case of the late Justice Marshall and Mr. Rauh, their widows) met privately with President and Mrs. Clinton for about half an hour's worth of customary pleasantries in the Blue Room. Wisdom thanked the president and assured him that whatever he had accomplished in his judicial career had been the work product not of just one judge but "judge and company," consisting of the other members of "The Four"—Elbert Tuttle, Dick Rives, and John Brown—as well as his collection of very able law clerks. And in the latter connection, Wisdom could not resist mentioning the name of his former law clerk and Clinton's potential Republican rival for the presidency, Lamar Alexander, who was one of Wisdom's invited guests. Clinton and Alexander had known each other when they were governors, Clinton of Arkansas

10. J. M. Wisdom [Friedman], December 10, 1993, 4.
11. Ibid., 7.
12. Remarks by The President in Ceremony Honoring Medal of Freedom Recipients, November 30, 1993, at 1.

and Alexander of Tennessee. In fact, when Wisdom and the president were shaking hands at the end of the ceremony, Clinton whispered to Wisdom, "Did you see Lamar over there?"[13]

Immediately preceding the entrance of the president and the honorees, Bonnie Wisdom and Hillary Clinton walked into the East Room together and sat next to each other in the first row of seats facing the podium. The image of these two accomplished women, matched in their powerful personalities yet distinguished by their vastly divergent political philosophies, sitting next to each other sent a titter through the crowd, particularly those located in the "Wisdom" section.[14]

Before bestowing each individual award, President Clinton offered a short description of the contributions made by Wisdom and his fellow recipients, journalist and author Marjory Stoneman Douglas, labor lawyer and civil rights activist Joseph Rauh, Jr., and former Supreme Court justices Thurgood Marshall and William Brennan. Turning to Wisdom, the president, with obviously deeply felt admiration and respect, offered this capsule biographical sketch: "John Minor Wisdom, a senior judge on the U.S. Court of Appeals at 88.5 years old, still handles a caseload as large as any judge on the bench. But he stands out among his peers as a truly first-class legal scholar who writes brilliant opinions, including his landmark opinion on voting rights in United States v. State of Louisiana in 1963, and his historic opinions to open the University of Mississippi to black students in Meredith v. Fair in 1962." Clinton continued: "He is a son of the Old South who became an architect of the new South. His father attended Washington College in Virginia when its students marched in the funeral of its president, Robert E. Lee. His background makes his progressive decisions all the more remarkable. Because I don't think the South could have made it through those trying times without leaders like Judge Wisdom."

The irony of a Democratic president being the one to confer the Medal of Freedom on this lifelong Republican was not lost on Clinton. He remarked, to an appreciative roar of laughter from those in attendance, that Wisdom "may be the only medal recipient today who was once a member of the Republican National Committee." The president then added that Wisdom "became the father of the modern Republican Party in Louisiana when he moved it away from reactionary isolationism to the moderation of President Eisenhower. His outspoken calls for

13. J. M. Wisdom [Friedman], December 10, 1993, 17.
14. Ibid., 19.

reform in government and public education and civil rights are some-thing of which all southerners and members of both political parties can justly be proud."[15] Finally, just before calling Wisdom, joined by his wife and their two daughters, Kit and Penny, up to the podium to re-ceive the medal, the president's military aide read the following citation: "Coupling intellect with compassion, Judge John Minor Wisdom has, throughout his distinguished military career and nearly four decades on the Federal bench, used his eloquence and expertise to illuminate the essence of American justice. Renowned for their clarity and reason, Judge Wisdom's opinions advanced civil rights and economic justice, and his inspired words echo throughout many of this country's most sig-nificant Supreme Court decisions." The aide noted: "As a gifted teacher and respected mentor, he has influenced and enlightened generations of younger lawyers, reflecting his extraordinary skills as an attorney and his reputation as a man of exemplary character. The United States Hon-ors Judge Wisdom's immeasurable contributions to humanity."[16]

Less than a year after President Clinton draped the Presidential Medal of Freedom around Wisdom's neck, Congress took an extraordinary step to manifest its recognition of Wisdom's distinguished service to the nation. On November 15, 1993, the House of Representatives passed H.R. 2868, "To designate the Federal building located at 600 Camp Street in New Orleans, Louisiana, as the 'John Minor Wisdom United States Courthouse'" by a voice vote. Its companion, Senate bill S. 1582, was similarly adopted by a voice vote on February 1, 1994, and Presi-dent Clinton signed the bills into law on May 25.[17] Within a month, on June 20, scores of federal judges and a multitude of friends, admirers, and relatives of Wisdom sat together in the Great Hall of the U.S. Post Office and Court House located across from Lafayette Square and Gal-lier Hall, the former site of New Orleans' City Hall. They had assembled for the official renaming of the courthouse in honor of its most illus-trious tenant.

The courthouse's Great Hall, lined with magnificent arched windows reaching thirty feet to its bronzed ceilings, was the site of the afternoon

15. Remarks by The President in Ceremony Honoring Medal of Freedom Recipients, No-vember 30, 1993, 3.
16. Medal of Freedom Citation to John Minor Wisdom, reprinted at Nick Marinello, *Honor-able, Indeed*, 14 TUL. LAW 1 (Spring 1994), at 6.
17. P.L. 103-256, 108 Stat. 690 (1994).

ceremony officially affirming what was already proclaimed on the building's exterior in big brass letters—the designation of this structure as the John Minor Wisdom U.S. Court of Appeals Building. The principal speaker was U.S. district judge Martin L. C. Feldman, who had served as Judge Wisdom's first law clerk after graduating, as Judge Wisdom did, from Tulane Law School. Feldman offered an eloquent and moving portrayal of his friend, colleague, and mentor: "John Wisdom's life is a celebration of law and justice. It has been a life so great, so grand, so deep and broad and divine that those of us who know him, those of us who are his privileged colleagues, those of us who learned from him and by his example, indeed, those of us who so unqualifiedly love and regard him, cannot be anything but overjoyed with this tribute to him today; putting his name to this great and grand building that symbolizes for us both the humility and the majesty of law and justice." Feldman continued: "John Minor Wisdom deserves this kind of fawning, the tribute we pay him today, because his special life, his unspoiled brilliance, his perfect scholarship and statecraft mean just one beautiful thing: one person can make a difference."[18]

In 1996, a now-ninety-old-year-old John Wisdom received the ABA Medal, awarded annually to an individual for "conspicuous service to the cause of American jurisprudence." At the awards ceremony, ABA president Roberta Cooper Ramo hailed Wisdom as a "moral and intellectual leader on a court that made heroic decisions despite strong pressures from regional political leaders of the times, and often risking personal harm." Furthermore, she continued, Wisdom's "courageous and significant contributions to this nation's progress toward equality among its citizens . . . still stand as bright beacons from a dark time."[19]

In the face of all of the awards that were bestowed upon Wisdom during his lifetime, it is apparent that one reward, perhaps the greatest prize that any attorney can obtain, always eluded him. Despite his decades of outstanding service on the most important federal appellate court in the country when it came to civil rights, his nationwide reputation as a thoughtful, scholarly jurist of impeccable integrity, and his ex-

18. Remarks of Judge Martin L. C. Feldman at dedication of John Minor Wisdom U.S. Court of Appeals Building, June 20, 1994.

19. This was not, however, the first time that Wisdom had been honored by his own profession. In 1990, the ABA's Litigation Section not only created the John Minor Wisdom Award for Public Service and Professionalism but also designated the award's namesake as its inaugural recipient.

tensive network of political connections, Wisdom never was appointed to the Supreme Court. Most observers and analysts, including Wisdom himself, agree that he was a victim, in large part, of bad timing. Despite his liberal credentials, he had been a Republican Party stalwart during his pre-judicial years and was, therefore, an unlikely prospect for nomination by a Democrat president. And by the time Wisdom had developed his well-earned reputation, Richard Nixon was living in the White House. It has been well reported that Nixon's attorney general, John Mitchell, the person primarily responsible for coming up with Supreme Court candidates, would have no part of John Minor Wisdom. At a dinner in Baltimore during the time of a pending Supreme Court vacancy, a reporter asked the attorney general, "What about Wisdom?" To which Mitchell replied, "That crazy son of a bitch? He would be worse than Earl Warren."[20]

But beyond his body of work that exceeded a thousand written opinions, more than all the honors and awards that he received throughout his distinguished career, the legacy that, at the end of the day, meant the most to Wisdom and to his wife was his relationships with, and the lifelong impact he had on, the scores of law graduates fortunate enough to have served as one of his law clerks. The association between judge and law clerk can vary in intensity and closeness. Judges rely on the work product of their clerks to varying degrees. They also range from one extreme to the other in the extent to which they involve themselves in the personal lives of their clerks. But if you ask anyone who clerked for Wisdom, you will invariably hear the word *family* among those used to describe the experience they shared for that one year.

On both sides of the equation, the clerks were much more than employees. They were treated, and felt, like loved and cherished members of the judge's family. From the quiet moments in the judge's home over coffee in the morning to the drive from his home to his chambers and then back again where the clerks shared private time with the judge to discuss law and every other subject under the sun, to the after hours conversations over drinks and dinner at the Wisdom home, a mutual respect and genuine affection developed that lasted long after the official term of the clerkship had expired. Nearly every former Wisdom clerk not only takes pride in the fact of the clerkship, but swears that the exposure to "the Judge" and Bonnie was a positive, life-altering ex-

20. J. M. Wisdom [Graham], La., March 7, 1981, at 3.

perience whose impact lasted throughout his or her life. Whether it was the judge's devotion to the intricacies of language, his and Bonnie's love of Shakespeare and opera, their passion for justice and equality, or just the fundamental decency of their character, each clerk remains forever changed by the experience of working with John Wisdom. And as these law clerks assumed the positions they now hold as federal judges, academics, attorneys, U.S. senators, and other public- and private-sector leaders, they brought the lessons learned from John and Bonnie Wisdom to their professional as well as personal lives.

On Saturday, May 15, 1999, just two days before his ninety-fourth birthday, John Minor Wisdom, the sole surviving member of "The Four," passed away. The death of this judicial giant generated more than a score of laudatory obituaries in media publications across the entire breadth of the country. One legal historian celebrated Wisdom as the "legal scholar who wrote opinion after opinion that desegregated courthouses throughout the Deep South and put blacks on juries, in the voting booth, in state legislatures and in integrated classrooms."[21] Congressman John Lewis, a veteran of the civil rights movement who had walked alongside Dr. Martin Luther King, Jr., in the civil rights marches and demonstrations of those history-making days in the 1950s and 1960s and whose firsthand knowledge of that struggle placed him in a uniquely qualified position to comment, declared that Judge Wisdom "represented a new breed of white judicial leadership, and he must be looked upon as a brave and courageous member of the bench who helped tear down the walls of segregation and the walls of racial discrimination. He represented the best the South had to offer."[22]

As a traditional New Orleans jazz band played "When the Saints Go Marching In," over four hundred friends and admirers, included fourteen of his Fifth Circuit colleagues, filed into the Great Hall in the courthouse bearing his name on May 27 for a memorial service to celebrate and honor John Wisdom's life. Judge Carolyn Dineen King, the chief judge of the Fifth Circuit, paid a moving tribute to her colleague. "Judge Wisdom's long and distinguished tenure on the bench of the Court of Appeals for the Fifth Circuit honored us all and has made the

21. Jack Bass, Obituary "John Minor Wisdom, Appeals Court Judge Who Helped to End Segregation, Dies at 93," *New York Times*, May 16, 1999, 45.

22. Kevin McGill, "Early Desegregation Judge John Minor Wisdom Dies at 93," *Commercial Appeal* (Memphis, Tenn.), May 16, 1999, B-7.

Fifth Circuit a great court in the nation's history."[23] Among the other encomia to Judge Wisdom was a letter read to the crowd from President Clinton in which the president acknowledged that "John Wisdom left his mark not only on our legal system, but on the generations of lawyers who served as his clerks and for whom he was a role model and mentor. He lived greatly in the law, showing the way to others through his extraordinary legal ability, his integrity and his courage."[24]

For seventy years, forty-two as a judge on the Fifth Circuit and twenty-eight as a prominent member of the bar and Republican leadership of his state, Wisdom had served his country with grace, style, intellect, humility, and, above all, humanity. Though born of upper-crust stock, he never forgot the lesson his mother had taught him about treating everyone with fairness and dignity. A hero to generations of those learned in and devoted to the law, Wisdom left a signal and impermeable imprint on American society. Reviving Louisiana's dormant Republican Party, working tirelessly and effectively for the election of his hero, Dwight Eisenhower, to the presidency of the United States, representing his clients with integrity and sagacity, and, above all, ensuring that every American's birthright to fair and equal treatment before the law was more than an empty promise, Wisdom brought a passion, eloquence, erudition, and dogged persistence to every task and challenge that he faced.

It is common nowadays to ask public figures how they wish to be remembered. In one of many interviews granted to historians and journalists anxious to interact personally with this living legend, Wisdom answered this question with his characteristic directness and honesty. "As one who attempted to judge according to his conscience and the law and was influential in bringing about an improvement in the social life of this country."[25] He accomplished all of this, and so much more, with grace, eloquence, sensitivity, and, of course, with wisdom.

23. "Hundreds Pay Tribute to Judge Wisdom," *New York Times*, May 28, 1999, B-11, col. 1.

24. Ibid.

25. J. M. Wisdom [Graham], March 7, 1981, 7; cited also in Robert Barnett, *John Minor Wisdom: O Rare*, 109 YALE L.J. 1261, 1264–1265 (2000).

INDEX

ABA. *See* American Bar Association (ABA)

Abrams, Creighton W., 166

Accomplice testimony, 120–21

Adams, Sherman, 40, 41, 89, 93–94, 96

Admiralty law, 121–23

Affirmative action, xi, 134, 220, 282, 319–30. *See also* Employment discrimination

African Americans: and bootleg whiskey possession, 118–20; as clients of Wisdom & Stone, 23, 23n37, 41; as Democratic political candidates in Louisiana, 213–14; disenfranchisement of, 44, 48, 125–30, 141–42, 272–302; employment discrimination against, 130–38, 134–35n79, 269n82, 318–30; exclusion of, from juries, 112–17; Ku Klux Klan violence against, 288–89; lynchings of, 132; and Mardi Gras, 13–14; military service by, 147; and pool closures, 232–36; and public recreational facilities, 231–36; and rape case, 112–17, 138–40; and Republican Party, 44, 48, 83–88; and segregation of public accommodations, 241–43, 241–42n141; and segregation of public transportation, 238–41, 254. See also *Brown v. Board of Education*; Desegregation; Racial prejudice and discrimination; Voting rights

Agriculture Department, U.S., 36

Ainsworth, Robert A., Jr.: appointment of, to Fifth Circuit Court of Appeals, 224, 358; on Ku Klux Klan, 289; on obscene materials, 310; and partition of Fifth Circuit Court of Appeals, 358; and *Poindexter v. Louisiana Financial Assistance Commission*, 196; on public transportation desegregation cases, 240; and *U.S. v. Jefferson County*, 223n72

Alabama: at-large municipal elections in, 299–301; *Brown v. Board of Education* implementation in, 206–12, 215–27, 246–53; civil rights movement in, 259–60, 284; demonstrations against segregation in Birmingham, 259–60; employment discrimination in, 134–35n79; expulsions and suspensions of student demonstrators in Birmingham, 259–60; public recreational facilities in, 236; racial gerrymandering in, 125–30, 273; segregation of buses in Birmingham, 254; voting rights in, 125–30, 273, 284, 287–88, 299–301

Alcohol cases, 118–20, 308–9

Alexander, Lamar, 373–74

Allen, O. K., 45–46

Allen, Violet, 108–9

Allen v. Republican State Central Committee of Louisiana, 52n26

www.ingramcontent.com/pod-product-compliance
Lightning Source LLC
Chambersburg PA
CBHW060959280326
41935CB00009B/757